CORPORATE CITIZENSHIP

Successful strategies for responsible companies

Malcolm McIntosh

Deborah Leipziger

Keith Jones

Gill Coleman

FINANCIAL TIMES
PITMAN PUBLISHING

FINANCIAL TIMES
MANAGEMENT
LONDON · SAN FRANCISCO
KUALA LUMPUR · JOHANNESBURG

*Financial Times Management delivers the knowledge,
skills and understanding that enable students,
managers and organisations to achieve their ambitions,
whatever their needs, wherever they are.*

London Office:
128 Long Acre, London WC2E 9AN
Tel: +44 (0)171 447 2000
Fax: +44 (0)171 240 5771
Website: www.ftmanagement.com

Washington Office:
1101 King Street, Suite 444, Alexandria, VA 22314
Tel: +1 703 519 2171
Fax: +1 703 739 6484
Website: www.ftmanagement.com

A Division of Financial Times Professional Limited

First published in Great Britain in 1998

ISBN 0 273 63106 3

British Library Cataloguing in Publication Data
A CIP catalogue record for this book can be obtained from the British Library.

1 3 5 7 9 10 8 6 4 2

Typeset by M Rules
Printed and bound in Great Britain by
Biddles Ltd, Guildford and King's Lynn

The Publishers' policy is to use paper manufactured from sustainable forests.

CONTENTS

Foreword by Alice Tepper Marlin, CEP   xi

About the authors   xv

Acknowledgements   xvii

INTRODUCTION: What is corporate citizenship?   xix

❶
SOCIAL RESPONSIBILITY IN A GLOBAL ECONOMY

Introduction   3

Examples of global organizations   4
    Levi Strauss & Co. · Nesté · Greenpeace · NEC · UK Ministry   4
      of Defence · Marks & Spencer

Some everyday events for individuals   6

The global economy and changing perspectives   7

Global sourcing   9
    Arbor International: supplying baby corn from the local to the
      local via the global   11
    The reverse brain drain – IT from India   11
    The floral revolution in Colombia – Ecoflor   12
    Global governance and the trade in illegal drugs   13

The developing world – rich and poor   14

What has become globalized?   18

Communicating in a global economy:
  learn to speak locally and globally   20

More globalization? What's the end game?   22

Global and corporate governance   23

The global company   24

What is the difference between international, multinational,
transnational, supranational and global companies?   26

  MANAGEMENT EXERCISES   27
  1 Two views of globalization   27
  2 Dilemma: a sticky situation   28
  3 Ethical dilemma: what would you do?   29
  4 Dilemma: Chinese bags   29

❷
THE NEW CORPORATE CITIZENSHIP

Introduction	35
Avon: managing in a multicultural world	37
London's Metropolitan Police	37
Who said this?	38
Corporate citizenship is for all organizations	40
Shell's global responsibilities	40
Economic, legal, social and environmental responsibilities	40
Renlon: winning new business	42
Moving up to social accountability: BT's social audit	42
Tomorrow's organization	43
Interest in social responsibility	43
Business for Social Responsibility (USA)	44
The Charter for Good Corporate Behavior (Japan)	45
The Asahi Foundation (Japan)	46
The Centre for Tomorrow's Company (UK)	47
Business as partners in development: The Prince of Wales Business	48
Leaders' Forum, The World Bank and The UN Development Programme	
The World Business Council for Sustainable Development:	49
Draft Principles for Social Responsibility	
Models of social responsibility	50
The Big Issue: *an alternative business on the streets*	51
Medecins sans Frontières: borderless care	53
MANAGEMENT EXERCISES	55

❸
PUTTING CORPORATE CITIZENSHIP AT THE HEART OF STRATEGY

Introduction	61
Brand image and reputation	61
Protecting reputations	65
Mercedes-Benz · Ford Pinto · British Airways · Heineken ·	
Prudential Assurance · Barclays Bank · Dow Corning	65
Managing risk	68
Bhopal and Union Carbide	69
Prince William Sound and Exxon	71

Quality, productivity and social responsibility   72
Quality and productivity: Premier Beverages   73

The learning organization   74

Successful strategies of long-lived companies   75

MANAGEMENT EXERCISES   76
1 Risk assessment and social responsibility   76
2 Company mission   77

❹

CRITICAL ISSUES IN CORPORATE CITIZENSHIP

Introduction   83

Corporate governance   85
Campbell's soup   90
CALPERS   90
The Cadbury Committee: the financial aspects of corporate governance   91
The Hampel Committee on Corporate Governance   92

The environment   95

The environment and the last 30 years   96
The Natural Step   98
The Coalition for Environmentally Responsible Economies:
    the CERES principles   103
The International Chamber of Commerce: Business Charter for
    Sustainable Development   104
Scandic Hotels: practising the Natural Step   105
Merck: investing in the rainforest   106
Century Textiles: greening the company secures key export markets   107
NatWest, Marks & Spencer, Bath Environment Centre, local
    government and the community – a partnership for the environment   108
Nortel: sharing technology   110
Novo Nordisk: dialogue with the stakeholders   111
SmithKline Beecham: cutting costs, cutting waste   112
The Tagua Initiative: may a thousand tagua buttons bloom!   112

Human rights and the workplace   113
The UN's 1948 Universal Declaration of Human Rights   117
Amnesty International: monitoring human-rights abuses globally   119
BP in Colombia   120
Shell in Nigeria   122
The International Labour Organisation   126

Nike   129
Levi Strauss & Co.: guidelines for country selection   131
The Apparel Industry Partnership   132
The Abrinq Foundation: rewarding child-friendly companies   132
Opportunity 2000   136
Churchill & Friend's disabled customer-care audit   140
Sexual harassment and ethics training in the US Army   145
Racism and sexual harassment in the British military:
   the changing of the guard   146
The National AIDS Trust Employment Initiative (UK) –
   a business charter for HIV/AIDS: Companies act!   148

Fair trade and ethical investment   150
Cafédirect: a story of fair trade   151
Max Havelaar: another success of fair trade   153
The Ethical Trading Initiative   154
Christian Aid's fair-trade campaign: how does your supermarket rate?   154
FairTrade   155
The Body Shop: are the fair-trade initiatives just cosmetic?   156
The Co-operative Bank: investing with a conscience   164
VanCity   166

The arms trade   167
Anti-personnel landmines: the Red Cross/Red Crescent campaign   169

Tobacco   172

Animal welfare and protection   173
Humane treatment of livestock: Hormel and Land O'Lakes   175
Animal testing: Tom's of Maine   175
The RSPB: over 100 years old and 1 million members   176

Education   177

MANAGEMENT EXERCISES   180
1 Dilemma: alcopops   180
2 Dilemma: employment   181
3 Dilemma: HIV in the kitchen   182
4 Corporate killing in the UK   183

❺

MANAGING CORPORATE CITIZENSHIP

Introduction   193
Key relationships and stakeholders   193

Who are stakeholders? 198

Out of touch with stakeholders? The House of Windsor
and the death of Diana, Princess of Wales 200
In touch with stakeholders? Environmental reporting for IBM (UK) 201
Environmental Risk Assessment for Sustainable Cities:
UNEP International Technology Center 203
Stakeholder management in military healthcare: the US
Department of Defense 203
Traidcraft plc 204

The inclusive company 206

McKay Nursery Co.: reponsibility to migrant workers 207
VW's "workholders" 207
Manganese Steel: closure and close-out are not the only options 208

Business and communities 209

The global and the local: Marks & Spencer's secondment policy 210
Levi Strauss & Co.'s Community Investment Team 211
Building Timberland in the USA 212
The London Benchmarking Group 213
The Corporate Community Index 214
Bata Thailand and the Thai Business Initiative in Rural
Development: shoe-in 215
Auchan: combating gang warfare 216
Unilever in Uttar Pradesh 216
Fondo Social del Empresariado Chihuahuense
(Chihuahua's Business Social Trust) 217
Phillips Van Heusen 218

Building partnerships 219

A partnership for progress: McDonald's and the
Environmental Defense Fund 219
A partnership in progress: Marine Stewardship Council (MSC) 225

Re-measuring wealth: auditing and accountability 227

Auditing business performance 232

Environmental auditing 234

Social and ethical auditing 237

BT's social audit: working within a "robust ethical framework" 238

The ethical audit 239

The Co-operative Bank's ethical audit of customers and non-customers 239
The Co-op's survey of ethics in business 240
The Body Shop: social-responsibility criteria 241

The social audit   241
   New Economics Foundation   243
   Accounting for a change: KPMG   244
   The CARE framework: Price Waterhouse   245
   The Body Shop's social audit   246
A new global standard for social accountability: SA8000   246
   The CEPAA's guide to SA8000   249
   SGS Yarsley and the development of SA8000   249
Developing global standards   249
Reporting company performance   251
   Corporate environmental disclosure:
     The Association of Chartered Certified Accountants 253
Managing the media: how to survive a boycott   255
   Lessons from "McLibel"   257
   MANAGEMENT EXERCISES   257
   1 Identifying your stakeholders   258
   2 Do you know what your stakeholders think of you?   259
   3 Auditing dilemmas   260
     (a) Ventilating an accountability issue in China   260
     (b) Keeping it in the family, Chinese style   261
     (c) House and home in Manila   262

❻

BUSINESS AS IF THERE'S A FUTURE

It is possible to envision different futures   271
Managing change and complexity   272
Five principles for corporate citizenship   277
Five management imperatives for corporate citizenship   278

Appendix 1: recommended reading   281

Appendix 2: glossary   283

Appendix 3: contact addresses   291

Index   305

FOREWORD

by Alice Tepper Marlin

Council on Economic Priorities

Milton Friedman, the prime advocate of the position that the responsibility of business is exclusively to maximize profit for shareholders, has lost the debate. Business leaders who once gave only a recalcitrant response to the feisty demands of activists now have developed an enlightened appreciation of the value of corporate reputation as a competitive advantage.

This savvy and cooperative approach has developed more or less independently in a number of countries, aided and abetted by a rapidly growing civil society, by media no longer universally fearful of naming companies, and by post cold war frameworks and strategies.

In today's business environment, the speed of transportation and communication has risen and costs have fallen dramatically. Literacy rates around the world have dramatically improved. Capital investment is so easily mobile that production anywhere in the world is practical and often financially advantageous. We've achieved more efficiency, lower costs, and new job opportunities in many locations.

But as assembly and manufacturing jobs move in response to market conditions, children and impoverished adults are hired at rock bottom wages to manufacture garments and toys, to weave rugs, and to cut stems and flowers, often for export.

The International Labour Organisation estimates that the 120 million children working worldwide are increasingly employed under dangerous, unhealthy, and inhumane conditions.

Public awareness and outrage have grown steadily and corporate reputations are now at stake not simply – like Texaco's – in a company's headquarter country, but wherever customers watch TV or log onto the Internet, and wherever ethical investors hold portfolios with an international exposure.

The momentum for global social change in this era of instant communications is unprecedented. Consider the Nike Corporation. In March 1998, the company announced that its financial performance had deteriorated substantially over the past year. One of the main reasons advanced by company management for Nike's decline was, in the words of the *Washington Post*, "resistance by customers because of persistent allegations that the company mistreats its factory workers."

Today's consumers are increasingly more sophisticated, and they are interested in more than just price. They are asking hard questions about the internal corporate practices behind the brand name products they buy. Many major corporations around the world already understand this and want to do the right thing. Management at many companies genuinely care about these issues.

They want to protect their reputations; they need to defend themselves from attacks; and they see social accountability as a competitive asset.

But companies find it extremely difficult to insist on the same standards of corporate responsibility from a network of hundreds of suppliers spanning the globe. Internal codes of conduct, pioneered by Levi Strauss & Co., have emerged as a partial answer to this dilemma. Toys 'Я' Us, Timberland, Liz Claiborne, Reebok and others have adopted first-rate codes of conduct. Nevertheless, there are several major flaws to this approach.

First, internal codes are inherently expensive and inefficient, because laws and customs vary widely in different countries and regions, and companies regard their sources and their audits as proprietary. Often, it is difficult for companies even to get reliable information. Factory owners, in turn, are taxed to have to perform multiple audits to differing sets of standards, each with its own requirements and paperwork. A recent Council on Economic Priorities' study of 360 US companies revealed that 77 have their own codes. The codes vary widely, with fewer than half covering compensation or limits on their work week. Fewer than a third are monitored at all. Virtually none are independently verified by third parties. Internal systems by their nature are neither transparent nor independently verified, resulting in credibility problems, instead of solutions.

The real solution is to adapt the same model that corporations use to ensure quality control on the part of vendors and suppliers. The solution consists of credible, verifiable, and certifiable standards that can be audited by expert third parties. ISO 9000, the best known of the management system standards, is now used in several hundred thousand facilities worldwide for quality control assurance. Social Accountability 8000 (SA8000) applies these same techniques to the assurance of social accountability, building on the same basic management system. Like ISO 9000, its systems for corrective and preventive actions encourage continuous improvement. They are incentive-based approaches. But distinct from ISO 9000 and ISO 14000 (for environmental management systems), SA8000 also has performance standards and these elements of the standard are quite stringent.

In many ways, SA8000 typifies the future of corporate social responsibility: it is consensus-based and requires substantial "transparency," or public reporting. In the world of SA8000, companies will need to do more than simply issue policy statements; they will need independent verification and consultation with stakeholders. This book provides an initial introduction to SA8000 and to the corporate environment which has created and fostered the standard.

Globalization poses major challenges to today's manager. Global approaches are needed which reflect the local context. By becoming better corporate citizens, companies can address both global and local issues, while connecting in new ways to consumers, investors, and employees. This book shows how companies can improve the bottom line by addressing the complex challenges posed by environmental degradation, poverty, and urban decay, to name a few.

The field of corporate social responsibility has changed dramatically in the past three decades. In the 70s, corporate social responsibility was considered a fringe issue, marginal and radical. Today, corporate citizenship is a mainstream corporate issue that has permeated the board room and the shop floor. *Corporate Citizenship* provides a road map for managers seeking to effect change within their companies and the world.

Alice Tepper Marlin
President, Council on Economic Priorities
Executive Director, CEP Accreditation Agency

ABOUT THE AUTHORS

Malcolm McIntosh is an independent teacher, writer and consultant on corporate citizenship. His clients include the UK government and large and small companies. He has produced films on social and environmental issues for BBC TV and published books and articles on global security, corporate social responsibility and environmental management. Now based in Bath, UK, he has travelled extensively and worked in Japan, Australia and Sweden. Dr McIntosh, FRSA is a Visiting Fellow of Bristol University and teaches at Bath and Lancaster universities where he runs courses on corporate citizenship, business ethics and sustainable communities. He is currently involved in a long-term study of global corporations that have survived the twentieth century.

Deborah Leipziger is the Director of the Council on Economic Priorities in the UK, a research organization devoted to promoting corporate citizenship. Ms Leipziger played an integral part in the drafting and launch of the first global social accountability standard, Social Accountability 8000, and its subsequent guidance document. A native of Brazil, Ms Leipziger earned a Master's in Public Administration from Colombia University's School of International and Public Affairs and a BA, magna cum laude, in Economics and International Studies from Manhattanville College.

Keith L. Jones is an Executive Manager with nearly thirty years' commercial experience across a wide range of sectors. He is a Lead Auditor and Sector Manager for SGS and was jointly responsible for pioneering, drafting, development and on-site auditing work for the ethical management standard SA8000. Dr Jones has degrees from the universities of Oxford, London and Durham and has researched and published extensively in business subjects.

Gill Coleman is Programme Director at the New Academy of Business which she joined at its inception in 1995. Previously she held the post of Director of Studies for the MBA in International Business at Bristol University. As a university teacher and researcher, she specialized in organizational dynamics and women's development, and has worked in the UK and Europe as a consultant to governmental and not-for-profit organizations. Since 1996, Gill has worked with Bath University School of Management, to establish and run the M.Sc. in Responsibility and Business Practice.

ACKNOWLEDGEMENTS

A project of this size inevitably involves a great many people. First and foremost we must thank our co-authors who have supported the writing and publication of this book over the last twelve months. As an international group of authors, we have worked as a team drawing on our different experiences, offering varying perspectives of the changing nature of corporate citizenship. This is reflected in the diversity of company profiles and examples of best practice in the book.

Next come those people who have given invaluable support in the form of research, writing and logistics. Many thanks to Alex Cutler for her work on various sections of the book. Our publishers, Financial Times Management, have allowed the project to develop from an initial concept and to see the author team expand. We are all very grateful to Pradeep Jethi at Financial Times Management for his insight and wisdom, but most of all for his boundless enthusiasm. He has had to suffer the development of the book as have two of his colleagues without whom this book would not have become reality. Elizabeth Truran, Managing Editor, has been as patient as is humanly possible and has been wonderful to work with, and David Hart, Marketing Manager, has worked hard to satisfy our demands. Others at Financial Times Management to whom we are grateful include Ron Davis and Lisa Nachtigall in the US, and Elie Ball and Kate Jenkins in the UK.

We have been given invaluable support and guidance by key people working on corporate citizenship issues including Chris Marsden at Warwick University, Jane Nelson at the Prince of Wales Business Leaders' Forum, David Murphy at the New Academy of Business and Alice Tepper Marlin at the Council on Economic Priorities.

In the process of checking the company profiles we received over one hundred responses and in particular we would like to mention the help we received from David Rice at BP, Emeke Achebe at Shell, Phil Wells at FairTrade, David Wheeler at The Body Shop and Sir Geoffrey Chandler at Amnesty International. Many, many thanks also to everyone else who took the time to update our profiles and send amendments. In the final analysis we hope we have incorporated the many comments we received, but if we have erred, we are sorry.

June 1998   *Malcolm McIntosh*
                                                                    Deborah Leipziger

INTRODUCTION
What is corporate citizenship?

This book provides you with an introduction to corporate citizenship, and the ways in which becoming a good corporate citizen can help your business. It is intended as a practical guide to issues and practices which fall under this title.[1]

One of the major differences between this book and other books on corporate citizenship, social responsibility and accountability is that we believe that significant initiatives are being made in organizations across all sectors, and in companies of many different types and sizes. For this reason, we have included profiles of McDonald's, The Body Shop, Marks & Spencer, Levi Strauss & Co., GrandMetropolitan (now Diageo), Tom's of Maine, BP, the US Department of Defense, the UK Ministry of Defence (MOD) *and* Greenpeace, along with many others. There are the beginnings of radical change in organizational behavior on a worldwide basis. Governments and global companies are being subject to greater scrutiny, and some recently formed pressure groups have become as influential as companies that are hundreds of years old. In many older, large institutional organizations, individual managers are struggling to cope with a changing external environment while their corporations are failing to adapt.

The profiles of companies and other organizations in this book are representative of the changes taking place. This book is not an attempt to be comprehensive, and while many of the profiles of organizations are exemplary, this book is an attempt to describe the world of global organizations and their collective contribution to corporate citizenship – whether they be private, public, governmental or non-governmental. We have started work on a project to identify and collate a more comprehensive collection of ideas and examples from around the world for our next book, and we look forward to hearing from people who want to be part of this new project for publication in the year 2000.

In researching this book and putting together the wealth of profiles, we have been made aware of the complexity of issues being faced by people at many levels in organizations all over the world. This book describes a radical alternative that is taking shape among people and organizations struggling with local and global responsibilities. Corporate citizenship is for us all, and this book provides signposts for a different future.

Corporate citizenship is concerned with the relationship between companies and society – both the local community which surrounds a business, and whose members interact with its employees, and the wider and increasingly worldwide community which touches every business through its products, its supply chain, its

> **Corporate citizenship is for us all – this book provides signposts for a different future.**

dealer network, its advertising, and so on. We will demonstrate in the chapters that follow that this relationship is changing rapidly, in ways which significantly affect business performance.

In talking about corporate citizenship, we are drawing a parallel between the individual citizen, and his or her responsibilities and rights as a member of a community and a company, which although made up of many people, acts as if it were an individual. We are suggesting that companies, too, have rights and responsibilities, which are undergoing change.

Historically and culturally, Western societies have tended to identify more corporate rights than responsibilities.[2] But this is a situation that is changing. For a variety of reasons, more is being expected of the corporation as a citizen. Some aspects of this new role – such as dilemmas over corporate involvement in human-rights issues in some developing countries – are complex; others – like the necessity to comply with more and more stringent environmental regulation – are becoming more clear. But all are having an increasing impact on how companies make and sustain their profits. Business leaders have long maintained that prosperity for all is best achieved through minimum regulation of business activity and maximum flexibility, and that the relationship between business and the rest of society best takes place through the market. We are suggesting here that this implicit contract is changing,

> **Prosperity for all in the future may paradoxically lie in business broadening its citizenship role and becoming a more conscious and informed social participant.**

and that prosperity for all in the future may paradoxically lie in business broadening its citizenship role and becoming a more conscious and informed social participant. This book is intended to help those working in business, and with businesses, to build that role. It is also intended to help government and civil society (non-governmental organizations, pressure groups and communities) to find new ways of working with business.

What is corporate citizenship?

Corporate citizenship, like individual citizenship, is an idea which ̖ practical and ethical dimensions. It includes basic business concerns, s ̗:

- risk avoidance and protecting reputation;
- insurance for the future;
- developing increased business competence, through:
  - managing diversity and complexity in a global economy
  - stabilizing the relationship between business and society
  - creating partnerships that span boundaries
  - having an integrated and consistent approach to corporate strategy
  - applying new metrics and reporting progress in meeting objectives.

It also includes:

- doing the right thing;
- a reflection of many people's belief that business organizations should express what is good in humanity, and be places where we can feel good about going to work.

A key feature of citizenship is that it involves a mutually reinforcing relationship between individuals and communities: individuals fulfil the responsibilities of citizenship, because some of their personal needs can only be met through communal action. Responsible citizens, for instance, dispose of their refuse in appointed places, rather than dumping it along the road or putting it on a neighbour's doorstep, because they need their neighbours to do the same. Corporate citizenship likewise suggests a two-way relationship between society and corporations: some of a corporation's needs will ultimately only be met by taking actions which are oriented towards meeting communal needs.

> **Corporate citizenship suggests a two-way relationship between society and corporations.**

We might think of corporate citizenship as forming a continuum, that stretches from "minimal" citizenship at one extreme (consisting of compliance with the laws governing the operation of the business, but nothing else), to a complex relationship of interlocking rights and responsibilities at the other (between a corporation and its communities, which has become an integral part of the functioning of the business). We will be suggesting that the successful companies of the future are likely to be those which discover how to make full use of this relationship as a normal part of running their business, and so will move along the continuum towards full citizenship.

MINIMALIST
Compliance with
legislation

DISCRETIONARY
Philanthrophy/
charitable giving

STRATEGIC
Citizenship
integrated into
business

Fig 1.1 The continuum towards full citizenship

In other words, it is possible to be a corporate citizen by merely complying with legislation, but full citizenship means that corporate citizenship has to become a strategic priority.

What is changing?

This is a book about change. At a time when academics are debating whether we are experiencing "paradigm shift" and "post-modernity," most readers of this book will have experienced some sense of awe at the speed with which everything, from family life, to ways of working and shopping are changing. Business is now having to deal with:

- a global economy – the movement of goods, money and people around the world;
- a technological revolution – underpinning the global economy with information technology, transportation, refrigeration;
- a proliferation of sources of information – from cable TV to the Internet, we have more information about each other than at any other time in history; whether we are any wiser is open to question;
- a huge growth in the size and scope of international business – the 100 largest *companies* in the world have turnovers that are greater than the GDP of half of the world's *countries*;
- signs of increasing environmental damage – global warming, loss of plant and animal species, problems with pollution of air, water and land.

These developments have had an impact on ways of doing business. For instance:

- single companies can now locate a head office in one country, research and development in another and production in yet another. The geographical connection between business leaders and the communities on which they have an impact is dissolving;

- competition is intensified, as cheap goods produced by low-wage workers are imported into high-wage parts of the world;
- ways of working have changed – many companies have stripped out layers of middle management and increased sub-contracting and the use of workers on short-term contracts, in an effort to achieve greater flexibility and reduce costs;
- companies can, and do, circumvent what they see as adverse trading conditions – such as government regulation – by relocating;
- campaign groups are able to get information about what businesses are doing in distant places, and are not afraid to use it to bring what they see as malpractice out into the open;
- consumers in affluent countries are able to choose their purchases from an increasing range of products, and are increasingly demanding, in terms of price and quality;
- new technologies mean that things can happen very rapidly – information is spread; reputations are strengthened or damaged.

This all produces a volatile and complicated environment. The following chapters illustrate how innovative companies are able to operate in it positively by developing their corporate citizenship.

Why we wrote this book

The four authors of this book have collectively worked in, and for, large organizations, private, public and voluntary, over several decades, in North America, Latin America, Europe, Asia and Australia. In our professional lives we spend a lot of our time trying to explain to managers, corporate executives and business students what corporate citizenship and corporate social responsibility is all about, and why it seems more important now than it did 20 years ago. We have been asked on numerous occasions by people to refer them to something they can read which will set out the territory – and although there are many excellent books on this subject, most of them are more detailed and more academic than most busy managers want. So we have written this book to fill a gap. In particular, the profiles in this book show

> **The profiles in this books show that corporate citizenship is now a strategic issue for all organizations.**

that corporate citizenship is now a strategic issue for all organizations. It is no longer discretionary.

How to use this book
....

Corporate Citizenship is intended as a source of ideas and examples, giving clear explanations of the issues and language currently dominating discussion about the social responsibilities of business.

We have gathered together a wide range of profiles from all around the world, to provide examples of how real businesses are moving towards active corporate citizenship, and how some notable companies have suffered serious bottom-line consequences through failing to notice what was going on around them. Examples are drawn from the USA, Japan, Africa, Brazil, India, France, Finland, Germany, Thailand, Britain and others; from a wide range of business sectors; from large multinational corporations; and from small businesses.

We see this as a practical book, containing ideas that you can apply yourself within your work environment. To facilitate this, we have provided a number of exercises or dilemmas within the text, which we invite you to work on. We have also made reference to organizations, associations, networks, interest groups and other bodies which are working on these issues, and which you can contact for further help, advice and support.

Chapter 1 provides an overview of the global economy, and how this has changed the nature of what is involved in running a responsible business. There are definitely winners from the globalization process and the prizes for business can be enormous, but there are also losers. The best possible future for people, the planet and business would be a situation where profitability is allied to strong, healthy communities.

Chapter 2 explores the issues and dilemmas faced by the corporate citizen in more depth, giving examples of how companies have dealt with the complex situation. It defines a new corporate citizenship which is not just for business, but also applies to public and voluntary-sector organizations. It ends with four models of socially responsible behavior.

Chapter 3 makes the connections between these broad developments, and core competences of business management – risk and brand management, quality, productivity, health and safety, employee morale and commitment.

Chapter 4 looks at the major critical issues in corporate citizenship – corporate governance, human rights, the environment, fair trade and ethical investment.

Chapter 5 considers the management of key relationships involved in running a socially responsible company. It explains what is meant by a "stakeholder" approach, and gives examples of innovative practice in handling these key groups. This chapter offers a toolkit, by which we mean examples of the most recent methodologies companies are using to measure and demonstrate their corporate citizenship. We believe this to be perhaps the fastest growing area of corporate social responsibility, and have provided best practice examples so that you can see what criteria are being used to judge performance, and what sort of evidence is relied on.

> This is not a book about altruism . . . it is a demonstration of how profits and ethics can go together.

Chapter 6 presents a series of options for the future.

It is not essential to read this book from beginning to end, and we envisage that for some people it will be most useful as a kind of dictionary or sourcebook, in which they can look up particular words and find an explanation of the concept, examples and ideas of where to go for further information.

At the end of Chapters 1–5 there are management exercises or dilemmas. It is hoped that the presentation of ideas in different ways will help facilitate understanding and change.

A couple of words about what it is not: this is not a book about altruism – although some companies are altruistic in their outlook – it is a demonstration of how profits and ethics can go together. It is also not a book containing simple answers or formulas. We seek to whet the reader's appetite, to point you in the direction of more information if that is what you need, and we cite the books where you will find a fuller discussion of the ideas we touch on.

Finally, we hope to convey to you that building corporate citizenship represents, in our view, a challenge and a real opportunity. It is a challenge to the existing ways of doing business, and so involves the difficult process of breaking habits and upending long-accepted ideas. It is an opportunity for business growth and personal development, for imagination and entrepreneurial flair. Most importantly, we believe it is an opportunity to develop a new business strategy that endeavors to leave a positive social footprint.

Notes

1 A corporation is a group of persons acting as an individual, whether for business or elsewhere. This means that corporate citizenship applies to organizations such as BP International Ltd, the British Broadcasting Corporation (BBC), Greenpeace and the US Department of Defense – OED.

2 See Korten, David C. (1995) *When Corporations Rule The World*. London: Earthscan.

1

SOCIAL RESPONSIBILITY IN A GLOBAL ECONOMY

Introduction

Examples of global organizations
Levi Strauss & Co. · Nesté · Greenpeace · NEC
UK Ministry of Defence · Marks & Spencer

Some everyday events for individuals

The global economy and changing perspectives

Global sourcing
Arbor International
IT from India
Ecoflor
The trade in illegal drugs

The developing world – rich and poor

What has become globalized?

Communicating in a global economy:
learn to speak locally and globally

More globalization? What's the end game?

Global and corporate governance

The global company

What is the difference between international, multinational,
transnational, supranational and global companies?

Management exercises

Introduction

"We perceive and deal with social issues in a non-traditional manner at Timberland. Timberland doesn't give money to charity. Instead we try to create a return. We integrate the notion of value creation into all our activities. We create values for ourselves as a company, our employees, our shareholders, our customers, the community and the non-profit organizations we co-operate with. The traditional notion of philanthropy is not adequate. It is not smart or wise to approach the social problems of society with the financial leftovers of companies. By integrating our social activities into our business strategies, we also provide these social activities with the sustainability that will see them through hard times, and harness business to work in another fashion." [1]

Something radical and exciting is happening when a leading footwear and clothing company such as Timberland, that is recognized around the world, says that there is another way of doing business. The same message is being communicated by McDonald's through its work with the Environmental Defense Fund, when Unilever promotes fish conservation, when Royal Dutch/Shell includes references to human rights in its business principles, and when Levi Strauss & Co. promotes ethical sourcing. All these successful companies see commercial advantage in being seen to care about the world's social and environmental problems.

Some social activists say that global companies such as Avon, GrandMetropolitan (now Diageo), BT, Shell, BP and Levi Strauss & Co. are following in the footsteps of smaller, socially active companies such as Ben & Jerry's and The Body Shop and putting corporate citizenship at the heart of strategic planning. However, some people in the business community argue that a major shift is taking place at the heart of global capitalism, that profitability can no longer be based solely on consumerism and competition. There is a growing understanding of the benefits of a proactive approach to social responsibility. Being seen to be a responsible corporate citizen is a competitive issue. Companies that have been exposed to global media scrutiny, such as Shell and McDonald's, know that the relationship between business and society is changing radically and rapidly. These companies are welcoming the growing rapport with human rights and environmental groups, because it sharpens their competitive edge, and makes them stronger players in the global market.

This chapter sets the scene for the new corporate citizenship that is developing for companies that take their own and the planet's long-term viability seriously. These companies know that operating in the global economy requires a new world view, a different set of management competences and a greatly increased sensitivity to issues, which previously were not thought of as pertinent to business.

Examples of global organizations
···

The examples below are all organizations with social and environmental responsibilities, whether they be commercial, in the public sector or single-interest pressure groups. They would all like to be thought of as responsible corporate citizens, and in some cases as exemplary; some of them claim to be models for the future. They should all be honest and accountable, and obey the law. Along with large companies are the environmental pressure group Greenpeace, and the UK's Ministry of Defence – a government ministry with a global reach.

Levi Strauss & Co. is the world's largest clothing company and the owner of Levi's, one of the best known global brands, and had reported sales of $7.1 billion in 1996. Being a global company and operating in 40 countries has had major implications and has led to the introduction of a code of conduct for the supplier companies which guarantees human rights, and promotes health and safety standards.

Nesté is one of Europe's largest petro-chemical companies. Based in Finland, it operates plants in the USA, Canada, France, The Netherlands, Mexico and China. In 1997 it issued its sixth annual environmental report, independently verified by SustainAbility, a leading environmental consultancy. To quote from the report: "Projects aimed at improving customer contacts, quality and work satisfaction support Nesté's environmental strategy, which strives towards business operations which are superior to our competitors . . . Society expects us to be socially responsible in all our operations."[2]

Greenpeace is one of the world's largest and most proactive environmental pressure groups. The group says that it has "the courage, inspiration and the global reach to defend Nature – by forcing industries and government to adopt the cleaner, more efficient solutions we all urgently want."[3]

NEC is the world's largest electronics manufacturer, and an original signatory of Keidanren's (the Japanese business association) Charter for Good Corporate Behavior (see Chapter 2). In NEC's words, "As we approach the 21st Century, the world is rapidly moving from regional interdependence to a global community, due to a highly developed infrastructure and the liberalization of governments. This can truly be called the generation of the 'global village' . . . NEC will contribute to a sound environment and a livable society through technology that harmonizes with nature and production that is environmentally friendly."[4]

The UK Ministry of Defence is one of the world's largest bodies and the second largest landowner in the UK. With a budget of $36.3 billion per annum, it shares responsibility for global security and peacekeeping with other governments on behalf of the UN. It operates nuclear-powered and nuclear-armed submarines and directly employs some 250,000 people around the world. MOD policy states that "the MOD protects and enhances the natural environment" and that it "strives to be a good neighbour at home and abroad."[5]

Marks & Spencer, the fourth most profitable retailer in the world, describes itself as "a thriving global organization operating successfully in many countries round the world." By the year 2000, it aims to have 120 franchise stores in 32 countries. Its non-UK sales already amount to $2.48 billion a year. The company says that, despite its higher prices, the organization lives up to its mission of "Quality Service Value" and "our customers choose us . . . We consider ourselves to be part of the communities we serve and actively contribute to creating a more prosperous and self-sufficient society."[6]

In a global economy, companies are now aware that contradictions in their operating practices in one country can expose their markets in another country. This book is concerned with the solutions that companies are developing.

"The world is a web of interconnected trades, organisations, labor markets and professions, not a division into one hundred and eighty autonomous and separate nations." [7]

We live in a global economy. The market is the spirit of the age we live in and corporations stride the world looking for new markets, new customers and cheaper resources. But what does this mean? What are the characteristics of the process of globalization that is now taking place? Do we have a shared understanding of the process and the outcome? What are the effects of the global economy on us as individuals, on organizations and business? How can we manage the complexities of the global economy when there is no clear view of the future? What competences must managers develop for the twenty-first century in order that our corporations remain profitable and remember their social responsibilities? With the advance of the global economy, corporations and countries, as much as individuals, must be careful not to become wholly captive to making money, rather than fulfilling other social and non-material needs. We must learn to manage the future. We can choose.

Markets are not enough; capitalism cannot provide for all of society's needs and business has to work hand in hand with good government to address environmental issues, distribute wealth more fairly, fight corruption, oppression and human-rights abuses. If business is the principle engine of society, it has a clear responsibility not to abuse its new freedom and global role. But even international agencies such as the World Bank and the International Monetary Fund, themselves evangelists for the market and trade liberalization, recognize that business cannot be asked to save the planet by itself.

Some everyday events for individuals

Individuals interact with the global economy on an everyday basis. Here are some of those situations:

- A woman withdraws money from a cash machine owned by a large bank which has investments all over the world. She is pleased that her savings grow every day because of the way in which the bank manages her money. She does not know how or where the bank invests its money. Should she care?
- A man does the weekly shopping at the supermarket, choosing from a wide variety of products sourced from all over the world and expensively wrapped in plastic and paper. He does not know how much pesticide was used on the baby corn, or how far the kiwi fruit has been flown, or how much the coffee-bean picker was paid. Does it matter?
- A manager lifts the phone to make a call, unaware that the company supplying the line has just opened an office in China, without considering abuses of human rights in that country. So what?
- A couple checks into a hotel for a holiday weekend unaware that the parent company which owns the hotel has no policy on caring for the

environment, that the company board is all male and that the flowers in the bedroom were picked by children in Colombia the day before. Would having this information have changed the couple's choice of hotels?

• People switch on the global television news unaware that the television company has helped to suppress information about human-rights abuses in one of its major future markets. Does it matter? Most people trust and believe TV news, and they watch it differently from other programs. Is this true across the world?

These stories are important because today many customers *are* asking crucial questions about global sourcing, about investments, and environmental policies. It only takes small changes in customer behavior to force companies to address these issues. The majority of customers may only be concerned about price and quality, but if 10 per cent switch products – this is significant. Non-governmental organizations (NGOs) and the media are interested in stories about the links between supermarket goods and local wage rates in distant supplier countries. Investors and companies are concerned to lessen the risk of exposure to environmental liabilities. Shareholders are increasingly wanting to know how companies are protecting their investments.

How does a bank that pays high interest rates invest its money? Does the bank have investments in an arms manufacturer supplying a country with an oppressive government? Have the apples been sprayed with a pesticide that can cause cancer? Do we want the Chinese to have the same access to news and information that we have? Does it matter that a television broadcaster tells its viewers that it is a caring company, while operating to a different tune in another market?

Businesses are becoming aware of a more transparent world where producers can link up with non-governmental organizations to brief governments, customers, and the media around the world. There is growing pressure on companies to acknowledge their global social responsibilities.

The global economy and changing perspectives

A list of events in the 1990s follows which illustrates some of the dilemmas outlined in this book. The list is a representative sample, covering many of the issues currently being discussed by organizations interested in corporate citizenship.

- Rio Tinto (previously known as RTZ), the world's largest mining company, and Freeport-McMoRan, an American corporation, are attacked by environmentalists and local people for their copper and gold mine in Irian Jaya, Indonesia. They disrupt Rio Tinto's annual shareholders' meeting and the press reports the dissension as well as the company's $2,460 million profit in 1995.[8] The lesson is that profits matter as much as environmental impact and that we live in a more transparent world.

- The International Monetary Fund (IMF) lends Mexico $17,000 million to repay foreign creditors. Deregulation of financial markets and privatization had allowed Mexican banks to borrow overseas against local assets. Foreign money poured in, knowing that in the last resort the IMF would not allow the Mexican economy to go bust. Private speculators were rewarded with high returns guaranteed by an UN agency intent on promoting free trade. In the end, the IMF will force Mexico to repay the debts, but it will not be the overseas speculators who pay, but ordinary Mexicans.[9] Making money out of money is the name of the game, but how do we protect labor, which cannot up and leave for higher returns elsewhere?

- Prime Minister Mahathir Mohammed of Malaysia calls for exchange-rate currency speculation to be outlawed at the IMF–World Bank annual meeting after his country's currency is hit by overseas speculators, as Mexico and Thailand had suffered earlier in the year. The US Treasury Secretary, Robert Rubin, calls for greater globalization of finance, not the reverse.[10] Some countries, most notably the USA, are not as affected by currency speculation as smaller, newly emerging economies. If the USA suffered the social disruption and political meltdown caused by massive currency speculation, would it change its position on globalizing finance?

- In 1997 Nomura, the Japanese finance house founded in 1925, becomes the largest owner of pubs in the UK paying $1,980 million to GrandMetropolitan (now Diageo) and Foster's. Along with previous acquisitions, this meant that Nomura owned eight per cent of British pubs (or bars), 4,309 establishments. Also in 1997 Nomura's president, Hideo Sakamaki, was arrested for breaking business law in Japan. The *Guardian* in the UK reported that along with 16 other directors, he admitted to having dealings with *sokaiya* (corporate racketeers). It was further reported that the *sokaiya*, linked to the Japanese Mafia, *yakuza*, had demanded protection money to allow Nomura to operate in Japan. Nomura was banned from being involved in certain business areas in Japan by the Japanese government from 6 August to 31 December 1997.[11] Should global links be made to connect behavior in one country by a multinational, with its behavior in another? Is this a question of both corporate and global governance?

- In October 1997 some 10 per cent of the British economy was subjected to corporate mergers, beyond the control of the government or most stakeholding groups, despite the fact that there is little evidence that such mega-mergers, based purely on share price, provide better long-term results for shareholders.[12] Who is rewarded by such large dislocations in national economies, and should governments be able to control such mergers?

● In Paris, France, on 1 October 1997, the French government ordered half of the private car owners not to drive, due to dangerously high levels of air pollution. This reduces the number of vehicles on the streets from 3 million to 2 million. One week earlier, on 24 September, the *Financial Times* survey of Europe's most respected companies had awarded BP and Royal Dutch/Shell second and eleventh places respectively. BMW came seventh.[13] Is a link being made between the petro-chemical economy and air quality? Who is responsible – the customer or the company?

● For several weeks in 1997, Malaysia, Singapore and Indonesia are almost brought to a standstill by smog which forced schools and the airports to close and people to stay at home. The World Health Organization gave a warning of respiratory and heart ailments. The smog is blamed on forest clearance fires which have got out of hand. In 1994, a similar situation arose and was found to be caused by clearing land to produce palm oil, paper and pulp for export.[14] Malaysia and Indonesia are competing in the global economy, partly by selling their natural assets. Now customers in Europe and North America are asking questions about timber sourcing that relate back to irresponsible and unsustainable forest clearance. What will the effect be on the producer countries?

Global sourcing
....

One of the key aspects of the globalization process involves sourcing (procuring and purchasing) from the cheapest market. While this is normally a major decision for a manufacturing industry, food importers are more able to change sources rapidly. The global economy has, of course, existed for hundreds of years and many European empires in the eighteenth and nineteenth centuries were built on trade and cheap overseas sourcing. The advent of refrigeration early in the twentieth century meant an increase in the range of tradable food products, and today vast quantities of perishable fruit and vegetables are air freighted around the world on a daily basis. The price to customers in the USA and Europe is composed of cheap labor costs in the source country plus a substantial proportion representing transport costs and the original cost of production. In the case of food, these costs, both to the customer and the environment, are referred to as "food miles."[15]

While money, sourcing and manufacturing may be mobile, populations and environmental resources normally are not. Money is attracted to high returns, manufacturing to low labor rates, trained workforces, quality production and sourcing to the cheapest, most reliable market. While investors, manufacturers and buyers may move on, populations remain behind, often having to live with the results of careless raw-resource extraction.

The sourcing of computing and information systems globally has fewer implications for long-term planning. As North America, Europe and some Pacific Rim countries become information and entertainment economies, they find themselves competing with countries such as India, Mexico, Egypt and, in the future, China. It is easier for a small percentage of the population of these countries to tool themselves up intellectually and compete in software systems than it is to set up a car factory.

Four examples of global sourcing

Here are four examples of global sourcing and distribution, all strikingly different, but all based on the truly global nature of the economy. The first explains how baby corn, or small maize, finds its way onto supermarket shelves in North America, Europe and Australia from Africa. The second concerns the post-industrial leap that countries such as India, Mexico and China have made into the information age which allows them to compete internationally in software products, and how they are gaining market share from North Americans and Europeans. The third shows how the search for the cheapest markets, and the necessity of developing countries to pay off overseas debts, have led to the development of industries which are in many ways harmful to the countries in which the produce is grown. In this case, the example cited is the flower industry and Colombia's contribution to the funeral of Diana, Princess of Wales. The fourth example looks at the other side of the global economy and points out that the trade in illegal drugs is now second only to the oil industry.

Multinational corporations and international agencies (such as the United Nations and the International Chamber of Commerce) are becoming more important in deciding how we all live, wherever we are in the world. As individual countries and empires become less powerful, international business, operating on a twenty-four hour basis, dominates the global economy.

Arbor International: supplying baby corn from the local to the local via the global

Maize is a known food throughout most of the world. Much of it is sourced in Africa and sold to supermarkets around the world.

In Australia, the UK or France, when you buy baby corn from the supermarket in the afternoon, it may have been picked in Zimbabwe the day before. The process starts at 6 a.m. when Hilbre Farm's managers, an hour's drive from Harare, Zimbabwe, link their electronic data interchange system to Arbor International's computers in Berkshire, England, and download the packing schedule for the day.

Arbor handles "responsibility for this product from the seed to the shopping trolley" for supermarkets around the world. With a turnover of $10.72 million a year, Arbor sells 120 tons of vegetables a month to industrial countries, mostly Britain, France and Australia. Arbor is paid $1.50 per kilo for vegetables that sell for $13.20 in the supermarket, the workers in Zimbabwe being paid up to $95.7 a month.

Most of the workers are women who also receive free food, fuel and lodging for as long as they want to stay. These workers receive more than the minimum wage. Even with airfreight costs, the women of Zimbabwe can easily undercut the market gardeners of Britain, although of course, baby corn is not grown in the UK because of the climate. In Marks & Spencer food shops in Britain, the bar code tells managers where the baby corn comes from, and which women picked it in Zimbabwe. As well as quality, supermarkets like Marks & Spencer require consistency.

At present, customers understand that their baby corn will look the same, taste the same and be available throughout the year. If major supermarkets adopt fair-trade[16] and ethical-sourcing principles and food labelling is improved, in future consumers may also be able to satisfy themselves as to the level of pesticides used on the crop, and the wages and living conditions of the women who pick them 8,000 kilometers away.[17]

The reverse brain drain – IT from India

One of the key aspects of the growing global economy is how changes in sourcing patterns are being driven by technological innovation on the one hand and by one of the world's most critical resources, education and training, on the other. In 1997, 25 per cent of the Fortune 500[18] corporations sourced some of their IT from India. This is an irony, given the fact that India is still rated very low on the UN's Human Development Index, but shows how a national economy can leapfrog industrialization and develop through enhanced labor skills.

Dewang Mehta, Executive Director of the Indian National Association of Software and Service Companies, says: "It's a reverse brain drain. After the US, India has the largest English-speaking scientific manpower pool, many of whom were trained in the US and have decided to return home." India's exports of software were $1 billion in 1996 and are expected to grow to $4 billion by 2000. As one software executive said: "We believe that the Internet is a leveller," because it allows countries like India to compete with more developed economies.

Other companies that have adopted India for software sourcing include British Airways (BA), which has invested $4.95 million in World Network Services in Mumbai, saving it $14.85 million on employment costs at its London centre. BA not only made significant savings, but also gained access to quality, experienced staff. Unilever has also outsourced to India the development of its mainframe conversion to handle the year 2000 problem.[19] Similarly, Reebok Europe used Indian software companies to solve a warehouse management system problem in 1993.

Countries with good education systems and a well-educated workforce, particularly proficient in computer and numeracy skills, are best able to compete in this global market. Also, as operating languages tend to be in English, and because Microsoft, the world leader, is American, countries such as India where the language of government is English, have a competitive advantage over countries such as China. The movement of software manufacturing to countries such as India redistributes wealth, but is dependent on quality provision and lowest cost. This benefits India, while creating unemployment in other countries. The UK, in particular, is learning to compete with Bangalore and Mumbai, India's Silicon Valley. Is this an example of the race to the finish, of outsourcing driving prices lower and lower to unacceptable levels?

However, infrastructure development is a long-term issue for countries competing in the outsource market, particularly in intellectual services like computing. Countries supplying computing services need reliable electricity supplies, which is not the case in many parts of India. Good healthcare provision, primary to tertiary education systems, and electricity supplies take years to establish. Should this be the responsibility of companies, such as British Airways or Reebok, that are happy to take advantage of cheap wages? When Indian wages rise, will these companies move on to even cheaper markets?[20]

The floral revolution in Colombia – Ecoflor

There are unexpected aspects to the global economy, which force us to question the sanity of leaving our lives in the hands of market forces. Is it an intelligent use of natural and human resources to fly flowers round the world on jumbo jets?

Britons spent $82.5 million on floral tributes to Diana, Princess of Wales, when she was killed in a car crash in 1997. Many of those flowers came from Colombia, in South America. Many Colombians were as moved by Diana's death as the British and some five million Colombians watched the funeral on television at 4 a.m. and a quarter of a million signed the book of condolence in Bogotá. Also significant was the 20 per cent rise in Colombian flower sales in Europe. According to the National Growers Association, Colombia contributed 3.5 million blooms to Diana's funeral, all of which were cut and flown to the UK.

Exports of flowers from Colombia contributed US$509 million in 1996, making it the second largest flower exporter after The Netherlands. Seventy per cent of Colombia's flowers go to the USA, 15 per cent to the UK and the remainder to Europe and the rest of the world.

Does the flower industry help Colombia's development? There are 400 farms covering 10,000 acres growing flowers, mostly in greenhouses. There has been indiscriminate use of agrochemicals and clean water now has to be collected from wells up to 100 metres deep. Even at that depth, the water supplies have been affected by toxins and, according to the World Health Organisation (WHO), concentrations of toxins in surface water exceed its guidelines. Much of the organic waste resulting from the flower production is fed to animals that increasingly suffer from low fertility rates and an increased number of miscarriages. Bovine milk and women's breast milk show chemical residues above WHO guidelines.

Most of the 70,000 workers in the greenhouses are women who receive the minimum wage and have to work overtime to earn a living wage. Most of them have little job security, and only 10 per cent are unionized.

However, a group called Ecoflor has captured 10 per cent of the market. Ecoflor's mission is to improve working conditions and reduce environmental damage. According to its Director, Marta Pizano: "We have succeeded in cutting pesticide use by 35 per cent and, by collecting rainwater, we use 40 per cent less groundwater. To our surprise, despite initial high investment, we are saving on production costs in the long term." A team from Bogotá's university says that with even greater efficiency they could make savings of up to 80 per cent on the use of water through microdrops and aspiration watering (involving discrete, well-targeted watering of crops).

Floriculture in Colombia is a cash crop which earns hard currency for the country but hardly raises the standard of living for those who work in it. It also causes environmental degradation and causes serious health problems. Responsible retailers in the USA and Europe could, at little cost to themselves but with great public relations value, announce that they were only going to purchase flowers from Colombia grown through Ecoflor. Everybody would be better off, including customers, who would be importing fewer toxic residues into their homes.[21]

Global governance and the trade in illegal drugs

The international trade in illegal drugs, as defined by the United Nations, represents 8 per cent of world trade, is bigger than iron and steel, and second only to the trade in oil. The UN Drug Control Programme says that although establishing the size of the illegal drugs trade is difficult, because all activities are outside the law, its estimates are as follows:

● The annual turnover is $4,000 million.
● By contrast, annual development aid amounts to $690 million.

- In 1996, an estimated 8 million people used heroin, 13 million used cocaine, 30 million used amphetamine-type drugs, 141 million used cannabis and 227 million used sedatives.
- World production of coca leaf more than doubled between 1985 and 1996, in the same period opium production more than tripled.

The business is highly globalized with producers and wholesalers able to switch trade routes and markets.

However hard international banks try to monitor the laundering of drug money, it is often impossible, though US laws on transparency are increasingly allowing drug enforcement agencies to track cash flows around the world.

As some of the main recipient countries for laundering drugs money, the USA, Britain, Italy, Switzerland and Canada have adopted common codes to help trace funds:

- Banks are required to report suspicious transactions.
- Employees are granted immunity from prosecution for breaking confidentiality laws.
- The sharing of seized assets with other interested governments is allowed.
- Non-banks must meet the same anti-laundering criteria as banks. [22]

Attempts to counter the trade in illegal drugs is evidence of global governance in action. This is a model for future developments in tracking money from illegal arms trading, or companies and countries engaged in human-rights abuses.

However the global economy is developing, whether by flying lilies round the world, money laundering or air-freighting baby corn, *the issue is one of accountability for business. How and where is money made?*

The developing world – rich and poor

Figures from the UN's 1997 *Human Development Report* show that the world is becoming increasingly polarized between the rich and the poor. Despite evidence that the gap doubled between 1981 and 1996, the apostles of globalization argue that the process benefits the whole world.

The figures that follow show the power and responsibility that global business has in working towards a fair distribution of resources and creating a sustainable world. The size and scope of large multinational companies and the relationship between governments and those companies must give pause for thought. The Governor of the Bank of England, Eddie George, did exactly that when he addressed the Institute of Petroleum: "The annual value of world oil output works out at something like $500 billion. That is more than the GDP of any country outside of the G7. On that basis you might find you are entitled to a permanent seat on the UN Security Council."[23] The business and management consultant, Charles Handy, paints a similar picture of the head of a large company being greeted at London's Heathrow Airport by a guard of honor and a fanfare: "I think we ought to treat them as heads of state because their 'states' are a damned sight more important than many other states."[24] The problem, as Handy sees it, is that "mega-organizations are like large countries but they are not accountable to anyone. They are not accountable to their citizens."[25]

Global business[26]

- The largest 100 companies have annual revenues that exceed the GDP of 50 per cent of the world's nation-states.
- General Motors has the same annual revenue as Austria.
- Korean motor manufacturer Daewoo – with a workforce of 91,000 – has the same annual revenue as Bangladesh, with a population of 116 million.
- Globally 358 billionaires have as much wealth as the poorest 45 per cent of the world's population.
- 359 corporations account for 40 per cent of world trade.
- Five companies in Britain receive almost 50 per cent of everything the British spend.
- The 12 most important global industries, such as textiles and media, are each more than 40 per cent controlled by five or fewer corporations.
- Ten corporations control almost every aspect of the worldwide food chain.

Moreover:
- Since the mid-twentieth century the world has consumed more resources than in all previous human history.
- The 48 least developed nations, with 10 per cent of the world's population, have 0.3 per cent of world trade.
- 1.3 billion people live on $1 a day or less.
- 160 million children are undernourished.
- 20 per cent of the world's population will die before they are 40 years old.
- Even in the UK, one in three children lives in poverty and the divide between rich and poor is greater now that it has been since 1886, and in 1997 it was the same in Britain as in Nigeria.[27]

> - In Bangladesh of the 16 million children under five, 14 million are malnourished and 700 Bangladeshis die every day of malnutrition.[28]
> - The world is divided into roughly three classes of affluence, regardless of the wealth of the country they inhabit. The super-rich overconsumers, middle-income "sustainers," and as many people living in poverty. These classes coexist in most countries.[29]

Business and government leaders now recognize that governments alone cannot solve problems of poverty and environmental degradation. The finger of blame cannot be pointed at one political system, one industrial sector or one philosophy for the state in which the world now finds itself at the end of the twentieth century. But as the UN's 1997 *Human Development Report* stated: "Globalization is being presented with an air of inevitability and overwhelming conviction. Not since the heyday of free trade in the 19th century has economic theory elicited such widespread certainty. The biggest winners have been multi-national corporations. Globalization has its winners and losers." In a similar vein, David Korten argues, in *When Corporations Rule the World*, that: "We are creating a world that is becoming more deeply divided between the privileged and the dispossessed, between those who have the power to place themselves beyond the prevailing market forces and those who have become sacrificial offerings on the altar of global competition."[30]

The problem embedded in the relative shift of power from governments to corporate bodies is – who is accountable, and to whom? As management guru Peter Drucker says, "No society has had so many centers of power as the society in which we now live . . . Therefore we come back to the old problem of pluralistic society: Who takes care of the Common Good? Who defines it?"[31]

It is clear that business operates best in democratic societies which operate under the rule of law, have low levels of corruption and an infrastructure of education, healthcare and crime prevention provided by central and local government. In other words, there has to be an understanding that only with government, civil society and business working together is it possible to build healthy, safe communities.

It is on this basis that a new model of global social development is emerging with partnerships between business, governments and communities at its heart. This is what GrandMetropolitan (now Diageo) means when it says: "What happens to society matters to us, because it happens to us,"[32] and when McDonald's says it has a "special responsibility to protect our environment for future generations" because "this responsibility is derived from our unique relationship with millions of customers."[33] With this understanding, these companies can expect that society will monitor their practice very carefully. Companies can turn societal concern to their competitive advantage by publishing an external social audit[34] to allay customer fears and to provide quality benchmarks. This proactive approach has been adopted by GrandMetropolitan (now Diageo) and BT, and it is actively being considered by parts of the Royal Dutch/Shell Group and BP.

The debate about global governance has moved on from the sterility of capitalism versus communism, of command and control versus the unfettered market, and from the Cold War. A more sophisticated approach is required, which is sometimes referred to as "the third way," that recognizes that the debate about the balance between freedom and order now has a world stage. As political philosopher David Marquand says: "Globally and nationally, we shall sooner or later have to choose between the free market and the free society." In a similar vein, John Gray argues that "in an open world" governments are unable to make choices between free markets and can only "struggle to reconcile them."[35]

For business the world is changing just as fast as for governments, hence the need for discussion about global corporate citizenship. As a chronicler of poverty over some 30 years, Peter Townsend articulates the problem for governments:

"As we approach the twenty-first century, a remarkable convergence of political and economic institutions has taken place around the world . . . Today virtually all advanced countries have adopted, or are trying to adopt, liberal democratic political institutions . . . In post-industrial societies further improvements cannot be achieved through ambitious social engineering."[36]

These sentiments are echoed by the Chairman of Nestlé, Helmut O. Maucher:

"The need to adapt and cast aside old behavior patterns is not confined to business. Governments, too, have to adjust to the new global realities which press urgently upon them . . . This internationalization of government decision making is the inevitable consequence of an integrated world economy in which tariff and other barriers to the free flow of goods and services have been progressively reduced."[37]

Just as governments cannot solve the world's problems on their own, without markets to motivate, innovate and inspire, so too business should not be expected to go it alone. As Handy says, "Capitalism is not capable of delivering a good life for all or a decent society. I don't think we should expect it to. It is a means not an end."[38]

What has become globalized?

How has the global economy developed, and what are its features? How is it that the process of globalization develops apace and governments and business sometimes claim that they have no control over their citizens' or organizations' destiny? How too can the elements of globalization be used to develop global corporate governance that leads to responsible corporate citizenship?

- *Telecommunications* – the growth of telecommunications through telephones, faxes and e-mail has made it possible to communicate electronically on a global basis. In one sense, this is more inclusive as it allows anyone, anywhere to participate in the information age, but many people do not have access to the hardware and software, or electricity and telephone lines.
- *Monitoring* – through the development of satellite technology, the world can be monitored for military movements, rainforest destruction and the effects of climatic change. Most of this information is freely available for individuals, governments and business.
- *Business* – business sources and operates globally.
- *Images* – images are flashed round the world, from Pepsi's colour change in 1996, to the Chernobyl explosion in 1986, and the Chinese government's crackdown in Tiananmen Square in 1989.
- *Disease* – through organizations such as the WHO, diseases such as smallpox are eradicated globally, while the elimination of the AIDS virus[39] becomes a global phenomenon, and deaths by car accidents are hardly mentioned, despite the fact that cars cause more deaths and accidents than many diseases.[40]
- *Ecology* – the sight of planet Earth from space has helped us to realize that we share one world and has enabled us to understand its fragility and our position in the universe.
- *Connectivity* – we are connected globally through shopping, travel, resource use, pollution and the media.

This global connectivity has three dynamics: movement, change and wealth disparity. The three business virtues of "resourcefulness, inventiveness and the courage to take risks"[41] are mirrored by the speed, agility and stamina required to operate successfully in the information economy.

Movement and mobility

Consider the following:

- Money is free to move, most labor is not.
- Capital flows from market to market.[42]
- Exchange rates change constantly.
- Business outsources to the cheapest suppliers or producers anywhere in the world.
- There is a rush towards an increasingly urbanized, world society.[43]
- Women are increasingly taking up paid work.
- There has been an increase in people working electronically from home, numbering 20 million in 1996; this is estimated to rise to some 200 million by 2016.
- There has been a rapid expansion of global business organizations.
- We are seeing the development of global, multilateral organizations and non-governmental organizations (NGOs).

Change

This can be summarized as:

- uncertainty about a lack of control over the future;
- a lack of job security, caused by constant restructuring, delayering and the relocation of companies;
- new products and processes are constantly being developed;
- there is a flood of new information about the world around us, so that just when we think we understand it, it changes.[44]

Wealth disparity

In essence:

- the trading blocs of Europe, North America and the Pacific Rim have grown in affluence to the virtual exclusion of other parts of the world;

● living standards have become polarized across national boundaries into three groups of overconsumers, sustainers and the impoverished.[45]

Communicating in a global economy: learn to speak locally *and* globally

Without English it is difficult, if not impossible, to make use of global communications systems, to use the Internet, or to have access to most of the world's stored information. More than 80 per cent of the world's information is stored in English. In the information society, knowledge is power and knowledge with intelligence means competitive edge and wealth. But who does English belong to? How is it developing? What might be the consequences if English became the only language spoken around the world?

1,700 million people speak English out of a total world population of 5,000 million. Of these, 470 million speak English as a first language and the remainder as a second or foreign language. English now has special administrative status in 70 countries. However, English is not the most common first language. More than 20 per cent of the world speak some form of Chinese as their mother tongue, and nearly 5 per cent speak Spanish; 4.5 per cent speak Hindi, followed by Bengali, Russian, Arabic, Portuguese, Japanese and French.

"It has all happened so quickly. In 1950, any notion of English as a true world language was but a dim, shadowy, theoretical possibility, surrounded by the political uncertainties of the cold war, and lacking any clear definition or sense of direction. Fifty years on, and 'Global English' exists as a political and cultural reality."[46]

The greatest promotion of English came initially through colonization and then through the influence of the printing press. In the nineteenth century Thomas Carlyle identified three events that he thought had shaped the west: gunpowder, Protestantism and printing. The first provided the power for the second to be taken outside the European continent, to be followed quickly by the printed word, often in the form of the Bible. The Chinese, who had invented both gunpowder and printing much earlier, and for whom Confucianism provides the equivalent of the Protestant work ethic, mainly kept all three developments to themselves. In the late twentieth century they are beginning to determine world trade patterns, becoming, for instance, net importers (rather than exporters) of grain in 1996.

Despite the ascendancy of China as a major world power, it is unlikely that any form of Chinese will become a global language because of the primacy that English has assumed. Not that the British, or those people for whom English is their first language should assume ownership of the language, because there is a multitude of forms of English spoken around the world with a variety of accents and dialects.

"Global English" is a limited affair of a few hundred words, confined to computer-speak, functional literacy but cultural illiteracy, vital communications but essentially banality. What is important is that in order for individuals and corporations to communicate on the world stage, they must use English effectively. Just as the growth of English was accompanied, or preceded, by military power so now world trade is largely conducted in English as the lingua franca.

In 1898, Otto Bismarck was asked what had been the most decisive factor in modern history. He replied "The fact that North Americans speak English." It was the development of computers coupled with the US military's need for a global satellite and communication navigation system that produced the Internet. As David Crystal pointed out in his book *English As A Global Language* "The development of computers has been almost entirely an American affair. The biggest setback to English would have been if Bill Gates had grown up speaking Chinese!"[47]

But as Crystal has also pointed out, the world must retain its indigenous languages, and English must be developed with local variations if we are not to become totally culturally illiterate. "If, in 500 years' time, English is the only language left to be learned, it will have been the greatest intellectual disaster that the planet has ever known."[48]

As a 1997 study by London's School of Oriental and African Studies (SOAS) showed, there are 10,000 languages in use in the world today. "We need a diversity of language because multilingualism is a healthy part of the way human society is organized. Language is a means of personal and group identity."[49]

For language to develop, it needs a cultural context. If English is to be capable of describing the world, how articulate we will be if it is left to air traffic control, Microsoft, Sony adverts and pop lyrics?[50] Mono-linguists, and particularly those whose first and only language is television English, will be at a disadvantage in the medium and long term, because, as the SOAS study shows "learning in two languages sharpens the wits."[51] Being conversant globally and locally implies competitive advantage. This book is written in English!

More globalization? What's the end game?

The growth of the global economy is based on the creation of conditions which will increase business activity. These conditions, it is argued by those who desire greater freedom for business to operate globally, will lead to more social development alongside increased world trade. There are those who argue that quite the opposite is happening, as the gap between rich and poor is no longer confined to one country versus another, but to the creation of greater disparities of wealth, health and security within every country. In other words, the creation of the global economy and the development of flexible labor markets, with business activity drawn to the cheapest labor, could be understood to mean the importation of the worst situations of the developing world – great wealth disparity, massive job insecurity and very low wage rates for a significant proportion of the population.

Those who argue in favor of an increase in global business activity, such as the World Trade Organisation, want to see:

- a level playing field for business; which means opposition to industrial subsidies, and opposition to higher regional regulations in areas such as health and safety, healthcare and environmental protection;
- deregulation of industrial sectors, such as airlines in the USA and electricity generation in the UK, as this creates greater competition;
- privatization of state services to introduce competition, business efficiency and market mechanisms to areas run on a public-service ethic. This has spread as far as the prison systems in the USA and UK;
- structural adjustment programs (SAPs), introduced by the International Monetary Fund for countries with deficits requiring loans from the IMF and the World Bank. These require cuts in government spending and the provision of public services to balance government budgets;
- the International Chamber of Commerce, the premier global business organization, with close links with the UN and the World Trade Organization, is "calling for 'a framework of global rules' covering essential issues such as business investment, competition, intellectual property rights, electronic commerce and the free flow of capital within and between markets."[52]

Global and corporate governance
· ·

With the partial demise of the state and the growing dominance of business, it has come to the attention of some business leaders that business prospers best under certain conditions. Unless the business concerned is active in trade in illegal drugs, rare animals, arms or illegally copied CDs, a 1997 World Bank report said that the best conditions for business were to be found in countries where the state was effective.

Perhaps the rolling back of the state has gone far enough? Indeed, the World Bank report found that countries with virtually ineffective state apparatus and a lack of democracy were the least likely to support a thriving business economy. Even people who have benefited most from free trade and opening markets, such as George Soros, who has made billions of dollars through currency speculation, feel that we "need discipline, some values to guide us in this potentially chaotic world." In conversation with the Director of the London School of Economics, sociologist Anthony Giddens, Soros said:[53]

> *Soros:* This open society is a precarious state of affairs, which is threatened from both sides. It's threatened by the imposition of dogma, fundamentalism . . .
>
> *Giddens:* And chaos on the other side . . . It seems to me that all our lives are like that now, sandwiched in this dilemma.
>
> *Soros:* There is a question of whether we can live with this knowledge of reflexivity[54] . . . I'm afraid that the prevailing view, which is one of extending the market mechanism to all domains, has the potential of destroying society . . . We have this false theory that markets left to themselves tend to equilibrium. It's not believed in practice.

To support the view that markets need governance, that the world needs both corporate, national and global governance, a World Bank survey in 1996 of 3,600 entrepreneurs in 69 countries in Latin America, Eastern Europe and Sub-Saharan Africa found that the vast majority of respondents thought that the institutionalization of the rule of law and fundamental human rights was good for business. In the 69 countries covered, the survey reported that the authorities failed to protect property and that the judiciary was dishonest or inconsistent. Forty per cent of respondents in these areas of the world said they had to pay bribes to survive, against 15 per cent in more affluent countries.

In other words, the fundamentals of good country governance are a lack of corruption, participation, a lack of civil war, a reliable judicial system and the maintenance of basic infrastructure, including communications, transport, education and healthcare beyond the vicissitudes of the market.

However, there are some multinationals which stand accused of operating to lower standards away from their home countries, and from benefiting from lower wage rates, lower health and safety standards and lax compliance with legislation. In recognition of the fact that some countries do not have reliable legal systems or legal aid, British law lords allowed a case to be brought by a Namibian against a multinational in the UK courts.

The case involved Edward Connolly, a Scottish maintenance engineer, who claimed that he was poisoned by uranium dust while working for Rossing Uranium, an RTZ (now known as Rio Tinto) subsidiary based in Namibia. RTZ is the world's largest mining company. In the House of Lords, the presiding judge said: "This is a case in which, having regard to the nature of the litigation, substantial justice cannot be done in the appropriate forum [Namibia], but can be done where the resources are available."

One judge, Lord Hoffman, dissented, putting his finger on one of the key global governance issues for multinationals: "The defendant is a multinational company, present almost everywhere and certainly present and ready to be sued in Namibia."[55] As the *Financial Times* reported: "If the presence of RTZ in the UK enabled it to be sued here, any multinational with its parent company in England will be liable to be sued here, in respect of its activities anywhere in the world."[56]

Is there a need for a world court, applying a level playing field and the rule of law based on the UN Declaration on Human Rights, to settle claims against large companies that can claim to have no geographical home?

The global company

Multinational corporations (MNCs) can be described in various ways: including by annual revenue, number of employees, presence in numerous countries and by other criteria. The UN Conference on Trade and Development (UNCTAD) constructs an "index on transnationality" by looking at a company's foreign assets to total assets, foreign sales to total sales and foreign employment to total employment. On this basis, some of the world's largest companies, and some of the best known brands, such as Coca-Cola, McDonald's, Shell and General Motors are excluded. According to UNCTAD's criteria, the world's top 15 multinationals are biased towards multinationals from smaller countries (see Table 1.1).

Table 1.1 UNCTAD's index on transnationality[57]

1	Nestlé	Food	Switzerland
2	Thomson	Electronics, telecoms	Canada
3	Holderbank Financière	Banking and cement	Switzerland
4	Seagram	Beverages, alcohol	Canada
5	Solvay	Pharmaceuticals	Belgium
6	ABB	Construction	Sweden/Switzerland
7	Electrolux	Electrical equipment	Sweden
8	Unilever	Food, detergents	Britain/Netherlands
9	Philips	Electronics	Netherlands
10	Roche	Pharmaceuticals	Switzerland
11	SCA	Paper, packaging	Sweden
12	Northern Telecom	Telecommunications	Canada
13	Glaxo-Wellcome	Pharmaceuticals	Britain
14	Cable & Wireless	Telecommunications	Britain
15	Volvo	Automobiles	Sweden

Despite this ranking the USA has the world's five largest public companies, ranked by the value of their shares. On this basis, the top 15 looks like that set out in Table 1.2.

Table 1.2 The top 15 public companies (ranked by share value)

1	General Electric	Electrical	USA
2	Microsoft	Computer software	USA
3	Exxon	Oil	USA
4	Coca-Cola	Soft drinks	USA
5	Intel	Computers	USA
6	NTT	Telecommunications	Japan
7	Toyota Motor	Automobiles	Japan
8	Royal Dutch Petroleum*	Oil	Netherlands
9	Merck	Pharmaceuticals	USA
10	Novartis	Healthcare	Switzerland
11	IBM	Computers	USA
12	Philip Morris	Tobacco and food	USA
13	Procter & Gamble	Detergents	USA
14	Pfizer	Pharmaceuticals	USA
15	Bristol-Myers Squibb	Pharmaceuticals	USA

* does not include UK Shell Transport & Trading; together these two companies would be second or third in this ranking.[58]

Foreign investment and share of world trade are reasonable indicators of the national origins of companies trading internationally. The USA and Britain are the largest recipients of foreign investment and they are the largest overseas investors, China also being one of the largest recipients of inward investment, but not, as yet, having many international companies. London is also the world's largest financial center, followed by New York, Tokyo and Frankfurt. Finance needs no physical logistics to travel, and the new entertainment and information industries do not need the bulk carriers required for heavy machinery, food and fossil fuels. Despite the enormous growth in entertainment and information industries, the bulk of trade between countries is with near neighbors (see Table 1.3). In 1996 Britain had 52.7 per cent of its trade with the European Union (EU), the USA had 21.3 per cent with Canada, and Germany 56.4 per cent with the EU.[59]

Table 1.3 Percentage of world trade 1996

USA	13.5
Germany	9.0
France	5.3
Britain	5.1
Japan	7.1
China	2.7
Hong Kong	3.6
Sweden	1.4

What is the difference between international, multinational, transnational, supranational and global companies?

An *international company* is one that is based in one country, but trades in other countries; a *multinational company* (MNC) may be based in one country, but has bases in other countries for management, manufacturing or distribution; a *transnational company* (TNC) is one that has its headquarters in one country, but operates most of the time outside that home country in a number of other countries (Nestlé for example, has only 2 per cent of its operations in Switzerland, its home base). There are also *supranationals* that appear to recognize no home base and operate in many countries. There are *global companies*, which may also be transnationals or supranationals, which manufacture different components in different countries to make a final product which is then sold globally. It is difficult in these cases to say "this product is 100 per cent American or Spanish." Most large automobile manufacturers and electronics companies are now global.

As every country adopts, or is forced to adapt to, liberal economics, it is up to business (whether it be domestic, a TNC, MNC, supra or global enterprise), as the prime beneficiary, to take the lead in social development that protects the environment and builds just and healthy local and global communities. The profiles in this book show that some businesses have accepted this challenge and are working for their own and the common good. In other words, the companies profiled here have accepted that there need not be a conflict between profits and shared values. Being socially responsible is a win–win situation. The environment and communities win, and business wins.

● MANAGEMENT EXERCISES ●

1 Two views of globalization

Do you agree with Alice, in *Alice in Wonderland,* that it depends on where we want to go to? Having read the two pieces below, by John Tusa and David Rothkopf, is it really a question of Mcfood versus diversity, and "winning the battle of the world's information waves?"

> *"Are we content with a world made safe for Mcfood and Waltculture and Rupertnews and Tedvision? Will we lie down before the high priests of globalization who create a new totalitarianism of taste, thought, experience and views using self-serving economic arguments decked out in the pseudo-democratic clothing of freedom and choice? . . . The homogenized global culture snuffs out species of artistic endeavour as surely as global enterprise threatens the biodiversity of natural species."* [60]

John Tusa, Managing Director of London's Barbican Arts Centre, formerly Managing Director of BBC World Service and for some 25 years a senior BBC TV newscaster

> *"The impact of globalization on culture and the impact of culture on globalization merit discussion. The homogenizing influences of globalization that are most often condemned by the new nationalists and by cultural romanticists are actually positive; globalization promotes integration and the removal not only of cultural barriers but of many of the negative dimensions of culture. Globalization is a vital step toward both a more stable world and better lives for the people in it . . . For the USA, a central objective of an Information Age foreign policy must be to win the battle of the world's information flows, dominating the airwaves as Great Britain once ruled the seas . . . Americans should not deny the fact that of all the nations in the world, theirs is the most just and the best model for the future."* [61]

David Rothkopf, Managing Director of Kissinger Associates, Adjunct Professor of International Affairs at Columbia University and senior official in the US Department of Commerce during the first term of the Clinton administration

▶

2 Dilemma: a sticky situation

What responsibility do you have for misuse of your product?[62]

H.B. Fuller is a Minnesota-based manufacturer of adhesives, sealants, coatings and paints. The company has a generally good reputation on community, environmental and workplace issues, and is a member of the Five Percent Club, meaning that it contributes 5 per cent of its pre-tax profits to its local community. It was one of the first Fortune 500 companies to commit itself to the CERES[63] principles.

Fuller produces, in all, more that 10,000 products. One of them, however, a solvent-based glue manufactured by a wholly owned South American subsidiary using a technology which is not used in the USA or Europe, has grabbed more than its fair share of attention. The product, which goes by the brand name of Resistol, was a widely used industrial glue. It also became a favorite among homeless children and orphaned or abandoned adolescents living rough on the streets of Central American cities, because one of its ingredients, toulene, gives off fumes which when inhaled, lead to intoxication and wild mood swings. Apart from being highly addictive, toulene is carcinogenic, and can lead to kidney failure and brain damage.

There is no doubt that the street children were using Resistol in a way that its manufacturers never intended or anticipated. Yet, the problem became so widespread and severe, especially in Guatemala, Honduras and some neighboring countries, that special assistance programs were established to try to combat the addiction problem. A group of protesters picketed the company's 1993 annual shareholder's meeting, claiming, with some justification, that Fuller's products were damaging children's health. But these were not just any children; they were children living in poverty, driven to seek escape from the degradation of their lives through solvent abuse – the kind of children, in other circumstances, that the company would be supporting through its contribution to programs.

The circumstances that lead to young children living unprotected on city streets are complex, and not the responsibility of an individual company, but manufacturing a product which adds to the danger and vulnerability experienced by those youngsters is not easily ignored. Yet, Resistol was an accepted and widely used product, and the manufacturer had relationships with legitimate customers which would be severely disrupted if it were suddenly withdrawn from the market. Indeed, some of Fuller's customers were small shoe manufacturers, that worked to specifications requiring them to use that particular adhesive, meaning that their businesses could not be run without it. Was this the manufacturer's responsibility? What should it do?

▶

3 Ethical dilemma: what would you do?

You are the chief executive of a major car company, with a subsidiary in Colombia. The subsidiary owns a banana plantation, whose workers have been the victims of violence by the government. The story hits the papers and you are being questioned.

Options:
● Sell the subsidiary, knowing that abuses are likely to continue.
● Bring in an expert negotiator.
● Press for change with local officials.

What do you decide to do? Why?

4 Dilemma – Chinese bags[64]

You are an accessories buyer for a cosmetics company, which often offers its products in brightly coloured cosmetics bags printed with the company logo. These are particularly popular at holiday times, when your sales are at their highest, and so are a firm favorite with your retail division.

Since the early days of the company, the bags have been bought from an importer, who sources them annually from a trade fair in Guangzhou, China. They are inexpensive, of consistent quality, and are considered a semi-durable packaging item. The supply has been reliable, and a stable trading relationship has been established with the importer.

Your company has recently started to be criticized by human rights groups for trading in China, because of the country's record of human-rights abuses. You fear that this could lead to a campaign which targets shoppers buying gifts at holiday periods, and your corporate affairs director is concerned about the possible impact on your reputation. You decide the best way forward is to try to establish that the cosmetics bags you are buying are produced under acceptable circumstances – that neither forced labor or child labor is involved. This proves very difficult to do: the importer who sells you the bags does not know exactly where they are produced, because he buys his stock from a trader at the trade fair. You dispatch a member of your staff to try to follow the trail in China, but there are many intermediaries involved, and it is impossible to get to see the place where the bags are actually produced.

Contacts in nearby Hong Kong suggest to you that in the area concerned it is unlikely that prison labor is being used. Instead, at least part of the production – stitching, for instance – is probably being done through a network of family-based outworkers. If this is the case, it is also reasonable to assume that these people have come to rely on the income they get from producing the bags, which you have been ordering at increasing quantities for more than five years now. They may

▶

easily have given up other forms of income generation to concentrate on meeting the demands of your market.

Which is the right thing to do – risk throwing family producers into poverty by overturning a stable trading relationship that has worked well for years, or risk your company's reputation by being seen to carry on trading when you are not able to establish beyond doubt that some of the worst excesses of human-rights abuses are not involved in this case?

Notes to Chapter 1

1 Freitas, Ken (Vice-President, Community Enterprise, Timberland) (1997) *Social Activities as a Business Strategy*; Freitas was interviewed for Partnership and Social Cohesion, Ministry of Social Affairs, Denmark, conference, 16-18 October. See also Timberland (1997) *Guiding Principles for Choosing Business Partners*. Hampton, USA: The Timberland Company.

2 Nesté (1997) *Corporate Environmental Report: Progress in 1996*. Helsinki: Nesté.

3 Greenpeace (1997) *Annual Review*. London: Greenpeace, July.

4 NEC (1991) *The NEC Environmental Charter*. Tokyo: NEC.

5 Portillo, Michael, Secretary of State (1996) *MOD Environmental Policy Statement*, JSP 418.

6 Marks & Spencer (1996) *Environment Report*. London: Marks & Spencer.

7 Townsend, Peter (1996) *Global Restructuring and Social Policy*. Bristol: Policy Press.

8 *The Economist* (1996) "The fun of being a multinational," 20 July.

9 Watkins, Kevin (1997) "Lender of last resort favours rich," *Guardian*, 22 September.

10 Elliot, Larry (1997) "A green light that means stop," *Guardian*, 22 September.

11 King, Ian (1997) "Nomura becomes UK's biggest pubs company," *Guardian*, 23 September; author's personal communications with Nomura International UK.

12 Brummer, Alex and King, Ian (1997) "Big business just got bigger," *Guardian*, 14 October.

13 BBC Radio 4 (1997) *The World at One*, 1 October; *Financial Times* (1997) "Europe's most respected companies," 24 September.

14 *The Economist* (1997) "An Asian pea-souper," 27 September.

15 "Food Miles" is a campaign run by SAFE, which aims to bring attention to the fact that some food sold in supermarkets contains fewer calories than the equivalent number required to get it from producer to supermarket shelf.

16 On fair trade, see Chapter 4.

17 Prest, Michael and Bowen, David (1996) "Vegetable magic," *Independent*, 7 July.

18 Fortune 500 companies are identified annually by the US *Fortune* magazine on the basis of profitability, size and growth.

19 The "2000 problem" refers to the fact that at midnight on 31 December 1999 most computers will think it is 1900, not 2000. This will probably wipe out many computer operating systems, including those in homes, offices, nuclear power plants and weapons systems.

20 Information Strategy (1997) *Offshore Options*. London: Information Strategy.

21 Lennard, Jeremy (1997) "Greenhouse defects," *Guardian*, 17 September.

22 *Guardian*, "Personal communications," 26 June 1997; *The Economist* (1997) "That infernal washing machine," 26 July.

23 George, Eddie, Governor of the Bank of England (1997) Address to the Institute of Petroleum, in Rowell, Andrew (1996) *Green Backlash – Global Subversion of the Environment Movement*. London: Routledge.

24 Donkin, Richard (1997) "Community spirit," *Financial Times*, 4 September; Handy, Charles (1997) *The Hungry Spirit: Beyond Capitalism – A Quest for Purpose in the Modern World*. London: Hutchinson.

25 Ibid.

26 UN (1997) *Human Development Report*. Oxford: Oxford University Press; *New Economics* (1996) Autumn; Korten, David (1995) *When Corporations Rule the World*. London: Earthscan; Elkins, Paul *et al.* (1992) *Wealth Beyond Measure*. London: Gaia.

27 Justice (1997) quoted in *Guardian*, 17 November.

28 UNDP (1998) "Poverty in the next century," *Choices*, January

29 Durning, Alan (1991) "Asking how much is enough," in Brown, Lester, R. (1991) *The State of the World*. New York: W.W. Norton.

30 Korten, David (1995) *When Corporations Rule the World*, London: Earthscan, p.214.

31 Drucker, Peter (1992) "The new society of business organizations," Harvard Business Review, September-October.

32 GrandMetropolitan (1997) *Report on Corporate Citizenship*. London: GrandMetropolitan.

33 McDonald's (1996) *Our Commitment to the Environment*. Illinois: McDonald's.

34 Social audit – see Appendix 2: Glossary and consult Index.

35 John Gray, Professor of Politics at Oxford University, reviewing Marquand, David (1997) *The New Reckoning: Capitalism, States and Citizens*. Bristol: Policy Press.

36 Townsend, Peter and Kwabena, Donkor (1996) *Global Restructuring and Social Policy*. Bristol: Policy Press.

37 Maucher, Helmut O. (1997) "Ruling by consent," *Financial Times*, 11 December.

38 Handy, Charles (1996) "What's it all for? Re-inventing capitalism for the next century," *RSA Journal*, December.

39 More than 30 million people were HIV positive in 1997, according to the UN. This figure represents one in every 100 sexually active adults.

40 In 1993, 885,000 people died in the world following a car accident. This is comparable with the annual deaths from malaria, cholera and TB.

41 Maucher – see note 37.

42 Between 1985 and 1995, the daily turnover of the New York, London and Tokyo financial markets increased from $190 billion to $1.2 trillion.

43 Tokyo is the world's most heavily populated city with 27.2 million inhabitants. In rich countries, 75 per cent of the population live in urban areas; 38 per cent in poorer countries. By 2030, 60 per cent of people will live in cities, compared with 46 per cent in 1997. However, urban residents are increasingly in poorer countries.

44 Francis Bacon said that "knowledge is power." Socrates said that "there is only one good, knowledge, and one evil, ignorance," but we must distinguish between information – of

which we have so much – and knowledge, of which we have so little. There is as much information in a sole edition of a newspaper such as the *New York Times*, the (London) *Guardian*, or the *Sydney Morning Herald* as the average person in the UK in the seventeenth century would have had to deal with in a lifetime.

45 See also *Newsweek* (1997) "All the world's a party," 6 October.

46 Crystal, David (1997) *English as a Global Language.* Cambridge: Cambridge University Press.

47 Ibid.

48 Ibid.

49 *Guardian* (1997) "Global study finds the world speaking in 10,000 tongues," 22 July.

50 *The Economist* (1996) 21 December; Smith, David G. (1992) "Modernism, hyperliteracy and the colonization of the word," *Alternatives*, 17.

51 *Guardian* (see note 49).

52 Maucher (President of the International Chamber of Commerce) – see note 37.

53 Soros, George and Giddens, Anthony (1997) "Beyond chaos and dogma," *New Statesman*, 31 October.

54 Reflexivity is described by Soros as "a two-way connection between what we think and what happens in the world." To Giddens, reflexivity is "the ideas that people have about their social world, about themselves, their future and the conditions of their lives, are not just ideas about an 'independently given' world – they constantly enter the world that they describe." See Maucher – note 37.

55 Vidal, John (1997) "See you in court," *Guardian*, 28 July.

56 Mason, John (1997) "RTZ ruling threatens other multinationals," *Financial Times*, 11 December.

57 *The Economist* (1997), 27 September. See also UNCTAD (1997) *World Investment Report: Transnational Corporations, Market Structures and Competitive Policy*, Geneva.

58 Morgan Stanley Capital International Database (*The Economist*, 1997).

59 *The Economist* (1997), 15 November.

60 Tusa, John (1996) "The agony and the ecstasy," *Guardian*, 6 June.

61 Rothkopf, David (1997) "In praise of cultural imperialism?," *Foreign Policy*, Summer.

62 Based on "A global vision," in Makower, Joel (1994) *Beyond the Bottom Line: Putting Social Responsibility to Work for Your Business and the World*, Business for Social Responsibility.

63 See Appendix 2: Glossary and Chapter 4.

64 Adapted from an exercise used by the New Academy of Business, devised by Jacqui MacDonald.

2

THE NEW
CORPORATE CITIZENSHIP

Introduction

Avon

London's Metropolitan Police

Who said this?

Corporate citizenship is for all organizations

Shell

Economic, legal, social and environmental responsibilities

Renlon

BT

Tomorrow's organization

Interest in social responsibility

Business for Social Responsibility (USA)

The Charter for Good Corporate Behavior (Japan)

The Asahi Foundation (Japan)

The Centre for Tomorrow's Company (UK)

*The Prince of Wales Business Leaders' Forum, The World Bank and The UN
Development Programme*

The World Business Council for Sustainable Development

Models of social responsibility

The Big Issue

Medecins sans Frontières

Management exercises

Introduction

······················

"A company which abuses its workforce, or a company which employs forced labour, is not only in breach of the Universal Declaration and the Vienna Declaration, but is flying in the face of civilized thinking all over the world. Such a company is acting irresponsibly in an area over which it has direct influence. And in a world of increasing transparency and global communications, such a company is also foolish if it thinks such behaviour will not attract attention."

Peter D. Sutherland, Chairman BP[1]

This chapter describes the new corporate citizenship that is developing as one of the consequences of globalization. As we saw in Chapter 1, globalization is not just concerned with the development of a global economy, although that is a major aspect, but also with ideas of connectivity through understanding the way our local and global communities and environments interrelate.

This book profiles a large number of companies and other organizations with a view to demonstrating the depth and breadth of thinking that is taking place on corporate citizenship. It is not the intention, in citing any particular organization, whether it be BP or Greenpeace, to argue that this or that organization is more responsible than another. Rather, we wish to show that a new model of corporate behavior is developing among concerned thinkers in all sorts of organizations. Within our large companies lurk radical thinkers, just as free thinkers in single-issue pressure group activists have been known to join the commercial world. This chapter is an analysis of the many organizational profiles that have been included in this book.

Let us be clear from the start that there *is* a new form of corporate citizenship. This is not about philanthropy, it is not about attaching a glossy community affairs report to the annual financial report. The new corporate citizenship is not an afterthought managed by public relations. The new corporate citizenship is about citizenship at the heart of strategic planning. The magnitude of the change that is necessary for this to be so might seem overwhelming, a little like trying to manoeuvre a supertanker in a small harbor.

BP's Chairman, Peter D. Sutherland, tackled this issue when, addressing a trustees' meeting of Amnesty International. He said, "Good business is sustainable, is part of global society not at odds with it, and reflects values which are shared across the world."[2] NatWest Bank is also on the verge of making a leap into a new future when it reports: "We believe that a balance between economic, environmental and societal goals is a key determinant of all our futures and we will take account of this in the way we run our business."[3] More radical still is when the chairman of Shell admits that his company has made "subtle, but in the end, far-reaching, mistakes in assessing developments"[4] over strategic decisions concerning Shell's operations in the North Sea and Nigeria. Why? Because of a "ghost in the global system" which, even though Shell runs one of the world's best known and well-managed companies, meant that on these two issues – if not others, its ability to make strategic decisions has been seriously flawed. These two events, in the North Sea and Nigeria, were followed by changes in Shell's decision making. It was decided that the Brent Spar oil rig would be cut up and used to build a Norwegian dock and the company adopted a commitment to human rights. But what did the chairman mean by a "ghost in the global system" – that Shell no longer knew the way forward? Or that in future it ought to be more sensitive to a wider range of stakeholder opinions?

For BP, NatWest, Shell and other companies there is a new future, not easily defined, not codified in traditional economics and management literature, which they must embrace if senior management is to be a comfortable and less vulnerable place to work.

The new model may well represent a paradigm shift,[5] although we are talking about radical evolution, rather than revolution. Nevertheless, a change of some significance is taking place in management which is being driven by factors that are only now being recognized around the world. The word "new" implies modernity, progress and development, but one of the qualities of the current corporate citizenship situation is its post-modernity: there is no clear view of the future and that rationality must be tempered with caution, emotion and unreason. Post-modernism relies on modernism for its explanation, and there is much of the modern in the company mission statements.

Certainly the mission statements of companies which claim to embrace a new model of business are as absolutist in declaring a new Utopia as the old models. For instance, The Body Shop stands for a clear set of values: "The pursuit of social and environmental change . . . to ensure that our business is ecologically sustainable . . . adopting a code of conduct which ensures care, honesty, fairness and respect . . . making fun, passion and care part of our daily lives."[6] Similarly, Ben & Jerry's Ice Cream mission statement (1996) talks about "profitable growth, increasing value for shareholders . . . the finest quality natural ice cream . . . improve the quality of life of a broad community."[7] Even the Timberland mission statement, quoted at the beginning of Chapter 1, refers to a new way of doing business, as if there is a specific alternative. But every example of a new way of doing business looks slightly different, and is based on an understanding of the uniqueness of external and internal factors for that company.

Avon: managing in a multicultural world

"To survive and prosper in this competitive marketplace, Avon must reflect the society its customers live in. And the American society, more and more, has become a microcosm of the entire world, as our population becomes even more diverse."

Walker Lewis, President Avon US[8]

With markets in 125 countries around the world, Avon sells cosmetics, jewelry, gift items, clothing, CDs, books and videos. Avon's products must suit the Filipino teenager in Manila, the African-American woman in Memphis and the man in Malaga. In order to meet the needs of all ethnic and racial groups, Avon works with minority vendors to ensure that its products meet specific needs. By supporting minority-owned vendors, Avon helps to support minority-owned businesses, thereby aiding minority communities, many of which form a significant part of the company's key markets.

Buying from minority-owned businesses also allows a company to innovate and develop new products based on demand from specific communities. By sourcing perfume from the minority-owned business of Howard Kennedy Enterprise, Avon has produced one of its major sellers – the largest single selling fragrance in Avon's history.

Purchasing from female-owned businesses is not as easy, according to Fitz Hillaire, Avon's Director for External Affairs. Such companies are not so readily identifiable. Minority-owned businesses in the USA must be 51 per cent owned by minorities, but there are no such requirements for female-headed businesses, making it harder to certify such companies.[9]

What is a minority?

In its US market, Avon defines minorities as Asian, Hispanic, African-American, Native American, and Aleutian Islanders.[10]

London's Metropolitan Police

The Metropolitan Police Service – known ubiquitously as "the Met" – has established an Ethics Committee and an Ethical Working Group to address the whole area of social and ethical accountability within its own operations across London.

The task is immense – the London police force consists of the equivalent of five regional forces together, with the attendant multiplicity of stations, diversity of command structures and, needless to say, daily ethical issues arising. Responsibility has been placed in the hands of the Deputy Commissioner of the Met – the UK's number two police officer, indicating that the issue is being taken seriously.

A Statement of Values has been produced, together with a detailed publication, *The Beat*,[11] covering ethical matters. At the time of publication, an awareness development program and a comprehensive future schedule of internal ethical audits are planned.

At this stage, the Met does not feel that an external accreditation is required, it already has enough of those in other areas, such as the government-inspired charter mark for service and, in any case, there are many external scrutineers of their activities, in the shape of every Member of Parliament and every investigative journalist, each one with a wealth of certain opinions about the work and responsibilities of the Met!

A confidential telephone line has been established and this has proved very successful. The invitation states: *"If it doesn't look right, if it doesn't seem right, if it doesn't sound right, if it doesn't feel right, ring the number and voice your concerns."* The public has made use of the number, and ethical issues have been raised and pursued to their conclusion.

The chief areas of possible ethical concern for the new Met Ethical Working Group include the prevailing "canteen culture" of macho male behavior. This is clearly a long-term task, but some successes have been recorded.

Other possible areas of ethical concern are the operations of the tactical support units whose remit is rapid response and enforcement, and the general police and public relationships where situations can be emotionally charged.

It is still very early days, but there are clear and hopeful signs that one of the world's most hard-worked and successful police forces is taking positive and progressive steps towards a more enlightened and values-driven approach to policing operations.

Who said this?

Who made the following statements? Was it the leader of an environmental pressure group, an academic, a leading politician or the boss of a major industrial giant?

> *"[Business] can only exercise freedom if governments have a legitimate and effective role. [Business] needs a framework of law within which to invest; a framework which provides the right incentives for the development of skills, for the right environmental policies and for the efficient use of resources. Without that companies have no power at all. Investment and anarchy do not mix."[12]*

"At [this company] we believe we have a special responsibility to help protect and preserve our environment for future generations. A business leader must be an environmental leader as well, which is why we analyze every aspect of our business in terms of its impact on the environment, and take what action is necessary to lead both in word and deed."[13]

These two statements emanate from two of the world's largest and most prominent business organizations – BP and McDonald's. They emphasize the responsibilities that business is attempting to face, sometimes not very successfully. BP has been accused of being involved in human-rights abuses in Colombia, and McDonald's has been accused of destroying the environment, providing unhealthy dietary advice and using poorly paid child labor. Both companies strenuously deny these claims, arguing, as in the statements above, that they are responsible global citizens with the social and environmental concerns at the center of their corporate strategies.

Managing today has been described as similar to flying an aircraft at high speed; it requires the ability to monitor constantly new information, to adapt quickly to changing circumstances and to develop organizational structures which are not fixed but flexible. As individuals we are all global citizens as consumers, investors, workers or victims of global climate change and economic forces beyond our control, but it is managers who have to face the day-to-day practical realities of managing in the global economy, an economy that never sleeps. In particular, this means developing and maintaining relationships with a diverse range of stakeholders.

Business needs to be developing a new brand of manager, sensitive to a new way of doing business, in a less deferential world with looser organizational boundaries and greater complexity. The competences of this new breed of global managers are crucial to effect the changes necessary for responsible corporate citizenship to become a reality and, therefore, remain profitable.

Managers who appreciate the new realities need:

● the ability to think as a global citizen;
● a genuine interest in diverse ideas and opinions;
● an ability to work with people from different backgrounds and with different world views;
● an ability to build relationships and construct new social and organizational structures;
● an ability to envision other social realities;
● an ability to manage in complex and chaotic environments;

- an ability to manage across geographic boundaries;
- an understanding of your own values, and an understanding that you are engaged in business with values.

Corporate citizenship is for all organizations

One of the themes of this book is that responsible corporate citizenship applies to all organizations, whatever sector they are in. For instance, the US Department of Defense is faced by the same equal opportunities challenges in its treatment of gays and lesbians as any other business.[14] For the UK's National Health Service (NHS),[15] Europe's largest employer, sourcing from around the world has similar implications to a large private-sector burger chain. And Greenpeace has the same responsibility to tell the truth, as it perceives it, as the major petroleum companies.[16]

Whether we are talking about a large manufacturing company, a local school, a national charity or a small family-run shop, all organizations have social responsibilities that make them corporate citizens, responsible or otherwise.

Shell's global responsibilities

The Royal Dutch/Shell Group of Companies operates globally and employs thousands of people. Its major impacts are in raw material extraction, employment and the environment. Its annual turnover is larger than many nation-state economies which means that it has responsibilities which go beyond the people it employs and the environment. There are issues of corporate governance, global sourcing and human rights, for instance. Indeed, for companies like Shell, managing its social responsibilities has become a strategic priority in order to protect its reputation, to protect its market share and to operate in a way which satisfies all its stakeholders – shareholders, employees, governments and customers.

Economic, legal, social and environmental responsibilities

Economic responsibility

All organizations have to be economic in that however their income is derived,[17] from the sale of automobiles or newspapers, through charitable donations or central/local government funding, they must remain viable and operate within their constitution or articles of association. All organizations have to provide certified accounts, set out on agreed criteria.

Legal responsibility

All organizations have to work within the law and be aware of their legal restraints. This is not just confined to their articles of association, but also to health and safety, trading standards, environmental legislation, employment law and other areas of life.

Social and environmental responsibility

Very few organizations operate simply on the basis of their financial and legal obligations; indeed it is difficult to imagine an organization that just works on such a basis. Organizations operate in a social environment in which ethical and philanthropic considerations are essential to their ability to operate. It is strange that while companies are held accountable financially and legally, there is only now a move to hold companies accountable for their operations which have an environmental and social impact. Of course, many organizations, in all sectors, fail to fulfil their financial and legal obligations.

To suggest that an organization just has to fulfil its financial and legal obligations for it to be a good corporate citizen is to misunderstand the role of business in society. One of the main points about the profiles in this book is that organizations that do not understand the other social responsibilities are far more likely to fail to fulfil their economic and legal responsibilities. Any business is both an economic and a social entity.[18]

No one would suggest that a company that knowingly damages a community, or sells a product that is harmful is a good corporate citizen. But this is not a simple matter. For example, in 1997 there was a strong consensus against the manufacture and sale of landmines, supported by the Red Cross and the governments of Canada and Britain, but this was not so previously when Britain and Canada, as members of NATO, supported both the landmines industry and their deployment – for instance, in the 1992 Gulf War and the Vietnam War in the 1970s. Corporate citizenship and managing a company's social responsibilities are, therefore, concerned as much with the shifting sands of public opinion as with moral management.

41

Renlon: winning new business

.ı timber-treatment company based in London with a turnover of $8.25 and 45 .es. Ten years ago its managing director decided that developing an environ- mⱸ ıly sustainable company would satisfy both his personal values and increase the profitability of the company. He knew that many of his customers were concerned about the use of highly toxic chemicals in their homes, so his decision to use non-toxins would, he knew, win more customers. However, being one of the first preservation companies to go down this route could have been dangerous, but, ten years on Richard Hall has not only succeeded in using water-based non-toxic treatments, but has seen the development of his business nationwide as he has satisfied customer demands, lowered his insurance costs, minimized exposure to risk and gained certification to British and European environmental management standards.

All organizations

Organizations:

- have a range of key relationships or stakeholders;
- are faced with ethical dilemmas, whether they recognize them as such or not;
- have statutory requirements;
- have to compete for markets or funding;
- are affected by the quality and excellence revolution, even if they are not directly involved.

Furthermore:

- many have adopted mission statements which articulate their values and purpose;
- are being forced or encouraged to re-think their relationship to the planet because of the state of the environment;
- are having to become more flexible to survive in a changing environment, in a vibrant, non-stop, global economy.

Moving up to social accountability: BT's social audit[19]

Late in 1996, the chief executive of BT, one of the world's largest telecommunications companies, announced to a surprised world that his company was going to conduct a full social audit. The company had conducted an environmental audit, published the results and been widely praised. The CEO's announcement had been sanctioned by the board but had not been talked through with senior managers. These managers had just learned the benefits of environmental audits – lower risk, increased efficiency, lower costs, improved employee morale, better public relations, etc. – now they were faced with developing a methodology for measuring the company's total impact, not just its environmental impact. BT's director of corporate relations explained that the social audit was part of a public relations campaign and that in his opinion, "social responsibility is a factor that we think is going to grow."

The task for BT's senior managers has been the same for any company concerned to understand its social and environmental impact. Where do we start? Are there any standards to apply? Is there a certification process? What methodology is best for us? For BT, the adoption of a social audit means that it is willing to be called to account for its operations in finance, the environment and society. (See also additional profile of BT in Chapter 5.)

Tomorrow's organization

A number of organizations have arisen in the last few years around the world which are interested in promoting a new way of doing business based on some of the principles of corporate citizenship outlined in this book. Among these are the Centre for Tomorrow's Company (in London), Business for Social Responsibility (in the USA), the Prince of Wales Business Leaders' Forum (in London), the New Academy of Business (in London) and the Council on Economic Priorities (in the USA). Older business organizations have also taken an interest in social responsibility because they perceive an interest from their members, the public and government. It is, after all, in the interests of business that they are seen to be socially responsible citizens and that that they support the rule of law and the role of government. "Investment and anarchy do not mix," as the CEO of BP has said.[20]

Before giving four examples of these initiatives it is worth noting that corporate social responsibility has become an issue for the public for a variety of reasons from corruption and fraud to environmental destruction largely as a result of pressure-group action.

Interest in social responsibility

Interest in corporate citizenship and social responsibility is growing as the role of business in society increases. The role of government is retreating to that of a referee, setting standards, originating legislation and working as a facilitator rather than a provider. A number of news stories have put corporate citizenship at the top of the agenda in recent years and alerted the public to issues of social responsibility.

Issues that have raised public awareness of corporate citizenship are:

- executive greed, in the form of share options and pay;
- corruption and fraud, represented by some high-profile owners and executives stealing from companies and employees;
- environmental degradation caused by some industrial practices;
- human-rights abuses, such as knowingly using child or prison labor to make clothes, shoes and sporting goods;
- fair trade, with some consumers becoming increasingly aware of the injustices of current global trade patterns;
- stakeholder empowerment, as shareholders demand more information and control over boards and customers are not content to accept company information as accurate or honest;
- product safety and labelling, as products are hastily withdrawn due to manufacturing mistakes and customers demanding more and better labelling on things such as genetic modification, irradiation, toxins and adulteration in food. In many countries, but particularly in the USA, there has been an increasing danger of legal liability and litigation.

Business for Social Responsibility (USA)

Business for Social Responsibility (BSR) is a US trade organization of over 1,200 companies that promotes corporate citizenship. With offices in San Francisco, Washington DC, Boston, Denver, New York and North Carolina, BSR seeks to "develop, support, advocate, and disseminate business strategies and practices that aim for high performance, innovation, and corporate prosperity. It focuses on policies that are responsible for the well-being of the bottom line as well as the workforce, the environment, and our communities." Its members constitute a wide spectrum of companies, both large and small, including Ben & Jerry's, Reebok, and Stride Rite.

BSR also runs the Business for Social Responsibility Education Fund, a non-profit research and education organization that promotes socially responsible business practice. BSR operates a resource center that contains information on best practice in six areas: ethics, the workplace, the marketplace, the community, the environment and the global economy. Members can access corporate codes of conduct and research papers. Another useful service is the weekly BSR *News Monitor* that summarizes news on corporate social responsibility from over 100 publications.

Founded in 1992, BSR has ten regional networks throughout the USA. It offers its members an annual conference, participation in working groups on major topics and a newsletter.[21]

The Charter for Good Corporate Behavior (Japan)

Keidanren, which began in 1946 during the American occupation, is Japan's largest and oldest business association. It has enormous political power within Japan and is recognized around the world as a significant non-governmental organization (NGO). After Japan was heavily criticized in the 1980s for its attitude to environmental issues, it established a Global Environmental Charter in April 1991. In September of the same year, it launched a Charter for Good Corporate Behavior in the wake of scandals involving securities companies.

The seven principles of the Charter are:

1 Endeavor to offer excellent goods and services that are useful to society.
2 Strive to make it possible for employees to lead comfortable and plentiful lives, and respect them as human beings.
3 Conduct corporate activities in a way that takes environmental protection into consideration.
4 Endeavor to make a contribution to society through philanthropic and other activities.
5 Work to improve social welfare in the community through business activities.
6 Firmly refrain from behavior that is counter to social norms, including having anything to do with organizations that have an adverse influence on social order and safety.
7 Always promote communication with consumers and residents through public relations activities and open hearings, and strive to make the principles of corporate behavior conform to social norms.

As Suzuki[22] pointed out, in 1996 there were some 4,500 environmental pressure groups in Japan, but social and environmental management was not a high priority for Japanese business. Surveys of Japanese companies looking at the implementation and monitoring of the Charter have generally failed to distinguish between *tatamae*, what the company says, and *honne*, what the company really thinks and does.

The relationship between business and society in Japan, which is at the heart of the social responsibility debate, is far closer than it may be in some societies, particularly the USA and Britain. For instance, when translating "corporate social responsibility" into Japanese, a corporation, defined in English as "a body of persons authorized to act as an individual,"[23] has its origins in "to meet at the shrine" and "to start a business," which together mean "society." In Japanese, a corporation and society are virtually synonymous, so that for a business to profit it must benefit the whole of Japanese society.[24]

That Keidanren thought it necessary to establish a Charter for Good Corporate Behavior at all is indicative of the massive changes taking place in Japanese society and the pressures on businesses to be seen to be scrupulous. Specifically, as one of the world's largest economies with enormous worldwide responsibilities to the environment and communities, there is concern to show that Japanese business operates to internationally agreed norms of behavior. These have been translated into the Charter.

The Charter is primarily targeted at senior managers and executives who it says have to "examine and discipline their own behavior and exercise leadership in keeping moral standards high in their corporations . . . Corporations must not only obey the law but also bring a social conscience to bear on their undertakings." Perhaps of greatest significance is the awareness that Japanese business practices were receiving a bad press overseas.

The Charter states that: "Japanese corporations need to rigorously reconsider traditional business practices so as not to give grounds for the criticism that Japanese business practices are exclusionary and opaque, it is urgent for us to work to achieve a free, transparent, fair market and establish confidence in Japan's economic system."

The Asahi Foundation (Japan)

An alternative to Keidanren's Charter for Good Corporate Behavior can be found in the work done by a special committee of the Asahi Foundation which annually rates companies using 12 categories:

1 Well-being of employees – including length of employment, new and old employees, full-time and part-time employment and the creation of opportunities.
2 Working conditions and fringe benefits – including paid leave, sick pay and medical services.
3 Flexibility of corporate system – including personal and professional support, community work and stress-relief leave.
4 Family benefits – including paternity leave, family-illness support, accommodation support, relocation support.
5 Opportunities for women – including women-only uniforms, marriage with co-workers, maternity leave, child-care leave and support, use of maiden names.
6 Treatment of elderly, disabled and part-time workers.
7 Internationalization – covering the employment of non-Japanese (which make up a significant minority in Japan).
8 Response to consumers' needs – including telephone complaint lines and attitudes to customers.
9 Community – including company participation in local communities and ability for employees to do community work in company time.
10 Disclosure – including information on all aspects of company performance on financial, social and environmental matters and the separation of advertising and PR departments.
11 Contributions to academic research and culture – including philanthropic donations to research and cultural programs.
12 Environment – including in-house conservation, management structure to deal with environmental issues and statement of corporate environmental objectives.

According to Asahi's 1997[25] evaluation, some of the internationally well-known Japanese companies that rate highly in many categories were:

1 Ito Yokado (retail)
2 Sony (electric)
3 Matsushita (electric)
4 Shiseido (cosmetic)
5 NTT (telecommunication)
6 Jasco (retail)
7 Sharp (electric)
8 Japan Airlines (airline)
9 Honda (automobile)
10 Tokyo Marine and Fire (insurance)

The Centre for Tomorrow's Company (UK)

The Tomorrow's Company Inquiry was set up in 1993 by the Royal Society of Arts Manufactures and Commerce (RSA) in London to address Britain's declining performance in terms of global competitiveness. The Inquiry headed by Sir Anthony Cleaver, Chairman of IBM UK, included representatives of many of Britain's largest businesses. They developed an Agenda for Action which was concerned with the relationship between business and the communities in which they operate.

In this respect the report mirrors much of the research into corporate citizenship at the heart of this book. Four of their findings are crucial to the new-world view which is emerging as the globalization process unfolds:

- First, the report referred to "the death of deference," meaning that employees, customers and communities increasingly expect their needs and values to be respected.
- Second, the efficient and responsible management of environmental resources is now of critical importance to all businesses.
- Third, flexible businesses are part of new organizational structures which require new management skills in working across geographic, sector and work-practice boundaries.
- Fourth, business has to earn its "license to operate," which means maintaining public confidence. In this regard, the report said that: "A company which undermines its *licence to operate* by the wrong behaviour exposes itself to a range of sanctions. Whatever the issue – from animal rights to executives' pay – companies seen to be insensitive to changing standards can find themselves at the centre of media and public outcry."

The report's recommendations would require a revolution for the vast majority of British companies because the recommendations not only advocate an inclusive approach to stakeholders, but also less reliance on financial measures of success. In the words of the report:

"The companies which will sustain competitive success in the future are those which focus less exclusively on financial measures of success – and instead include all their stakeholder relationships, and broader range of measurements, in the way they think and talk about their purpose and performance."

While the purpose of the Centre for Tomorrow's Company is "to inspire and enable British business to compete with the world's best through applying the inclusive approach," its message of the inclusive company is one which is being adopted by the most visionary companies around the world. Its focus on Britain's competitiveness may relax as it comes to appreciate that the companies it is keenest to make more competitive are global players whose interests in creating healthy, sustainable communities lie as much outside Britain as at home. Indeed, the evidence shows that for British business to prosper, it needs stable, prosperous markets – many of which are being created through inward investment and outsourcing from Britain's largest corporations, which are beginning to take their corporate citizenship beyond the parochialism of national boundaries and to consider the development of global society.

A further development by the Centre for Tomorrow's Company is the abandonment of the term *stakeholder* in favour of the *inclusive company*, because of a preference for an emphasis on the development of key relationships with employees, customers and communities. The Centre's explanation of the inclusive company is that customers are accountable to shareholders, but have a responsibility to other stakeholders. Some companies, such as BP, have also opted to refer to *key relationships*, rather than stakeholders.[26]

Business as partners in development: The Prince of Wales Business Leaders' Forum, The World Bank and The UN Development Programme

This partnership of three global organizations states that "the private sector has become the principal motor of development" and asks: "Can profit-driven companies be expected to play a leadership role in sustainable development, beyond the minimum expectations of operating within the law and contributing directly to economic growth through their core business activities?" Its conclusions are that successful business will in the future be based on economic growth and participation, environmental sustainability, social cohesion and human development, and that business has a crucial contribution to make in these areas.

The report underlined four principles which businesses needed to achieve these aims:

1 Reputation management

"Reputation is built on a complex base of intangible attributes such as reliability, quality, honesty, trust, social and environmental responsibility and credibility. Despite the fact that many business leaders would agree that reputation adds value, most companies still adopt a fragmented and PR-driven approach to reputation management."

2 Relationship management

"In today's global economy the relationships which a company has with its primary and secondary stakeholders are becoming increasingly complex, covering a wider range of stakeholder groups and issues than ever before. Most companies need to build more integrated strategies, structures and systems for stakeholder management and consultation."

3 Responsiveness

"A company's ability to understand and respond innovatively to market trends, future opportunities and stakeholder needs, plays a key role in building reputation and competitiveness. Linked to this, there is a growing emphasis on 'lateral thinking' and on systems approaches, aimed at building innovation around 'service needs' or 'customer benefits,' rather than product specifications. Such approaches often require co-operation with non-traditional partners."

4 Resource efficiency and enhancement

"A company's ability to access high-quality resources – be they human, natural, physical, financial or informational – and to adopt managerial and technical processes which add value to these resources efficiently, effectively and responsibly, will influence the company's reputation, responsiveness and relationships, its cost structure, the quality of its products and services, its environmental impact and productivity."

The World Business Council for Sustainable Development: Draft Principles for Corporate Social Responsibility[27]

Building on its Charter for Sustainable Development, a voluntary non-verifiable set of principles, the World Business Council for Sustainable Development has drafted a set of principles on social responsibility based on the premises that "changing public concerns about corporate social responsibility require a proactive approach by WBCSD members" and that "such an approach may generate commercial advantages."[28]

The draft principles cover:

- social responsibility as a corporate priority
- integrated management
- process of improvement
- employee education
- prior assessment
- products and services
- public information
- facilities and operations

- research
- precautionary principle
- contractors and suppliers
- emergency preparedness
- transfer of best practice
- contributing to the common effort
- openness to concerns
- compliance and reporting.

Models of social responsibility

Central to corporate citizenship is the relationship between business, government and civil society.[29] Often the relationship between these three groups is seen as the foundations of society as a whole.[30]

All companies that act within the law and remain profitable are in the most limited of senses acting in a socially responsible way. With the demise in Eastern Europe and Asia of state-run, command-and-control economies, business is increasingly the engine of society, devising new products, carrying out research and funding education.

Four models of social responsibility

In terms of social responsibility and, therefore, corporate citizenship, business activity can be grouped under four headings.

These categories are not mutually exclusive, but are helpful in understanding how different business organizations can be assessed as corporate citizens. They are:

1 *Business is amoral*, based on profit-making, and has no responsibility other than its economic and legal obligations.
2 *Business is a moral activity*, based on profit-making, and has an obligation to act for social betterment, meaning the betterment of the whole of society.
3 *A business is a community*, based on a corporate identity, which may be just for profit, not just for profit, or not for profit, and which recognizes that a business has a social and economic role.
4 *A business is a network* – it does not have a corporate identity and is neither moral not amoral in its purpose; it is fluid and may be transitory and based on project management.

The amoral or responsive business

Such a business:

- has no responsibilities other than economic and legal obligations;
- sees social responsibility issues as problems for reputation and public relations management;
- believes that its only stakeholders are its shareholders;
- has directors which act as trustees for shareholders;

- does not believe in stakeholders, but instead has key relationships, because stakeholder theory implies some ownership of the company;
- is managerial and action oriented;
- bases action on empirical research;
- is essentially responsive/reactive to changes in values of society;
- is founded on the principle of improving business and capitalist performance;
- regards rewarding earnings per share as the primary purpose of the company.

Business as a moral and responsible activity

Here a business would have the following beliefs/goals:

- Business has an obligation to strive for social betterment;
- Business should act beyond compliance with economic and legal obligations;
- Business should be philanthropic;
- Business is the engine of society;
- Business has economic, political and social power;
- Shareholders are the primary claimants, with a range of other claimants who may be called stakeholders;
- The directors are trustees for a range of claimants, including the shareholders.

The Big Issue: an alternative business on the streets

The Big Issue magazine was set up in 1991 in London as an alternative to begging and to give homeless people the means to earn an income. A street paper sold by homeless people, it aims to encourage self-help, believing that homeless people possess the potential to change their lives. By giving them a chance to make choices and learn new skills, in selling *The Big Issue* the hope is that it will help individuals to move off the streets, into a home, a job or training.

With a national circulation of 280,000 a week (in the UK), *The Big Issue* was inspired by a street paper in New York that was moderately successful. In order to address the UK's problem of marginalizing social failures, *The Big Issue* is aimed at challenging the very idea of social failure, insisting that instead of handing out money to the disenfranchised, giving them a "hand up," by providing them with a chance to earn a regular income, constructively addresses the problem.

The editorial content of *The Big Issue* has been vitally important in making it a success. As with any magazine, readership and circulation are extremely important and to increase these, editorial quality must be aimed strategically. As a magazine aimed at disenfranchised people and sold by homeless individuals, it is apolitical unless criticizing a particular policy. It focuses on issues of street-level importance, often picking up stories before the mainstream press. New trends, fashion and clubs are covered, as well as a double-page spread, "street lights," written by homeless people, which allows them to air their views. The magazine is a business and so must make money in order to support the other work it carries out.

In addition to selling *The Big Issue*, vendors have access to a huge network of support services. Training in office skills, building confidence, helping vendors find employment, writing skills, street work, outreach, counselling, housing help and access to furniture projects are all facilities available. In 1995, in order to expand this support work, The Big Issue Foundation was established. As a registered charity, it provides an umbrella support for those who have moved on and into accommodation, and the above support services.

Group work among vendors includes creative writing workshops, art workshops, women's groups, photography and drama workshops. Access and referral to training organizations in the community, funding for adult-education courses, in-house training courses including adult literacy, temporary and permanent work placements, interview training and CV development are organized by *The Big Issue*. Help with housing and resettlement are vital services, some of which are carried out in partnership with housing associations, self-build projects and joint fundraising schemes. Outreach work includes direct practical and emotional support, as well as counselling and welfare and legal-rights advice. Drug and alcohol counselling is also available.

The Big Issue also operates on an international basis running a network – the International Network of Street Papers (INSP) which provides a consultancy service for its partner papers and gives advice on setting up street papers and support for other homeless initiatives. The idea of *The Big Issue* is now being emulated in other cities around the world and has been launched in Australia, South Africa and the USA.

A business is a community

A business run on this ethos:

- is based on a set of values which include economic and legal obligations;
- is often based on some concept of business supporting social justice, equity and public service;
- includes for-profit, not-just-for-profit and not-for-profit organizations;
- is often family or co-operatively owned.

The network or partnership business

This business:

- is often based on the management of a specific piece of work or project;
- is often based on an electronic network;
- has virtual organization;
- does not necessarily have any corporate identity;
- is transitory, flexible, and has an indeterminate social structure;
- occupies holes in established social structures, both inside and outside existing corporate structures;
- recognizes diverse values within the network and aims for commonality of purpose, not a commonality of values;
- often operates on trust and love rather than formal contracts;
- recognizes both individual and shared constructs of reality;
- unlike the other models of business, does not necessarily have a unified, clear view of the future – apart from completing the project in hand;
- has loose organization that is non-absolutist and does not have a view as to the direction society is, or should be, heading in;
- often operates in the space between organizations, and sometimes in the space between the market and the state;
- is not always based on financial reward, but the pursuit of an idea;
- encourages social entrepreneurism;
- is often cross-border and international in nature, and does not recognize national boundaries or regional differences;
- often crosses global time lines and traditional work-practice time schedules.

Medecins sans Frontières: borderless care

Established in 1971, Medecins sans Frontières (MSF) is an independent, non-profit, international humanitarian organization whose objective is to provide medical aid to populations in crisis. It is largely made up of volunteer health professionals and prides itself on its independence from all states and institutions, as well as from political, economic or religious influences. It is an example of an international aid agency working across borders, in the zones created by conflict between rival nations or ethnic groups.

The objective of the organization is to rapidly respond, with medical teams of doctors, surgeons, anaesthetists, specialized nurses and logistics experts, to wars and man-made or natural disasters which occur throughout the world. Funded largely through private donations, it launches campaigns using galas, concerts, exhibitions and book or record sales to raise funds and promote the reputation of MSF, although it also receives funds from some governments and international organizations, such as the EU and UNICEF.

The basis of the organization is a strong network, with independent sections in Belgium, Spain, France, The Netherlands, Luxembourg and Switzerland. Volunteer teams on site work under the responsibility of a co-ordinator who manages the operations and relations with local health authorities and relief organizations. Delegate offices around the world disseminate information, fundraise and recruit healthcare professionals, and liaison agencies in New York and Geneva are in charge of relations with international organizations and institutions. An international network reinforces the human, logistic and financial resources of each section and guarantees their independence.

MSF operates in a number of different ways. In conflicts, sites will have already been assessed by reconnaissance outfits, although problems of security and difficult living conditions, combined with storage of medicine and equipment, sanitization of premises, installation and maintenance of operating theatres and training of local auxiliary personnel, mean that intervention is delicate and complex.

In refugee camps, both curative and preventive healthcare is carried out with other partners. In disaster regions, immediate implementation is essential and logistics planning is extremely important in allowing MSF to react so rapidly. Logistic means at their disposal are constantly available and the range of means (shelter, communications, water processing, sanitation, food, power supplies) give diversity to the operation.

Also involved in long-term medical aid, MSF works in countries where medical facilities are currently non-existent or poor. Because of the nature of MSF's work, it possesses a particular specialization – the use of mass medicine – which enables the organization to establish training courses in nutrition, immunization, water, hygiene and waste elimination, which are organized both in Europe and on site.

An increasing number of initiatives is being established in this non-corporate world, and it may be that this is the area of growth for social responsibility. It is in this area that business sees advantages in working with stakeholders. Rather than seeing former antagonists as "the enemy," in this model of social responsibility it is possible for two organizations with conflicting views of social reality to work together for some discrete social betterment.

We can give two examples here, but there are many more. When McDonald's and the Environmental Defense Fund in the USA decided to work together (see profile in Chapter 5), it was a milestone in terms of consensus decision making, in terms of working as inclusive organizations and in terms of recognizing that some elements of the social responsibility, agenda – in this case sustainability – can be agreed. Similarly, a second example is Unilever's decision to work with the World Wide Fund for Nature (WWF) to conserve global fish stocks. This was a step in a new direction. In both of these examples, and in the many others that are now emerging, there are those on both sides who see the whole process as flawed – they are deeply cynical about the motives on both sides, but it is clear that a common agenda of concern for the one planet we occupy is shared by people in all organizations – business or pressure group. Finding a way forward is the basis of the new style of business operation that is emerging. Hence, we have called this type the Network or Partnership Business, where there are profits to be made, but they are to be measured in both the short and the long term, and in terms of the health and wealth of local and global communities.

● MANAGEMENT EXERCISES ●

1 Which of the following three mission statements most closely replicates your organization's policy of social responsibility?

Johnson & Johnson:
> *"We believe our first responsibility is to doctors, nurses and patients, to mothers and all others who use our products and services . . . We are responsible to the communities in which we live and work, and to the community as well."*

The Hanson Trust:
> *"'In our company management's overriding objective is to increase earnings per share annually . . . Increasing shareholder value will increase the wealth of the company, and thus, of society."*

GrandMetropolitan (now Diageo):
> *"Corporate responsibility is not a fringe activity. Business success cannot be defined solely in terms of earnings, growth and the balance sheet. A truly successful company is sensitive to the concerns of all those on whom it depends; investors, employees, customers, trading partners and the countries and communities in which it does business."*

2 Look at the four models of corporate social responsibility in this chapter. Do any of the organizations you know fit any of the categories?

3 What are the implications of the following statement from Helmut O. Maucher (1997), Chairman of Nestlé and President of the International Chamber of Commerce, for companies operating in countries with poor human rights or environmental standards? If he is correct, how then can companies influence irresponsible governments?
> *"Business has no political power and aspires to none, although we clearly are interested in the social and political balance and the stability of the countries we work in."*[31]

▶

4 Dilemma: building a road

You are a civil engineer working in the construction industry. Your role is to manage large-scale construction projects, many of them under government contracts. The industry as a whole is just coming out of recession, and your company, like many others, has got rid of all but essential staff, and is now trying to operate as a leaner, fitter operation. It is essential for your survival that you gain new contracts.

The company has just been invited to submit a tender for a road-building project. Under the terms of government contracts, the job will be awarded to the cheapest bidder, and if your bid is successful, it will be your job to project manage it. You know that this particular scheme is going to provoke extensive public protest, from both some sections of the local community, which do not want their nearby woodlands ruined by a new road through the middle of it, and by environmentalists, who believe that several rare species of plant will be lost as a result of the building. The official planning process has been undergone in the usual way, and the project which came out of it was probably the least bad option. Nevertheless, protesters are likely to come from many miles away to join local people in causing as much disruption and delay in the project as possible.

The cheapest way of dealing with the likely problems is to erect a barbed wire fence around the site, employ security guards and get on with the job as quickly as possible. But you know that this is likely to further inflame the feelings of the protesters, could possibly put the safety of your staff at risk, and damage your company's reputation as a good corporate citizen. The last thing you want is to get into battle with members of the local community, and you feel there are things which could be done to alleviate the situation, but they would take time and money, and the terms of the contract allow no financial leeway. You feel resentful of the fact that while you, the contractors, are not responsible for deciding to put the road there, only for building it, you are likely to become the target of people's anger.

You are about to go to a meeting to discuss with your senior colleagues whether to take up the invitation to submit a tender or not. What should you do?

Notes to Chapter 2

1 Peter D. Sutherland, Chairman of BP, address to Amnesty International. Dublin, 26 September.

2 Ibid.

3 NatWest (1996) *Environment Report*. London: NatWest.

4 Herkströter, Cor, Chairman of Shell (1996) "Dealing with contradictory expectations – the dilemmas facing multi-nationals." Amsterdam, Shell International Ltd, 11 October.

5 Paradigm shift, which has become a cliché through overuse, was invented by Thomas Kuhn (1970) in *The Structure of Scientific Revolutions* (Chicago: Chicago University Press) when he said that all scientific thinking operated within theoretical or holistic frameworks,

or paradigms. A paradigm shift, therefore, is when the overview or framework within which understanding is gained changes because of both empirical knowledge and sensory perception.

6   The Body Shop, (1995) *Our Agenda*. Littlehampton, UK: The Body Shop.

7   Ben & Jerry's (1996) *Ben and Jerry's Mission*. Digital release on www.benjerry.com

8   Avon (1995) *Diversity: A Special Publication for Associates of Avon*. Annual Report. New York: Avon.

9   Hillaire, Fitzroy (1997) Interviewed by Deborah Leipziger. New York, 18 June.

10 See note 8.

11 Directorate of Public Affairs and Internal Communication (1997) *The Beat*. London: Metropolitan Police Service.

12 E.J.P. Browne, Group CEO of British Petroleum plc (1997) *Corporate Responsibility in an International Context*. Address to the Council on Foreign Relations, 13 November.

13 McDonald's Restaurants Ltd (1994) in Murphy, David F. and Bendell, Jem (1997) *In the Company of Partners*. Bristol: Policy Press.

14 See profile in Chapter 4.

15 The NHS (National Health Service) was introduced after the Second World War to provide free healthcare at the point of contact for all British people, because it had been found that the health of the populace was too poor to provide fit young men to fight in the armed forces (or work in industry). In other words, healthcare support provides business with basic infrastructure.

16 The conflict between Greenpeace and Shell is profiled in Chapter 4.

17 For instance, see Carroll, Archie B. (1991) "The pyramid of corporate social responsibility: toward the moral management of organizational stakeholders," *Business Horizons*, July/August.

18 See Carroll, note17; Schumacher, E.F. (1972) *Small is Beautiful: Economics as if People Mattered*. London: Blond & Briggs; Goyder, George (1993) *The Just Enterprise. A Blueprint for the Responsible Company*. London: Adamantine Press.

19 Social audit – see Appendix 2: Glossary.

20 See Browne, note 12.

21 Makower, Joel and Business for Social Responsibility (1994) *Beyond the Bottom Line: Putting Social Responsibility to Work for your Business and the World*. New York: Simon & Schuster.

22 Suzuki, Hideyuki (1996) *Corporate Responsibility and Environmental Management in Japanese Business*. September. Unpublished report commissioned by Malcolm McIntosh Associates and the New Academy of Business. Presented as a final report at Bristol University.

23 *Oxford Dictionary* (1969) Oxford: Oxford University Press.

24 Suzuki, see note 22.

25 Tepper Marlin, Alice (1995) *The Asahi Foundation Report*. London: Council on Economic Priorities.

26 The Centre for Tomorrow's Company – see list of organizations in Appendix 3.

27 World Business Council for Sustainable Development (1998) *Corporate Social Responsibility:*

A Pro-active Approach. A discussion paper prepared for the working group on the CSR of the WBCCSD with permission from Professor Alyson Warhurst, International Centre for the Environment, MERN, University of Bath. Draft, January.

28 Ibid.

29 The term "civil society" refers to that part of society which is non-military, non-governmental and non-ecclesiastical, and is concerned with citizens and community.

30 See, for instance, Cannon, Tom (1992) *Corporate Responsibility*. London: Pitman Publishing; Logan, David, Roy, Delwin and Regelbrugge, Lauri (1997) *Global Corporate Citizenship*. Tokyo: The Hitachi Foundation; Marsden, Chris and Andriof, Joerg (1997) *Understanding Corporate Citizenship*. Unpublished paper. University of Warwick; Maucher, Helmut O. (1997) "Ruling by consent," *Financial Times*, 11 December.

31 Maucher, see note 30.

3

PUTTING CORPORATE CITIZENSHIP AT THE HEART OF STRATEGY

Introduction

Brand image and reputation

Protecting reputations

Mercedes-Benz · Ford Pinto · British Airways · Heineken
Prudential Assurance · Barclays Bank · Dow Corning

Managing risk

Bhopal and Union Carbide
Prince William Sound and Exxon

Quality, productivity and social responsibility

Premier Beverages

The learning organization

Successful strategies of long-lived companies

Management exercises

Introduction

For many people responsible corporate citizenship is an ethical issue, but there are also compelling arguments for adopting a responsible approach simply because it is good business. The profiles of companies in this chapter that have fallen foul of public opinion on issues of social responsibility are testimony to the fact that responsible corporate citizenship should be a strategic issue for all companies. There are enormous markets for globally branded products, but the brand image has to be maintained – globally. There are many themes to a book on responsible corporate citizenship, but two linked aspects stand out. The first is that we live in a more transparent world; it is difficult to escape scrutiny. The second is accountability to a wide range of stakeholders. Both these issues require companies to monitor their entire supply chain to see if their partners, contractors, suppliers and perhaps clients conform to basic standards on a range of corporate citizenship issues.

The retailer that is not sure of where its shirts have been manufactured, the restaurant chain that cannot certify the safety of its burgers and the cosmetics company that cannot guarantee that its products have not been tested on animals are potentially all at risk. Being aware of these issues is not a question of altruism on the part of business; these issues matter to many consumers – public opinion is shifting, from Los Angeles to Tokyo to London.

This chapter looks at the advantages of the responsible corporate citizenship approach. It provides examples of corporate citizenship as risk, brand, reputation and asset management. It also considers corporate citizenship as a logical progression from quality assurance.

Brand image and reputation

Brand image and reputation have become more of a strategic priority in a global economy where one product may be sold in many different markets. The advantages of being able to sell one brand worldwide are counterbalanced by the possibility of that brand losing its reputation. This is particularly true of products that appeal to young urban professionals with significant amounts of disposable income (see Table 3.1 on p. 64). Many of the worst brand mismanagements in recent years have involved corporate-citizenship issues ranging from human rights to corporate governance and the environment.

Some companies have made a virtue of being seen to be more concerned and caring than their competitors. So The Body Shop positions itself as more ethical, IBM as providing solutions to planetary problems, McDonald's as being sensitive to local cultures and Nike as empowering individuals to do better. But all these companies, as global brands, have been accused of breaking that precious trust with the buying public. The Body Shop was accused of overstating the level of fair-traded[1] products it sold, but The Body Shop denied this and acted swiftly to counteract such claims in the future; IBM nearly collapsed in the 1970s through its board being out of touch with the personal computer market; McDonald's has had to defend itself all over the world against accusations of rainforest destruction, reliance on child labor and selling poor quality food,[2] and Nike has re-written its global trading principles as a result of bad publicity over the use of child labor in the manufacture of its footwear.[3] These companies have all denied the claims and worked hard to ensure that these accusations do not continue.

Now that the General Motors Corporation has chosen four brand names for its automobiles worldwide (Chevrolet, Opel, Saab and Cadillac), GM has to be careful not to suffer the fate that has befallen Mercedes-Benz and its "A" Class car which allegedly toppled over when swerving to avoid moose that strayed onto Nordic roads, or that which happened to Ford with its explosive Pinto in the 1960s and 1970s.

According to a survey of British managers, in the highly competitive global economy, the three key issues for business success are (1) customer service, (2) the training, development and retention of key personnel and (3) efficiency and cost control.[4] As businesses have become leaner, tighter organizations with fewer staff, key relationships and brand image are the company's greatest assets and their management becomes more important.

When the company espouses clear values in its advertising, or through its mission or vision statements, it must be prepared to be accountable for its actions. The human resources director for one of the world's largest advertising agencies has said that: "With many organizations now pared to the bone, what differentiates them from their competitors are concepts like values, mission, passion and beliefs – once thought too 'touchy-feely' to have anything to do with business."[5] In companies which have downsized, decentralized or now operate in many varied markets, it is easy for

management to take its eye off strategy while it manages th
procedure of getting the product to market.

John Kay in *Foundations of Corporate Success*[6] said that the
that last are those that manage their key relationships well and fo
reputations. This means that maintaining vigilance over quality and reputation becomes even more vital to business success. The global company can
now be structured on a horizontal, rather than a vertical basis, with different components being manufactured in different parts of the world,
assembled locally or regionally and managed from the most desirable location, rather than in a home country or on top of the factory. In the not too
distant past, many large business conglomerates owned, or had an interest
in, the mine that produced the ore to make the ships that were marketed
worldwide through their own offices. In other words, they were structured
vertically and had control of the complete supply chain.

As the world seems to get smaller, the manufacturer may find it cheaper
to source raw materials in one country, manufacture in another and sell in
a third. This requires closer management of the supply chain, if quality and
reputation are to be protected. As the profiles of Premier Beverages, Levi
Strauss & Co. and Nike show, there are distinct advantages to be gained
from accounting for working practices at all stages. Management today may
be like flying an aircraft at speed, but in order to do so, more, not less, information and control is required. So, much of the drive to put corporate
citizenship at the heart of strategic planning is concerned with providing
managers with more information about the company's total impact and,
therefore, with protecting company reputation and enhancing brand image.

Brand image is everything. What do you think of Nike, Virgin, Volvo,
Greenpeace, Amnesty International or Coca-Cola? These organizations work
hard at promoting "brand" image. Virgin's image is flexible, exciting, young
and based on good service. Volvo is seen as safe and well engineered.
Amnesty International is known to be honest, accurate, reliable and
committed.

In a world where the same shop that sells socks also sells shares, and
where you can cash a check as you pick up the tomatoes, there is greater
emphasis on brand image. For instance, General Motors sells both automobiles and runs a credit card; American Express provides financial services
and vacations, while in the UK Marks & Spencer sells clothing, food, pensions and insurance; and the Virgin brand sells airline seats, pop music and
investment opportunities. It is brand image that sells a range of products, not
a single item, and increasingly global brand image requires constant care

⌐nd attention. It is easily damaged by global media reporting, just as issues can easily become important because of celebrity support. Using Michael Jackson to promote a product and then finding that he has been accused of child abuse is the sort of nightmare any company wants to avoid. In the same way, the Red Cross was delighted that Diana, Princess of Wales chose to highlight a major global social responsibility issue, the sale of anti-personnel land mines, which is leading to agreements to ban their manufacture and sale around the world.

The world's most powerful brands are mostly American, and others may have a national image but be owned by a second country. For instance, most people in the UK and Japan would think that Burger King (Hungry Jack's in Australia) and Pizza Hut are American, but they are owned by GrandMetropolitan (now Diageo), a UK company.

Table 3.1 The world's most valuable brands[7]

Coca-Cola	US	Soft drinks
Marlboro	US	Tobacco
IBM	US	Computers
McDonald's	US	Fast food
Disney	US	Entertainment
Sony	Japan	Electronic equipment
Kodak	US	Film and camera equipment
Intel	US	Computers
Gillette	US	Shaving and personal care products
Budweiser	US	Beer
Nike	US	Sports footwear
Kellogg's	US	Breakfast cereal and food
AT&T	US	Telecommunications
Nescafé	Switzerland	Food
GE	US	Electrical
Hewlett-Packard	US	Computers
Pepsi	US	Soft drinks
Microsoft	US	Computer software
Frito-Lay	US	Food
Levi's	US	Clothing based on denim

Most of these brands are based on lifestyle image. We all need food and clothing, but we do not have to buy McDonald's and Levi's.

A brand image works for a company internally and externally. Inside the company the brand image acts like a glue and a heartbeat, persuading employees that their product unites them in their daily endeavors, and is something to believe in. Externally, brand image also provides customers with "something to believe in," to quote the Volvo advertisements of the 1990s. For both constituents, brand means more than the product itself – it also represents lifestyle, values and helps to shape their lives. As Interbrand, a leading brand agency, says: "People don't have to pay 30 per cent more for a Disney T-shirt. But they do so because the brand means more to them than the T-shirt – it embodies the Disney magic."[8]

Protecting reputations

Mercedes-Benz

To most observers in 1997, the inability of Mercedes-Benz to predict that its new "A" Class car allegedly toppled over when avoiding moose on Nordic roads was extraordinary. The company compounded the problem when it waited three weeks before withdrawing the car from the market. The company lost 2,000 pre-sales, worth some $200 million. The car had cost $1.65 billion to develop.

The issues were obviously safety, but also the management of key relationships, particularly the media and potential customers, and so fits into the category of corporate governance. Perhaps the most telling comment came from Mercedes' rival, BMW, which said: "We are not gloating about this as this affects the reputation of our entire German industry. It could well be us next time and Mercedes will be on the defensive for a long time."[9]

Ford Pinto

Twenty years earlier, in 1978, Ford was convicted of knowingly selling a car, the Pinto, with a fuel tank that was likely to explode on rear impact. The court verdict was criminal homicide against Ford. By 1978, Ford had sold hundreds of thousands of the Pinto model and had paid out thousands of dollars in compensation to previous accident victims. At stake for the company was the influx of cheaper sub-compact vehicles into the North American market from Japan and Europe, particularly from VW. Ford rushed to market knowing that its car could be made safer, but calculating that the improvements would cause a delay in the launch of the car and that compensation claims would be cheaper than the cost of improvements.[10]

At the time of the Pinto incident in the USA, a safety expert estimated that there were more than 40 European or Japanese sub-compacts on sale there with safer fuel tanks. At this time overseas competitors captured a substantial proportion of the US small automobile market.[11] Twenty years after the Pinto incident, manufacturers are still miscalculating the effect of negative media coverage and litigation.

British Airways

The "world's favourite airline" was found guilty of poaching customers from its trans-atlantic rival, Virgin, owned by Richard Branson, and conducting a campaign of "dirty tricks." The Chairman of British Airways, Lord King, who had successfully taken BA from a nationalized industry to privatization, was thought to have handled the media disastrously.[12]

The issue was one of honesty and integrity and, as a consequence of the incident, British Airways issued *The Way We Do Things: The Code of Business Conduct* to all staff, which included advice on honesty: "This goes beyond simply telling the truth to ensuring that any misrepresentation is quickly corrected."[13]

Heineken

In January 1996, Heineken, Dutch makers of world-famous beer, sent a fax to a television production company, Planet 24, concerning the company's sponsorship of a programme called *Hotel Babylon* which was to be adapted for various European audiences. The fax referred to the fact that some members of the audience were black and therefore not, as Heineken thought, representative of a typical Italian audience, for whom this particular pilot was made. The fax stated that there was "too high a proportion of Negroes." In Britain the programme was to be shown on Channel 4.

Heineken realized that the fax, which was leaked to a newspaper, was offensive and discriminatory and the CEO, Vuursteen, made a public apology. Although it has been claimed that Heineken's beer sales were affected by this outbreak of corporate racism, the company claims that there was no drop in sales.

Prudential Assurance

In 1996 and 1997, British TV viewers were regaled with images of Peter Davis, the Chief Executive of the Prudential, Britain's largest insurance and pension provider, riding around London on a motor bike. The image projected was of the mobile corporate executive, old enough to be wise, young enough to be a biker, the company that was safe and honest enough to be trusted with viewers' pensions.

The Prudential, alongside other pension companies, was found guilty of mis-selling personal pensions worth $6.6 billion. Peter Davis admitted that he was "ashamed" of what had happened. It was, he said, "probably the worst thing that had happened to Prudential" and "we're sorry that there have been problems and we're determined to put them right."[14]

In 1997, the Prudential was forced to apologize after it was "named and shamed" by the incoming Labour government. The affair will cost the company up to $750 million. The theme of Peter Davis' previous TV appearances had been "trust me." It will take some time to repair the damage to Prudential's image after a scandal which directly involved 60,000 customers, many of them on low to medium incomes.

Barclays Bank

The British bank was forced to withdraw from South Africa in November 1986. With its origins in Africa, and with Quaker founders, this was an enormous humiliation for Barclays, which was targeted by anti-apartheid student protesters at British universities. Students in higher education are seen to be the future higher earners, thus the bank decided that rather than lose their custom, it would withdraw from a country which at that time did not look ready to reform itself.

The jury is still out on which companies helped the most to destroy the evil of apartheid. Was it the companies that withdrew from the country, or was it the companies that remained in the country, but put pressure on the white minority regime to reform, while keeping South Africa in the global economy?

Dow Corning

In 1997, Dow Corning was reported to have misled women by concealing information about the health risks associated with breast implants. The company offered to pay $2.4 billion to settle the claims filed against Dow Chemical, the parent company. These claims had a major impact on the future of the company.[15]

Richard Branson maintains the image of Virgin as innovative, fun, caring and good value by attempting to balloon round the world, British Airways displays its international credentials on its tail fins and McDonald's likes to be thought of as good value, fun and fast. A couple of plane crashes could ruin the image of either airline, just as an outbreak of food poisoning at a McDonald's restaurant could deal a mortal blow to its global business.

The results of a survey of customer loyalty in the UK showed that people trusted individual brand names, such as Kellogg's and Heinz, but did not trust multinational companies in general (see Table 3.2). Indeed, people trusted their breakfast cereal more than the police, judiciary, local council or Parliament. As Richard Branson has said: "Brands must not be built around products, but around reputation, quality and price." On this basis he has used the name Virgin (a name which, in 1984, he was told could not possibly launch an airline) to launch a whole range of products within the Virgin family.[16]

Table 3.2 Brands: who do you trust in Britain?[17]

Your GP (local, general doctor)	85%
Kellogg's	83%
Boots (pharmacy)	83%
Heinz	81%
Sainsbury's (supermarket)	74%
Tesco (supermarket)	71%
Bird's Eye (frozen food from Unilever)	70%
The Police	62%
The Judiciary	43%
Local council	24%
A multinational company (MNC)	**13%**
Parliament	10%
The Press	7%

Managing risk

All companies conduct assessments in areas they know in which they could be at risk, but rapid changes in globalization have exposed companies to new risks – that they may not have thought existed. We have already mentioned in Chapter 2 Shell's recognition, after the Brent Spar incident and the exposure of its role in Nigeria, that over 30 years it had been paying too little attention to the growing power and influence of global non-governmental organizations.

The specific risk here is that a company may be found to be operating with a different set of values away from its home base, or that it may be sourcing from, or working with, another company which has irresponsible practices.

The risk of exposure in areas such as the exploitative use of child labor, human-rights abuses or environmental protection is far greater now that electronic communications have diminished the power of national governments to control information. Oppressed indigenous populations, non-governmental organizations and single-issue pressure groups and the media can all make easy use of global communications systems.

Risk and reputation

Here are two profiles involving two major companies, Union Carbide and Exxon, where environmental disasters could have been avoided, could have been handled differently and which have cost both the companies concerned a great deal of money and a significant loss of reputation.

Bhopal and Union Carbide

On 2 December 1984, a Union Carbide plant in Bhopal, India, released 42 tons of toxic gas causing 2,000 immediate deaths, and leading to a further 4,000 deaths. In addition, 200,000 people were seriously injured, 60,000 permanently.[18] Union Carbide has been described as "the perpetrator of the world's worst industrial disaster."[19] Although there have been many other industrial accidents which have had similar consequences, they have not resulted in so many immediate deaths. These include the Exxon Valdez oil spill in 1989,[20] the Seveso chemical plant explosion in Italy and Love Canal in the USA in 1976, the Chernobyl nuclear accident in 1986 and the Ford Pinto car in 1978.[21] To apportion blame for these accidents to the company suggests either deliberate malpractice or incompetent management. In all these cases there is clear evidence that the cost of better risk management would have been far smaller than the cost of the clear-up.[22]

In the case of the Bhopal tragedy Union Carbide, which had a 50 per cent stake in the Indian company, had a reasonable "parental" code of conduct, but its overseas management of plants, such as at Bhopal, was poor.[23] The factory was covered by a maze of local regulations in the state of Madhya Pradesh, but there were only 15 safety inspectors to cover the state's 8,000 plants.

The damage to Union Carbide's reputation

The Bhopal plant closed immediately after the accident. One of the main gates has been painted with a large skull with the caption "Killer Carbide." Across the street a two-and-half metre high statue of a woman in anguish clutching a dead baby was erected. Union Carbide's chairman admitted in 1988:

> "[In the 1970s] our safety record was unequaled among manufacturers. Our employees were healthier than most other people, and we were aggressively establishing ourselves competitively in the markets of the world. Then, in a few short years, our world seemed to change. Today, we are one of the most feared and misunderstood industries in the history of the planet."[24]

Eight months after the accident at Union Carbide, as if to prove that it was not just local Indian management that was at fault, an incident at a Union Carbide plant in West Virginia led to 120 people being hospitalized.[25]

In the period from 1984 to 1992, the company reduced its workforce from 98,400 to 12,000 and sales fell from $9,900 million in 1984 to $4,800 million in 1992.[26]

Union Carbide's solution

In 1989, five years after the accident, Union Carbide agreed to pay the Indian government $470 million in compensation, to be divided among victims and their families, and agreed to build a hospital to be opened in 1998. Although many Indians thought the company had paid substantially less than it would have had to pay had the accident happened in the USA, the company said: "We feel we fulfilled our obligations in 1989."[27]

Five years after the agreement, the courts had rejected 75 per cent of the 615,000 claims, and those families that had been successful were receiving about $3,500 for each fatality. The extreme delays in compensating families and victims has resulted not just from inefficiency and corruption in the Indian judicial and administrative systems, but also from the way events unfolded in the hours and days after the accident.

The local hospitals, struggling with inadequate resources in a poor country, were overwhelmed by the tens of thousands of people suffering from the effects of the toxic gas. Doctors dealt as best they could with the living and failed to identify the dead. The next day government workers burned hundreds of bodies on a municipal funeral pyre. Many people were cremated quickly and autopsies were not allowed in keeping with religious tradition. Satisfying claims has, as a consequence, been an extremely difficult business. In addition, Union Carbide claims that its investigating officials had no access to the site immediately after the accident. An investigation in 1988 reported that: "The results of this investigation show, with virtual certainty, that the Bhopal incident was caused by the entry of water to the tank through a hose that had been connected directly to the tank. It is equally clear that those most directly involved attempted to obfuscate these events."[28]

The wider issues

The question that arises from this case concerns not just internal management issues such as health and safety in the plant, but also the company's wider responsibilities for dealing with contingencies such as the accident at Bhopal. To what extent should a company prepare contingencies to cope with an accident of this magnitude? Is it the responsibility of the company, especially when operating in a country with lower levels of public healthcare than in its home country?

The issue arose in 1997 with tobacco companies negotiating deals with some states in America to pay reparation for damage caused by smoking cigarettes over many decades. In this case, it transpired that the tobacco companies knew they could be causing damage to their customers. Although that was not the case with Union Carbide's Bhopal plant, the issue remains the same. *If society "licenses" industry to operate, then whose responsibility is it to deal with the consequences*?

Prince William Sound and Exxon

On 24 March 1989, the Exxon Valdez oil tanker ran aground in Prince William Sound in Alaska spilling 10.8 million gallons of crude oil, causing one of the world's worst environmental disasters. On the same day, Exxon's UK subsidiary, Esso, was helping to launch a coffee-table book on coastline conservation with the National Trust![29]

Over the next eight years, Exxon's clean-up costs amounted to $1 billion, as well as $3 billion for settling claims, and not including the time and energy devoted to the clean-up operation and subsequent litigation claims by Exxon managers. Despite the efforts of the oil company, the local fishing community and environmentalists, it is estimated that some 15–20 per cent of the oil remains in the Prince William Sound and the Gulf of Alaska.[30]

The petro-chemical economy

Partnerships with environmental organizations are becoming more common, but it is fair to say that some oil companies such as Royal Dutch/ Shell have been working on conservation issues for over 50 years. Despite Esso's work with the National Trust in the UK, the Exxon Valdez incident was a public-relations disaster for the company both in North America and Europe. The way in which Exxon has managed its affairs over the 100 years it has been in business has significant lessons for people interested in the longevity of companies.

We live in a petro-chemical economy, and without fossils fuels, particularly oil, our lifestyles would be radically different. Oil is hardly challenged by the world's second largest industry, the trade in illegal drugs. Oil is vital to the world economy and we have been unable to turn off the pumps, despite the oil-price shocks of the 1970s and 1980s. Starting out as Standard Oil of New Jersey, Exxon prided itself on being run by geologists and engineers along rigid lines which dictate that there is a technical fix for every problem.

Exxon and other oil companies

Exxon's great rival over the years has been its oil colleague, Royal Dutch/ Shell, with whom it has level pegged on sales and profits over the years. What distinguishes the two companies is the fact that Shell has been more adventurous, which may reflect the reality of Shell's position as a European company. While Shell has invested in natural gas and liquefied natural gas, Exxon has, in the main, stayed in oil.

As oil prices have remained flat in the last few years and the industry has had to invest in clean technology to meet tighter environmental regulations, Exxon has also been challenged by the other oil companies to cut its bureaucracy. It has followed the fashion of the 1980s and 1990s and downsized, delayered. This means that since 1980, the company has cut one third of its staff, cut down on management hierarchies, reduced its central office staff by 50 per cent, but has succeeded in making more money from what it does best – extracting and refining oil.

Who pays for clean-ups?

Exxon exemplifies the theme of this book: the world's global corporations carry enormous responsibility for their activities, and even for the state of the world. The Exxon Valdez went down in Alaska and has been subject to US litigation and pressure through the media from environmental pressure groups. Companies do not always have to bear their burdens so publicly when their mistakes occur in countries which do not uphold the rule of law. What would have happened to Exxon had the disaster happened in Nigeria? Given that Exxon's daily oil production worldwide is almost the equivalent of Nigeria's daily output, this is an interesting comparison. Other figures tell the same story: Exxon's annual turnover is three times Ireland's, and it daily markets enough oil to supply all of France's and Germany's needs.[31]

Quality, productivity and social responsibility

Imagine a restaurant: candle light, good company, delicious food – then at midnight you and your partner end up in the back of an ambulance on the way to a hospital because of acute food poisoning.

The restaurateur had bought what she thought was good food from a wholesaler, who had bought it from an importer who had bought it from a distributor in another country, who had sourced the food from hundreds of farms in the producing country. At what point had the infection crept into the food? Who was responsible? How could the infection be traced?

Just such cases happen all too often nowadays as food is sourced globally, passing through numerous middle men before ending up as meals. In 1996, thousands of Japanese school children suffered from food poisoning which was eventually traced to their packed lunches. In Britain people will continue to die from infected beef for decades to come, caused by feeding infected animal matter to herbivore cattle, and the Spanish have learned to be suspicious of cheap cooking oil after many people died from cheap adulterated oil in the 1970s.

In a case in the USA, school children were found to be suffering from hepatitis which originated in their school lunches. The problem was traced to frozen strawberries from Mexico. The workers packing the strawberries had such poor living conditions and were being paid such low wages that that they were ill, and their sickness was being transferred to the goods they were handling.[32]

In all these cases there is a question of liability, which could prove extremely costly in terms of reputation and litigation. It is for this reason that

Fitzroy Hilaire from Avon Cosmetics says that "cheap labor becomes very expensive in the long run."[33]

Toys 'Я' Us, which supplies 25 per cent of toys in North America, was faced with situations where it had to be sure of the quality of its products or face commercial meltdown. Along with other toy sellers, it discovered that not only were workers in developing countries, such as China, suffering from illnesses caused by toxic ingredients in the products, but that the products were emitting toxicity to children in US homes. At both ends of the supply chain there was a need to link quality assurance to issues of environmental protection, workplace rights and consumer law. Toys 'Я' Us has now insisted that all its suppliers be certified to Social Accountability 8000 (SA8000), the new global ethical trading standard pioneered by the Council on Economic Priorities in New York.[34]

The case of Premier Beverages is another example of quality with a direct link to productivity, workers' rights and consumer sales.

Quality and productivity: Premier Beverages

Premier Beverages is part of the Typhoo/Cadbury group of companies, and stands among the top five of the UK tea producers. Much of the tea produced by Premier reaches the market as "own-label" brands sold by supermarkets. In the mid-1980s, Premier changed the way it bought tea: until this time, like its other major competitors, it bought 80 per cent of its tea by auction at the London tea market. But it was prompted by the need to overcome market variations and exert more quality control to move towards buying directly from tea producers. This change brought the company's tea buyers into significant contact with tea estates for the first time, and enabled them to begin to make connections between the conditions in which tea is produced and the quality of the product.

In 1991, a major quality assurance project (QAP) was put in motion at Premier Beverages. This extended quality processes beyond the normal aspects of the product specification, taste and consistency, and manufacturing processes involved in tea production, to include management systems, hygiene and safety standards, and social conditions on estates. In order to help to put this into practice, the company took the unusual step of working alongside FairTrade. The tea trade as a whole had been the subject of attention from international development agencies, which criticized the fact that prices paid to developing country producers were not keeping pace with rising levels of affluence in the west, and contrasted the cramped and unhealthy conditions in which tea-pickers lived on many estates with the comfort of western tea drinkers. Premier's need for consistent quality standards meant that it was willing to explore unconventional routes to establish enduring relationships with tea growers, and

FairTrade offered assistance in doing this. Improving health, education and housing benefits for estate workers was linked, through the QAP, to achieving a preferred supplier status. A clear assessment system with which estate managers must comply was put in place, with an emphasis on continuous improvement.

For Premier Beverages, the defining element of the company's buying strategy remains quality assurance: it recognizes that establishing the terms of a relationship which is mutually beneficial to both producers and buyers is key to getting its quality requirements met. Premier's chief tea buyer and the champion behind the QAP, Phil Mumby, describes this ethical sourcing approach as simply good business, which has enabled Premier's market share to grow. The relationship with FairTrade has not been without difficulties – for a while in the mid-1990s it broke down completely, after a national newspaper carried an advertisement from several NGOs attacking the tea industry's treatment of tea growers – but the strength of the commercial case for pursuing the high-quality/fair-trade connection led to the re-establishment of the partnership. Premier is now working by explicit and published FairTrade principles, and is preparing to submit itself to external audit against these.[35]

The learning organization

Companies that are transparent, accountable and ahead of the game are constantly learning and aware that in order to remain successful they have to make use of the information economy. There are lessons to be learned from those companies that continue to be successful despite changing external conditions. How have they survived?

Peters and Waterman's (1982) ground-breaking book, *In Search of Excellence: Lessons from America's Best Run Companies*, reported that excellent companies were flat, anti-hierarchical structures, innovative and entrepreneurial, have small corporate and middle management staffs, reward systems based on contribution rather than length of service or hierarchy, brain power rather than muscle power and strong, flexible cultures. They also pointed out that their research of 62 of America's most successful companies showed: "The idea that profit is a natural by-product of doing something well, and not an end in itself, is almost always universal."[36]

Peters and Waterman's view that the successful company is flexible and rewards intelligence, learning and merit is central to the concept of the learning organization. As de Geus, writing on "the learning organization," points out, the company that acts like a living organism will naturally be a learning organization absorbing and reacting to information in an evolutionary manner. Companies that are conceived of as machines, rather than living organisms, are unlikely to be aware of external shifts in public opinion or be sensitive enough to their key relationships, because they will not be sensitive to the unexpected.

Corporate citizenship requires companies to be aware of their social responsibilities, and this is only possible if companies are learning organizations.

The learning organization:
- continually builds its skills base;
- regards employees and other stakeholders as essential sources of new ideas;
- sees employees as people, not just as human resources or raw, disposable materials;
- measures the success of the organization by indicators other than just financial accounting, because this may be a better indicator of future profitability;
- recognizes that decision making is learning – therefore, in theory, all organizations learn all the time. However, it is necessary for organizations to learn how to learn from mistakes and successes.

According to Peter Senge: "As the world of work becomes more interconnected and business becomes more complex and dynamic, work must become more 'earningful.' It is no longer sufficient to have one person learning for the organization . . . The organization that will truly excel in the future will be the organization that discovers how to tap people's commitment and capacity to learn at all levels in the organization."[37]

Stakeholders and key relationships are sources of strength and innovative ideas for the company. All workers at all stages of the supply chain have a vital part to play in the continuing viability of the company.

Successful strategies of long-lived companies

In *The Living Company: Growth, Learning and Longevity In Business*, de Geus pointed out that most companies die after 40–50 years, but that there are some that are over 200 years old. Why? How have they survived?

He also contends that companies with long, successful lives have four characteristics:

1 Sensitivity to the external environment, which allows the company to learn and adapt;
2 Cohesion and identity, which allow the company to be a community and have a personality;
3 Tolerance and decentralization because the company understands its own ecology; this enables it to build new relationships in and outside the company;
4 Conservative financing which allows the company to govern its own growth and evolution.[38]

In another piece of research on long-life companies, *Built To Last*, Collins and Porras (1998) said that "visionary companies make more money than the more purely profit-driven comparison companies."[39] This study looked at the "successful habits of visionary companies" and showed that the visionary US companies analyzed had similarities:

● They showed resilience and stuck to their core ideology.
● Profit maximization was not the dominant driving force or primary objective.

Responsible corporate citizenship can enable companies to take advantage of the new business climate – stick to core values, engage with stakeholders and put corporate citizenship at the heart of strategy – and be profitable.

● MANAGEMENT EXERCISES ●

1 Risk assessment and social responsibility

NatWest (1995) in the UK says that as "environmental responsibility is a corporate priority, environmental risks are a part of normal risk assessment and management." As a consequence, it has been engaged in developing FEMAs (Financial Eco-Management and Audit) and RPAs (Reportable Performance Assessment).[40] However, like most banks, NatWest has a serious problem in terms of accountability.

The nature of the banking problem is this. While 50 per cent of most banks' working capital is sourced from customers' accounts, the remaining 50 per cent is sourced globally, and any attempt to trace the source of the banks' money can prove virtually impossible. Given that banks like NatWest are interested in decreasing their risks and have made a commitment to environmental sustainable

▶

development and human rights, what can they do to assess their full exposure on issues of social responsibility?

The profiles in Chapter 4 of VanCity Union and the Co-operative Bank may prove helpful.

2 Company mission

A few words on mission statements

Any organization, in order to be effective, needs to have a mission which is well-explained and widely understood. This enables people to be clear about what the company is trying to accomplish, and offers some touchstone against which policies on social, environmental and ethical issues can be measured.

> *"A mission statement is a general declaration of the purposes of the organization and the very long-term objectives that its leaders want to achieve. The best examples are written in inspirational tone to provide a focused and motivating document for the organization's employees."*[41]

Mission statements are widely used to communicate a company's mission, but not all statements are meaningful and understood by employees, shareholders, customers and suppliers. There is a difference between a mission and a vision, the former describes the organization's tasks and way of operating, while the latter provides some idea of the long-term goal of the company.

In order to be useful, a mission statement must:

- be short and simply expressed – if the statement is long, full of qualifications and written in inaccessible language, it will not be memorable;
- be widely available – a statement which appears only in the annual report, or is given to new employees at their induction and never seen again is not doing its job; in order to motivate, the statement must be visible;
- be renewed regularly – a good mission statement is a living document, which company leaders can identify with and employees can understand and relate to.

Exercise

It is often not easy to identify an organization from its mission statement. See if you can identify the from the statements below:

A: "[We] recognise a responsibility to society to conduct business as responsible corporate members of society, to observe the laws of the countries in which we operate, to express support for fundamental human rights in line with the legitimate role of business and to give proper regard to health, safety and the environment, consistent with their commitment to contribute to sustainable development."

▶

B: "[This company] believes that one of the main reasons it has been successful is its long-term commitment to [Third World] countries. The track record which has been established as a socially responsible, apolitical and trustworthy employer has proved invaluable in dealings with governments worldwide and has undoubtedly contributed to the success of the international business."

C: "The way we trade creates profits with principles."

D: "Our corporate value is to be a good neighbour concerned for the community and the environment."

E: "We strive to be a good neighbour at home and abroad."

F: "Environmental management continues to be a corporate priority, fully integrated into business. We believe sound environmental practice is a key factor demonstrating corporate management."

G: "Our customers choose [our] clothes and furniture because our designs are excellent quality and our values are outstanding. Manufacturing to these standards demands very close attention not just to the appearance of the finished goods but to the methods, materials and processes used to produce them."

H: "We will devote our human resources and technology to create superior products and services, thereby contributing to a better global society."

(The answers can be found in note 42 at the end of this chapter.)

Does your company have a mission statement? If so, do you know it, and can you write it down?

If you don't know, who would you approach to find out?

How do you evaluate the mission statement? In what ways could it be made into a more effective tool?

Notes to Chapter 3

1 Fair trade – see Appendix 2: Glossary.

2 See Chapter 5 for a ground-breaking partnership between McDonald's and the Environmental Defense Fund.

3 See Chapter 4 for a profile of Nike's position on trading.

4 These are echoed by a MORI survey (1996) *The Key to Business Success*, a UK survey of top business leaders for SGS-Yarsley International Certification Service Ltd, with the figures of 53 per cent, 41 per cent and 33 per cent respectively for the three categories.

5 Royston, David, Human Resources Director for Ogilvy & Mather, in Simpson, Liz (1997) "Call in the cops," *British Airways Business Life*. London: British Airways.

6　Kay, John (1993) *Foundations of Corporate Success.* Oxford: Oxford University Press.

7　According to Interbrand, a brand-image consultancy, reporting in a highly simplified form (*Financial Times*, 17 October 1997).

8　Ibid.

9　*The Economist* (1997) "Mercedes Bends," 15 November; *Guardian* (1997) "Moose test topples Mercedes," 13 November.

10　Hoffman, W. Michael and Mills Moore, Jennifer (1990) *Business Ethics: Readings and Cases in Corporate Morality.* Maidenhead: McGraw-Hill.

11　Ibid.

12　King, Ian (1997) "Great corporate calamities," *Guardian,* 13 November.

13　British Airways (1995) *The Code of Business Conduct.* London: British Airways.

14　Davis, Peter (1997) on "The Money Programme," 16 November.

15　Rolana, Olna (1997) "Dow Corning seeks to settle implant cases," New York Times, 26 August.

16　Branson, Richard (1997) "Brand new world" in *The World in 1997.* London: Economist Publications.

17　The Henley Centre, *Planning for Social Change 1997/8.* Henley, UK: The Henley Centre.

18　Moore, Molly (1993) "The second disaster in Bhopal," *Business & Society Review,* reprinted from *The Washington Post.*

19　Dembo, David, Morehouse, Ward and Wykle, Lucinda (1990) *Abuse of Power: Social Performance of Multinational Corporations: The Case of Union Carbide.* New York: New Horizons Press, p.5.

20　See profile on p. 71.

21　Hoffman, Michael (1990) "The Ford Pinto," (1990) *Business Ethics.* Maidenhead: McGraw-Hill.

22　Wheeler, David and Sillanpää, Maria (1997) *The Stakeholder Corporation.* London: Pitman Publishing.

23　Moore (see note 18) and Dembo *et al.* (see note 19).

24　Dembo *et al.*, p.1 (see note 19).

25　Reputation Management (1994) *Union Carbide: Ten Years after Bhopal, Still Dealing with the Fall-Out,* PR Central, January/February.

26　Ibid.

27　Moore (see note 18).

28　Garrett, Alexander (1997) "Business buys its way to a greener image," *Independent on Sunday,* 10 November.

29　Kalelkar, Ashok S. (1988) *Investigation of Large-magnitude Incidents: Bhopal as a Case Study,* Arthur D. Little Inc., Cambridge, Massachusetts, presented at the Institution of Chemical Engineers Conference on Preventing Major Chemical Accidents, London.

30　*Chemistry & Industry Magazine News* (1996) "What became of the Exxon Valdez Oil?," 2 January; *The Economist,* (1994) "Inside the empire of Exxon the unloved," 5 March.

31　*The Economist,* (1994) "Inside the empire of Exxon the unloved," 5 March.

32 Deborah Leipziger, quoted in Matthews, Virginia (1997) "Framework for ethical sourcing," *Financial Times*, 12 December.

33 Ibid.

34 See Chapter 5 for details of SA8000.

35 Mumby, Phil, Premier Beverages and Wells, Phil, Fair Trade Foundation (1997) Speech at Ethical Business Seminar, London, 11 March; Adams, Richard (1993) "Typhoo Puts the 'T' in TQM" in Centre for Social Management and New Consumer, SAUS (1993) *Good Business? Case Studies in Corporate Social Responsibility.* Bristol: Policy Press.

36 Peters, T. and Waterman, R. (1982) *In Search of Excellence: Lessons from America's Best Run Companies.* London: HarperCollins. Writing a few years later, they admitted that many of their most successful companies had gone out of business a few years after the book's publication because they had been sold, merged or unable to react fast enough to changing external conditions.

37 Senge, Peter (1990) *The Fifth Discipline: The Art and Practice of the Learning Organization.* London: Century.

38 de Geus, Arie (1997) *The Living Company: Growth, Learning and Longevity in Business.* London: Nicholas Brealey, p.16.

39 Collins, James C. and Porras, Jerry I. (1966) *Built to Last.* London: Century, p.8.

40 NatWest Bank (1995) *Environment Report.* City?: NatWest Bank.

41 Levicki, Cyril (1996) *The Strategy Workout.* London: Pitman Publishing.

42 A: Shell; B: British American Tobacco; C: The Body Shop; D: British Airways; E: UK Ministry of Defence; F: NatWest; G: Marks & Spencer; H: Samsung.

4

CRITICAL ISSUES IN CORPORATE CITIZENSHIP

Introduction

Corporate governance

Campbell's Soup
CALPERS
The Cadbury Committee
The Hampel Committee

The environment

The environment and the last 30 years

The Natural Step
The Coalition for Environmentally Responsible Economies
The International Chamber of Commerce
Scandic Hotels
Merck
Century Textiles
NatWest, Marks & Spencer, Bath Environment Centre,
local government and the community
Nortel
Novo Nordisk
SmithKline Beecham
The Tagua Initiative

Human rights and the workplace

The UN's 1948 Universal Declaration of Human Rights
Amnesty International
BP in Colombia
Shell in Nigeria
The International Labour Organisation
Nike
Levi Strauss & Co.

The Apparel Industry Partnership
The Abrinq Foundation
Opportunity 2000
Churchill & Friend
The US Army
The British Army
The National AIDS Trust Employment Initiative (UK)

Fair trade and ethical investment

Cafédirect
Max Havelaar
The Ethical Trading Initiative
Christian Aid
FairTrade
The Body Shop
The Co-operative Bank
VanCity

The arms trade

The Red Cross/Red Crescent campaign

Tobacco

Animal welfare and protection

Hormel and Land O'Lakes
Tom's of Maine
Royal Society for the Protection of Birds

Education

Management exercises

Introduction

At the heart of the current interest in corporate citizenship is concern about the way in which our large corporations behave. How they operate is central to the development of local communities and the evolution of global society. Just as most people believe that government should be accountable to the people, so too more and more people now want business to be accountable for its actions. On the fiftieth anniversary of the Universal Declaration of Human Rights in 1998, it is clear that there are many abuses of the Declaration, but there is also increased discussion about universal human rights.

In an increasingly global economy, how can the world take forward workers' rights? Should workers have the same rights in Angola as in the USA, France and Japan? Should the rules that govern a company's behavior in Britain apply when that company operates in Nigeria or China? Should environmental standards be higher in an advanced industrial society, such as Germany, than in developing countries, such as Colombia or Vietnam? The British may be concerned about animal welfare, but does this matter in Thailand? Does the arms industry keep the world at peace, or help foment war? Do we need land mines? Is all trade in tobacco immoral?

This chapter begins by looking at corporate governance. As corporations are asked to assume some of the roles that governments perform, new rules are being developed by business to maintain their self-regulation. In Chapter 1 the point was made that business operates best where there is a "level playing field," where the rule of law operates, in the absence of corruption, and where government provides good infrastructural support in the form of healthcare, social security, education, transport, housing and communications.

Corporate governance is essentially concerned with the relationship between business and society, or specifically between a company and its owners. It is not surprising then that responsible business is increasingly involved in ensuring that good government is maintained and that society has a sound infrastructure. It is, after all, essential to the long-term survival of business.

Of course there are companies that are only interested in making money and are oblivious to their other responsibilities. These companies often

ld's environment and abuse workers. But some of the
companies are slowly waking up to another world where
accept their responsibilities and rise to the challenge of global
because they not only see that it is good for business but also
ey like the idea of the pre-eminence of business. The partnership
betwe business, governments and society needs new rules. Global corporate governance is an issue for business, government and society.

Categories of corporate citizenship

There are numerous critical issues in corporate citizenship. Throughout this
book we have highlighted many issues which fall within the broad remit of
corporate citizenship.

They can be categorized in different ways. For instance, from the company's point of view, they can be seen as falling into five areas: economic,
environmental, social, ethical and human relations,[1] but for those individuals within companies or in communities affected by a company's actions,
there may be a primary interest in issues such as fair trade, disclosure, environmental damage or employment.[2] Indeed, corporate citizenship can be
viewed from the starting point of social justice, environmental responsibility
or community welfare. We can make the company and business performance central to concerns about corporate citizenship, or the community.

Corporate citizenship is viewed from different perspectives depending on
where the individual stands. It is often the case that in the affluent North
(see "North–South dialogue" in Appendix 2: Glossary) people have different
perspectives depending on what they are doing at any moment during the
day. For example, while at work an employee sees matters in one way, but
the same person may not have the same perspective while purchasing

Table 4.1 The critical issues in corporate citizenship

1 Corporate governance
2 The environment
3 Human rights and the workplace
4 Fair trade
5 Ethical investment
6 The arms trade
7 Tobacco
8 Animal welfare and protection
9 Education

goods from a supermarket, withdrawing money, share trading at a bank, driving home in the car, or attending a political meeting in the evening. The vast majority of people in the North and South do not work directly for the largest corporations, but they are affected by the various impacts in economic, environmental, social and ethical spheres.

In this book we have put corporate governance, the environment, human rights and fair trade at the top of the list of issues, but we have also included material on the arms trade, tobacco, animal welfare and education for corporate citizenship (see Table 4.1).

Corporate governance
● ●

In recent years certain events have called into question the ability of the boards of public companies to operate effectively. A direct link is being made between the way companies are run and the way government works. If the latter should be accountable and well run, why should the same standards not apply to business? The link between the way in which government and companies are run is important because, in the age of the global economy, business increasingly dominates most people's lives, whether they be in New York, Cape Town or Beijing.

Good corporate governance is central to responsible corporate citizenship. In most cases, the major investors in public companies are either institutions such as insurance companies, pension funds or banks. The public increasingly want to know where they are investing their funds and what criteria are being applied in making investment, research and manufacturing decisions.

Some businesses have progressed from being domestic, to international, to multinational, to transnational.[3] How then do we ensure that transnational companies are accountable? And to whom should they be accountable? As leading US shareholder activist Bob Monks says: "In the centuries to come, as multinational companies create the borderless world of global markets, the focus will be on ensuring that corporate power is compatible with the rights of individuals."[4]

Opinion polls show that the public have little confidence in business leaders, and this is common in most leading industrial countries. A survey in the UK in 1997 found that only 15 per cent of the public trust large multinational enterprises to be honest and, as the leader of the UK's Institute of Directors has said, "Low trust carries a high cost . . . We have a problem. It's to do with the perception of [business behaviour] which is undermining business and wealth creation and thus society as a whole."[5] In the USA, confidence in company directors has focused on corporate pay and shareholder returns, while in Japan bribery, corruption and fraud have featured prominently in media coverage of business activity.

Despite Milton Friedman's declaration (1962) in *Capitalism and Freedom*[6] that the only responsibility of corporate officials is to "make as much money for their shareholders as possible," many shareholder activists, particularly those that are non-institutional, argue that corporate officials have too much power and not enough accountability for the social and environmental impacts of their decisions.

Inside companies, managers who are stressed because of job insecurity caused by takeovers, downsizing, delayering and reengineering, have also begun to express unhappiness at the way corporate power is wielded in the boardroom. Many of them feel that directors are often out of touch with management and other employees.

Corporate governance includes issues such as:

- how transparent should boards be in their decision making and to whom should they be accountable?
- who are boards working for? Shareholders? Themselves? A wider range of stakeholders?
- what competences should directors have?
- how do companies hold their employees accountable?

While it is true to say that the subject of corporate governance is under discussion in most countries where multinationals are based, and in some countries where multinationals operate, it is clear that good government aids good corporate governance, that the rules governing company formation and boardroom structure vary from country to country, and culture to culture, and that in some countries boards have more power and control than in other countries.

There are, however, some common issues associated with boardroom power in most countries:

- Many boards are self-perpetuating and control nominations of new members.
- Many people are appointed to boards as a reward for long service or loyalty, rather than because of competence.

- In some cases, board members are appointed to support over-powerful chief executives, who do not want to be questioned too closely.
- Board members can become too familiar with each other and develop a common mindset.
- Many board members do not have the necessary competences to serve as directors and trustees of the shareholders' and society's interests.

There is a great deal to be learned about the structure, role and competence of boards in different countries and in different companies. Surveying company boards on the basis of country may not, however, prove totally enlightening, because, as Jonathan Charkham found in *Keeping Good Company*,[7] a study of corporate governance in the USA, UK, Germany, France and Japan, many transnational corporations are now more supranational. He cites Nestlé, Glaxo, Shell, Unilever, Toyota and Volkswagen as being more active outside their home countries than they are at home. Although, interestingly, we think of each of those companies as having a national image.

His conclusion is that: "In all circumstances the effectiveness of corporate governance is a factor in the tendency of companies to survive and prosper or falter and fail." In other words, good governance means good business. Also good government sets the tone for good corporate governance. Just as government can be corrupt, so too can directors of companies. The one naturally leads on from the other, but attitudes to bribery provides an interesting difference in opinion and regulation. In Germany, for instance, bribes overseas are tax deductible if correctly accounted for, while the Organization for Economic Co-operation and Development (OECD) would like to see bribery become a criminal offence. Others say that if the bribe is invoiced, at least it is audited and so accounted for; any other form of payment risks the charge of corruption.[8]

Other issues also set companies and systems of corporate governance apart:

- In Japan and Germany hostile takeovers are forbidden.
- Britain has the most lax regulations when it comes to takeovers, followed by the USA but some US states have tighter regulations than others.
- While in all countries institutional shareholders form the majority, in the USA individual shareholders still retain over 40 per cent of shares on the stock market.
- Institutional shareholders in the USA and the UK are likely to be insurance companies and pension funds; in Japan and Germany they are more likely to be banks.

Britain has been more proactive in reforming the essentially nineteenth-century rules of corporate governance than other countries, but this is linked to Britain's role in global finance and its trading position. London is still the pre-eminent world finance center and Britain, despite its size, is still a significant trading nation. Britain has commissioned two reports on corporate governance and executive pay, while US reform has focused more on rewarding shareholders and executive pay; Japan has sought to make business operate more ethically (see profile in Chapter 2 on Keidanren's Code of Corporate Behavior).

The essence of the US reforms, and much of Britain's, has been focused on the issue of liquidity. Shareholders in the USA and the UK expect to be able to buy and sell their shares with ease, whereas the relationship between shareholders and society in countries like Germany and Japan is much more one of being in the same ship together. There is less taking to the lifeboats by shareholders when times get tough. This means that the relationship between those who direct and those who invest varies from country to country.

Increasingly in the USA and the UK, shareholders have been demanding that boards be more accountable for losses. There is also a tendency for shareholders to bypass the board and talk directly to managers about the way in which funds are being managed. Action by shareholders is not just confined to those who want higher earnings per share, but also those people or organizations, such as human-rights organizations and churches, who want to know where and how the company has been investing and operating.[9]

Specific cases in the last few years have brought this issue to a head because it has become clear that boards are not always in touch with their managers or aware of the way in which their company runs. The story is told of an institutional investor confronting the board of IBM, when things were not going too well in the 1980s, and being horrified that few of the directors actually used the company's product, or a personal computer at all.[10]

More significant, and of a completely different nature, in recent years two banks have collapsed, BCCI and Barings, and there was Robert Maxwell's fraudulent use of pension funds. These cases all involved fraud, but they also brought into question the culture of boardroom complacency. In each case a dominant individual was able to operate with little accountability over a considerable period of time. In order that accountability, honesty and scrupulousness are part of everyday operating procedures, it is important that the tone be set by the board. Just as in government, dominant individuals, who may be very effective leaders, need to be held accountable for their actions, and their decisions need to be made with a team. In cases such as those cited here, there was little internal or external auditing of either decisions or management systems. Unreined bosses and managers can impair company performance just as much as incompetent boards.

The division of labor and responsibility between government and business is important because business can only operate within the rules of the game as prescribed by society. As Sir Adrian Cadbury, ethics prize winner, and author of the UK's 1992 *Cadbury Report on Corporate Governance*, said: "Society sets the ethical framework within which those who run companies have to work out their own codes of conduct. Responsibility for decisions, therefore, runs both ways. Business has to take account of its responsibilities to society in coming to decisions, but society has to accept its responsibilities for setting the standards against which those decisions are made." [11]

It is clear that in all established markets investors are demanding more information and greater accountability on the part of boards of companies, both public and private. This information is also required by a number of other key claimants or stakeholders involved in significant relationships with the company. One of the main conclusions of the Tomorrow's Company 1996 Inquiry was that companies must speak with the same voice to all stakeholders. [12] No longer is trust enough, such that boards can be packed with the great and the good; boards must be competent, accountable and professional, as must their reporting procedures to shareholders and other stakeholders.

Increasingly shareholders are asking to bypass boards and deal directly with management, despite the fact that directors are supposed to represent shareholders' interests to management. This move, coupled with the fact that investors and other groups, such as pressure groups and the media, are becoming more methodical and organized, means that the revolution that is taking place in boardrooms has to continue. Those inside are discovering that their positions and the acceptability of the company's business activities, including the profitability, are being closely monitored.

Campbell's Soup

An example of good corporate governance raising profits and accountability is that of Campbell's Soup. Campbell's is a major US-based food manufacturing company. In 1990, the global brand of soups had not been performing well for several years. A new chief executive was appointed who believed that accountable bosses manage better.

He persuaded the board that corporate governance and accountability were priorities in turning the company round.

The reforms he introduced included:

● performance payments for senior management;
● performance targets, including industry benchmarking and beating the opposition;
● independent board members paid in company shares;
● maintaining a close dialogue with shareholders.

Since these reforms were introduced, the share price has soared as have the board's payments and that of the new chief executive.[13]

CALPERS

Given that the majority of shareholders in public companies in most industrial countries are often institutional, it is not surprising that they have begun to exert pressure on boards for better performance, especially as their members are often pensioners.

One such institutional investor is CALPERS (California Public Employees Retirement Scheme), which has major investments of $74,000 million in companies around the world. Every year it draws up a list of the dozen worst performers in which it has investments. Then it demands to talk to management about improving the performance of the named company and, if necessary, then mounts a campaign for change. CALPERS has been joined by other fund holders including TIAA-CREF (the US teachers' pension fund) with investments of $100,000 million.

A review of CALPERS' campaigns between 1987 and 1992 shows that the campaigns have yielded significant returns. On an investment of $500,000 a year in corporate governance activism, it has succeeded in increasing the fund's returns on an average investment by $2.4 million.

Obviously, there may be a downside to such activism, because demanding a seat on the board of companies may blur the distinction between investors and management, and may sacrifice the essence of Anglo-American shareholding, namely liquidity.

Having found success in the USA, CALPERS has moved its public campaigns to Britain, France and Japan where in 1996 it had investments of $5,775 million. In the UK, CALPERS is suggesting that British directors stand for re-election every year, so that shareholders can easily remove badly performing directors or register protests about excessive pay. Annual votes should be confidential and announced. It also recommends increasing the number of independent non-executive directors, improving director training and restricting the number of boards that directors can sit on.

In Japan, the discussion about independent non-executive directors has only just begun, but if investors such as CALPERS have their way, there might some time in the future be a global code of conduct for boardroom corporate governance.

The Cadbury Committee: the financial aspects of corporate governance

While reforms in the UK have been focused on making directors of public companies accountable, now the emphasis, through the Hampel Committee (see below), is on accountability and rewarding shareholders by making them rich. In 1992, the Cadbury Committee drew up *guidelines on corporate governance* which were designed to radically change the relationship between boards and shareholders. As the bulk of shareholdings in companies on the London stockmarket are institutional boards of directors, who are, in effect, entrusted with the public's hard-earned savings because the institutional investors are insurance companies and pension fund managers, the UK's Pensions Investment Research Consultants (PIRC) have pointed out that shareholders are "the guardians of public savings" and directors the trustees. This emphasizes the social role of companies and highlights the accountability standards that are expected from corporations that the public chooses to support through its savings, insurance schemes and pensions provisions.[14]

The committee's guide to best practice for management
The board

● The board must meet regularly, retain full control over the company and monitor the executive management.
● There should be a clearly accepted division of responsibilities at the head of a company, which will ensure a balance of power and authority, such that no individual has unfettered powers of decision. Where the chairman is also chief executive, it is essential that there be a strong independent element on the board, with an appointed leader.
● Non-executive directors should be of a high caliber and respected.
● The board should have specific duties, to ensure its full control of the company.

Non-executive directors

● Non-executive directors should bring independent judgement to bear on matters of strategy (performance, executive pay), resources and standards of conduct (ethics).
● The majority of non-executive directors should be free of business or financial connections with the company, apart from their fee and shareholding.
● Terms should be specific and reappointment should not be automatic.
● Non-executives should be able to take independent advice on company matters.
● Appointments should be through process and approved by the whole board.

Executives

- Directors should not serve for more than three years without shareholders' approval.
- Directors' fees and other payments should be made public.
- Executive directors' pay should be decided by non-executive directors.

Controls and reporting

- There must be an effective audit committee.
- Directors must report on the company's internal financial control.
- The board's relationship with auditors should be objective and professional.
- The board must present an accurate view of the company's position.
- The board must explain its responsibility for preparing the accounts next to the auditor's report on the board's responsibilities.
- The board should state if the business is viable.
- The chairman of the audit and remuneration committees should be responsible for answering questions at the Annual General Meeting.

The principle that underlies corporate governance is:

> *"[The managers] must be free to drive their companies forward but exercise that freedom within a framework of effective accountability."*

Failure to conform to Cadbury

When the Cadbury committee published its findings, PIRC[15] found that 25 per cent of the largest companies failed to meet the criteria. Most of the failures fell into three categories:

1 The roles of chairman with chief executive were combined into one.
2 There were cross-directorships on the boards of companies with links to each other.
3 There were not enough non-executive directors.[16]

The Hampel Committee on Corporate Governance

Following on from the Cadbury Code on corporate governance, and the Greenbury Code on executive pay, the former Chairman of ICI, Sir Ronald Hampel, reported on corporate governance in August 1997. In his preliminary report his emphasis was that: "corporate prosperity comes before accountability,"[17] a view that contradicts the growing tendency to see the two issues as closely linked. If anything, the Hampel view of corporate governance moves away from greater scrutiny of directors' actions, away from separating the chief executive's functions from those of the chairman and is rooted in the short-term profitability of the company, rather than the short *and* long-term viability and profitability for all stakeholders.

When the Hampel Committee submitted its final report in January 1998, the chairman said that there was no convincing link between good corporate governance and good financial performance, thereby flying in the face of the evidence. Central to the criticism of Hampel's final conclusions was the fact that the committee had hardly moved from the nineteenth-century concept of boards of directors being solely responsible to shareholders. PIRC, pensions consultancy, said that there were "many questions unanswered," and the Centre for Tomorrow's Company said that the committee had "missed a golden opportunity to broaden the approach to governance of British companies" while the UK's Trade Union Congress said it was "a complete abdication of British business leadership."[18]

The UK sees itself as a leader on corporate governance and the new government (elected by a landslide in May 1997) is now intent on clarifying company law and increasing accountability for companies. It is clear that the Hampel Committee failed to meet the mood of the time and that companies, and possibly the London Stock Exchange, will face increased legislation to cover what is at present a voluntary code of corporate governance.

Corporate corruption – and governance

Cases such as Robert Maxwell's theft of millions of pounds from his employees' pension funds, the collapse of BCCI, the Sumitomo copper trading case, the Guinness fraud and the bankrupting of Barings Bank have brought to the public's attention the issue of corporate control of senior managers and directors. In some of these cases, the deception has been for personal gain, but in others the deception has taken place because of a desire to cover mistakes and because of a lack of management procedures to monitor corporate decisions.

Barings is a case in point. In 1996, as one of the oldest banks in the world, Barings was forced to sell up after one of its traders, Nick Leeson, based in Singapore, managed to run up debts amounting to billions of dollars. Leeson appeared to be making huge profits for the parent company based in London, when actually he was losing money on a daily basis. Nobody questioned the fact that he seemed to be able to make more money than other banks operating in the same sector and geographical region.

Despite the fact that five months before he bankrupted the company an internal audit report showed that he was out of control, there was no attempt to check his work. He was able to run both the front-room trading side of the business and the back-room accounting side. Although Leeson was responsible for the fraud that took place, his senior managers and the directors of the bank were also culpable because it was they who were the guardians of the company's position. Leeson, having got himself into a difficult position, was simply trying to cover his losses, not to enrich himself. The company in London not only failed to manage its employee, but did not understand what he was doing. The senior managers did not respond to warning signs; they did not have a fraud-response plan.

The accounting and consultancy firm KPMG has a list of what it calls "the seven deadly sins," which KPMG says are the result of the "opening of economies and the globalization of markets" which "have created significant opportunities for business and for fraudsters."[19] The seven items are based on their experience of investigating cases such as Barings, where companies venture into unknown overseas markets (see Table 4.2).

Table 4.2 KPMG's list of "seven deadly sins"

1   The control and ethical environment of the new market is out of line with the rest of the group.
2   The company has an ambivalent attitude to kickbacks.
3   There has been shallow research into new markets.
4   Control is limited because of language barriers or remote locations.
5   There is a misunderstanding of local legislation.
6   There is limited awareness of local scams.
7   There has been poor due diligence of joint-venture partners.

Moreover, in KPMG's experience, there are two common characteristics in such cases:

● the abuse of power by an individual;
● the manipulation of accounting records.

Sometimes what is seen as corruption in one country is not seen as such in another, and this is particularly so in the case of bribes for contracts.[20] But if business works best when there is a level playing field and when the rule of law applies, and if there now exists a global economy in which all businesses are potentially players, then there is an argument for working towards a corruption-free, bribe-free trading system. This would not only benefit business, but also the populations of countries where bribery is endemic.

Transparency International, a Berlin-based consultancy working against corruption, argues that it is the poorest people in the poorest countries who suffer most because of corruption. This is because bribery normally means that, in the case of government contracts, the best value, best quality contract is not awarded and the country as a whole then suffers.

Transparency International rates countries on their corrupt business practices. In 1997 it rated the ten most corrupt countries for business to operate in as Nigeria, Bolivia, Colombia, Russia, Pakistan, Mexico, Indonesia, India, Venezuela and Vietnam.[21]

Corruption in business may be a natural way of doing business, but as long as any company has to maintain a wide range of stakeholder or key relationships, there are going to be demands on that company to declare its principled position on issues like bribery, and to open its books. More questions are going to be asked about the structure and composition of the board of directors and on the competence of directors and senior management to run the company.

It would seem that any risk assessment of a company's viability is now going to include close scrutiny of the often semi-secret boardroom in order that companies become more accountable to shareholders and other stakeholders alike.

Corporate governance is also a matter of global governance. Large businesses operating in countries with despotic regimes can set a tone for good management and send a moral message to oppressed people that business and life is better where there is accountability on financial, environmental, social and management issues.

The environment
....

Many companies would say that environmental responsibility has become a strategic issue due to increased pressure on business to account for its environmental impact. Some of this pressure has come from consumers and some through increased legislation, standards and benchmarking. Given that people and companies are beginning to understand that they have a moral responsibility to protect the environment, many people would put environmental protection and sustainability at the heart of the corporate citizenship movement.

While issues such as fair trade and child labor have come to the public's attention in the last few years, and occupied the minds of some politicians, the environment has exercised people's minds for well over 30 years. Just as exploitative child labor is not a recent issue, so environmental pollution, particularly of air and water, has been discussed since the industrial revolution in the eighteenth and nineteenth centuries.

The change in business and government behavior towards the

environment has been a long time coming, but a revolution is taking place which will radically change the way in which companies go about their business.

However, there is a problem. The Scandinavian Natural Step movement, outlined in the profile later in this chapter, started from the premise that most people did not understand the fundamental conditions for life on Earth. A similar survey of scientific understanding[22] in the UK in 1996 revealed that 34 per cent of the population thought that the sun went round the Earth and 65 per cent thought anti-biotics kill viruses *and* bacteria. There had been great change in scientific understanding over the last ten years, although people educated in the 1960s had a better understanding than older generations, particularly on genetics.

The environment and the last 30 years

The image of earth from space now stares out at us from news broadcasts, advertisements for washing machines and any book on the environment or the global economy. The first astronauts on the moon spent more time staring at the earth than they did out into space. Never before had our home been photographed in such beauty and clarity. Never before had we been able to see its isolation and fragility. Space photography brought the world a new reality. As the earth rose over the moon, so a new awareness of the vulnerability of earth arose in our minds.

It was only in 1972 that the state of the world's environment, as a single entity, was discussed for the first time at a conference of world leaders at the UN Conference on the Human Environment in Stockholm. Despite the concern shown in Stockholm on issues like acid rain, desertification, water, poverty and population between 1972 and 1992, by the time of the Earth Summit in Rio de Janeiro in 1992, the state of the environment had depreciated. The post-1945 enthusiasm for industrialism and technology, embraced both by free-market and communist economies, was founded on the use of natural resources and expanding the frontiers of scientific progress and consumerism.

If there was one thing that the photograph of the earth from space and the Stockholm Conference conveyed, it was that the world was no longer an open frontier for continual, unlimited development, but that instead it was seen as an interrelated system, limited in its capacity to supply endless raw materials and absorb toxic wastes.

But it has taken since the 1970s and the publication of numerous important reports on the limits to population growth and resource use for much to change.[23] Only now at the end of the twentieth century are we beginning to face the challenge of living in a sustainable way.[24] The publication in 1987 of *Our Common Future* by an international committee chaired by Gro Harlem Brundtland, as a prelude to the 1992 Earth Summit, allied sustainability to development. A hundred years, even 50 or 25 years ago it did not seem urgent to understand the relationship between economic development and a healthy planet because resources appeared to be infinite and nature seemed to capable of absorbing any waste we produced.

We now know that we have adversely affected our climate and planet through industrial activity and that we are suffering the effects of acid rain, ozone layer depletion and global warming. We knew some of these things over 30 years ago, but failed to act swiftly. It is worth quoting from Rachel Carson's ground-breaking book *Silent Spring*, published in 1962, which analyzed in great detail the effects of toxic chemicals on wildlife and on us through the food we eat:

> *"The question of chemical residues on the food we eat is a hotly debated issue. The existence of such residues is either played down by industry as unimportant or is flatly denied. Simultaneously there is a strong tendency to brand as fanatics or cultists all who are so perverse as to demand that their food be free of poisons."*[25]

Carson was campaigning against the use of DDT, which has since been banned, along with other supposed technological advancements of the twentieth century, such as asbestos and CFCs, which have also proved disastrous.

Now there are agreements on the phasing out of CFCs under the Montreal Protocol (except that China, among other countries, is allowed to continue using them for 20 years), asbestos and DDT have been banned (but are still present in our houses, soil and food). Now the focus of international attention is on greenhouse gases that cause global warming. In 1992, at the Earth Summit, 108 governments agreed to develop policies to save the earth. The rich countries agreed that by 2000 their greenhouse-gas emissions, particularly carbon dioxide, would be no higher than in 1990. Two of the worst offenders, the USA and Australia, argued against mandatory targets (see Table 4.3).

Table 4.3 Carbon dioxide emissions 1990–2000[26]

	CO_2 emissions / m tons 1990	2000	% change 1990–2000	m tons 2000 per person
Upward projections				
Australia	265	328	+24	17.7
United States	4,895	5,449	+11	20.3
Japan	1,068	1,128	+6	8.9
Finland	54	69	+28	13.5
France	379	417	+10	7.1
The only downward projections				
Britain	584	563	−4	9.5
Germany	983	945	−4	11.55
Switzerland	44	42	−5	5.8

Britain's reduction has come about because of the move from coal to gas-fired electricity power stations, and Germany's reduction has been as a result of closing dirty industries in the former East Germany.

By any measure, the rich countries' ability to tackle what most people see as one of the most important issues facing the world is failing, in some cases dramatically. It is impossible to ask the emerging "Big Five"[27] to limit their emissions of greenhouse gases if 75 per cent at present are produced by a small affluent majority who live in North America and Europe. As the wealth in those affluent countries is produced by transnational corporations, whose responsibility is it to reduce greenhouse emissions? Business or government? Or should consumers stop buying automobiles and washing machines?

How is it that Australians and North Americans manage to produce twice as much CO_2 and other greenhouse gases as the average Japanese or European? That economies are built on added value, and that adversity can produce greater efficiency, is shown in the fact that Japan produces more than three times the GNP per ton of oil equivalent than the USA, and a third more than Germany.[28]

The Natural Step

The principles of the Natural Step movement have been adopted by companies like IKEA, Scandic Hotels, Electrolux and the Swedish McDonald's. The organization, or movement as some supporters like to think of it, was founded by Dr Karl-Henrik Robert, a cancer specialist who noticed a dramatic increase in childhood cancers and wondered why. As a consequence, he developed a set of non-negotiable principles, or systems conditions, for environmental sustainability. The value of cyclical, rather than linear, processing was agreed by a group of leading Swedish scientists and supported by the King of Sweden. Every house and school in Sweden received a booklet and a cassette explaining the Natural Step philosophy.

The starting points were that there were certain impediments to change, around the world:

● a general lack of knowledge regarding the fundamental conditions of life;
● an absence of a comprehensive overview of environmental science which leads away from integration to arguments over detail, rather than agreement on principles;
● negative expectations and resignation;
● the individual's sense of disempowerment; "I can do nothing!."

The Natural Step conditions

The principles which underpin the conditions are scientifically non-negotiable, and are based on a cyclical, systems approach.

1 Stored mineral deposits no longer accumulate in the biosphere. This means mining no faster than the slow depositions of nature.

   Scandic Hotels: We cannot take more from the soil than that which is regenerated.

2 Persistent artificial compounds no longer accumulate in the biosphere. This means not producing products that cannot be processed by natural systems.

   Scandic Hotels: We must not use nature-hostile substances, for example freons, PCBs and DDT.

3 The physical state of nature must be maintained. This means not encroaching into natural areas. We must maintain the earth's surface and vegetation.

   Scandic Hotels: A rich animal and plant life is a prerequisite for the cycle and the ecosystem.

4 The metabolism of nature rests within that of nature. This means that we all share the one biosphere, and we all rely on, and are entitled to, the same life-support systems.

   Scandic Hotels: We must use the resources effectively and fairly.

There are now Natural Step organizations in the USA, Britain, Canada and Australia. See the profile of Scandic Hotels later in this chapter.

Gaia: business for the future?

Gaia theory has not, as yet, been adopted by any large companies, but the implications are as profound for the management of large organizations as understanding the fundamental principles of life enshrined in the Natural

Step. Gaia theory, or geophysiology, is attributed to James Lovelock, an inventor and one-time NASA scientist. Awarded many prizes around the world for his work, he has yet to be accepted by many mainstream scientists.

Simply put, Gaia, the Greek goddess of life (a name given to the theory by novelist William Golding), states that conditions on Earth are unique and self-supporting. Life on Earth is adaptable, continuous and self-regulating, relying on creating life-sustaining order out of complexity and chaos. It is not, therefore, Darwinian because it does not argue the case for evolutionary changes or that living things evolved simply by adapting to their environment. Despite the fact that some outside events have changed, for instance the sun has got considerably hotter over a period of time, the environment on earth remains much the same. Life on earth self-regulates itself. Earth is "alive."

The difference between Gaia and conventional science is that the former is holistic and most scientists are reductionists – which means that there is a failure to see the earth and its life systems in total. In that sense, it echoes the Natural Step in recognizing that we all share the same environment. But Gaia theory says that humans may destroy *their* environment, but it could be only *their* environment that they destroy, because the earth will regulate itself and continue.

If Lovelock is correct, then Gaia is the ultimate organism, providing the framework within which other organisms, including transnational corporations, can operate. These organizations are bee colonies, or ant hills, as are cities and villages. Operate outside the earth's self-regulation, and it will not be possible for these social organisms to survive. It should not be possible for us to destroy the complexity and chaos on which Gaia thrives, but, as Lovelock says, a planet like Mars, with limited life, could not be self-regulatory. Destroying the diversity of life on earth, as modern agriculture does, is to destroy the basis of life on earth – for humans, despite the ability of the earth to sustain and renew itself.

Sustainable development

Sustainable development, a term first discussed in the 1960s and 1970s by, among others, Herman Daly and Barbara Ward, was described by the Brundtland Report: "Sustainable development is development that meets the needs of the present without compromising the ability of future generations to meet their needs."[29] While this provides a useful starting point for discussion, and is often quoted in company environmental reports, it begs as many questions as it answers.

The three sustainability shifts

It is more realistic to focus on three fundamental shifts in perception involving issues of social justice and equity:

1 Value the environment for the contribution it makes to life on earth, whether in terms of physical resources, recycling, beauty, amenity or religious significance.
2 All people have a right to environmental resources, including materials and beauty.
3 Decision making about the use of environmental resources must be based on an awareness of all those who may be affected by the decision, including people in other parts of the world and unborn generations.

Sustainable business and the environment

Environmental policy and practice is one of the key measures both of business performance and of business's sense of corporate citizenship. Not only are there performance measures and certification procedures enshrined in the European Eco-Management and Audit Scheme (EMAS) and the ISO 14000[30] series, but it is now widely recognized that protecting the environment can also brings significant business benefits. They are shown in lower resource costs, cheaper waste disposal, increased markets, better employee relations and decreased liabilities.

The revolution that has taken place over the last 30 years, which heralded the introduction of environmental management systems, is the transition from "end-of-pipe" solutions to whole-system approaches. This means that rather than dealing with pollution after it has been created, and paying for disposal or mitigation, enlightened companies are designing processes that minimize waste, limit resource use and work towards closed-loop systems.

Rather than seeing the earth as a "sink," which can absorb any amount of waste, business has begun to take responsibility for its own waste. Just as some natural resources have been found to be finite, so the ability of the planet to absorb unnatural toxic waste has become apparent. This means that business is increasingly being encouraged to *internalize its externalities* – in other words, to be responsible for its total environmental impact from raw material procurement, through process and disposal at the end of the product's life.

Steps towards sustainable business

To this end, companies can:

- introduce environmentally friendly practices, processes and products;
- adopt the polluter-pays principle and the precautionary principle.[31] This means not passing on environmental costs, understanding the full environmental impact of new practices, processes and products and internalizing externalities;[32]
- use closed-loop technology, which means recycling all wastes within processes;
- make products with as long a life as possible;
- practice the six "Rs": return, re-use, recycle, reduce, re-think, re-design;
- refrain from using toxic chemicals;
- take responsibility for the lifetime of products and decisions;
- think of business as providing a lifetime service, rather than a product (for instance, BMW now sells "mobility," not automobiles, and in the USA Inferface, a major carpet seller, is responsible for the total lifecycle of the floor covering);
- adopt recognized accountability and reporting standards on environmental impact.

The ecology of commerce

Paul Hawken's book, *The Ecology of Commerce*, was a bestseller when it was published in 1994. Sub-titled *A Declaration of Sustainability*, the book was about business's failure and inability to tackle the environmental crisis facing the planet. "Despite the fact that the environmental issues are now accepted internationally as the most pressing problem of our age, the institutions that embody and guide our economic progress [business] have hardly responded at all. . . .To change this state of affairs, business will have to deal directly with the three issues of what it takes, what it makes and what it wastes."[33]

Hawken's objectives for business are as follows:

"1 Reduce absolute consumption of energy and natural resources in the rich North by 80 per cent over the next 50 years. This means making things last twice as long with half the resources.

2 Create secure, stable employment as poverty and insecurity cause environmental degradation.

3 Build self-actuating systems, rather than regulations and control, as humans will always want to flourish and prosper.

4 Honor market principles because sustainability will not come about through trying to change the dynamics of the market.

5 Allow people to be more creative, participative and rewarding.

6 Exceed sustainability by restoring degraded habitats to their full bio-diversity.

7 Rely on current incomes because sustainable human communities should act like natural ones, living within the natural ebb and flow of energy from the sun and plants.

8 Business has the ability to create beauty and achieve aesthetic outcomes as much as parts of society, but business, governments and other organizations cannot create a sustainable society. This can only be achieved through the eager participation of millions of people."

The Coalition for Environmentally Responsible Economies: the CERES principles

The CERES principles, formerly known as the Valdez principles, were created in 1989 as a result of the Exxon Valdez oil-spill disaster in Prince William Sound, Alaska.[34] The initiative came from The Coalition for Environmentally Responsible Economies (CERES) and the principles are now known as the CERES Principles. These Principles were modelled on the Sullivan Principles, which were introduced in 1977 to urge American companies to make changes to workplace practices in their operations in South Africa.[35] Unlike the Sullivan principles, the CERES Principles were not backed by major corporate supporters, although they were backed by growing companies like Domino's Pizza Distribution Corporation, VanCity Investment Services, Metropolitan Sewer Corporation and Smith and Hawken. However, they can be seen as important trend setters and a precursor to the guidelines (see below) of the International Chamber of Commerce's *Business Charter for Sustainable Development*.[36]

The CERES principles cover:

1 protection of the biosphere
2 sustainable use of natural resources
3 reduction and disposal of waste
4 wise use of energy
5 risk reduction
6 marketing of safe production and services
7 damage compensation
8 disclosure

9　the appointment of environmental directors and managers

10　assessment and audit.

CERES conducts an annual survey of environmental reports based on their principles and in 1996 said that the five best reports they had received in the preceding years were from: Sun Company 1995, Polaroid 1994, Vancouver City Savings Credit Union 1993, General Motors 1994, Louisville and Jefferson County, Kentucky and Metropolitan Sewer District 1994.[37]

The International Chamber of Commerce: Business Charter for Sustainable Development

In 1991 the International Chamber of Commerce launched its *Business Charter for Sustainable Development*, designed more as a checklist for companies than a certificate of compliance with sustainable principles. It is based on the principle that "economic growth provides the conditions in which protection of the environment can best be achieved," and that there is "not a conflict between economic development and environmental protection."

The principles or objectives are as follows:

1　Environmental management is a corporate priority.

2　The environment must be integrated into all aspects of business.

3　Strive for continuous improvement taking regard of scientific developments, consumer needs and community expectations.

4　Employees must be educated on the environment.

5　Assess environmental impacts for new projects.

6　Develop products and services that have no undue environmental impact.

7　Provide customers with information on the safe use, handling and disposal of products.

8　Develop facilities and activities that are efficient and minimize impact and waste.

9　Conduct research on the impact of materials, products and processes.

10　Adopt the precautionary approach in order to prevent irreversible environmental degradation.

11　Encourage contractors and suppliers to comply with the company's standards.

12　Maintain emergency plans to deal with accidents.

13　Transfer environmentally sound technology throughout industrial and public sectors.

14　Contribute to the common effort.

15　Foster openness and dialogue with a range of key relationships on environmental matters.

16　Conduct environmental audits and inform key relationships.[38]

The business case for environmental management

It is not difficult to find examples of radical initiatives where business has risen to the challenge and is working towards some form of sustainability. When these examples are analyzed it is not entirely clear why more businesses are not rushing to adopt both environmental responsibility, to raise compliance and lower liability, and environmental best practice, given the public relations potential and the cost savings.

The profiles presented here range from Scandic Crown Hotels' adoption of the Natural Step to Merck's investment in the rainforest. Also included are Marks & Spencer's and NatWest bank's investment in a community environment center, the tagua nut, Century Textiles, Novo Nordisk and SmithKline Beecham. All these cases in their different ways show the wealth of creativity that now exists in environmental management.

Ecotourism, the Scandic Hotel Group and the Natural Step

According to the World Tourism Organization, tourism will be the world's biggest business by the year 2000. In 1996, 592 million travellers spent $423,000 million.[39] Only some 5 per cent can be defined as ecotourism, and Australia is the only country which has established an accreditation system for tour operators, rating them on their approach to the environment. Some so-called ecotourism is decidedly environmentally unfriendly. For instance, tourists to the Brazilian Amazon rainforest are changing the ecosystem; strict controls have been introduced in the Barrier Reef in Australia; and walkers in the UK's national parks are often guided up clearly marked paths when climbing popular mountains so as to minimize damage. Ecotourism, according to the Ecotourism Society in the USA, is "responsible travel that conserves natural environments and sustains the well-being of local people."[40]

Scandic Hotels: practising the Natural Step

Given that all tourists have to stay somewhere, the Scandic Group's approach has proved attractive, cost-saving and beneficial to the environment.

The Group's ambition is to "become one of the most environmentally friendly hotels in the world," and believes that "We are all temporary guests in time."[41]

Its environmental measures include:

● soap: instead of individually wrapped soaps, most of which gets wasted, the hotel supplies gentle, natural-based soap and shampoo products in reusable plastic dispensers manufactured by Ecover. Savings: 30 tons of soap and shampoo per annum, reduced packaging waste by eight tons per annum;

● cleaning: most hotels use as many as 15 different cleaning products, all individually packed and containing environmental poisons. By using concentrated products from Henckel Ecolab, which are combined to different strengths for different uses, savings have been made on packaging, transport and use;

● dishwashing: concentrated dishwashing substances require less energy to deliver and less packaging. Also Scandic's washing machines regulate the amount of water used depending on the task involved;

● paper and natural products: "Wood fiber can be recycled eight times. It does not make sense to make toilet paper from it the first time." Scandic uses recyclable paper, rather than chlorine-bleached, white-paper sheets made from unbleached cotton, and furnishings from natural materials.

Merck: investing in the rainforest

Fewer than 10 per cent of the species of plants, animals and microbes on this planet have been described, still fewer studied, and the tropical rainforests are home to the vast majority of species. For centuries, the rainforests have provided medicines for indigenous peoples. Many key medicines in use today are derived from rainforest plants.

Alarmed over the rapid destruction of the world's rainforest, Merck has formed a partnership with a Costa Rican research centre to preserve and study plants and insects in Costa Rica's rainforest. Unlikely partners, Merck is one of the largest pharmaceutical companies in the world; the National Biodiversity Institute (INBio) is a private, non-profit research centre.[42]

Since 1991, Merck has provided INBio with funding and technology. In exchange, INBio collects a limited number of plants, insects and bacteria, and provides them to Merck for further scientific exploration. Such specimens may contain valuable compounds that may lead to a breakthrough in the development of new drugs. Ten per cent of the research budget and 50 per cent of the potential royalties go to support the Costa Rican rainforest.

Merck–INBio represents a winning partnership. INBio receives funding and technology; Merck receives potential sources of new drugs. Costa Rica's rainforests are preserved and its plant and insect species are catalogued. Similar agreements have been forged between a tropical country, a university, a US institution and multinational corporations, including Bristol Myers Squibb, American Cyanamid, Monsanto, and Shaman Pharmaceutical.

These new types of partnership that unite various kinds of organizations, both non-profit, profit, and governmental, with partners in other countries are essential if we are to address the problems and opportunities of globalization.

Century Textiles: greening the company secures key export markets

For companies in emerging markets, the growing environmental and social awareness of consumers in the USA and Europe can bring competitive advantage and new export markets. Century Textiles and Industries Limited,[43] based in India, is a major manufacturer of cotton textiles, yarn, and rayon. With 6,900 employees and a turnover of $113 million, Century Textiles is a key exporter of textiles to the European market. Founded in 1897, Century's textile unit is the largest in India, and is its most significant exporter of cotton textiles. Seventy-five per cent of Century's output is exported.

Century believes that its focus on quality is the key to the company's success. The manufacturer has won many quality awards, in addition to ISO 9002 certification. The company's commitment to modernization is also impressive. In the past 15 years, it has spent $70 million to upgrade its technology.

In Europe, consumers were beginning to demand clothing that did not harm the environment. Of growing concern was the pesticide use associated with growing cotton, which is harmful to the environment as well as to workers. A reliance on azo dyes, which are thought to cause cancer and allergies, was also a grave concern, posing a threat to both workers and consumers. Textile production requires significant water resources, producing copious levels of effluent.

A strong emphasis on quality and efficiency facilitated the company's transition to becoming more environmentally aware and able to react to consumer demands and environmental legislation. In 1991, India banned the use of PCP (pentachlorophenol), a chemical preservative which causes cancer. According to Mahesh Sharma, a manager in Chemical Technology, "The PCP ban was not much of a problem for Century" because of its inherent focus on quality.

In 1993, Germany banned certain harmful azo dyes. One of the major German clients, Otto Versand, placed an order for azo-free product, leading Century to seek Eco-Tex certification – which requires compliance with 17 environmental criteria and parameters, including bans on pesticide use, carcinogenic and allergenic dyes.[44]

In 1995, Century became the first Indian textile company to receive Eco-Tex certification. According to Sharma, achieving certification was simple, as the company had already begun to search for substitutes.

The advantages of Eco-Tex certification have been significant. By making changes to the dye recipes, the company made significant strides in improving quality. By carrying the Eco-Tex label on its product, the company is now able to charge a premium of 8 to 10 per cent. In 1996, the market for Eco-Tex certified product grew by 10 per cent. The market continues to grow throughout the EU.

NatWest, Marks & Spencer, Bath Environment Centre, local government and the community – a partnership for the environment

Why did NatWest and Marks & Spencer support a major community initiative involving the community to the tune of $825,000? Why did they decide to work with local government and environmental pressure groups?

There are many such initiatives being formed involving the business, public and voluntary sectors which provide opportunities for dialogue and debate about shared social and environmental problems. Here is an example of a successful project.

The Bath Environment Centre is an example of a community project funded by a partnership between private business, local government and volunteers. After two years of planning and fund-raising, the Centre held its first event in 1994, under the title of "Reclaim the Streets." The next year it opened as a Centre in a disused bank in the middle of Bath offering exhibitions, seminars and an information resource on environmental themes. It also ran local projects based on international initiatives, such as a global action plan (GAP), inspired by the United Nations Environment Programme, and a schools traffic accident reduction (STAR) program, which started as a Bath initiative and has since been adopted in many other parts of the UK.

In the first two years the Centre had 30,000 visitors. As the Centre grew, other projects were started, including joint ventures with Bath University's International Centre for the Environment; Bath Spa University College; and a business environment association (BEAB).

Bath has a unique history and has been given the status of World Heritage City by UNESCO, because of its 2,000 year history, Roman spa baths and seventeenth-century architecture. More than 2 million people visit the city every year as tourists or shoppers, and the region earns more than $610,500,000 a year from these visitors.

However, for a variety of geographic and political reasons Bath has been incapable of tackling some long-standing environmental problems. Its position at the bottom of a valley and the volume of traffic passing through the city mean that the air quality is particularly poor, often well below WHO guidelines. A main road runs through the middle of the city and since the deregulation of buses, public transport has become both inadequate and very expensive. Despite the evidence from other British and European cities, many of the city's retailers are opposed to increased pedestrianization. Environmental activists in the city were the first in the UK to promote annual "car-free days," which have now been adopted in many other cities as a way of engaging the public in radical alternatives to private transport.

The Centre has been at the forefront of efforts by the local community and local government, now Bath and North-East Somerset Council, to promote Local Agenda 21.[45] For example, the Centre, in partnership with the Council, has recently started running farmers' markets, selling produce from within 50 kilometers, which have proved extremely popular. This is perhaps a sign that, to a certain degree, globalization can be slowed, if not reversed, the quality of products on sale can be raised (most of the vegetables are organic), the environmental burden can be reduced, people can be put back into the local food-production chain and the hegemony of supermarkets can be challenged. What is more significant is that this a very local initiative supported by global business. This is what is being called "*glocalization*."

Bath Environment Centre was set up in 1994 by a volunteer group, with a small amount of core funding from Bath City Council. In the two years before the Centre opened its doors, it had raised some $825,000,000 (including $287,000 from NatWest which allowed the Centre to occupy a disused bank for two years), $198,000 from Marks & Spencer (which seconded a mid-career manager for two years) and other funds from the local council and charitable foundations. To cement the idea of partnership between different sectors, the Centre has been set up as a charity with a board of trustees which has included representatives from the whole community. The Centre is wholly independent and owned by its members, that is, anyone who cares to join.

In 1997, the Center was assured of continuing funding from Marks & Spencer, NatWest, local government and other local businesses. More important, it has continued to be run largely by volunteer staff numbering over 200 since its opening. Important too is the award of national lottery funding for three years, amounting to $231,000.

Bath Environment Centre has been successful for a number of reasons:

● It is not a campaigning organization; it is a center for information, facilitation and debate.
● It has brought together groups from across the city to find common solutions to issues of sustainability.
● It is independent and, therefore, has had to earn respect from local government, the business sector, the educational sector, the public and environmental activists to survive.
● It has combined operating as an information resource and a place to visit, with the running of projects both inside and outside the Centre. By this method it has begun to reach out into the community and into people's homes and workplaces.
● It has maintained a positive media image both through the local newspaper and through local television and radio.
● It has been supported by a list of patrons, some of whom are nationally recognized figures.
● The business partners have been able to raise their profile in the community, to learn from people outside their businesses (including sitting down face to face with protagonists) and increase their knowledge of the environment and communities.
● It has succeeded in raising finance from individuals, local government, small and large businesses, the UK's national lottery and the EU.

Nortel: sharing technology

In 1987, 24 countries pledged to reduce ozone depleting gases by signing the Montreal Protocol. However, many developing countries, among them Mexico and China, did not have access to the technologies and processes for reducing CFC use. Through the Industry Cooperative for Ozone Layer Protection (ICOLP, now the International Co-operative for Environmental Leadership), a non-profit organization composed of 22 companies, Nortel funded conferences and provided experts to transfer technologies developed by Nortel to companies in Mexico, China, Brazil, India and Vietnam.[46] As a result of these conferences, several developing countries were able to make substantial progress in meeting the Montreal Protocol.

How can a multinational corporation benefit from technology transfer? Nortel is a high-growth Canadian communications company seeking to expand its operations in emerging markets, where demand for the company's services is booming. Nortel, however, has found that it was not well-known relative to its competitors in some emerging markets. Promoting technology transfer helped to enhance Nortel's reputation and name recognition in some of the company's most valuable markets. By broadening the constituency of those affected by industrial actions, in both time and space, Nortel realized that it could add value for its stakeholders, increasing its competitiveness in the long run, while promoting sustainable development.

The process of achieving the ambitious targets of the Protocol has required substantial co-operation among many, including industry, governments from around the world, and non-governmental organizations. The complexity of the CFC problem and the high stakes involved illustrate the need for extensive co-operation between companies. According to Dr Margaret Kerr, VP for Environment, Ethics, and Quality: "We also recognize that the CFC issue is too complex to solve by ourselves. The only way to advance the agenda is to get value for all companies through continual improvement."

According to Dr Margaret Kerr, the company's senior environmental officer, Nortel was a small company that has enjoyed rapid growth. It now has an annual turnover of $8.15. "The corporate culture is based on entrepreneurship, innovation, and adding value. We foster new ideas by encouraging our people to be open-minded and avoid bureaucracy. We like to be leaders. We like to win, and hence we encourage technical innovation and risks if there is a promise of a breakthrough."

There is a clear understanding throughout the company of commitment to stakeholders, including not only employees and shareholders, but also customers, suppliers and communities. Nortel's environmental policy recognizes the relationship between economic growth and a healthy environment. Increasingly each product is designed and produced with the environmental impact of its lifecycle in mind. This commitment has created a corporate culture that fixes environmental management as every employee's responsibility, with annual awards given to those employees who exhibit leadership in meeting the corporate commitment to the environment.

Novo Nordisk: dialogue with the stakeholders

Based in Denmark, Novo Nordisk is the world's largest producer of insulin and enzymes for healthcare and industrial purposes. Novo Nordisk has companies and offices in 61 countries, with manufacturing facilities in seven countries. It manufactures treatment for people with diabetes (insulin), hormone-replacement therapy for women, and human growth hormone. Novo also discovers, develops, manufactures and markets industrial enzymes for detergents, starch, textiles, etc. With 13,395 employees, Novo's net turnover was DKK 14,873 million in 1996. The company has grown steadily since 1992.[47]

Novo Nordisk has had an independent environmental department since 1974, and in 1996 published its fourth environmental report. Novo estimates that only 200 companies worldwide publish environmental reports. Novo's outstanding environmental record won the company the prestigious Corporate Conscience Award from the Council on Economic Priorities in 1997.

In 1991, Novo Nordisk initiated annual consultations with environmental stakeholders. With its chairman present, Novo executives convene a group of a dozen leading environmental leaders. Among the participants are directors of ethical investment portfolios, research organizations and campaigners. By convening this dialogue with stakeholders, Novo is able to observe trends and respond to environmental allegations *before* they are publicized.

According to Marianne Gramstrup of the Corporate Environment Department, "towards the end of the 1980s it became clear that it was no longer merely the authorities with which the company needs to maintain a dialogue on its environmental responsibilities. We began to see growing interest among other groups in society: customers, neighbors, environmental organizations, students, investors, and in particular, our employees."[48] The company had learned the hard way just how dangerous it is to ignore public opinion. In the 1970s, a US campaign alerted consumers not to purchase detergents made with enzymes. While no health risks had been documented, Novo's sales dropped 50 per cent. One-fifth of its workforce was made redundant. Two years later, the US Food and Drug Administration concluded that there was no risk associated with enzymes in detergents.

Novo is a leader in environmental reporting; rather than just tracking emissions, the report tracks the use of inputs such as water and energy. Novo has also developed an enzyme which allows paper producers to reduce the use of chlorine in bleaching. Such environmental innovation is related to the company's ongoing dialogue with stakeholders.

Novo prides itself on its dialogue with stakeholders. When visited by NGOs it often has to face very tough questions which it tries to answer frankly and honestly. If they do not know the answer – they say so! The company claims to learn from stakeholder input.

SmithKline Beecham: cutting costs, cutting waste

SmithKline Beecham's 300-product range includes such household names as Ribena, Lucozade, Horlicks, Panadol, Night Nurse, Macleans and Aquafresh, and its 1994 turnover was $11.55 billion. In 1994, it hired a young biologist, Gary Parker, to look into the business benefits of lifecycle analysis (LCA). LCA involves looking at products and packaging from cradle to grave, to assess their total environmental impact from source of materials, energy use in production, to disposal. Surprisingly, this sort of analysis did not become a major business tool until the mid-1980s. The benefits can mean lower raw material and energy costs in production, decreased transportation costs, easier recycling and significant public-relations benefits.

The figures in the case of SmithKline Beecham speak for themselves. Through the application of LCA to an existing rigid polystyrene pack a new lightweight PET blister pack for one of its toothbrushes resulted in a 70 per cent reduction in material consumption per pack. Americans buy 16 million of these toothbrushes every year, and the company saved 160 tons of plastic and 6,000 tons of emissions to the atmosphere per year. The energy saving of 116 million megajoules was the equivalent of energy required to light every US home for one hour.[49]

The application of technology and knowledge based on sustainability principles and sound business management has produced higher profits for the company and lowered its environmental impact.

The Tagua Initiative: may a thousand tagua buttons bloom!

What do The Banana Republic, Gap, Jones of New York, and DKNY have in common? They are among the 60 companies that use tagua nut buttons in their garments.[50] Cut from thin slices of tagua nut, these buttons are a fashionable substitute for plastic buttons.

Tagua trees grow naturally in a region of Ecuador that is rich in biodiversity but extremely poor. The Tagua Initiative addresses this contradiction through a joint venture between Conservation International (CI), a US-based NGO that seeks to promote biodiversity and an Ecuadorian NGO, the Foundation for Socio-Environmental Training, Research and Development (CIDESA). CI provides links to national and international markets; CIDESA provides training and technical assistance in marketing, as well as financing.

Since 1990, the joint venture has sold over 70 million buttons, totalling over $5 million, while employing 2,800 people. Five per cent of the profits ($300,000) have been reinvested in conservation projects.

A significant amount of product testing was needed to make the initiative succeed. In the early stages of product development, garments made with tagua nut buttons were washed, and lo and behold, an odd thing would happen. By adding water and heat, the buttons would sprout!

Most companies that use the tagua buttons do not publicize the fact – their motivation for using the buttons is based on price (the tagua buttons cost only slightly more than plastic), quality and fashion trends.

What makes the Tagua Initiative so successful? By dealing with ten major whole-salers, the initiative operates on a large scale, rather than furnishing a niche market. Industry provides access to markets, critical information on quality control, thereby ensuring the viability of the venture. NGO support allows a disadvantaged community to protect biodiversity by protecting their livelihoods. Despite the link between industry and the NGO sector, there is a risk that efforts to promote biodiversity may be under-mined by the local government's drive to build roads.

Human rights and the workplace

In the age of the global economy in the affluent North (see "North–South dialogue" in Appendix 2: Glossary) many parents are paying to leave their children in playschools and nurseries so that they (the parents) can return to work, but in the poorer South, many children as young as five and six have to work and do not have access to education, adequate healthcare or clean water, and are often the main income earners in their families. Human-rights issues have become issues for business because organizations such as Human Rights Watch and Amnesty International have highlighted abuses in countries where multinational corporations are operating.

Recent cases have involved brands such as Nike, Gola and Reebok, with stores like C&A and Marks & Spencer being accused of knowingly profiting from the use of exploitative child labor in the manufacture of their products. These companies denied being involved with their knowledge or agree-ment, and have sought to ensure that they are not caught in this media trap again. Non-governmental organizations such as Christian Aid and FairTrade have targeted some companies and products in the hope of shaming them into managing their supply chains ethically. In most cases, this involves com-panies simply understanding their supply chains.

At the end of the 1990s most large companies have a policy on the envi-ronment, and those that do not are seen as lacking a sense of social responsibility and of failing to address a key management issue. It is now the case that transnational companies are also beginning to have a policy on human rights. Recent events have highlighted the need for companies to be aware of growing concerns about human-rights violations and business's role in hastening the adoption and implementation of human rights around the world. Increasingly, the information revolution means that individuals and organizations are armed with expert information and eyewitness accounts of human-rights violations.

It is not only governments that can stand accused of failing to uphold fundamental freedoms. Citizens, be they individuals or corporations, can also be complicit if they fail to acknowledge or take action on known violations. As Geoffrey Chandler, former senior executive at Royal Dutch/Shell and now Chairman of Amnesty International's UK Business Group, says: "Companies are citizens of the country in which they operate. They are subject to the laws of that country. But they are not subject to all its customs and practices if these transgress internationally accepted standards."[51] His view is that this is not just a question of managers suddenly discovering morality, but that "companies have nothing to lose and much to gain. All they need is a clear perception of the way world opinion is changing, a widening sense of corporate self-interest and responsibility, plus some leadership and moral courage."[52]

If corporations are citizens, from which we derive the concept of corporate citizenship, then they bear witness just as individuals do. If it is wrong for a person to turn away in the face of injustice, it is wrong for a corporation to do so. If you see your neighbor beating up another neighbor, do you do nothing? If a company operates in a country where there are systematic human-rights violations, should the company remain silent? The absolutist approach is for companies to withdraw from countries where there are such violations, but many would argue that a gradualist approach produces better results, over a period of time.

Nevertheless, one aspect of this discussion has recently changed radically. In the past, it was transnational corporations and bodies such as Amnesty International and Human Rights Watch which bore witness and reported on what they had documented. In most cases, business failed to report until the evidence was produced by human-rights organizations. Now, however, the oppressed, pressure groups and the media are making use of the open information system that exists via satellite communications and the Internet to bring eyewitness accounts as they happen. Few people will forget the television pictures transmitted from Tiananmen Square in 1989 of China's suppression of the students' uprising or the police beating of a driver, Rodney King, in Los Angeles in 1991 which led to street uprisings.

The arguments against action or condemnation, either by governments or companies, against other countries which abuse their own citizens are twofold. First, one nation should not interfere in another nation's internal affairs. Second, in defense of corporate inaction, the financial imperative comes before all others, and the responsibility of a company to protect its investment becomes paramount. However, as the profiles in this book show, and as Chandler, just quoted, says, the financial imperative is now beginning to be governed by the imperative to be proactive on human rights. Bad press on human rights can seriously damage the bottom line.

Governments are complicit with business when it comes to the condemnation of countries with human-rights abuses, but also with lucrative markets. Often soft targets are chosen, like Myanmar (Burma), because such condemnation does not threaten investments or trade, while harder targets, such as Saudi Arabia, are hardly mentioned. Even when President Clinton tried to link human rights to trade in China, business lobbied hard to negate such a linkage. In the UK in the 1980s, maverick defence minister, Alan Clark, wrote in his diaries: "Earlier today, a creepy official who is in charge of South America, came over to brief me ahead of my trip to Chile. All crap about human rights. Not one word about the UK interest."[53]

The UK's interest is, in theory, enshrined in the 1948 Universal Declaration of Human Rights and it is to this Declaration that business should be looking when formulating their own human-rights policies. Human rights are not just a matter for nation-states and governments. There are human-rights issues in every workplace, and every business is closely involved in implementing fundamental freedoms and ensuring the there are no abuses of human rights. This is true, for instance, on issues like equal pay, on freedom of thought, equal opportunities, exploitative child labor which prevents children from going to school, the right to marry and have a family, earning a living wage and on the right to trade-union recognition (see the profile that follows on the Universal Declaration on these issues). Human rights are as much a workplace issue for business, as a question of foreign policy and international diplomacy for government.

The 1948 Universal Declaration has its roots in the agony, horror and injustices of two world wars, and in American ascendancy as a result of those wars. It is so similar to the US Constitution that it can be viewed as an American-global constitution, a script written for the ensuing 100 years.

The origins of the 1948 Universal Declaration lie in the first codification of human rights in 1215 in the Magna Carta. While certainly not making all men and women equal, the Magna Carta put in writing the concept of the rule of law: "No freeman shall be taken or imprisoned . . . or exiled or in any way destroyed . . . except by the lawful judgment of his peers or (and) the law of the land."[54] The English Civil War and the English Bill of Rights, more than 450 years later, further advanced the rights of individuals to fundamental human rights. The American Revolution and the Bill of Rights in 1791, followed by the French Revolution in 1789, were both inspired by Yorkshireman Thomas Paine's, *The Rights of Man*, which enshrined civil rights in the constitution of countries on both sides of the Atlantic.

In 1919 US President, Woodrow Wilson, said of his country that its founders had "set this nation up to make men free, and we did not confine our conception and purpose to America." This global ambition was repeated by another President, Harry Truman, in 1949: "We must embark on a bold new program for making the benefits of our scientific advances and industrial progress available for the improvement and growth of underdeveloped areas. The old imperialism – exploitation for foreign profit has no place in our plans. What we envisage is a program of development based on the concepts of democratic fair dealing."[55]

It is not surprising that the United Nations, established in the aftermath of the Second World War and on the ashes of the failed League of Nations, should adopt a declaration on human rights that parallels the US Constitution, given the position that the USA found itself in 1945. Since then, a number of US Presidents, including Kennedy and Carter, have attempted to make human rights central to their administration's foreign policy. In the 1980s and 1990s Bush and Clinton have promoted human rights, although both have found it easier in the final result to adopt President Reagan's realist position to human rights, arguing that gradualism will win the day eventually. Central to this argument is the idea that increased world trade means increased interrelatedness, and that soon the whole world will follow the liberal economic model in which human rights are seen as the basis for successful markets.[56]

As the world moves towards global standards for business on human rights the 1948 Universal Declaration is seen as the template, and the world moves towards adopting the US Constitution. Does the history of human rights indicate some inevitability? Are we inexorably moving towards a situation where governments and corporations reach the same conclusion – that the expansion of business worldwide will meet fundamental freedoms and human rights in a marriage of convenience?

If this is so, then business, as much as any individual, organization or government must be part of the revision of the 1948 Universal Declaration, because there are some serious omissions which have become apparent through our continued destruction of the environment, some scientific discoveries and the growth of information technology.

If human history is seen as the lust for power and the balance between freedom and order, then current developments require the consideration of the addition of new articles to the Universal Declaration.

The need for additional human rights

Here follows some suggestions for additional human rights:

- The right to an unpolluted environment, including access to clean water and air and the right to shelter.
- A right to privacy away from spying eyes in the sky, and on the Internet.
- A right to the integrity of one's own genetic inheritance.
- The right not to consume or be part of the global financial system[57] and a recognition that we are social as well as economic animals.
- That multinational corporations and other transboundary organizations are corporate citizens, and have rights and responsibilities similar to individuals, governments and communities, and should be accountable for their decisions and actions.

In the information age, knowledge is power, more than labor, capital or materials, and this knowledge is principally used now to manipulate people and nature. The Universal Declaration does not specifically cover the abuse of corporate power or environmental protection. Some may see calls for the inclusion of clauses on these issues as steps towards global governance. As global agreements are increasingly forged without the participation of governments, for instance on Internet standards and the new social accountability standard SA8000, it is worth considering additional human rights which take account of changes over the last 50 years.

The UN's 1948 Universal Declaration of Human Rights

Preamble

- Unless we understand that every person in the human family has equal rights, freedom, justice and peace cannot exist.
- During the history of mankind many people have been oppressed. We must aim for a world where all people can enjoy the right to say what they think, to choose their own beliefs, to live without fear and without want.
- Human rights must be protected by law.

- Men and women have equal rights, and we must work for social progress and better living standards.
- All the members of the United Nations have agreed to these things, and must fully understand the implications.

Proclamation

Each and every member of the United Nations and individuals in each country must teach respect for human rights and ensure protection under the law.

Article:

1 All people are equal.

Everyone has a right to:

2 fair and equal treatment.
3 life, liberty and freedom.
4 be free from slavery.
5 freedom from torture.
6 be regarded as a person.
7 equality before the law.
8 legal protection.
9 freedom from arbitrary arrest, detention or exile.
10 fair trial, held in public.
11 to be judged innocent until proved guilty.
12 privacy.
13 freedom of movement.
14 political asylum.
15 a nationality.
16 marry and have a family.
17 own property.
18 freedom of belief and religious practice.
19 freedom of opinion, including receiving and imparting information across borders.
20 assembly.
21 political activity.
22 social security including economic, social and cultural rights.
23 work, including the freedom to choose work, equal pay, sufficient wages to ensure an existence worthy of human dignity, and the right to join a trade union.
24 leisure, rest and paid holiday.
25 a decent standard of living, and mothers and children deserve special care.
26 education, which must be free and compulsory at elementary level and promote human rights and fundamental freedoms.
27 culture and copyright of their own artistic and scientific achievements.
28 expect an international order which protects these human rights.

29 Everyone has a duty to the community in which they live and in a democratic society, a person's rights should only be limited so far as to protect others' human rights.

30 No government, organization or individual may destroy this Declaration.

Amnesty International: monitoring human-rights abuses globally

Amnesty International was founded in 1961 after the publication of a letter in *The Observer,* London's oldest Sunday newspaper. Peter Benenson, a lawyer, wrote an article entitled "Prisoners of Conscience" on 28 May 1961, in which he said: "Open your newspaper any day of the week and you will find a report from somewhere in the world of someone being imprisoned, tortured or executed because his opinions or religion are unacceptable to his government . . . The reader feels a sickening sense of impotence. Yet, if these feelings of disgust all over the world could be united into a common action, something effective could be done."

The organization now has supporters in 150 countries and has won the Nobel Peace Prize.

Amnesty International's UK Business Group

AI's Business Group, which was established in 1991, is chaired by Sir Geoffrey Chandler, former senior executive of Royal Dutch/Shell, and supported by Richard Branson, founder of the Virgin Group, and Anita Roddick, founder of The Body Shop, Sir John Harvey-Jones, former Chairman of ICI, among others.

> *"The Business Group believes that companies should be aware of the human rights context of the countries in which they operate, a context which will increasingly influence the investment climate. It seeks to use its influence to prevent human rights violations, to encourage awareness of human rights throughout the business community and promote Amnesty International's aims."*

Human rights guidelines for companies

Amnesty International's Business Group have issued *Human Rights Guidelines for Companies*[58] which recognize that "companies frequently operate in countries where human rights are violated and where security is an issue." Because such issues "contribute to civil unrest and uncertainty in the investment climate," companies have a "direct self-interest in assisting respect for human rights to prevail."

Most important is for companies to be aware of human rights, or the lack of them in the countries they operate in and to use their influence in support of human rights (as outlined in the Universal Declaration). While "Amnesty International takes no view on boycotts or disinvestment, nor does it criticize companies engaged in legitimate business in any country . . . it believes companies have a responsibility to use their influence to protect human rights."

"This can be done by:

- including specific support for human rights in their internal codes of conduct;
- ensuring that their personnel and security policies are in line with international guidelines;
- voicing explicit support for the Universal Declaration of Human Rights;
- engaging in discussion on human rights issues in the countries in which they operate."

More specifically, the guidelines contain information on taking responsibility for human rights *internally* and *externally*. They also cover security arrangements for companies operating in countries where there are security problems.

On 10 December 1997, President Nelson Mandela of South Africa signed a personal pledge as part of a campaign by Amnesty International for the fiftieth anniversary of the Universal Declaration which read: "*I promise to do everything in my power to ensure that the rights in the Universal Declaration of Human Rights become a reality throughout the world.*"

How about the world's leading corporations, or their leaders, committing themselves to the same pledge?

The business case

Many of the oldest and most revered companies operate in countries with appalling human-rights records where their commercial operations outlast a passing array of despotic, unelected governments. What should they do? Do they have no political power, as Helmut Maucher, President of Nestlé and of the International Chamber of Commerce wrote in the *Financial Times* in December 1997?[59]

Here are two cases of oil companies operating in two countries which are renowned for corruption and abuses of human rights. First, BP in Colombia, followed by Shell in Nigeria.

BP in Colombia

In the lush eastern foothills of the Andes, BP is drilling for oil in a remote and politically unstable region of Colombia known as Casanare. BP is a contractor to the Colombian government, and other partners are the state oil company, Ecopetrol, Total and Triton; current production averages around 300,000 barrels per day. Both of Colombia's main guerilla groups, the ELN and FARC have a presence in Casanare. The guerrilla organizations have several revenue streams, among them are: narcotics, kidnapping and extortion. Companies refusing to pay for "protection" suffer the consequences – as a result of failure to pay, oil pipelines are routinely destroyed. BP's policy on corruption is strict: the company refuses to engage in corrupt practices. According to David Rice of BP, six times the amount of oil spilled in the Exxon Valdez has been spilled due to guerrilla activities.[60] BP is not the only target: Occidental Petroleum's oil fields were attacked some 40 times in the first eight months of 1997.[61]

To protect its oil fields and personnel, BP employs security personnel and also requires the protection of the Colombian military and police. According to Rice, "The military is accused of human rights violations and BP condemns all abuses of human rights from whatever quarter. However, we suffer from guilt by association."[62] The presence of a large security force also breeds mistrust among the local community.[63]

BP has been accused of providing the military with intelligence on local community leaders. It is alleged that this transfer of information led to the subsequent torture and disappearance of several people. BP denies that it turned over any intelligence to the military, but has stated that it has provided videotapes of meetings with local community leaders as part of its environmental assessment. These videotapes are made with the consent of the local communities, in order to document the commitments the company makes to the local community. BP now tracks all videotapes. Human-rights organizations have asked BP not to videotape meetings, thus presenting BP with a dilemma which places the needs of one stakeholder group, the local community, in contradiction with another group, human-rights organizations.

In addition, a British Member of the European Parliament has testimony from local people alleging that BP's security staff had committed human-rights violations, and that a number of community leaders who were critical of BP had been murdered.[64]

In November 1996, BP itself requested Colombia's independent Prosecutor General to investigate all the allegations against the company. In February 1998, the Human Rights Unit found no evidence to sustain any of the accusations including that of passing photographs to the army. Moreoever, far from being "murdered," one of the individuals named by the British MEP was, in fact, alive.

A report by the *Independent on Sunday*[65] reveals that one of the human-rights organizations which has campaigned against BP, the Colombian Human Rights Committee, is run by a Asdrubal Jimenez Vacca, a man described as a guerrilla commander by Colombian press reports. A Colombian exile, Jimenez denies that he is affiliated with the Popular Liberation Army (EPL).

BP is one of the most admired companies in Europe, according to the *Financial Times*. With 56,000 employees in 100 countries, BP operates in three main areas: exploration and production of oil and gas, refining and transporting oil and gas, and manufacturing petro-chemicals. Once known as British Petroleum, the company produces one of every 12 barrels of oil produced in the USA, making it the largest US producer. In the UK, one in every five barrels is produced by BP.

With its significant current and potential future reserves in Colombia, BP is unwilling to leave the country because of problems with human rights. Instead, BP and its partners are investing in the development of the region through a program known as

"Casanare 2000." The region is poor, with 47 per cent of the population having unsatisfied basic needs, and annual income has historically been far lower than that for Colombia as a whole.[66] However, the advent of substantial royalties (now over $100 million a year) directly to Casanare should help promote the long-term sustainable development of the region. BP and its partners have invested $17 million in four years to promote the protection of the environment, healthcare, education and infrastructure.[67]

The case of BP in Colombia demonstrates the extreme difficulty of operating in a poor region undergoing a violent guerrilla war. The company has taken the following actions to deal with the crisis:

1 BP has extended an invitation to journalists, activists and politicians to visit Casanare. This openness is key to allowing major stakeholder groups access and information.
2 BP has also promised that if the company receives evidence of human-rights abuses, it will report them to the key authorities.
3 BP's CEO, John Browne, has met with President Samper of Colombia and raised the issue of human rights while expressing BP's commitment to them.
4 BP has made some unusual commitments to foster human rights and non-violence. It is promoting civil-rights awareness and disarmament, developing a training program for soldiers in environmental management and first aid, providing soldiers with pocket-sized human-rights cards that list the fundamental rights of people.
5 In April 1998, BP launched its own statement of policies in five areas: "ethical conduct, employees, relationships, health, safety, environmental performance, and finance and control." Support for the Universal Declaration of Human Rights is included in these policies.

Shell In Nigeria

"Shell is here on trial . . . The Company has ducked this particular trial, but its day will surely come and the lessons learnt here may prove useful to it for there is no doubt in my mind that the ecological war the Company has waged in the Delta will be called to question sooner rather than later and the crimes of that war be duly punished."[68]

Ken Saro-Wiwa's last speech to the military court
before he was killed by the Nigerian government

Shell in Nigeria is a case of rapid organizational learning on the part of the company, and rapid global understanding on the part of consumers and producers. It is difficult to dispute that this case stands as a watershed on global and corporate governance.

In 1958, Shell discovered oil in Ogoni in Nigeria, and between then and 1993, when production ceased in that area, extracted $5.2 billion worth from five oil fields. Some 40 per cent of the oil goes to the USA, and the revenues are shared by the Nigerian government and the oil companies under a joint partnership arrangement by Shell. Apart from the fact that Shell has been willing to operate in a country where there are systematic human-rights abuses, Nigeria is rated as the most corrupt country in the world in which to do business,[69] the World Wide Fund for Nature (WWF) also estimates that the burn-off of gases from Shell's oil wells is one of the single largest causes of global warming.[70] Shell says that gas flaring is "perhaps the largest environmental challenge facing Nigeria," and as a shareholder in the country's Liquefied Natural Gas Company, there are plans to stop "all unnecessary gas flaring by 2008."[71]

Another source of pollution suffered by the people of Ogoni comes from leaking pipelines. When Shell was first accused of neglecting its environmental responsibilities, it said that "they were OK when they were installed."[72] In retrospect the chairman of Royal Dutch/Shell admits that they should have been more sensitive – and buried the pipes.

It has been estimated that it will cost between $3.3 billion and $6.6 billion to clean up the damage caused by leaking pipelines over the last 40 years, but the damage to Shell's reputation has been more significant. Shell says it is spending $100 million a year on environmental improvement; now the policy is to remedy pollution incidents as they happen, but it admits that historical cases still need to be addressed.

Shell has admitted that facilities which were acceptable up to the early 1980s are not acceptable now. Shell, and the world, have moved on with regard to environmental protection.

Shell has been charged with being complicitous in the deaths of Ogoni activists, including Ken Saro-Wiwa, who were campaigning against the Nigerian government and against Shell's despoilation of their land, and calling for a greater share of the profits from Shell's extraction of oil. Shell has been at pains to say that in no way did it condone the killings, and that it actively intervened to stop the executions taking place.

Nevertheless, perhaps the situation is summed up in a quote from one of Shell's general managers in 1996:

> "I am afraid I cannot comment on the issue of the Ogoni 9, the tribunal and the hanging. This country has certain rules and regulations on how trials can take place. Those are the rules of Nigeria. Nigeria makes its rules and it is not for private companies like us [Shell] to comment on such processes in the country."[73]

In reply one of the Ogoni activists said:

> "But there lies the political and moral dilemma. Shell is a private company but it is also the source of the country's wealth. And whether it likes it or not, Shell is intimately bound up in the life and death struggle for the future of Nigeria."[74]

According to Shell's figures, about 90 per cent of Nigeria's foreign exchange is generated through oil revenues, which accounts for 80 per cent of the government's total income.[75] Shell is naturally sensitive about the way in which its activities have been portrayed in the media in Europe and North America. It is clear in retrospect that there has been some misrepresentation and inaccurate reporting of the facts, but it remains the case that enterprises such as Shell see their roles as responsible citizens as encapsulated in the following quote from Shell:

"We believe our role as a responsible Nigerian company is to work with the communities in our areas of operation to complement and add value to this central core of government-driven development [our stress]. We do provide a substantial community support, but we believe our most effective contribution to Nigeria is through the taxes and royalties we pay and the wealth we generate in the economy [our stress]."[76]

This event has forced Shell to rethink and rewrite its business principles to include statements on sustainability and human rights. However, there was no effect on Shell's share price because of this débâcle, despite reports to the contrary in some newspapers.[77] Perhaps the company has taken note, but shareholders do not yet see human rights as an issue which could affect profitability.

On this point it is interesting that one of the largest institutional investors in Shell, Prudential Assurance, did not support calls from PIRC (Pensions and Investments Research Consultants) for Shell to be subjected to an externally verified social and environmental audit. This was despite the fact that in 1990 the then Chairman of the Confederation of British Industry and former head of the Prudential, Sir Brian Corby, had argued that "environmental auditing can make significant commercial and environmental gains."[78] These issues were discussed at Shell's Annual General Meeting in 1997 and, as PIRC's managing director, Ann Simpson said, "Shell is putting a huge effort into winning this one . . . They have had a crash course in why the environment and human rights need to be integrated into business strategy and fully reported to shareholders."[79]

Public outrage at Shell's activities in Nigeria indicated changing attitudes about what is acceptable and what is not. In May 1997, 18 pension-fundholders controlling 1 per cent of the shares filed a shareholder resolution at the Annual General Meeting against Shell pressing it to establish an independent audit of its human-rights and environmental policies. A campaign group alleged that Shell had been implicated in the deaths of 2,000 people in Ogoni, as well as causing widespread environmental damage.

For the first time in the UK, a shareholder resolution based on social grounds was front-page news. The motion was defeated, but supported by 10 per cent of shareholders (with 6 per cent abstaining). Shell's outgoing Chairman, John Jennings, supports independent verification. The proverbial line in the sand is being redrawn. In future, Shell will publish an environmental and community report which will have been verified externally.

Business action on human rights

The definition of human rights is expanding from strictly civil and political rights to include economic, social and cultural rights.

The decision to conduct business in countries in which the state explicitly or implicitly condones a pattern of pervasive violations of human rights is one fraught with risk. Companies are increasingly assessing human-rights conditions in countries in which they source, and are assessing the potential danger to their brand image that sourcing from such countries presents.

In countries with gross violations of human rights, companies have three options:

1 To withdraw their operations.
2 To influence and press for reform.
3 To maintain operations without instituting any changes.

Over 30 companies have decided to leave Myanmar (Burma) due to abuses of human rights perpetrated by the military junta. Several companies, Liz Claiborne among them, have withdrawn operations due to the prevalence of corruption, because of human rights abuses by the government. Cynics reply that the decision to leave Myanmar is fairly easy, given that it is not an economic power in the same way that South Africa is.

In many countries with prevalent abuses of human rights, the government is involved in every sphere, including business. In order to invest in such countries, it is often necessary to form a joint venture with the government or a family member of a dictator. Dictators who violate human rights can lure investors into a web of complicity in corruption and human-rights violations. To what extent is a multinational corporation responsible for the violations of its joint-venture partner? The answer to this question is changing. In March 1997, a US court ruled that Unocal was liable for the violations of human rights by its partner, the Myanmese government. While this decision may be overruled, it suggests that a fundamental change in perception is taking place.

When pressured to withdraw from Myanmar, a major soft-drink company responded with the following claim: corporate decisions are "guided by our firm belief that trade is one of the best ways to build bridges between peoples. It aims to help open lines of communication, find common ground, stimulate dialogue, and thus bring people and their nations closer together."[80]

It is impossible to believe that BP and Shell did not know that they were operating in countries with serious abuses of human rights. It is much more likely that they did not see these issues as a priority, or that they saw their presence as benign. Now that some shareholders and other stakeholders have made human rights an issue, companies are less complacent. The lessons are clear: activism does work and companies must be more aware and more sensitive. Alas, Ken Saro-Wiwa and his colleagues are dead.

The International Labour Organisation

Established in 1919, at the end of the First World War, the International Labour Organisation (ILO), won the Nobel Peace Prize in 1969 for its work on promoting human rights, particularly in the workplace.

There are some 75 ILO Conventions on issues such as minimum working age, forced labor and collective bargaining, the principles which form the bases of these were established in the 1944 Declaration of Philadelphia which asserts that:

- labor is not a commodity;
- freedom of expression and association are essential to sustained progress;
- all human beings have the right to pursue their material and spiritual development in conditions of freedom, dignity, economic security and equal opportunity.

Child labor

"Many things we need can wait, the child cannot. Now is the time his bones are being formed, his blood is being made, his mind is being developed. To him we cannot say tomorrow. His name is today."

Gabriela Mistral, Chilean poet and Nobel Prize Winner

Child labor is on the rise, though it remains largely invisible. The ILO estimates that there are about 250 million children under the age of 15 working full- and part-time around the world, about 95 per cent of them in developing countries. Child labor is also becoming a significant problem affecting immigrant communities in many industrialized countries.

Definitions are important in assessing the problem: standards for minimum employable age established by the ILO have been ratified and incorporated into national legislation by many countries. Briefly, the age standards for developed countries are set out in Table 4.4.

Table 4.4 Minimum employable age in developed countries (ILO)

13 years old	for light work
15 years old	for regular work
18 years old	for hazardous work[81]

For countries where social and educational services are not well developed, the age standards differ and are set out in Table 4.5.

Table 4.5 Minimum employable age in developing countries (ILO):

12 years old	for light work
14 years old	for regular work
18 years old	for hazardous work

Increasingly, the standard for industrialized countries, 15 years of age, is being applied without qualification to producers in developing countries.

For companies which are interested in taking a proactive approach, there are four main types of action they can employ, usually in this order:[82]

1 Ascertain whether or not there is a problem.
2 Provide immediate protection for working children.
3 Shift under-age workers out of the workplace, setting up procedures and guidelines to halt new hires.
4 Find long-term alternatives to the use of under-age workers.

Ascertain whether or not there is a problem

The first concern is to establish whether a problem exists, and then, how serious it is. It is not easy to know at first glance whether an industry or plant has a serious problem with under-aged workers. Workers can appear younger or older than they are. Children may be present at the worksite, but may not be working. In addition, local contractors may try to hide an under-age workforce when inspectors are present or may use sub-contracting arrangements that, when brought to light, could embarrass the company.

Detection, then, is the first challenge. The company needs to know the extent of the problem – how many children are working – and it needs to know the nature of the problem – what they are doing, for how long, at what tasks, whether under hazardous conditions, and so on.

Assessment is a difficult challenge, given the ease with which birth certificates and work permits can be falsified. Furthermore, in some remote areas, such documentation is not routinely kept. Surprise site visits can also be of limited value, since children in the factories may look younger than their counterparts in the industrialized world, due to malnutrition.

Given the complexity of detection, some companies hire the services of local researchers, NGOs, or a certification agency to conduct simple question-and-answer surveys in the areas where workers live, asking them about the school and work activities of the younger members of their households. Direct interviews with children can also be helpful. Do they remember a major event, such as a fire or earthquake that happened ten years ago?

Provide immediate protection for those working

The first priority is taking action to protect under-age children in exploitative conditions, without undertaking any precipitous action that could harm the children. If children are working, a company will want to make sure that they are kept away from any dangerous equipment and that the conditions of work will not endanger their health. Immediate steps that companies take include safeguarding children from dangerous equipment, toxic chemicals, and excessive working hours. Protection of children travelling late at night is another concern. However, these represent interim measures; they are not solutions. An audit of the factory or work area may reveal health and safety problems which need to be addressed.

Shift under-age workers out of the workplace, setting up procedures and guidelines to halt new hires

Medium-term actions are designed to remove child workers from the factory floor in such a way that they do not suffer more than if they were to remain working. *The best interests of children* should be the guideline. Throwing children out of work abruptly when they are the sole breadwinner in the family is not a solution. While it is not the responsibility of companies to provide adequate schools or day-care facilities, they can serve as catalysts to support local schools or day-care facilities. Companies can work in partnership with local government and NGOs to provide adequate alternatives to work.

Wherever possible, companies should seek a greater understanding of the local reality. In many countries, child labor thrives because parents are unemployed. In such scenarios, hiring the parents or older siblings is an alternative.

Find long-term alternatives to the use of under-age workers

Child labor is rife where there is poverty. Healthy industry and a strong relationship between industry and society are the only means of eradicating child labor without victimizing child workers.

Companies can invest in communities to assure mutual benefit. Some companies are exploring the possibility of solving the problem of poverty by providing incentives, disincentives and alternatives. They prepare adults to take jobs in the industry through fast-track training programs. At the same time, they support NGOs that create schools for children. The two are linked in a pact: if the children are not in school, the adults will remain unemployed.

Latin America: An estimated 15 to 20 per cent of all children work in garment, shoe, mining or assembly plants. Countries with serious problems include: Brazil, Colombia, Guatemala and Mexico.

Asia: Almost half of the world's working children are found in South and South-East Asia, in the food processing, carpet and garment industries. Countries with serious problems include: Bangladesh, China, India, Indonesia, Nepal, Pakistan, Philippines and Thailand.

Africa: Children comprise 17 per cent of the continent's workforce. Export industries include garment, mining, carpet and food processing. Countries with serious problems include: Egypt, Lesotho, Ivory Coast, Morocco, Tanzania and Zimbabwe.[83]

Business and the workplace – overseas

Some businesses have been caught in the spotlight and been able to maintain their market position while introducing radical reforms in their supply-chain management. Nike and Levi Strauss & Co. are two companies which have had to act fast.

Nike

Nike is an example of a new trend, made manifest by globalization. By subcontracting all of its production to Asia, Nike only operates marketing, design and financial departments in the USA. Nike has pared down all of the poorly compensated parts of the assembly line, while retaining executive positions. Nike's strategy has made it a highly successful company. While Nike has benefited financially from globalization by developing a global assembly line using Vietnamese, Chinese, Thai and Indonesian labor, increased telecommunications allow for a spotlight to be placed on the company. In the USA, Italy, the UK and elsewhere, campaign groups have targeted Nike.

According to the Asia Monitor Resource Centre and the Hong Kong Christian Industrial Committee, the workers bear the costs:

"Companies like Nike and Reebok benefited in every way because they do not have to deal with production: they distance themselves through subcontracting, benefiting from low production costs without any direct lines of responsibility. Subcontracting also allows these sports shoe multinationals to respond quickly to changing styles and fashions, while passing on all of the uncertainty and insecurity to their subcontractors and ultimately the workers themselves." [84]

Protest continues to mount, with 18 October 1997 declared Worldwide Day of Action against Nike, and cartoonist Garry Trudeau devoted several weeks' worth of cartoon space to Nike factories in Asia in newspapers around the world. In the Wellco factory, one of Nike's Chinese subcontractors, some workers earn less than the Chinese minimum wage, earning $30–$42 per month, without overtime. The official minimum wage is $42 per month. [85] Part of the rage consumers feel is due to the high cost of shoes (often as much as $100 a pair), contrasted with the share a worker receives. In most cases, the person who makes the shoe could never afford to purchase a pair. A well-known brand, which graces the feet and backs of some of the leading sports figures in the world, is vulnerable because it sets its brand off as "the best." In the 1996–97 fiscal year, Nike's sales totalled around $9.5 billion, nearly doubling its sales since 1995. [86] Nike is vulnerable, with other shoe companies, on its formula and the fall in demand.

In the face of mounting criticism, Nike hired Andrew Young, from Goodworks International, to monitor its factories. Young is a very well-respected African-American civil rights leader who marched with Martin Luther King and served as mayor of Atlanta in Georgia, and as US Ambassador to the United Nations. Young is a household name in the USA. In Young's report, the following overall finding is made: "Nike is doing a good job in the application of its Code of Conduct. But Nike can and should do better." [87]

Nike's attempt to hire an independent monitor is laudable, but it falls short on several accounts. First, independent monitoring must be done by people with professional auditing training who understand the industry, in conjunction with local grassroots organizations and unions. Auditing for social concerns is a growing field, with evolving standards. While Young certainly has credibility, he is not an auditor, nor is he an expert

Doonesbury

BY GARRY TRUDEAU

Universal Press Syndicate © 1997 G.B. Trudeau

on the shoe industry, nor is he familiar with working conditions in Asia. Nike is to be commended for issuing a report on the Internet; this degree of reporting is unusual, but in order to have credibility the report needs to be done by professionals and experts and verified independently.

What are the factors which companies should consider in deciding where to conduct business? Levi Strauss & Co. and Timberland have decided to adopt guidelines for country selection.

Levi Strauss & Co.: guidelines for country selection

The following country-selection criteria address issues which Levi Strauss & Co. believe are beyond the ability of the individual business partner to control.

1 *Brand image*
We will not initiate or renew contractual relationships in countries where sourcing would have an adverse effect on our global brand image.

2 *Health and safety*
We will not initiate or renew contractual relationships in locations where there is evidence that company employees or representatives would be exposed to unreasonable risk.

3 *Legal requirements*
We will not initiate or renew contractual relationships in countries where the legal environment creates unreasonable risk to our trade marks or to other important commercial interests or seriously impedes our ability to implement these guidelines.

4 *Political or social stability*
We will not initiate or renew contractual relationships in countries where political or social turmoil unreasonably threatens our commercial interests.

Since adopting these guidelines, the company has phased out production in China and Burma, due to pervasive human-rights problems. In Spring 1998, Levi Strauss & Co. reversed its decision on China. The company temporarily halted production in Peru, for fear that the Shining Path guerrillas were a threat to the personal safety of employees.

Multinational corporations exert significant influence over the government of host countries. Because such governments court foreign investment, multinationals are often in a position to meet with high-ranking government officials, including cabinet ministers and ambassadors. These meetings represent an excellent opportunity for company executives to press for better working conditions. A large US clothing manufacturer has used such meetings to encourage the host government to employ additional labor inspectors and to emphasize the need for adherence to local labor law. By making the point that they are committed to human rights and worker rights, companies can and do exert significant power. Companies can also assure that government services and funding are channelled to communities in need.

The Apparel Industry Partnership (USA)

In 1996, President Bill Clinton established the Apparel Industry Partnership (AIP), composed of representatives of clothing companies, unions and human-rights organizations. Members of the AIP include many of the most well-known apparel companies in the USA, including Reebok, Liz Claiborne, Nicole Miller, LL Bean and Nike. Other members include Business for Social Responsibility (see profile in Chapter 2) and the Interfaith Center on Corporate Responsibility. The aim of the partnership is to eliminate sweatshops by developing a code "which prohibits child labor, forced labor, and abuses of workers' rights, while promoting adequate health and safety standards." The AIP recognizes the right to join a union, permits only a sixty-hour working week apart from "exceptional circumstances," and requires that workers earn the minimum wage.

The AIP is establishing an organization to monitor the agreement. The AIP has been criticized for several reasons. First, the minimum wage in many developing countries is no protection against poverty. Second, 14-year-old children are still able to work under the agreement. Third, a sixty-hour working week is still permitted.[88] The AIP's exclusive focus on apparel companies in the USA limits its scope in ways that undermine the initiative. Apparel companies in other parts of the world can continue practices that are not allowed under the agreement. Furthermore, the focus on apparel ignores other industries where there are serious problems, such as the toy industry.

The Abrinq Foundation: rewarding child-friendly companies (Brazil)

Abrinq represents a new model for social change. Rather than operating as a charity, Abrinq engages with the private sector to affect major change in the life of Brazilian children. Abrinq's mission is to increase awareness and mobilize society about children through private-sector engagement and political action to defend children's rights. The Foundation has benefited 240,000 children and adolescents throughout Brazil by promoting child and maternal health, creating libraries, and working to abolish child labor.

The Foundation operates on the principle that in order to improve the rights of the child, manufacturers, suppliers and retailers need to get involved. Abrinq works with 400 "child-friendly companies" – providing incentives to companies to fight against the exploitation of child labor while investing in projects to improve the quality of children's lives. Companies certified as "child friendly" can advertise their commitment to consumers, on their products, bags, stationery, and signs.

With funding from the International Labour Organisation, Abrinq produced a book, a video and an exhibition on child labor to educate the business community about the damage done to children who work. Since companies are part of the problem, they must become part of the solution.[89] Abrinq asked companies to pledge to ban child labor and to require the same of their suppliers. A database was created to gather information on best practice in combating child labor. A media campaign was also launched to mobilize public awareness. Over 400 companies have been certified as "child friendly," in a wide range of industries, taking in agriculture, services, finance, airports and public-sector organizations.

In order to receive the "child friendly" seal, the following measures must be observed:

1 Children under the age of 14 are not allowed to work for the company/organization.
2 The company/organization must ensure that suppliers and clients adhere to the commitment.
3 The company/organization must develop or support social programs aimed at training children and teenagers.

These commitments are investigated by Abrinq's partners, including unions, employees and NGOs. After the decision is made to grant a company the seal, there is a public ceremony, to which press, celebrities, high-ranking officials, and television are invited. The seal is valid for one year, after which time a company or organization can re-apply.

Some of the success stories include Natura, Brazil's largest cosmetics company, which has adopted a primary school, Matilda Maria. Natura has helped to train teachers, develop an environmental awareness campaign, and develop the library and video center. As a result of the partnership between Natura and the school, the drop-out rate has decreased from 38 per cent to 6.5 per cent.[90] The Power Company of São Paulo was the first public-sector company to become certified. The construction company Oliveira Roxo has convinced other companies to finance a Fund for Children's and Adolescents' Rights through a 1 per cent income tax.

Consider some of the reasons given by participating companies for their role in Abrinq's campaign:

[The use of the seal brings] "commercial benefit when other serious companies, alerted by our . . . work with the seal, awake to their social responsibilities and seek . . . a closer relationship with our company."[91]

[The Refinery Santa Elisa] "belongs to a sector whose image is rather distorted in the Brazilian socio-economic environment. There is a stigma of more than 4 centuries which utilizes the media to picture the sugar-alcohol sector as being pro-slavery, feudal, possessive and which disrespects children. We understand that it may be harmful for the sector if this image is not extinguished or if urgent *measures are not taken with that purpose. [However, the central reason for joining is due to] the conviction of acting in a more humanitarian, more correct manner in the education of youngsters."*

Cristina Dias, of the Refinery Santa Elisa[92]

"[W]e requested the seal only to document the work we have done for some years . . . and to show the public the difference between Paratodos and other transport companies."

Fatine Chamon A. Siquiera[93]

The Child Friendly Campaign has made impressive inroads in industries where child labor is a serious problem, among them citrus production and the manufacturing of shoes and charcoal. The Campaign has proved a major success, in part because of its timing. In the early 1990s, Brazil ratified the International Convention on the Rights of the Child. The legislature approved the Children and Adolescents Statute, and the ILO launched the Brazilian operation of its International Programme on the Elimination of Child Labour.

The Foundation was established in 1990 by Oded Grajew, a social entrepreneur. At the time, Grajew was President of Abrinq, the Brazilian Association of Toy Manufacturers. In 1989, he read a report that would change his life and the face of Brazil: UNICEF's *Report on the State of Children*. The report revealed dismal problems in education and health. Brazilian children were worse off than children in other Latin American countries. Grajew decided that it was time for business to get involved.

One of Abrinq's first campaigns was to promote a serum that combats childhood dehydration, a leading cause of death for Brazilian children. Two major supermarket chains, (Pão de Acucar and Sendas) publicized the campaign on 10 million shopping bags. One million measuring spoons were distributed, along with stickers.[94]

Equal employment opportunities

"Diversity is neither altruism nor affirmative action. It is a bottom-line issue. Companies that prosper in the future will be those that recognize the increasingly powerful role that women and minorities have in economic decision making."

Jon C. Madonna, Chairman and CEO of KPMG Peat Marwick

What does your organization look like? Your employees are the face of the organization, the face the customer sees. Does your company reflect the society in which it is based?

One of the most fundamental changes facing the workplace in the North (see "North–South dialogue" in Appendix 2: Glossary) is the rise of the multicultural and global society. The US Department of Labor estimates that 75 per cent of new entrants to the labor force will be women and minorities throughout the 1990s.[95]

The business case

A diverse workforce:

- allows a company to anticipate the needs of diverse groups in society and to develop new products and markets. As society becomes increasingly multicultural and business becomes more global, understanding niche markets is of the essence;
- enables the company to manage and benefit from change;[96]
- maximizes talent – by recruiting and promoting people of different backgrounds, companies can tap into a broader range of talent;
- is a sign of a caring and ethical company;
- with the proper training and procedures in place, can avoid embarrassing legal action;
- builds employee loyalty and commitment.

A 1992 survey of leaders in the British financial community revealed that their ideal company to invest in was one that provided equality of opportunity. Other factors included corporate ethics, being a good employer and training.

Why equal opportunities for women and minorities?

One of the greatest changes in employment over the last two decades has been the substantial growth of women in paid employment. How companies and countries handle this varies greatly.

For example, in Japan one of the key factors in rating companies is whether or not companies require females to wear uniforms, but not their male counterparts.

The freedom for a woman to use her maiden name is another factor used to rate the policies of Japanese companies towards women. Neither of these practices is considered by research organizations when evaluating companies in the USA or Europe.

While the specifics of how women are treated vary, the notion that discrimination should not be tolerated is a basic right. A key issue is representation for women at all levels of the company, from the boardroom to the shop floor. The other major issue is the availability of benefits which promote the special needs of families, and which help those engaged in childcare to have fulfilling work roles.

The definition of *minority* varies enormously from culture to culture and country to country. For example, in Japan, a key concern is the regular employment of non-Japanese and the promotion of foreign employees. In other societies, the use of the term "minority" can be misleading, as a small minority may hold positions of power which exclude the vast majority from being represented.

Discrimination and *un*equal opportunities

- According to the UN, women do 70 per cent of the world's work, earn 10 per cent of the world's wages, and own less than 1 per cent of the world's property.

- In the USA, a fully employed woman earns 71 cents for each $1.00 earned by a man, and women with college degrees earn the same average salary as men with only high school diplomas.

- In 1993, according to the US Bureau of the Census, Black Americans earned an average $370 per week; Hispanic Americans earned $335 per week. White Americans earned $478 per week.

Opportunity 2000

Opportunity 2000 is a business-led campaign, launched in 1991 in the UK by Business in the Community. Its objective is to increase the quality and quantity of women's employment opportunities in private and public-sector organizations. The campaign arose from investigative work done by an influential group of business leaders, which concluded that organizations which fail to fully utilize the country's female resource are compromising their competitive performance.

The goals of the campaign are that by the year 2000:

- member companies will have made a measurable improvement to the quality and extent of women's employment at all levels in their organization;
- membership will comprise employers from all sectors, and involve medium and smaller businesses;
- members will have influenced other businesses – for instance through the supply chain – and encouraged them to strive for a better balanced workforce;
- the campaign will have achieved a significant culture change among its members by sharing knowledge, and by raising awareness of issues of women's participation in the workforce and the benefits of being a family-friendly employer.

Employers joining the campaign are required to make a public statement of their ambitions and goals for improving women's representation at all levels in the workplace, and to demonstrate how they will achieve them through an action plan. Employers monitor progress towards their goals each year, and Opportunity 2000 carries out an annual progress review with its membership. In 1998, this will include benchmarks, against which members can assess their performance.

Opportunity 2000 reports that research carried out by the Institute of Management in the UK showed that in 1997, only 15.2 per cent of all executives were women, and 4.5 per cent of directors. Among Opportunity 2000's members, however, women accounted for 31 per cent of all managers and 11 per cent of directors in 1996.

WHAT CAN COMPANIES DO TO PROMOTE DIVERSITY?

1 Develop a policy on equal employment.
2 Set a strategy with time-specific goals for achieving targets in recruitment and promotion.
3 Provide diversity-awareness training.
4 Develop mentoring programs (these exist at many companies, including Avon, General Mills and IBM).
5 Develop and implement strategies for recruiting diverse employees.
6 Purchase from minority-owned business (see the profile on Avon in Chapter 2).
7 Offer generous family benefits.
8 Examine your charitable contributions: to what extent do you promote women's groups and minority groups? (For example, do you fund the boy scouts but not the girl scouts?).
9 Promote diversity at all levels, from the board to shop floor.

Diversity on company boards

In the early 1990s, a study of 806 Fortune 500 companies assessed the views of CEOs on the question of diversity on corporate boards.[97] What they had to say is revealing not just about boards, but about diversity in general: "The CEOs we interviewed stress that diversity is no longer just a matter of equity, but also an important economic consideration."

Here's why according to the study:

● Companies need diversity to succeed in the marketplace.
● Diversity at every level of the corporation – including its governance – helps a company to develop the sensitivity to cultural, linguistic and social differences that is required for successful marketing.
● Consumers want boards that understand their needs.
● Business leaders tell us that their customers are rapidly becoming more knowledgeable, not only about product quality and the value they receive, but also about corporate performance. Increasingly, they

understand the influence that comes with buying power, and they know how to exert leverage on these matters.

- Investors trust boards that grasp the full range of their interests.
- Today's active consumers are far more likely to attend public board meetings, or to make their demands known through institutions, such as pension funds, that hold large blocks of stock. More and more, they are demanding economic reciprocity – and boards that understand their needs and reflect the range of their communities and interests. This is especially true at a time when the business media are focusing attention on corporate boards, and the public is more aware than ever of the role of boards and their composition.
- Business leaders need the expertise of all available qualified candidates.
- In today's competitive environment, CEOs want to benefit from the widest possible talent base – including outstanding nominees who do not fit the usual demographic profile.

Disability

"Treat disabled people as intelligent human beings. Give them some dignity. One of the most hurtful things to me, as a carer, is when other people fail to give a person with a disability any respect. I have even been asked the classic: 'Does he take sugar?'"

Lorna, a financial consultant at Prudential and a carer

Disability is a complex topic because each disabled person is unique, with different needs. Prudential's employees' handbook on disability explains:

"Disability is a wide term: it can include people with speech and language, reading and writing or learning difficulties; being blind or deaf; those who have difficulty in moving around or who use a wheelchair; people with mental health problems; those who have conditions like multiple sclerosis, epilepsy, or muscular dystrophy; or people who look different, whether it's something they were born with, or the result of an accident."[98]

On the disability front, organizations need to be aware of the needs of disabled employees and disabled customers. A strong business case can be made for the need to address the concerns of both of these sectors.

A person is *disabled* if a *physical* or *mental* impairment has a substantial and long-term adverse effect on his or her ability to perform a job or carry out normal day-to-day activities.

Facts and figures on disability

- In Europe, there are 50 million disabled people, representing 11 per cent of the population, a number equivalent to the population of Denmark.
- By 2030, the population of Europe will have increased by 7 per cent, but the number of people over 65 will have increased by 40 per cent.
- In the USA, there are 43 million disabled people, and the market in products for disabled people is valued by IBM at $100 billion per year.[99]
- In the UK, a conservative estimate of this market is $50 billion per year.
- In the UK, one of every four potential customers is disabled or has a disabled person in his or her immediate circle.[100]

As the population ages, the market share represented by people with disabilities is growing rapidly and becoming difficult to ignore. Expectations of fair treatment are also rising as discrimination against disabled customers is less and less tolerated. In many countries, strong legislation against such discrimination is being enacted or strengthened.

This market is significant for several reasons. First, a disabled customer is likely to bring along family members and friends – so the lack of access to a restaurant or hotel, theater or supermarket can signify the loss of an entire family or social circle. Second, care of the disabled is a strong indication that a company or organization is caring and responsible. A menu in Braille or a supermarket cart for someone in a wheelchair leaves a positive impression on customers, a "feel-good factor." Such actions speak very loudly. The absence of such caring also speaks volumes.

In order to attract disabled customers, some service providers are training staff in how to treat customers with special needs. Many companies are issuing guidebooks for their staff on how to treat disabled employees. Prudential's employees' handbook, for example, quotes a financial consultant who has deaf customers: "We've done a lot of work with the deaf community, and have invested time in learning sign language. It really is a question of gaining trust and proving you are worthy of that trust. In our experience, deaf people view their disability as a slight problem that can be overcome."[101]

Barclays has received an award for training 250 managers in deaf awareness. The bank has agreed to make such training available to all cashiers. NatWest bank reports that 14,000 customers receive their bank statements in Braille, and another 10,000 in large print.[102] More than 100 employees at the

UK supermarket Sainsbury's have registered for courses in sign language.[103] Tesco, one of the major supermarket chains in the UK, provides parking, toilets, and shopping carts for disabled customers. In one of their stores, they are piloting 24-hour home shopping for their customers who are homebound.

A study commissioned by British Gas shows that customers are willing to pay up to 12 per cent more for services if they know the company is providing good service for the disabled.

Churchill & Friend's disabled customer-care audit

Churchill & Friend, a disability training consultancy, has developed a disability customer-care audit which poses interesting questions:

1 Does your organization have a statement declaring the organization's intent as to making your goods, services and facilities accessible to disabled people?
2 Is your complaints procedure accessible to disabled people?
3 Do your design and development teams receive disability-equality training?
4 Do you liaise with a working party of disabled people to check that your goods, services and facilities meet their needs and are easily accessible to them?
5 Do you involve disabled people in the production of your printed material? Audio-visual material?[104]

Disabled employees

> *"Technology has expanded the horizons of the disabled beyond our wildest dreams. It's done for us what the Wright brothers first flight did for travel."*
> Leye Chrzanowski, editor of a US
> disability newspaper, *One Step Ahead*[105]

Despite all of the compelling statistics and the rise of legislation, disabled people continue to face discrimination in hiring and promotion, leading to a high rate of unemployment and under-employment among the disabled. The consequences of discrimination are severe, since employers lose considerable talent by narrowing their hiring base.

Only 17 per cent of people with disabilities were born disabled, with the majority of disabilities occurring during a person's working life. Given the high cost of medically retiring an employee, companies are increasingly retaining workers who have become disabled in the workplace, either through re-training or retro-fitting the workplace.[106]

Hiring disabled employees can also boost a company's reputation, whereas legal action against a company for discrimination can seriously damage even the best reputation.

Many companies are reaping the benefits of hiring disabled employees. Both the Pizza Hut and Red Lobster restaurant chains have hired significant numbers of disabled staff. Ben & Jerry's sources its brownies from a bakery that employs workers with learning difficulties.

"The prevalence of people with disabilities increases markedly with age, to the extent that in the US there is a growing tendency to call non-disabled people 'temporarily able-bodied (referred to as 'tabs'). This reversal in perception means that access is automatically planned for everyone; it is transgenerational."[107]

As a result of technological advances such as the Internet, computers which read aloud, and other facilities, the workplace and universities are becoming more flexible and able to accommodate disabled people. But are our perceptions adapting to fit the technology?

The buildings of the future will be built by architects who can promote accessibility for all customers. Accessibility is not expensive when it comes to designing new buildings; it is a question of planning.

- Three-quarters of the major US manufacturing, communications and technology companies employ disabled people.[108]
- 87 per cent of companies who hired disabled employees encouraged other companies to follow their example.[109]
- Nearly 90 per cent of employers and employees polled were so pleased with disabled workers that they favored policies to increase the number of disabled recruits.[110]
- 69 per cent of changes made to accommodation to provide access to disabled employees cost less than $500.[111]

ACCESSIBILITY CHECKLIST:
HOW CUSTOMER-FRIENDLY IS YOUR COMPANY?

Many of these modifications suggested apply not only to the disabled, but to parents of small children.

Employing disabled workers can provide many business advantages. Disabled employees often have additional skills in problem-solving skills, attained by managing their own lives. In addition, disabled workers will be better suited to address the needs of disabled customers. Surveys show that disabled employees are likely

▶

to remain with the same employer for longer periods of time and to have fewer absences due to sickness and other reasons.[112]

Parking

1 Do you have any designated parking spaces for people with disabilities?
2 Is a percentage of parking space designated?
3 Are the designated spaces as near to the main entrance as possible?
4 Does the space meet with recommended specifications?
5 Is the designated parking clearly indicated both at the entrance and at the bay itself?
6 Is it sheltered from the weather?

Getting to the building

1 Is the pathway from the parking lot to the entrance as short as possible?
2 Is it clearly signposted and well lit?
3 Is there a dropped curb or slope between the parking area and the pathway?
4 Is there tactile paving at pedestrian crossings on the pathway?
5 Is the pathway surfaced with a suitable material?
6 Is the pathway kept clear in winter?
7 Is the pathway wide enough for a wheelchair?
8 Are any grates on the pathway hazardously placed?
9 Are there resting places on the pathway?
10 Are your reception staff trained in how to assist wheelchair users who drive their own cars to the entrance, for example, are they ready to arrange for the car to be driven to the car park?[113]

Ageism

As the population ages, companies are faced with ageing employees. Age is also an equal-opportunities issue. Hence, most companies with policies on equal opportunities pledge not to discriminate on the ground of age.

In the UK, a 1998 survey found that four out five people over 50 believe that they have been discriminated against on the basis of age when applying for work.[114] As 40 per cent of the UK's workforce is 45 years old or over, the implications are serious. The UK, in common with many other countries, may be failing to utilize key resources – maturity, knowledge, training and low absenteesim.

A number of companies are developing very creative policies on incorporating an ageing population in the workforce. B&Q, the British home-improvement chain, has a policy of hiring older workers who have worked in construction. Given their previous careers, they are well-informed about timber and home improvement, and so are better able to advise customers.[115]

Sexual orientation

Many companies are adding sexual orientation to their policies on equal opportunities, but changes are slow. One of the demands made by gay and lesbian groups in the USA is that gay and lesbian partners of employees should receive the same benefits as married employees.

Disney is one of the companies providing benefits to gay and lesbian partners – which has angered Southern Baptists in the USA who have called for a boycott of the company. This is a hotly contested issue. Another controversy arose with United Airlines, one of the major sponsors of the Gay Pride parade in the UK, and official airline of the parade. The company was targeted in the media for not providing the gay and lesbian partners of their employees with the same travel privileges as it gives to employees with spouses.

> *"Employers who do well addressing gay and lesbian issues are the organizations that will excel in the years to come. They will outshine their competitors. They will grow and develop profitably in their industries. They will find creative new ways to flourish in the uncertain marketplace of the 1990s and the new millennium beyond. Why? Talent. Plus openness and an ability to change. This doesn't mean that companies will excel only because they are good with lesbian and gay issues. But it is a revealing indicator. Organizations that address gay and lesbian issues demonstrate a willingness to listen and respond to the concerns of all of their employees."*
>
> Ed Mickens, *The 100 Best Companies for Gay Men and Lesbians*[116]

The key questions on corporate policies regarding gays and lesbians are:

1 Are gays and lesbians included in the company's anti-discrimination policy?
2 Does the company offer benefits to partners of gay and lesbian employees?
3 Does the company regard the gay and lesbian market as important?
4 Is the company able to attract this market in a sensitive manner?[117]

While most elements of the sexual orientation policies of US companies re-state federal laws, discrimination against gays and lesbians is illegal in only a few locations. In 1974, IBM became the first company to add sexual orientation to its discrimination policy. According to a major survey of 1,000 US companies, half of the companies included the term "sexual orientation" or "sexual preference" in their policies.

In 1991, Lotus Development Corporation became the first large, publicly traded company to offer domestic-partnership benefits, after a number of universities and municipalities began to do so (see Table 4.6).

Domestic-partnership benefits include health insurance, family leave and relocation assistance, among others. Some companies, such as Ben & Jerry's, offer domestic-partnership benefits to all couples who live together, whether they are married or not.

Table 4.6 Some US companies which provide domestic-partnership benefits

Apple	MCA
Ben & Jerry's	Microsoft
Borland	Oracle
Boston Globe	Quark
Charles Schwab	Silicon Graphics
Disney	Sun Microsystems
Fannie Mae	Time Warner (some divisions)
Genentech	United Airlines
International Data Group	Viacom
Levi Strauss & Co.	Village Voice
Lotus	Ziff-Davis

In the USA, the size of the gay market is estimated to be between 5 and 20 million. With many gay couples residing in urban areas, without children, they fall into the groups known as "yuppies" (young urban professionals) or "dinkies" (dual income no kids). Alcohol, tobacco and clothing companies are among the key industries marketing to this sector, often playing a key role in sustaining gay publications.

Sexual harassment

"Sexual harassment involves unwanted behavior of a sexual nature, and a perception by the victim that it has become a condition of work, or creates a hostile, intimidating and humiliating working environment. It can involve physical contact, expression of sexual innuendos, sexually colored comments and jokes, the exhibition of pornography, or unnecessary and unwanted comments on a person's appearance."[118]

Twenty years ago, sexual harassment was not identified as a problem, its definition was unclear and the law afforded little protection against it. While the vast majority of victims are women, cases are also reported of women harassing men, and people harassing co-workers of the same sex. It is difficult to estimate the extent of sexual harassment, since the majority of its victims remain silent. Estimates suggest that millions of women suffer from sexual harassment. In the USA, there were over 15,000 allegations of sexual harassment in 1996. In the late 1980s, there were 61,000 cases per year. Several factors are causing an upsurge in women's reporting cases of harassment, and campaign groups and NGOs are speaking out on this issue. In 1995, the Fourth Women's Conference in Beijing addressed the issue of sexual harassment, highlighting its incidence worldwide. As more and more employees win cases, others are encouraged to address the problem.

The ILO does not have a convention on sexual harassment, but addresses the issue under a convention banning discrimination. Thirty-six countries protect employees from sexual harassment. Companies are increasingly developing specific guidelines on sexual harassment and developing training programs to combat problems. Universities, police departments and military units are also developing prevention programs.

Sexual harassment and ethics training in the US Army

Since the 1980s the reputation of the US military has suffered from accusations of sexual harassment. In 1996, several women at the Aberdeen Ordinance Center in Maryland charged their supervisors with abuses, including rape and bullying. According to Togo West, the Secretary of the Army, "what happened at Aberdeen was an aberration. Sexual abuse is not endemic throughout our Army. Sexual harassment, however, continues to be a problem."[119]

Twenty-five years ago, the US Army became one of the first major US organizations to implement a formal equal-employment-opportunities program. Since then, the Army has experienced serious problems, with 72 per cent of the women and 63 per cent of the men interviewed reporting that they had experienced "sexist behavior," with 47 per cent of the women and 30 per cent of the men experiencing "unwanted sexual attention." Fifteen per cent of the women and 8 per cent of the men had experienced "sexual coercion," with 7 per cent of the women and 6 per cent of the men having experienced sexual assault.[120]

In order to address the problems at Aberdeen, the US Army has taken the following measures:

1 Basic training has been extended to include a week of training on basic human rights.
2 More chaplains are being added to training units so that they may be best placed to change behavior.
3 Drill sergeants will be exposed to stricter screening to remove people with records of violence or sexual harassment.

4 A national hot line has been established to receive formal complaints. In seven months, the hotline received 1,288 calls, of which 353 have resulted in criminal investigations.

5 The Army is "reengineering" its equal-employment program.

6 The Army is developing awareness programs to alert women and men of their rights and to assist them in reporting abusive behavior.

Racism and sexual harassment in the British military: the changing of the guard

On 14 October 1997 the British Army invited anyone interested to come to Buckingham Palace to find out "how committed we are to making the Army a better place for ethnic minorities to work." The British Army currently has only 1 per cent ethnic representation, compared with 5 per cent in the civil service. The Chief of General Staff, Sir Roger Wheeler, said that "whether we like it or not, there is a perception that the army is a racist organization . . . We are determined to provide genuine equality of opportunity to everyone."[121] The perception is confirmed by cases.

After Prince Charles complained about the lack of ethnic-minority guards outside Buckingham Palace, Richard Stokes said that he had resigned from the Household Cavalry because of racial abuse, hate mail and having had banana skins thrown at him during a rehearsal for Trooping The Colour.[122] Mark Parchment left the Royal Marines in 1988 having been forced to exercise carrying a spear rather than a gun because he was black. In 1994, the Household Division lost Mark Campbell after 17 months of active service when his bed was urinated on; he was continually called "nigger" and he received hate mail.

The initiatives undertaken by the Army include:

- an equal opportunities action plan that implements measures to ensure equality of opportunity is an environment free from harassment;
- a team to investigate non-criminal complaints of racial or sexual harassment and discrimination;
- a confidential helpline for soldiers, staffed by civilian welfare workers;
- an overhaul of the Army's equal opportunities training, plus leaflets explaining the policy and a complaints procedure;
- an ethnic minorities recruitment team to visit areas with a high representations of ethnic population;
- soldiers to be evaluated for their understanding of equal opportunities as part of overall performance evaluation.

An incident in 1997 caused the Navy to be heavily criticized for initiation rites committed on new joiners to a ship's company which included tying up sailors and sexually abusing them. The defending lawyers said that that humiliating initiation rites were a routine part of Navy life. Under a ruling from the European Court of Justice, the Ministry of

Defence has also had to pay compensation to women who were discharged for becoming pregnant while they were serving as members of the armed forces, and may have to pay compensation to men and women discharged for being gay or lesbian.[123]

AIDS and HIV in the workplace[124]

By the year 2000, it is estimated that 40 million people worldwide will be HIV positive. The majority of people with HIV are in their working years, generally, between the ages of 25 and 40. These facts will require employers to consider the effects of AIDS on the workplace and to develop appropriate policies for dealing with AIDS and HIV.

AIDS is affecting the bottom line. According to the Terrence Higgins Trust, a UK charity which assists employers in dealing with HIV and AIDS, "Ignorance and misunderstanding about HIV and AIDS could have a significant impact on your business through discrimination, harassment and work disruption. Education and policy development can help minimize the damaging effects of such activities on the productivity of your business and the effectiveness of your employees." [125]

Sir Geoffrey Mulcahy, chairman and CEO of Kingfisher Plc which runs supermarkets and other services in the UK, recognizes the effects of the workplace: "The risk of widespread disruption and in the longer term, lower morale, motivation, productivity, and indeed profits, is very real."[126]

Medical innovations are allowing people with HIV to remain at work for longer periods, making the issue of AIDS in the workplace one that is unlikely to disappear in the near future.

What should employers do to manage a disease that is complex and misunderstood?

1 Develop a policy.
2 Train employees about prevention.
3 Develop strategies for continued employment.
4 Develop community-wide programs.

Developing a policy

The development of an official company policy is important for guaranteeing that employees are treated equally and fairly and that management understand the correct procedures. In some instances, companies find that HIV and AIDS issues can be incorporated into existing policies on equal opportunities and health. Creating a policy can be an excellent vehicle for discussion and education within the company. In order for the policy to succeed, it is essential that senior management support the policy and set an example. Consultations with key parties, including staff, healthcare providers and unions, are also essential. Clear communication to staff about the policy is also vital to successful implementation. Once the policy is implemented, management needs to monitor and evaluate its effectiveness.

What issues should be included in a policy on AIDS and HIV?

- *Confidentiality*: an employer needs to ensure that information about an employee's health is confidential.
- *Discrimination*: the employer cannot discriminate on the basis of HIV and AIDS status.

The National AIDS Trust Employment Initiative (UK) – a business charter for HIV/AIDS: Companies act!

Below is a sample policy of a company which was signed up to Companies act!, a business charter for HIV/AIDS, developed by the National AIDS Trust Employment Initiative.

Company A is fully committed to the principle of non-discrimination when dealing with an employee or potential employee with HIV.

We are also committed to the principle that confidentiality should be strictly adhered to in relation to anyone with HIV or AIDS, and that employees or potential employees with AIDS will be treated in exactly the same way as any other member of staff with a comparable disease.

As signatories to Companies act!, we demonstrate our commitment through our employment policy on AIDS, in the form of either a separate policy document or specific references within broader employment policies, and by implementing at least one of the following within one year of signing:

Internally by:

- providing access to education on HIV/AIDS
- publicizing proven senior management commitment.

Externally to play our part in the community by:

- raising awareness of HIV/AIDS in the business community;
- actively and financially supporting Companies act!;
- supporting the work of the national AIDS Trust through sponsorship, donations or help in kind;
- providing practical assistance to agencies working with HIV/AIDS through help in kind, such as secondments (see Glossary) or funding.

Over 50 companies in the UK have signed up to Companies act! They include:

Barclays Bank	IBM
The Body Shop	The Independent
Bromley Hospitals NHS Trust	Levi Strauss & Co.
Calibre Films	Marks & Spencer
City of Cardiff	Midland Bank
English National Ballet	Saatchi & Saatchi
Glaxo Holdings	J. Sainsbury
HarperCollins	Sotheby's
Honeywell	Virgin Atlantic Airways

Training employees on prevention

In the USA, only 20 to 25 per cent of companies have developed training programs on HIV/AIDS. In the UK, approximately one-fifth of the Companies act! signatories have provided training. Polaroid has won a Corporate Conscience Award from the Council on Economic Priorities for its AIDS education programme. Established in 1987, the company's policy has been extended to employees in Australia, Brazil, Mexico, and New Zealand. The company has set up support groups for employees, as well as an AIDS information policy which provides referrals and counselling.

Increasingly, companies are utilizing internal publications to provide information to employees about prevention. Some companies are providing training on an annual basis, often on World AIDS Day. Some companies, such as The Body Shop, are utilizing a theater company to increase awareness about AIDS.

Develop strategies for continued employment

There is mutual advantage for both the employee and the company in keeping employees with HIV at work. The employee is able to maintain an income and relationships with work colleagues. A sense of purpose can also assist with preventing depression. The employer also gains by not having to hire and train additional staff. One approach used by employers is to allow people with HIV and AIDS-related illnesses to work from home.

The rise of AIDS and HIV grants employers the opportunity to provide leadership in one of the major crises of the century. For example, Companies act! encourages companies to use their economic leverage to pressure insurance companies to cover HIV and AIDS.

Develop community-wide programs

As companies develop their own internal programs for combating AIDS, discrimination and ignorance about the AIDS virus, these companies are finding opportunities to extend these programs into the community. Polaroid is a founding member of the New England Corporate Consortium for AIDS Education, and the company also encourages employees to volunteer in community organizations which assist people with HIV.

Fair trade and ethical investment

Fair trade

"FairTrade is a little flash of genius, a touch of human rights in a wholly unjust global trading system that exploits the weakest. Fair trade is simple enough: small-scale coffee producers are paid a guaranteed price, which is always higher than the international market and never drops below a set minimum. The producers deal directly with the buyers, and the first world consumer pays little more than 1 p (2 cents) per cup extra. It's the closest thing to hope there may be. Under this system, everyone wins."

John Vidal[127]

Fair trade is based on the principle of rewarding producers for their efforts. At present the world trade system fails to pay many producers a living wage for basic commodities like bananas, coffee, chocolate, peanuts and tea. Fundamental to the fair-trade movement is the fact that supermarket shoppers have a choice; they can choose to buy fairly traded products for reasons of ethics, quality, price or lifestyle. Consumers can make a difference. By rewarding producers at source and strengthening their position through direct trade, fair prices and the provision of credit, fair trade is seen as the best way of promoting development.

The development of countries like Brazil, India, China, Indonesia and Russia may have a momentum of its own, but other areas of the world in Africa and Latin America require affluent consumers to exert pressure on transnational corporations such as Nestlé, Unilever and Philip Morris. Exploitative child labor, health and safety and working practices are at the heart of the fair-trade movement, just as much as fair pay is for a day's work.

Coffee: a study in global economics, poverty and fair-trade initiatives

As the profiles of Cafédirect and Max Havelaar in this chapter show, coffee has become an important test of the market for fairly traded products. Through this product, and a few others, consumers around the world are being asked to understand how world trade works and to make an ethical choice about the brand of choice of coffee they drink. It is also hoped that they will try brands such as Cafédirect, and decide that they taste as good, if not better, than other brands.

The best way to explain how the trade in coffee works, and how world trade works, is by the three-point illustration from 1997 set out in Figure 4.1.[128]

Seventy per cent of total coffee production goes onto world markets controlled by a few large food transnationals. In 1995, the USA consumed 21.9 per cent, Germany 16.6 per cent, France 7.6 per cent, Japan 6.8 per cent and the UK 4.4 per cent.[129]

Cafédirect: a story of fair trade

Cafédirect was initiated in 1993 in the UK by four alternative trading organizations (ATOs): Oxfam, Traidcraft, Equal Exchange and Twin Trading. By 1996 it was able to claim that its coffee, both instant and ready ground, was available in 1,400 outlets in the UK, including most mainstream supermarkets. Cafédirect says it "buys coffee directly from growers' cooperatives, not from middlemen. So growers gain more influence, security and income."[130]

The comparison with the usual coffee case outlined in Table 4.7 is instructive: Cafédirect makes the following guarantees:[131]

● Green coffee is bought on internationally recognized fair-trade terms.
● A minimum fair price is paid of $1.26 / lb for arabica coffee beans, and $1.06 / lb (1996 prices) for robusta beans, however low the market falls.
● The price is guaranteed as 10 per cent over the market rate.
● Pre-payments up to 60 per cent of the minimum price are available to aid cash flow and help cut out middlemen.
● Only small-scale producers are involved where producers have control. No brokers are involved.

By the end of 1996, Cafédirect was able to announce that it was sourcing coffee from seven countries (Nicaragua, Costa Rica, Dominican Republic, Peru, Mexico, Uganda and Tanzania) involving 460,000 growers. Some 162 million cups of coffee in the UK had been fair-trade coffee since the launch in 1996. Cafédirect has a FairTrade Mark from FairTrade (see profile later in this chapter).

1 For every dollar or pound spent on coffee

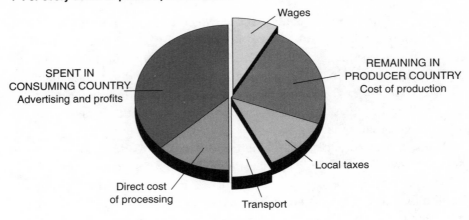

Wages

REMAINING IN
PRODUCER COUNTRY
Cost of production

SPENT IN
CONSUMING COUNTRY
Advertising and profits

Local taxes

Direct cost
of processing

Transport

2 Coffee sales in the UK

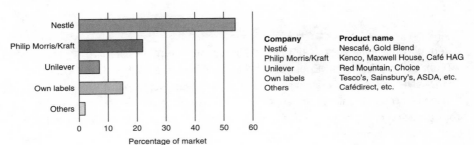

Company	Product name
Nestlé	Nescafé, Gold Blend
Philip Morris/Kraft	Kenco, Maxwell House, Café HAG
Unilever	Red Mountain, Choice
Own labels	Tesco's, Sainsbury's, ASDA, etc.
Others	Cafédirect, etc.

3 Coffee producers and the buyer

Producers	GNP per capita $	Coffee as % of total exports
Uganda	250	95
Colombia	1,200	56
Costa Rica	1,780	35
Brazil	2,540	10
Ivory Coast	790	25
Indonesia	500	4
Kenya	360	35
Buyers		
UK	$14,610/capita	4.4% of world consumption

Fig 4.1 How the coffee trade and world trade work (1997)

Max Havelaar: another success of fair trade

In just seven years, Max Havelaar has made fairly traded coffee available in 90 per cent of all supermarkets in The Netherlands, with 2.5 per cent of the market share. The coffee is sourced from 270 co-operatives in 18 countries throughout Africa and Latin America. Although it is best known for its coffee, Max Havelaar also provides fairly traded chocolate, cacao products and honey. These products are now also available in Belgium, Switzerland, Denmark, France and Luxembourg.

The Max Havelaar Foundation owns the quality mark that certifies that the products are fairly traded. The Foundation does not purchase or sell coffee or cocoa, rather the Foundation ensures that importers meet the following five criteria:

1 Products are purchased directly from small-farmer organizations.
2 A premium is paid to farmers.
3 A minimum price floor is established.
4 Farmers can receive advance payments for their harvest (up to 60 per cent).
5 Producers and importers work to develop long-term trading relationships.

According to the Foundation, "empowerment of the farmers is as important as a fair price for their products. Empowerment is more than just a higher standard of living. It is important that farmers develop a long-term perspective and that their resilience is strengthened. Their position . . . has to improve, resulting in more control over their own lives."

The director of the Max Havelaar Foundation tells a moving story about his work with an indigenous tribe in rural Mexico. "They had never met a white man before I arrived in their village. Nor had they ever seen their own reflection in a mirror. After years of producing coffee, they have greatly improved their standard of living. But wealth can cause change and conflict. Many villagers have bought televisions and now watch Brazilian soap operas. As a result, they are losing touch with their own rich cultural heritage."[132]

Visiting Bangladesh, one of the world's poorest countries, in September 1997, the UK government's Secretary of State for International Development, Claire Short, said that "fair trade is not just about types of coffee." The Ethical Trade Initiative (see profile later in this chapter) with support from her department and major retailers, meant that "fair trade will be taken onto a much bigger canvas. Ethical and sustainable business is good business." Using Bangladesh as an example Short said: "If we are to tackle poverty across the world, we must succeed in Bangladesh."[133]

Bangladesh has a population of 120 million and the highest recorded level of child malnutrition in the world. Some six million children under the age of 14 are estimated to be employed in factories and on the streets in

Bangladesh. The conundrum for the fair-trade movement was that boycotting goods made with exploitative child labor, as had happened with footballs and jeans, was not the answer, as this made children and their families even poorer.

One answer is to introduce global standards and codes of conduct which raise expectations on child labor and health and safety, and to make sure that workers in countries like Bangladesh receive enough money to allow their children to go to school. Only an educated workforce can compete in the global economy and help themselves to develop their own economy, one free from poverty and the need for development aid, and not vulnerable to manipulation by transnational corporations.

The Ethical Trading Initiative

The Ethical Trading Initiative (ETI) was established by the Monitoring and Verification Working Group, a forum composed of several development and campaigning organizations in the UK, including: the New Economics Foundation,[134] FairTrade (see profile overleaf), the World Development Movement, Oxfam, Christian Aid (see profile below), the Catholic Institute for International Relations, and Consumers International.

The aim of the ETI is to improve working conditions by developing a forum for discussion, analysis and training. The ETI is a process rather than a product, providing a common framework for addressing codes of conduct and monitoring. The Initiative hopes to provide a "road map" for companies seeking to develop best practice in the area. Training for auditors and conflict resolution are among the services the ETI hopes to provide.

The ETI has invited a wide group of UK-based companies and NGOs to participate in ongoing dialogues. Among the companies represented are J. Sainsbury and the Co-operative Wholesale Society. Save the Children, Action Aid and The Council on Economic Priorities[135] are also part of the ETI framework. Claire Short, the Secretary of State for International Development, has endorsed the Ethical Trading Initiative and her department has provided significant financial support.

Christian Aid's fair-trade campaign: how does your supermarket rate?

Christian Aid is campaigning for British supermarkets to give workers in developing countries a fairer deal. They are shaming supermarkets, through publicity, into changing their policies on fair trade. They are calling on all supermarkets to "adopt independently monitored codes of conduct guaranteeing minimum working conditions for their brand suppliers." In October 1997 their published, and well-advertised list of supermarket chains that had made serious moves in the right direction ranked the top ten:

1 Tesco
2 Safeway
3 Sainsbury
4 Co-op (Co-operative Wholesale Society)
5 Asda
6 Waitrose
7 Kwik Save
8 Somerfield
9 Morrisons
10 Marks & Spencer[136]

FairTrade

The objective of FairTrade (the organization based in London) is to alleviate poverty in developing countries by encouraging both industry and consumers to support fair trade. The organization was established in the UK by Christian Aid, CAFOD, New Consumer, Oxfam, the World Development Movement, and Traidcraft Exchange in 1992. It has developed standards that ensure that products carrying their FairTrade Mark meet minimum wage requirements, ensure adequate housing and guarantee minimum health, safety and environmental standards. FairTrade's terms of trading include: a minimum price, credit terms and a long-term trading commitment.

FairTrade checks that products meet these standards. In the UK, the FairTrade Mark has been awarded to several brands, allowing consumers to purchase fairly traded chocolate, coffee and tea. The majority of these products are available in UK's leading supermarkets. FairTrade has played a key role in research on fairly traded textiles, orange juice, bananas and flowers.

Fair trade coffee, Tikki Café, but not a brand having the FairTrade mark, is now available in the House of Commons. The seven founding organizations of FairTrade have called on their membership (a total of half a million) to ask for fairly traded coffee.

In April 1997, the Fair Trade Labelling Organization International was established to co-ordinate efforts throughout Europe on fair trade, including work by FairTrade and other groups in other countries. This body will set criteria and manage relationships with producers, allowing for greater transparency and co-operation throughout the European market.

FairTrade is working on several pilot projects with British companies, including Sainsbury's, the Co-operative Wholesale Society and Premier Beverages.[137] Together with companies, FairTrade is developing acceptable standards for each country and sector, accompanying company officials on joint monitoring visits to suppliers.

The Body Shop: are the fair-trade initiatives just cosmetic?

The Body Shop has a Fair Trade Department "to help create livelihoods, and to explore trade-based approaches to supporting sustainable development by sourcing ingredients and accessories direct from socially and economically marginalized producer communities."

The Fair Trade Department purchases products from around the world: Brazil-nut oil from Ghana and Brazil, jute containers and clay bowls from Bangladesh, Ghana-shea butter from Ghana, sisal from the Y'apetheti Producers' Association in Mexico City and paper products from Nepal. Many of these products are sourced from indigenous peoples and women's co-operatives, through the Community Trade Programme involving 35 suppliers in 20 countries.

The Body Shop has been criticized in the press for overstating the extent of its fairly traded products. It has subsequently undergone a very comprehensive social audit to measure the extent to which its policies and practices coincide, but measuring social impact is not always clear-cut. One of the possible measures is to demonstrate the extent to which The Body Shop purchases products at a premium from disadvantaged local communities. The Body Shop purchased 10 tons of a bean harvested in several different countries at $1,725 per ton, whereas the world price on the New York futures market ranged between $1,240 and $1,270.

According to the company's social-audit report:

> "One thing that stands out in this social audit process is the difficulty of measuring the intangibles. The experts try to do it, the development agencies try to do it, we have tried to do it. How do we measure human development? Where are the instruments that are capable of measuring the search for new awareness and greater strength in organisation? How can we determine where to plant the seed of greater equality so that it grows into something bigger and better? These are elements of development which defy statistics but which are clearly observable in the communities we have encountered along our journey."

As part of its social audit, The Body Shop received a great deal of feedback from the local communities where it sources materials, and published both positive and negative reactions. For example, according to members of the Nahnu tribe in Mexico:

> "In my community, every day the trust amongst the men and women increases. In the meetings they [men] were the only ones who talked. Now it seems that things are changing because it is us, the women who talk the most now. It is nice to see how the women are waking up after so many years of being asleep."

> "If The Body Shop withdrew and did not give us more work, the families and communities involved would be in serious trouble."

According to a member of the Santa Ana Pueblo:

> "The money is not substantial, although it does generate employment, both here and at other pueblos."[138]

Ethical investment

Linked to fair trade, another significant development since the 1960s has been the rise of a new form of investment. In it a wide range of non-financial concerns are taken into account: concern about the environment, human rights, social repercussions, working conditions and animal welfare, for example. While socially responsible investing first started in the 1960s, with the anti-Vietnam-war political protest movement, it soon gained importance as first tobacco and defense, then anti-apartheid and finally environmental issues, helped the movement gain momentum. It has now reached a point where total packaged ethical funds under management in the UK have increased by 26 per cent since 1994. Ethical investment only represents 1 per cent of all investment in the UK, but the issues involved are seen as indicators for business and management to be considered in future strategy. In other words, understanding ethical investment criteria is as good a way as any for senior managers to be aware of vulnerability to attack from pressure groups, NGOs and the media.

Ethical and green investment funds on the whole can be differentiated from conventional funds by the criteria that are used for making a decision to invest. In addition to the usual financial performance criteria, certain specifically chosen criteria can be used when assessing a company's suitability. On the whole, a fund may use negative criteria, positive criteria and/or active dialogue with companies.

Negative criteria

A set of criteria, which may include issues such as alcohol, animal testing, oppressive regimes, pornography and tropical hardwood, may be drawn up from which companies with interests in them, are excluded. Negative criteria vary from fund to fund, and on the whole it is up to the investor to decide which issues are important when drawing up an investment plan. The difficulties associated with negative screening are that companies included by default (i.e. those companies not excluded by the criteria) may still not be the sort of companies an ethical investor might wish to invest in, so a degree of laxity is present.

Positive criteria

The use of positive criteria encourages companies demonstrating commitment to a variety of issues such as community involvement, education/

Table 4.8 Examples of ethical-investment criteria in four funds

	NPI Global Care Unit Trust[139]	ABF Het Andere Beleggensfond	Community Growth Fund	Biogrond Beleggensfond: Triodos Bank
Specialist research	x		x	x
Independent committee	x		x	x
Geographical spread	International	International	South Africa	The Netherlands
Country of origin	UK	The Netherlands	South Africa	The Netherlands
Launch date	Aug. 1991	1991	1992	April 1990
Fund value	66.4 million		Rand 812 million	
Negative criteria				
Alcohol	x			
Animal testing	x			
Armaments	x			
Fur	x			
Gambling	x			
Genetic engineering	x			
Greenhouse gases	x			
Irresponsible marketing	x			
Meat/dairy production	x			
Mining	x			
Nuclear power	x			
Oppressive regimes	x			
Ozone layer	x			
Pesticides	x			
Pornography	x			
Road building	x			
Tobacco	x			
Tropical hardwood	x			
Water pollution	x			

Table 4.8 *cont.*

Positive criteria	NPI Global Care Unit Trust[139]	ABF Het Andere Beleggensfond	Community Growth Fund	Biogrond Beleggensfond: Triodos Bank
Benefit to animals	x			
Community involvement	x			
Education/training	x	x	x	
Job creation			x	
Participation of women		x		
Pay structures		x		
Working conditions		x		
Employment opportunities		x		
Shared decision making		x		
Effective corporate governance	x		x	
Energy conservation	x			
Good employee relations	x	x	x	
Health/safety equipment	x		x	
Healthcare services	x			
Mass transit systems	x			
Multimedia/telecommunications	x			
Policy statements/audit/transparency	x	x		
Pollution monitoring/control equipment	x			
Process-control equipment	x			
Progressive relations/strategy	x		x	
Recycling services	x			
Water management	x			
Sound environmental practices			x	
Environmental chain management		x		
Organic land				x

training, good employee relations, waste management and recycling services. This allows the investor, rather than excluding the undesirables, to indicate the types of companies it wishes to invest in, therefore, indicating a positive agreement with the companies' commitment.

Active dialogue

Some fund managers, when deciding which companies to include in the portfolio, may find organizations which nearly meet the investment criteria but not quite. By participating in an active dialogue with the company, there is encouragement for positive improvement, thereby effecting change.

The difference between ethical, green and environmental funds is generally in the criteria used for assessment, although there may be a degree of overlap. An important factor in ethical investment is the level of research used to investigate both potential companies and the criteria against which to rate them. Evidence of independent research, or use of a specifically selected in-house research team lend credence to the fund's reputation.

A selection of four funds is reviewed in Table 4.8 (see page 158), from the viewpoint of corporate responsibility. These four funds have been chosen to show the diversity of issues considered in ethical investment, and the use of negative and positive criteria. The list of criteria will prove useful to managers in understanding how some stakeholders may see their company, and where the company may be vulnerable. Have you, as a manager, thought about all these issues?

Definition of criteria used in the comparison of four ethical investment funds

Community involvement: Companies active in the community with programs which may include staff secondment, support of Business in the Community, the Per Cent Club, charitable giving and fund raising.

Education and training: Companies supplying education or training services to enhance the quality of life and opportunity in the workplace.

Healthcare services: Companies supplying medical equipment, specialist nursing services, care for the elderly or holistic therapies.

Health and safety equipment: Stricter legislation and corporate focus on employee safety has created a demand for equipment which can lessen the risk of industrial accidents and improve workplace conditions. We look for companies supplying specialist equipment or devices which have a health, safety or environmental application.

Good employee relations: Companies with good industrial relations records and policies which include, for example, measures to encourage employee participation, support for women and minorities and employee share-ownership programs.

Policy statements, audits and openness: Companies with clear policies and systems of accountability. For example, those which publish a statement of business ethics or a code of conduct, have environmental management systems (such as EMAS or ISO140001)[140] or conduct social audits and make them publicly available, and respond fully to external inquiries.

Progressive relationship and strategy: Companies which clearly explain their corporate strategy and its environmental and social implications. Companies which actively promote the interests of staff, such as maternity/paternity leave, counselling services, pension schemes or other welfare services; customers, for example those with eco-labelling of products; suppliers, such as those implementing audits for environmental performance and fair trade; and the public, such as those which contribute to community activities.

Effective corporate governance: Companies which demonstrate accountability to their investors and are seeking compliance with the recommendations of the Cadbury, Greenbury and Hampel Committees on corporate governance.

Benefits to the environment

Energy conservation: Companies engaged in the supply of energy conservation services such as domestic or industrial insulation, or electronic energy-efficiency devices.

Mass transit systems: Companies engaged in the provision of bus and rail services, or the manufacture of bicycles.

Multimedia and telecommunications: Companies which are directly involved in transforming the use of information, communication or ways of working, including developments in CD-ROMs, teleworking and mobile telephony.

Pollution monitoring/pollution-control equipment: Companies engaged in the manufacture, supply or operation of pollution-control equipment or monitoring devices.

Process-control equipment: Companies engaged in the manufacture or supply of efficiency-improvement devices which provide water, energy or materials savings.

Recycling services: Companies engaged in the collection and recycling of waste, or which use a high proportion of waste in their products.

Water management: Companies involved in the protection and provision of water supplies, or the provision of water-purification services or equipment.

Benefits to animals: Companies active in processing or retailing vegetarian foods. Companies developing alternative textiles to leather.

Negative criteria

See explanation above.

Alcohol: Avoidance of companies involved in the production of alcoholic drinks or of companies which generate more than 10 per cent of their turnover from its sale.

Gambling: Avoidance of companies with activity related to gambling, including the National Lottery and ownership or operation of betting shops, horse and greyhound racing tracks, licensed bingo halls, casinos or gaming clubs.

Irresponsible marketing: Avoidance of companies which have consistently had public complaints against them upheld by the Advertising Standards Authority (ASA) or which have irresponsibly marketed products, such as breast-milk substitutes, to developing countries.

Armaments: Avoidance of companies involved in the sale or production of strategic goods or services for military weapons or operations.

Oppressive regimes: Avoidance of companies with subsidiaries or associated interests which support the activities of oppressive regimes, or companies which use forced labor.

Pornography: Avoidance of companies which publish, print or distribute newspapers or magazines, or distribute films or videos, classed as pornographic.

Tobacco: Avoidance of companies which engage in activities related to the production of tobacco products or which generate more than 10 per cent turnover from tobacco sales.

Impact on the environment

Greenhouse gases: Avoidance of companies generating high emissions of carbon dioxide, the main greenhouse gas, including the extraction, refining or distribution of fossil fuels except natural gas; oil exploration and distribution; and fossil-fuel power stations which use coal or oil.

Mining: Avoidance of companies directly involved in mining or quarrying.

Nuclear power: Avoidance of companies which are involved in the uranium fuel cycle, the treatment of radioactive waste, or the supply of nuclear-related equipment or services for constructing or running nuclear plant or facilities.

The ozone layer: Avoidance of companies which make or sell ozone-depleting chemicals (dates have yet to be set for their phasing-out).

Pesticides: Avoidance of companies which manufacture, store, wholesale or retail pesticide products in the UK which are on the Department of the Environment's "Red List," or which have been restricted in five or more countries, or those which have been implicated in incidents by the Health and Safety Executive.

Road builders: Avoidance of companies generating more than 10 per cent of turnover from road building.

Tropical hardwood: Avoidance of companies active in the extraction, clearing, processing or import of tropical hardwood products.

Water pollution: Avoidance of companies consistently exceeding discharge consents.

Impact on animals

Animal testing: We avoid companies which manufacture pharmaceuticals, medicines, vitamins, cosmetics, soaps or toiletries, unless they make it clear that their products and ingredients are not tested on animals.

Fur: Avoidance of companies involved in the sale or manufacture of animal-fur products.

Meat/dairy production: Avoidance of any companies involved in the production or processing of meat products, and meat/poultry-related products, including dairy products and eggs, or whose primary activity involves their sale.

Genetic engineering: Avoidance of companies whose primary activity is research into life forms involving the transfer of genes across species and alteration of plant or animal genes for commercial use.

Banking with a conscience

Here are two examples of companies in the financial sector; one is a British bank and the other is a Canadian credit union, which both operate on an ethical basis. Both are successful, both have seen an increase in customers, both are being emulated in small ways by the major banks. Neither the Co-operative Bank nor VanCity has suddenly arrived on the scene to benefit from the new global concern for social and environmental issues; they are both building on a heritage of responsible banking. Banks like them, and others like SBN in Denmark and Triodos in The Netherlands, have shown that it is possible to operate ethically in the global trading system and offer investors a choice about how their money is used.

The Co-operative Bank: investing with a conscience

The Co-operative Bank surveyed its customers to assess their ethical priorities. Over 70,000 customers responded, and thus was born the bank's ethical policy, based on the founding principles of the bank.

Established in 1872, the Co-operative Bank, often referred to as The Co-op, is part of the co-operative movement. With 130 outlets, it operates the largest telephone banking service in the UK. The bank is considered to be a major innovator, having been the first to introduce free banking and to pay interest on current accounts (checking accounts). In 1995, pre-tax profits totalled £36.7 million, ($58.72 million), 9.2 per cent higher than the previous year.

Why did the Co-operative Bank develop its ethical niche? In the early 1990s, it was losing market share. To survive it needed to:

● develop an identity;
● increase awareness;
● increase customer loyalty, and;
● expand customer base.

The brand map told the story well:

● Big Four[141] – considered arrogant.
● Co-operative Bank – considered downmarket.
● Regional banks – too small.

The company faced three options:

1 Emulate the Big Four.
2 Concentrate regionally.
3 Invent a new brand.

The marketing staff knew that it would be impossible to emulate the larger banks at home and abroad, the Co-op could never be like Lloyds or Citibank. Nor did the Co-op want to be a regional bank. The team decided on option three and developed a new kind of brand. They would "brand the truth," not just extract value, but add value. Information about its customer base reinforced the decision. The bulk of the Co-op's personal customers was in the caring professions, teachers and health workers, as a result of its historical legacy and place in the market. Forty per cent of the general public were prepared to pay a premium for ethical products, and of these consumers, a majority were young and well-off.

Co-op Bank's ethical stance emerged from a business problem and a marketing opportunity. While the bank does sometimes have to turn away business for ethical reasons, its ethical stance attracts customers. One in ten of its customers made a decision to bank with the Co-op because of its ethical stance. The Co-op Bank has also worked with some companies it invests in to show them alternatives to using rainforest wood or to intensive factory farming.[142]

The Co-operative Bank's ethical policy

Following extensive consultation with customers, with regard to how their money should and should not be invested, the Bank's position is that:

● it will not invest in or supply financial services to any regime or organization which oppresses the human spirit, takes away the rights of individuals or manufactures any instrument of torture;
● it will not finance or in any way facilitate the manufacture or sale of weapons to any country which has an oppressive regime;
● it will actively seek and support the business of organizations which promote the concept of "Fair Trade," that is trade which regards the welfare and interest of local communities around the world;
● it will encourage business customers to take a pro-active stance on the environmental impact of their own activities, and will invest in companies and organizations that avoid repeated damage of the environment;
● it will actively seek out individuals, commercial enterprises and non-commercial organizations that avoid repeated damage of the environment;
● it will actively seek out individuals, commercial enterprises and non-commercial organizations which have a complementary ethical stance;
● it will welcome suppliers whose activities are compatible with its Ethical Policy;

- it will not speculate against the pound using either its own money or that of its customers. It believes it is inappropriate for a British clearing bank to speculate against the British currency and the British economy using deposits provided by their British customers and at the expense of the British tax payer;
- it will try to ensure that its financial services are not exploited for the purpose of money laundering, drug trafficking or tax evasion by the continued application and development of its successful internal monitoring and control procedures;
- it will not provide financial services to tobacco product manufacturers;
- it will not invest in any business involved in animal experimentation for cosmetic purposes;
- it will not support any person or company using exploitative factory farming methods;
- it will not engage in business with any farm or other organization engaged in the production of animal fur;
- it will not support any organization involved in blood sports, which involve the use of animals or birds to catch, fight or kill each other, for example, fox hunting and hare coursing;
- in addition, there may be occasions when the Bank makes decisions on specific business involving ethical issues not included in this policy.

See also profile of the Co-operative Bank in Chapter 5.

VanCity

VanCity is Canada's largest credit union with US$4,800 million in assets and over 230,000 members. Established in 1946, Vancouver City Savings Credit Union provides financial products and services. Among the financial services it now provides are direct banking services via the Internet.

VanCity's mission statement:

> *"Vancouver City Savings Credit Union is a democratic, ethical and innovative provider of financial services to its members. Through strong financial performance, we serve as a catalyst for the self-reliance and economic well-being of our membership and community."*

The management philosophy contains commitments to:

- a superior service delivery through an entrepreneurial and innovative approach and a commitment to well-trained, knowledgeable, friendly, fast and efficient staff;
- financial soundness and stability through adequate capitalization, prudent lending and risk management;
- a responsibility to members through being able to respond to current and future financial needs;
- a responsibility to the wider community through investments in grassroots community

activity, staff involvement and corporate financial support, as well spreading the word about the role of credit unions in community economic development;

● the role of ethics in our culture through integrity, professionalism, equity and democracy, which promote personal growth and development and a team approach to management.

VanCity is a signatory to the CERES principles[143] and will only support companies that are socially responsible. The *Ethical Criteria* have evolved through consultations inside and outside the company. The *Criteria* for choosing funds to invest in covers:

● progressive individual and employee relations (including adherence to employment equity, labor safety practices and child labor laws);

● operate within countries and regions that support equal opportunity and adhere to non-discriminatory hiring practices;

● derive a majority of their income from non-tobacco-related products;

● engage in civilian, non-military activities;

● utility companies that derive their income from non-nuclear forms of energy;

● adhere to environmental regulations and use technologies or products that are environmentally responsible.

During 1996, VanCity reinvested US$2,508,000 or 7 per cent of its consolidated net earnings, after income taxes and distribution to its members, in the local community. Funding included:

● a community partnership and donations program for projects that promoted economic self-reliance, ecological responsibility and social justice, self-reliance loans.

Access to credit was extended to very small business starting up, based on character not assets or cash flow and peer group lending based on groups of individuals forming teams to apply for loans.

The arms trade

The sale of arms is an issue that features in the list of criteria for ethical investment, but it has also become an issue important to those who might not previously have looked critically at one of the world's largest industries. When Diana, Princess of Wales decided to support the Red Cross's anti-personnel mine campaign, she managed to focus huge media attention on one aspect of the global arms trade.

Despite the fact that the arms trade employs thousands of people around the world, opponents argue that it takes resources away from work which could be more productive, such as in providing clean water, hospitals or schools in developing countries; mass transit systems; research into alternatives to fossil fuels, cures for cancer or AIDS in developed countries.

The world's top arms manufacturers include the USA, the UK, Russia, France and Germany. Apart from manufacturing arms for their own use, they also sell weapons to their allies and to many other countries. This includes selling weapons to countries that have little respect for human rights and whose records have been documented and condemned for many years by organizations such as the United Nations, Amnesty International and Human Rights Watch. Countries that have been condemned for human-rights abuses, but who are still supplied by the main weapons-manufacturing countries, include Saudi Arabia, China and Malaysia.

A change of ethical policy in the UK?

With the UK being the second largest exporter of arms, Britain's Foreign Secretary, Robin Cook, announced a new ethical basis for Britain's arms sales in 1997. He said that the fundamental human rights that had to be respected were:

- the right to life;
- freedom from arrest without due process;
- freedom from torture;
- the right to freedom of thought;
- the right to freedom of religious practice;
- the right to vote for one's government.

Echoing the US Constitution, he said that the British government held these rights to be self-evident: "These are rights we claim for ourselves and which we therefore have a duty to demand for those who do not enjoy them."[144] However, Britain and the other arms exporters sell weapons to countries with systematic human-rights abuses.

In cutting arms sales, any country is faced with the paradox that President Ronald Reagan addressed in 1981 when he sanctioned the sale of high-technology arms sales to South America: "Our policy must reflect the world as it is, not as we would want it to be."[145] The reality that Britain faces in cutting arms sales is that Britain's $8.25 billion annual exports support 90,000 jobs directly and 415,000 jobs indirectly in the UK, and that if Britain does not supply weapons, other less discriminating countries will happily fill the gap to boost their economies.[146]

The business of arms sales

Here are three examples of arms sales featuring Saudi Arabia and Indonesia and the sale of anti-personnel mines worldwide.

Anti-personnel landmines: the Red Cross/Red Crescent campaign

Banning the use, production or stockpiling of anti-personnel mines has been a Red Cross / Red Crescent campaign for many years and has received worldwide attention. According to the US-based group Human Rights Watch, in 1997 those US companies which agreed to stop being involved in some part of the production of landmines include Motorola, Hughes Aircraft, Olin Ordnance, Kemet, Microsemi, AVX, and Dyno Nobel. Those companies which had refused this call include General Electric, Alliant Tech-systems, Lockheed Martin, Raytheon, and Thiokol.[147]

The Canadian government initiated the Ottawa Treaty, which in 1997 was signed by 120 countries, including two of the world's largest arms suppliers, France and Germany. Banning anti-personnel mines has been opposed by the USA and Japan on the ground that their use is necessary in areas such as the border between North and South Korea. The British government, while generally supporting the ban, has argued for delay in clearing landmines laid by Argentina in The Falklands. Britain has also argued that its anti-runway mine is not targeted at people and that their priorities are Cambodia and Angola.

There are estimated to be some 100 million active landmines waiting to go off embedded in the ground in some 70 countries, of which 20 million have been in the Sinai desert for the last 25 years, and others in Cambodia and Vietnam. According to Frank Ryding, a Red Cross doctor, 2,000 people a month are killed or maimed by mines, many of them children.

If the world can agree to ban anti-personnel landmines, can it not work towards the banning of other anti-personnel weapons which may or may not be as indiscriminate?

Businesses not involved in arms manufacturing can help. In September 1997 when Ted Turner, founder of Cable News Network (CNN), offered the United Nations $1 billion he specified that his chosen causes were children, refugees and landmines.[148]

Flogging weapons in Saudi Arabia

In September 1997, Britain's largest arms sale was threatened by abuses of human rights in Saudi Arabia. Under the Al Yamamah arms deal, negotiated by Prime Minister Thatcher in 1985, Britain agreed to supply $66,000 million worth of arms to Saudi Arabia in return for oil. The main beneficiaries of the deal are the arms manufacturers British Aerospace, Vosper Thorneycroft, and Vickers Defence Systems, but other industries also benefit from Britain's trade with Saudi Arabia including transport, power generation and telecommunications.

Two British nurses were found guilty in a Saudi Arabian court of murdering their colleague, Yvonne Gilford. One of the nurses was sentenced to be flogged 500 times in public, and the other to be publicly beheaded. Outrage in the British and international media caused British Aerospace's shares to fall sharply and threatened Britain's lucrative trade with the Gulf kingdom. As one British newspaper said: "(Saudi Arabia) has provided a rich gravy train for British industry, especially arms manufacturers, and anything which threatens to upset that causes alarm in the City of London."[149]

This case highlights both the problems of world trade and how countries and companies operate within their own codes of conduct. If countries only allowed trade with like-valued countries, much world trade would cease. The question also remains as to how much leverage business can put on countries to operate in accordance with the UN Declaration of Human Rights. Certainly, in the case of Saudi Arabia, human-rights abuses are common and well-documented.

Arming Indonesia

In 1975, Indonesia illegally occupied the former Portuguese colony of East Timor. For two decades the military government, led since 1966 by General Suharto, has systematically repressed and tortured all those who have opposed its occupation.

In 1994, the US government stated that it would no longer sell small arms, including rifles, and crowd-control equipment to Indonesia. According to Amnesty International, British companies continue to supply such weapons for use against civilians including the MP5 sub-machine gun, designed in Germany but manufactured in Britain.[150] In 1996, Germany led arms exports to Indonesia with sales of $342 million, followed by Britain with sales of $186 million and the USA with sales of $6 million.[151] The main beneficiary of Britain's arms sales is British Aerospace, through the Hawk fighter aircraft. Many of these weapons are used against the pro-democracy movement, which is upholding the fundamental rights enshrined in the UN Declaration of Human Rights.

Following the unveiling of its "ethical foreign policy" in September 1997, the British government announced a rejection of export licenses for a limited range of arms equipment worth just $1.65 million, including armored personnel carriers and sniper rifles to Indonesia. The reason given was that these items would be used for internal oppression. Amnesty International has called for a complete ban on the supply of lethal training equipment by the British Ministry of Defence to Indonesia and an end to the export of machine guns, surveillance equipment, water cannons and armored personnel carriers.

Possible solutions

The solution may lie in the strategies being discussed in Washington and adopted in London of linking aid budgets and arms sales to provide carrots and sticks which force arms purchasers to change their behavior. Britain's Department for International Development (DfID) is also trying to target overseas aid directly at non-governmental and civil rights groups, to bypass corrupt, illegitimate governments. As a member of the UN's Security Council, Britain is also intent on enlarging the Council and using its weight in UN agencies such as the World Bank and the International Monetary Fund to link economic development to social and ethical development. Secretary of State for International Development, Clare Short, said in May 1997: "We want to see a global moral community where economic endeavour goes hand in hand with accountable government, the rule of law and strong civil society."[152]

Controlling arms sales

Amnesty International has suggested specific mechanisms for controlling arms sales:

- new arms and security export controls based on human-rights assessments
- a public register of all arms exports
- the inclusion of clauses on human rights in contracts for end-users.[153]

In September 1997 the UK's Foreign Secretary, Robin Cook, supported by Lionel Jospin, the French Prime Minister, proposed the establishment of a European code of conduct to regulate the arms trade. This would require the setting up of the mechanisms advocated by Amnesty International, if initially only on a European basis. This would certainly help prevent the sale of torture equipment to countries such as China and Saudi Arabia.

Tobacco
· · · · · · · · · · · · ·

"Nicotine is an acute poison."
British-American Tobacco

The above statement comes from an internal document written by scientists at British-American Tobacco (BAT) in the 1970s who were looking at commercial alternatives to cigarettes. It was made public on 16 February 1998 in Minnesota, when the state was seeking to recover healthcare costs from tobacco companies.[154]

● Tobacco-related illnesses are the number one cause of death in the USA.

US Center for Disease Control

● Second-hand smoke is responsible for the deaths of 3,000 Americans per year.

US Environmental Protection Agency

● 200 million people of the next generation worldwide will die from smoking.

World Health Organization

The statistics above on tobacco-related illnesses speak for themselves as a cause of premature death, but things are changing, for there has been a major alteration in how smoking and the tobacco industry are perceived. A major example of this change is the 1996 decision by the American Medical Association to encourage investors to divest from tobacco. This campaign focuses on 13 company stocks and the 1,474 mutual funds that hold tobacco stocks.[155] In the USA, 23 states have filed lawsuits against tobacco companies in an effort to reclaim the funds government has spent on medical care, estimated at $50 billion per year. For Florida alone, the cost to the government of smoking-related illnesses is $12.3 billion.[156]

INFACT, a Boston-based citizens' group, has encouraged a boycott of the tobacco industry. INFACT criticizes tobacco companies for marketing cigarettes to teenagers and children through the use of cartoon characters and by giving away free samples at rock concerts and sporting events.

The big tobacco concerns, however, have been under siege since one of the smaller companies, Ligget Group, reached a compensation settlement with a clutch of state governments that had been suing it to recover the extra health costs with which they say smoking has burdened the public purse. To meet the growing threat, the industry has set aside a compensation fund of $300 billion.[157]

It is not only happening in the United States. SPP, one of Sweden's largest insurers with assets worth more than $30 billion and a four per-cent stake in Swedish Match, the cigarette manufacturer with over 50 per cent of the market share, is seeking assurances from the tobacco company. These include proving that it is working on less harmful cigarettes and avoiding marketing campaigns targeted at young people.[158]

One charge made against the tobacco industry is that it is increasingly marketing tobacco products to the poor in developing countries. With the overall number of smokers in the USA falling, tobacco companies are turning to eastern Europe, Asia, Latin America and the emerging African nations. According to Barbara Zolty, smoking analyst of the World Health Organisation, "Africa is one of the areas now being targeted by the multi-nationals," a view confirmed by a newly arrived corporate advertising executive who stated, "The market (in Africa) is growing hugely. Tobacco companies have nowhere to go, with legislation in their own backyards." And one authoritative report has confirmed that Jeeps emblazoned with the Marlboro logo and other tobacco brand names have turned up in African forests, where even the Coca-Cola Company is rare.

There are other accusations, too. In 1997, the *New York Times* ran a story linking tobacco companies with smuggling operations. One-quarter of the cigarettes sold in foreign markets are filtered through smuggling networks which evade taxes. The result is a significant loss of revenues, estimated at $16 billion per year.[159]

The power of the tobacco concerns and their lobbyists (such as the former British Prime Minister, Margaret Thatcher) should not be underestimated, but the tide of opinion is now all the opposite way. A familiar site now in city precincts during business hours is the small group of smokers puffing away together, ostracized from their place of work by health and safety decrees, not unlike adherents of some obscure sect whose time has passed.

Animal welfare and protection

Interest in animal welfare is growing rapidly in many countries in the North (see "North–South dialogue" in Appendix 2: Glossary). The concern ranges from the rights of animals to live humane lives, to food quality and safety to the protection of endangered species.

In Britain, Europe and the USA[160] bovine spongiform encephalopathy (BSE, or mad cow disease) has put the spotlight on the meat-processing industry, raising concerns over food safety and animal welfare. In Hong Kong and China, one million chickens were slaughtered when it was suspected that they carried a deadly infection. Both mad cow disease and Chinese chickens have educated the public, and business, on supply-chain management, as they have involved tracing the infections back to their sources.

The trade in protected species highlights the making of profit from animals thought to be exotic or having special properties, and the testing of cosmetics and medicines on animals is an issue that is high on the political agenda in some countries, but irrelevant in others.

- Ninety-three per cent of adults in the USA believe that animal pain should be reduced as much as possible, even if the animals are going to be slaughtered.[161]
- Fifty per cent of shoppers in the UK say that their purchasing decisions are influenced by the conditions under which animals are maintained.[162]
- Two-thirds of UK adults would like to see improved conditions for animals, with seven out of ten willing to pay more for meat if farm animals are treated more humanely. Forty-two per cent are willing to pay 50 pence (70 cents) more for a pack of meat costing £2 ($3.25).[163]

Welfare of farm animals

In response to growing consumer concern over animal welfare, various food retailers are adopting codes of conduct. McDonald's now requires its suppliers to adhere to humane standards.

What is the business case for respecting animal welfare, other than consumer pressure? According a report by the Council on Economic Priorities, industry experts are noticing a correlation between animal welfare and food safety when companies require suppliers to meet standards. Just as standards for human rights tend to improve quality, animal-welfare standards send a powerful message to suppliers: we care and if you want our business you should care too.

Humane treatment of livestock: Hormel and Land O'Lakes

Both Hormel, a major US meat producer and Land O'Lakes, a major US butter manufacturer have developed codes of conduct. Hormel Foods Corporation has a policy for suppliers which requires that all animals be treated humanely: "Any part of the marketing chain not complying with this policy will be excluded from doing business with HFC."[164]

In 1991, Land O'Lakes developed an Animal Welfare Statement:

"Land O'Lakes promotes humane treatment of animals by all segments of the livestock industry – producers, handlers, and processors – and works with a coalition from within and outside the livestock industry in developing sound animal care guidelines."[165]

Animal testing

"To make sure a new shampoo or shower gel doesn't sting, it is squirted into the eyes of animals. Rabbits are preferred because they cannot produce enough tears to wash away the irritants.

Why are these tests that started over 50 years ago allowed to continue, when up to 8,000 cosmetic ingredients are already known to be safe? Do we really need more?"

British Union for the Abolition of Vivisection

Each year in Europe 30,000 animals die as a result of cosmetic testing. The British Union for Abolition of Vivisection (BUAV) has developed an international standard for certifying that companies do not test on animals. Over 100 companies have agreed to these standards, among some of the most well-known in the USA are: Tom's of Maine, John Paul Mitchell Systems and Kiss My Face; and in the UK: The Body Shop, and supermarket chains Sainsbury's and Tesco. A number of German companies have also signed on.

Public pressure to ban animal testing has become so intense that the issue is being taken up by the European Union. The European Parliament has agreed a ban on animal-tested cosmetics to be enacted in 1998. The ban has since been postponed by the European Commission.

Animal testing: Tom's of Maine

"Tom's of Maine makes a full line of natural care products which are free of animal ingredients and which are tested for safety without using animals. In formulating our toothpastes, deodorants, and other products we make an effort to choose simple, naturally derived ingredients which have a long history of safe use."

Tom's of Maine is a US-based company whose products are also available in the UK. It has a clear policy on animal testing and makes the following points:

- While Tom's only uses natural products, many cosmetic ingredients have been thoroughly tested for safety, and the US Food and Drug Administration (FDA) has a list of "generally recognized as safe" (GRAS) substances. There is no need to repeat these tests on humans or animals.
- Animal testing is not always an accurate indicator of toxicity, carcinogenicity or irritancy in humans.
- There are alternatives to animal testing, such as using *in vitro* testing procedures with cell and tissue cultures.
- The company has supported the introduction of legislation to promote alternatives to animal testing in many US states.
- The company received the National Anti-Vivisection Society's highest honor in 1992 in recognition of its leadership and compassion in helping the public to adopt a cruelty-free lifestyle.

Tom's of Maine is a values-based company which has grown through niche marketing of natural care products. It is a company with a loyal customer base: people buy because they believe not only in the issues, but also because of the quality of the product. The issue of animal testing is only one reason why Tom's has succeeded. It also markets its products on their natural ingredients, all of which are well labelled. In this case, Tom's scores in terms of corporate citizenship for having put a number of societal concerns at the heart of the business: disclosure and openness, natural ingredients, lifestyle and animal testing.

The RSPB: over 100 years old and 1 million members

The Royal Society for the Protection of Birds (RSPB) is Europe's largest wildlife conservation charity. It was formed in 1889 in an embryonic form, and published its first report in 1891. It has over a million members, and takes particular action for wild birds and the environment in a number of different ways.

The YOC (Young Ornithologists Club) for juniors and RSPB *Phoenix* for teenagers (the only environmental club in Britain exclusively for teenagers) make up over 180,000 members, which, with the support of member groups and school and community groups, make significant contact with a new generation of society.

The RSPB operates on a number of different levels. It relies almost entirely on the support of its membership to finance conservation work: in 1995/6 this generated £12 million ($19.8m) in subscriptions; £9.5 million ($15.6m) in legacies; and £6 million ($9.9m) in business support, charitable trusts and grants. Grant income nearly doubled to £3.2 million ($5.28m), due to contributions from the Heritage Lottery Fund.

The money is spent on a variety of activities. Informing and educating the public is particularly important, through its members' magazine, *Birds*, and through the junior magazine, *Bird Life*. Volunteers – over 7,000 every year – assist in running programs for children, and local RSPB groups organize 5,000 outdoor trips and indoor meetings every year.

Managing nature reserves plays a large part of the RSPB's work. Throughout the UK, 97,000 hectares are covered, safeguarding sites of conservation importance and protecting the habitats of 30 of the 36 most rare or threatened birds in the UK. The RSPB also manages lowland wet grassland and coastal lagoons, and campaigns to safeguard the remaining 1 per cent of Scottish pinewoods.

Detailed studies of species and biological and economic research and monitoring are used to campaign and advise key decision makers, and policy reports and comment papers range from protecting the marine environment to forestry.

On an international basis, the RSPB has helped to develop BirdLife International conservation projects worldwide, funding work in Europe, the Middle East, Africa and Asia. They work extensively in Europe influencing policy by briefing government and EU officials, promoting solutions and changes to UK and EU legislation.

Education

As issues of corporate social responsibility become an increasingly important part of business life, there are a growing number of organizations which are providing education and training to managers and entrepreneurs, as short executive courses, or as complements to university-based management and business degrees. They are also producing materials which can be used as part of in-house management development programs. Many MBA programs now offer elective courses on environmental management and business ethics. Several leading business schools – such as Harvard and Wharton in the USA, and London and Manchester in the UK – have established academic posts and associated research programs in business ethics. There are also courses which are moving beyond these to consider broader issues of sustainability and corporate citizenship.

What follows is an illustrative selection, from a fast-developing area (for full address details, see Appendix 3).

USA

The Business Enterprise Trust

A non-profit organization created to highlight and promote the study of good business practices. The trust makes an annual award to outstanding companies and individuals, and produces video documentaries, business-school cases and educational materials to illustrate how sound management and social vision can result in business success.

Center for Corporate Community Relations at Boston College

A non-profit membership association serving corporations committed to community involvement and corporate social responsibility. Services include professional development, custom research and information services, and an annual International Leaders' Conference.

Ethics Resource Center (ERC)

The Ethics Resource Center is a non-profit, non-partisan educational organization whose vision is an ethical world. Its mission is to serve as a catalyst to improve the ethical practices of individuals and organizations from the classroom to the boardroom. The organization fulfils its mission through three distinct areas of expertise: as a leader in the fields of organizational/business ethics consulting; as a provider and facilitator of character education programmes; and as an ethics information clearing-house.

World Business Academy (WBA)

A research and educational institution that engages the business community in a better understanding and practice of the new role of business as an agent for social transformation. The WBA delivers self-learning educational resources, and conducts research projects, forums and seminars in the areas of corporate social responsibility, leadership, and the development of human potential at work.

Canada

Human Rights Research and Education Center

Headed by Professor Errol Mendes, the Center operates a range of programs, corporate round tables, research and publications, in the belief that university-based centres can act to bridge the mechanism between the corporate community and the public sector/civil society. It offers a program on business ethics and stakeholder relations.

UK

New Academy of Business

The New Academy of Business was founded in 1995 by Anita Roddick, CEO of The Body Shop International. It is an independent educational body, whose mission is not to act as a "corporate university" for the company which brought it to life, but to help to chart a path towards business practice which is both profitable and part of building a just and sustainable world.

The New Academy's work falls into four main themes:

1 The challenge of globalization – developing international trade in a way that also enhances social justice and human rights.

2 The need to protect our environment and pursue sustainable development.

3 The responsibility of business towards its own local and national communities.

4 The development of creative and humane workplaces.

Together with high-quality business management, these themes form a leadership agenda for the future, which the New Academy promotes through a range of courses and activities, which include:

- a master's degree – the M.Sc. in Responsibility and Business Practice, developed and taught in partnership with the School of Management, University of Bath. This is a part-time programme, run over two years, for experienced managers, entrepreneurs and educators;

- an Innovation Network – linking together companies to act as a forum for the research, development and sharing of best practice, and as a source of information to others;

- learning sets for managers seeking to adopt a profit-with-principles approach to business;

- courses of social and environmental responsibility in business for MBA students on university programs;

- management development programs tailored to the needs of particular client organizations, from senior executives to young activists;

- research, publications, conference papers and teaching materials.

Through these activities, the New Academy seeks to promote individuals and their employers to build a positive role for business in relation to wider society, and at the same time to encourage business educators to think creatively about the skills, knowledge and awareness needed by tomorrow's business leaders.

Ashridge Centre for Business and Society

Situated within Ashridge Management College, the Centre conducts research into the link between corporate competitiveness and accountability to stakeholders, and the role of business as a stakeholder in society.

BP Centre for Corporate Citizenship, Warwick University Business School

Established in 1996, its mission is to promote good corporate citizenship through active involvement with companies, research and teaching. Corporate citizenship is defined as understanding and managing as positively as possible a company's external influences for the benefit of both itself and society as a whole on society

The Netherlands

The European Institute for Business Ethics

Established in 1994 at Nijenrode University, the Institute is a joint venture between the University and the European Business Ethics Network. It aims to produce high-quality teaching, research and consulting which is relevant to the European business community, and which enhances ethical awareness, assesses progress and outcomes, and increases ethical accountability.

● MANAGEMENT EXERCISES ●

1 Dilemma: alcopops

In 1995, several British brewers introduced a new range of alcoholic drink, targeted at younger drinkers. The drinks are as intoxicating as strong beer, but are flavoured to taste like soft drinks such as lemonade and cherry soda – hence the name "alcopop." The labels on the bottles were designed to appeal to young people, carrying cartoon characters and bright colors, and have humorous names; the two leading brands were "Hoopers Hootch," produced by Bass, and "Two Dogs," produced by cider-makers Merrydown. The product was a great success, and commanded a market in the UK worth around $578 million a year.

▶

However, a problem emerged. Although alcopops were aimed at drinkers in the age range of 25 to 35 years old, it became apparent that they were very appealing to under-age drinkers. Teenagers liked their fruity flavours and sweetness, as well as the bottle designs, and parents became very concerned that their children were prey to a cynical marketing ploy by brewers. Concern was expressed that people might drink alcopops unknowingly, thinking they were drinking a soft drink. The newspapers carried stories of drunken children as young as 11 or 12 being found wandering the streets carrying bottles of alcopops. The issue was widely debated on television, radio and in the newspapers.

Brewers responded that their product was a legal one, appealing to a niche market of younger drinkers bored by the taste and image of more traditional beers and ciders. They were not responsible, they said, if these drinks were illegally sold to under-age young people.

In response to the media furore, a few national supermarket chains decided to refuse to stock alcopops, and some public houses removed them from their stock. Sales in the first part of 1997 fell by around 11 per cent as a result, but the brewers are confident that a buoyant market remains.

The appearance, packaging and taste of alcopops make them seem fun and fashionable, and appeal to children who would not otherwise be interested in alcohol.

(i) Should brewers produce drinks specifically designed to appeal to young people?

(ii) Should such products be openly available in supermarkets and corner stores, where teenagers will see the eye-catching labels, and where they may not have too much trouble getting past the busy check-out assistant without being challenged about their age?

(iii) Should retailers take an independent decision on this, and refuse to sell alcopops, even though they may lose some business, and possibly come under pressure from the suppliers, or is it up to parents to exercise control over their children?

2 Dilemma: employment

You run a small business producing children's clothes, which employs 15 people. Most of them have been with you since you started the company five years ago, and have families which depend on the wages they earn. You take your responsibilities as an employer very seriously.

When you had a sudden rush of orders the summer before last, you took on a new member of staff on a two-year fixed-term contract. She has turned out to have a poor sickness record, with frequent and unpredictable short absences, and an uneven temper – although you know that she has difficult home circumstances, with three young children. Until recently, when she entered a new relationship, she has been bringing up the children alone.

▶

Her contract is due to expire within a few weeks, and she has come to you asking for it to be renewed. But you are worried: if you renew the contract, you will have employed her continuously for more than two years, and she will become entitled to full employment protection under UK law. Your profitability is only just acceptable at the moment, and you are under pressure from cheap foreign imported clothes, which means you really cannot increase your prices.

Your margins are very narrow. What will happen, you wonder, if she were to go sick for more than a few days, or even worse, if she were to get pregnant and want to take maternity leave? The loss of production this would cost you could be critical, and could threaten the viability of the whole company. What about the jobs of the other employees, all of whom desperately need this work too? The consequences for them could be desperate. In many ways you would be safeguarding their futures better if you let this person go, and took on someone new on a temporary basis. The right thing to do is obviously to offer her another contract – but is that fair on the other workers?

3 Dilemma: HIV in the kitchen

You run a busy restaurant in the city center. Many of your customers by day are office workers, who call in for sandwiches and salads for their lunch. In the evening you cater for people who are going to the movies or to shows. You pride yourself on providing good nutritious food and excellent, fast service. Most of your staff have been with you since you opened up, about three years ago, which is unusual in an industry characterized by casual contracts and high turnover. You consider this stability to have played a major part in your being able to assure quality and consistency to your customers.

Now one of your chefs has come to you, and told you, in confidence, that he has discovered he is HIV positive. He is very distressed, and you have been doing what you can to listen to him and reassure him, but another thought is also troubling you – should you let him go? It can only be a matter of time before the news leaks out. What effect will his presence have on the other staff? This is an environment in which kitchen knives are used and occasionally someone gets cut, despite safety precautions and good attention to hygiene. Suppose the other staff feel unsafe in this environment, and begin to look for other positions? It could seriously disrupt your way of working and affect your customer service. Do the staff, in any case, have a right to know if they are working with someone who has been tested positive? As a good employer, what is your responsibility? How can you be fair to the staff, and at the same time be responsible towards the chef in question? You know that if you ask him to leave he is bound to have to conceal his HIV status from another employer.

Furthermore, what would happen if some customers somehow become aware

▶

that one of your chefs is HIV positive? You have no reason to believe that your customers are well-informed about the ways in which HIV can be transmitted. Some of them will think they are at risk from eating food prepared by, or handled by, someone with the virus. Even if they don't really know, they may decide they will play safe and eat somewhere else. It could seriously damage your customer base, particularly the regular lunchtime trade, and once your reputation suffers, your competitive edge is lost.

You dislike yourself for even thinking these things, at a time when your chef, as a valued member of your staff team, needs your support, but what should you do?

4 Corporate killing in the UK

No successful prosecutions followed in these six British disasters[166] listed below.

- May 1985: Bradford FC soccer stadium caught fire: 56 people died
- March 1987: a Zeebrugge ferry, The Herald of Free Enterprise, capsized in the English Channel: 188 people died
- November 1987: King's Cross underground rail station caught fire: 31 people died
- December 1988: Clapham Junction rail crash: 35 people died
- August 1989: the pleasure boat Marchioness sinks in the River Thames: 51 people died
- September 1997: Southall train crash on the London to Cardiff line: 7 people died.

Corporate negligence has not been proved in all the cases presented here, but the questions remain:

(i) Should it be possible to prosecute directors of companies for corporate manslaughter in these and other cases if corporate negligence is proved to be a significant cause of the deaths?
(ii) Should anyone be held accountable for deaths like these?

Notes to Chapter 4

1 See, for instance, the work of Chris Marsden, head of BP's Corporate Citizenship Unit at Warwick Business School, who talks about the company's "ripple effect." For contact details see "BP Centre for Corporate Citizenship" in Appendix 3.

2 See, for example, pages 157–64 in this book, criteria for judging companies based on various issues, but from the position that corporate citizenship begins with the premise that the company is part of society and that social responsibility needs to be viewed from the point of view of society. The company's view is only one of many.

3 See Chapter 1, page 26 for the differences between international, multinational, transnational, supranational and global companies.

4 Monks, Robert and Minnow, Nell (1966) *Watching the Watchers: Corporate Governance for the 21st Century.* Oxford: Blackwell.

5   Melville-Ross, Tim (1997) "Can business do more to project its purpose and values? RSA Forum on Ethics in the Workplace." *RSA Journal*, June.

6   Friedman, Milton (1962) *Capitalism and Freedom*. Chicago: University of Chicago Press.

7   Charkham, Jonathan (1995) *Keeping Good Company: a Study of Corporate Governance*. Oxford: Oxford University Press.

8   Cadbury, Sir Adrian, ethics prize-winner (1987) "Ethical managers make their own rules," *Harvard Business Review*, September–October, p.72.

9   For instance, Greenpeace owns shares in many companies, and various churches have had shares in arms manufacturers. See Mackenzie, Craig (1993) *The Shareholder Action Handbook. A New Consumer Guide*. Newcastle upon Tyne: New Consumer.

10   *The Economist* (1994) "Corporate governance: the invisible hand," 8 October.

11   Cadbury, p.73 – see note 8.

12   See the profile on the Centre for Tomorrow's Company and its *Tomorrow's Company Inquiry* in Chapter 2.

13   *The Economist* (1994) "Survey of corporate governance," 29 January.

14   Buckingham, Lisa (1992) "Of boards, buddies and bad practice," *Guardian*, 13 June.

15   PIRC – Pensions Information Research Consultancy, London.

16   *The Economist* (1994) "Survey of corporate governance," 29 January; *The Economist* (1994) "Corporate governance: the invisible hand," 8 October; *Guardian* (1992) 14 March; *Guardian* (1992) 28 May; *Guardian* (1992) 13 June; Charkham – see note 7.

17   Committee on Corporate Governance, chaired by Sir Ronnie Hampel, *Preliminary Report*, August 1997; Barnett, Anthony (1997) "Hampel Report snubs pleas for tougher rules," *The Observer*, 21 December.

18   Buckingham, Lisa, Gow, David and Crowe, Roger (1998) "Harsh words greet soft-line Hampel Report," *Guardian,* 29 January.

19   KPMG (1997) *Fighting Fraud*. No.7. London: KPMG.

20   See Chapter 4 for a discussion of different views on bribes.

21   *The Economist* (1997) "Who will listen to Mr Clean?," 2 August.

22   Bauer, Martin, *1996 Survey on Public Understanding of Science*. London: London School of Economics.

23   For example, Ehlich, Paul (1968) *The Population Bomb*. New York: Ballantine Books; *The Ecologist* (1972) "Blueprint for survival," 2, London; Meadows *et al.* and The Club of Rome (1972) *Limits to Growth*. New York: Universe Books.

24   Sustainable development: the term was developed by economist Herman Daly in the 1960s and 1970s through his discussion of "steady-state economics," and used by Ward, Barbara and Dubois, Rene (1966) *Spaceship Earth*, but it was brought into common use by the Brundtland Report (Harlem Brundtland, Gro (1987) *Our Common Future*. Oxford: Oxford University Press).

25   Carson, Rachel (1962) *Silent Spring*. Harmondsworth: Penguin, p.162.

26   Source: IEA, see *The Economist* (1997) "A warming world," 28 June.

27   India, China, Brazil, Mexico and Russia.

28   Brown, Lester *et al.* (1992) *Vital Signs 1992–3*. London: Worldwatch Institute Earthscan.

29 Harlem Brundtland, Gro (1987) *Our Common Future*. Oxford: Oxford University Press.

30 ISO 14000 series – see Appendix 2: Glossary.

31 See Appendix 2: Glossary.

32 See Appendix 2: Glossary.

33 Hawken, Paul (1994) *The Ecology of Commerce: A Declaration of Sustainability*. London: Phoenix (Weidenfeld and Nicolson). Paul Hawken was the winner of the Small Businessman Award from the American government for his book and seventeen-part TV series, *Growing a Business*, which was shown in 115 countries.

34 See Chapter 3 for a fuller profile of the Exxon Valdez story.

35 Rajib, N. Sanyal and Neves, Joao S. (1991) "The Valdez principles: implications for corporate social responsibility," *Journal of Business Ethics*, 10:883-90.

36 International Chamber of Commerce (1991) *The Business Charter for Sustainable Development*. Paris: International Chamber of Commerce.

37 SustainAbility and UNEP (1996) *Engaging Stakeholders*. Vol.2. London: SustainAbility & UNEP.

38 For a full copy of the principles, contact the ICC at its headquarters in Paris.

39 *The Economist* (1997) "A good trip?," 30 August.

40 Ibid.

41 Scandic Hotels (1996) *We Now Take a Natural Step*. Stockholm: Scandic Hotels.

42 Leipziger, Deborah and Wells, Phil (1995) *The Merck-INBio Partnership for Biodiversity*. Research Working Papers; *The Transnational Corporation in a Host Country: Policy and Practice in Developing Countries*. London: New Consumer and CEP.

43 Robbins, Nick and Roberts, Sarah (1997) *Unlocking Trade Opportunities: Changing Consumption and Production Patterns,* Case Studies of Export Success from Developing Countries by the International Institute for Environment and Development for the UN Department of Policy Co-ordination and Sustainable Development. New York, May, pp. 23–24.

44 Eco-Tex was established by the German Hohenstein Institute and the Austrian Textile Research Institute, with support from groups in Denmark, Sweden and Switzerland. An international research consortium, Eco-Tex specifies a rigorous standard. In order to receive a certificate, companies must be certified on an annual basis.

45 Agenda 21 was a key document signed by all the heads of government attending the 1992 Earth Summit in Rio de Janeiro. As a prescription for how the world might work towards sustainability, Agenda 21 covers environmental issues, world trade, community campaigns, health, education, government and other issues of global-local significance.

46 Leipziger, Deborah (1996) *Partnerships for Change: Companies and Non-Profits Team up to Address Global Problems*. Research Report on Economic Priorities. October–November. New York: Council on Economic Priorities.

47 Novo Nordisk (1996) *Novo Nordisk Environmental Report*, Denmark, p. 1

48 Gramstrup, Marianne and Corporate Environmental Department (1995) *Novo Nordisk and the Environment*. p.4.

49 SmithKline Beecham (1996) *Integrating LCA into Packaging and Product Development*. ENDS Report 255. London: ENDS, April.

50 Robbins and Roberts – see note 43.

51 Chandler, Geoffrey (1996) "Human rights have everything to do with business," *The Observer*, 19 May.

52 Ibid.

53 Clark, Alan (1996) *Diaries*. London: Weidenfeld and Nicolson. Clark was a defence minister in the Thatcher government.

54 Clause 39 of the Magna Carta was signed by King John at Runnymede in 1215 AD.

55 Sachs, Wolfgang (1992) *The Development Dictionary: a Guide to Knowledge as Power*, 2nd edn, London and New Jersey: Zed Books.

56 Fukuyama, Francis (1992) *The End of History and the Last Man*. Harmondsworth, UK: Penguin. See Fukuyama among others, for this thesis.

57 In so far as such a system exists. See Korten, David (1995) *When Corporations Rule the World*. London: Earthscan.

58 Amnesty International UK Business Group (1997) *Human Rights Guidelines for Companies*. London: Amnesty International.

59 See Chapter 1, note 37.

60 Rice, David, Senior Policy Adviser: External Affairs and Communications, BP (1997) Interviewed by Deborah Leipziger, 3 September and subsequent personal communications with Malcolm McIntosh.

61 Raynor, William "A lethal brew of oil and blood," *Independent on Sunday*, 31 August.

62 See note 60.

63 *The Economist* (1997) "BP at war," 19 July.

64 Ibid.

65 See note 61.

66 Estimated Economic Index 1995, published in *Casanare 2000: una vision al futuro* (1996) Colombia: BP, Ecopetrol, Total, Preussag Energie and Inaquimicas.

67 BP (1997) *BP in Colombia, The Facts*. London: BP.

68 Allen, M. (1993) "Worldly wisdom," *New Statesman & Society*, 21 May.

69 See Transparency International's rating available from Transparency International, Berlin.

70 This represents a burn-off of 75 per cent in Nigeria, against a burn-off of only 6 per cent in the USA on similar oil wells.

71 Shell Petroleum Development Company of Nigeria, The (1997) *Ogoni and the Niger Delta*. Nigeria Brief. August. Lagos: Shell Petroleum Development Co. of Nigeria Ltd.

72 *The Economist* (1997) "Shellman says sorry," 10 May.

73 Imomoh, Eckbert, General Manager: Eastern Division, Shell Petroleum (1996) on *Africa Express*, Channel 4 TV, UK, 18 April.

74 Fani-Kayode, Toyin (1996) on *Africa Express*, Channel 4 TV, UK, 18 April.

75 See note 71.

76 See note 71.

77 Compare Caulkin, Simon (1997) "Amnesty and WWF take a crack at Shell," *The Observer*, 11 May with *The Economist* (1997) "Shellman says sorry," 10 May.

78 Plender, John (1997) "How can we be sure of Shell?," *New Statesman*, 23 May.

79 Caulkin, Simon (1997) "Amnesty and WWF take a crack at Shell," *The Observer*, 11 May.

80 PepsiCo, (n.d.) digital release on www.pepsi.com.

81 At the time of going to press, the ILO had not developed clear definitions of light and hazardous work.

82 Leipziger, Deborah and Sabharwal, Pia (1995) *Child Labor: The Cutting Edge of Human Rights*. Research Report. November. New York: Council on Economic Priorities.

83 Sources: United Food and Commercial Workers Union.

84 Asia Monitor Resource Centre and Hong Kong Industrial Committee (1997) *Nike and Reebok Subcontractors Violate Chinese Law: Working Conditions in Sports Shoe Factories in China Making Shoes for Nike and Reebok*. Hong Kong: digital release, p.2.

85 Ibid., p.6.

86 *The Economist* (1997) "Trainers, sneakers and shoes: in the vanguard," 7 June.

87 Goodworks International "The Nike Code of Conduct. A report on conditions in international manufacturing facilities for Nike, Inc.," *Executive Summary*, digital release on www.nike.com.

88 *The Economist* (1997) "Dress code," 19 April.

89 Rodrigues dos Santos, Benedito (1996) *Entrepreneurial Mobilization for the Eradication of Child Labor in Brazil: A Study of the Strategies Developed by the Abrinq Foundation for Children's Rights*. Sao Paolo UNICEF, Brazil, p.12.

90 Ibid, p.18.

91 Ibid, p.22.

92 Language modified slightly to improve on awkward translation in these three quotes; (Ibid, p.20).

93 Ibid, p.21.

94 Ibid, p.8.

95 Council on Economic Priorities (1994) *Shopping for a Better World*. San Francisco: Sierra Club.

96 Equality Foundation (1997) *Equal Opportunities Quality Framework: The Complete Guide to Employers*. Bristol: Equality Foundation.

97 Heidrick and Struggles Inc. (1993) *The New Diversity: Women and Minorities on Corporate Boards*.

98 Prudential Assurance (n.d.) *Disability*, London, p. 70.

99 Lyon, Nicola (ed.) *Fact Sheet*. Employers' Forum on Disability.

100 Ibid.

101 Prudential – see note 98, p. 10.

102 *Employers' Update* (1997) "Disability initiatives at NatWest," newsletter of the Employers' Forum on Disability, Summer.

103 *Employers' Update* (1997) "Sainsbury's issues guide to stores in move to raise awareness," Spring, p. 5.

104 Churchill & Friend (1994) *Measuring Best Practice Regarding the Provision of Foods, Services and Facilities to Disabled People*, Disability Customer Care Audit, London, May.

105 Quoted in Wolfe, Kathi (1997) "Enabling the disabled: where there's a wheel, there's a way," *Hemispheres*, June, p.123.

106 The British Post Office estimates that it costs $60,000 to medically retire an employee.

107 Employers' Forum on Disability and The Bucknall Group (1997) *Open for Business: A Best Practice Guide on Access*, compiled by Bennett, D. and Tolfree, P., London, p. 8.

108 According to a 1995 survey by the Global Strategy Group, quoted in Employers' Forum on Disability (1997) *Employers' Update*: "US firms discover the benefits." Summer, p. 13.

109 Ibid. According to a 1995 poll conducted by Mason-Dixon in *Employers' Update*.

110 Ibid.

111 Ibid.

112 Lyon – see note 99, p. 1.

113 Disability Customer Care Audit.

114 Milne, Seamus (1998) "Stand against ageism," *Guardian*, 3 February.

115 Centre for Social Management and New Consumer, McIntosh, Malcolm (ed.) (1995) *Good Business? Case Studies in Corporate Social Responsibility*. Bristol: Policy Press.

116 Mickens, Ed (1996) *The 100 Best Companies for Gay Men and Lesbians*. New York: Pocket Books.

117 Baker, Daniel, O'Brien Strub, Sean and Henning, Bill, in association with the National Gay and Lesbian Task Force Policy Institute (1995) *Cracking the Corporate Closet*. New York: HarperCollins

118 Jane Aeberhard-Hodges, Equality and Human Rights Co-ordination Branch: ILO, interviewed in *World of Work* (1997) "Unwanted, unwelcome and increasingly illegal: sexual harassment in the workplace," no.19:8.

119 Knowlton, Brian (1997) "Army to teach 'ethics' to avert harassment," *International Herald Tribune*, 12 September.

120 Ibid.

121 Advertisement in all UK national newspapers on 14 October 1997.

122 *Guardian* (1997), 14 October; *London Evening Standard* (1997), 14 October.

123 Beaumont, Peter and Mills, Heather (1997) "About turn in ban on service gays," *The Observer*, 23 November.

124 Sources: Sir Geoffrey Mulcahy, Chairman and CEO of Kingfisher plc, in Mulcahy, Sir Geoffrey (1993) in *HIV and AIDS, Briefing Notes*. London: Terrence Higgins Trust; Hussey, Julian (1996) *Employment and AIDS: A Review of the Companies Act! Business Charter on HIV and AIDS*. August. London: National Aids Trust, p.4; Will, Rosalyn (1995) *Stellar Companies: The 1995 America's Corporate Conscience Awards*. Research Report. May. New York: Council on Economic Priorities, p.4.

125 Terrence Higgins Trust and the Industrial Society (1993) *HIV and Aids: Positive Management, Briefing Notes*, London.

126 Ibid.

127 Vidal, John, *Guardian* quoted in FairTrade brochure, 1997.

128 Sources: Oxfam (1997) *Shopping for a Fairer World*. Oxford: Oxfam.; Traidcraft (1997) *Drink to Fair Trade*. Oxford: FairTrade (1997) *Shop for a Fairer World*. London: FairTrade; Barret Brown, Michael (1993) *FairTrade*. London: Zed Books.

129 *New Internationalist* (1995) "Coffee spilling the beans," September.

130 *Coffee for sale:* a Cafédirect poster featuring Mr and Mrs Gomez of Casa Gomez, San Juan del Oro, Peru.

131 Direct (1996), Leaflet, Cafédirect, Autumn.

132 Meeting with Hans Bolscher (1997) Social Venture Network, Berlin, 31 May.

133 Boycott, Owen (1997) "Supermarkets join global fight against sweatshops," *Guardian,* 20 September.

134 See the profile on the New Economics Foundation in Chapter 5.

135 See Index for entries under Council on Economic Priorities.

136 *Supermarkets' Ethical Progress* (1997) London: Christian Aid.

137 See profile of Premier Beverages (in Chapter 3).

138 Body Shop, The (1997) *Our Agenda.* Littlehampton, UK: The Body Shop.

139 The negative criteria are not absolute in all cases. They indicate the issues that give rise to environmental or social concerns and are considered in the research process when assessing companies. For further details of the criteria for NPI Global Care's family of funds, contact NPI Global Care (see Appendix 3 for address details).

140 See Index and Appendix 2: Glossary.

141 The "Big Four" banks in the UK are the Midland, Lloyds, Barclays and NatWest.

142 Williams, Simon, Director of Marketing and Butterfield, Leslie, Chairman of BDDH Advertising (1997) Speech given at Social Venture Network Conference. Berlin, 31 May.

143 See Appendix 2: Glossary and the section on the environment earlier in this chapter.

144 Lloyd, John (1997) "Into the ethical dimension," *New Statesman,* 25 July.

145 *The Economist* (1997) "Your friendly neighbourhood arms-dealer," 23 August.

146 White, Michael (1997) "Indonesia export deal blocked," *Guardian,* 26 September; *The Economist* (1997) "The arms trade: business as usual," 2 August.

147 Human Rights Watch Arms Project (1997) *Exposing the Source: US Companies and the Production of Anti-Personnel Mines.* New York: Human-Rights Watch, April.

148 *The Economist* (1997) "Ted Turner saves the world," 27 September.

149 Fairhall, David (1997) "Blow to £40,000 million weapons programme: outrage over sentence fuels city jitters," *Guardian,* 27 September.

150 Crowley, Michael (1997) "Making a killing," *Amnesty,* July/August.

151 Bellamy, Christopher (1997) "Human rights and wrongs make profits a question of conscience," *Independent,* 23 May.

152 Lloyd – see note 144.

153 Crowley – see note 150.

154 Boseley, Sarah (1998) "Tobacco firms' secrets smoked out," *Guardian,* 16 February.

155 Thorsten, Richard "INFACT's next challenge: taking on big tobacco," *Boycott Quarterly,* Summer.

156 *New York Times* (1997) "Philip Morris Chief admits smoking deaths," 22 August.

157 *The Economist* (1997) 19 April.

158 *Financial Times* (1997) 25 September.

159 Bonner, Raymond and Drew, Christopher (1997) "Cigarette makers are seen as aiding rise in smuggling," *New York Times*, 25 August.

160 We should make it clear that at the time of going to press, there have been no proven cases of BSE in the USA. The example is used here because of the global debate, including in the USA, about food-health issues such as BSE, salmonella and listeria. The USA banned the import of beef when BSE was first discovered.

161 1995, Opinion Research Corporation for Animal Rights International; 'What humans owe animals', quoted in Will, Ros (1996) *Consumers to Industry: Curb Farm Animal Suffering.* Research Report. January/February. New York: Council on Economic Priorities.

162 Survey in 1997 of 2,000 adults conducted by the Royal Society for the Prevention of Cruelty to Animals (*Independent* (1997) "Shoppers placing more value on compassionate farming," 30 June).

163 Ibid.

164 Ibid.

165 Ibid.

166 *Independent* (1997) 2 October.

5

MANAGING CORPORATE CITIZENSHIP

Introduction

Key relationships and stakeholders

Who are stakeholders?

The House of Windsor
IBM (UK)
UNEP International Technology Center
The US Department of Defense
Traidcraft plc

The inclusive company

McKay Nursery Co.
VW's "workholders"
Manganese Steel

Business and communities

Marks & Spencer
Levi Strauss & Co.'s Community Investment Team
Building Timberland in the USA
The London Benchmarking Group
The Corporate Community Index
Bata Thailand and the Thai Business Initiative in Rural Development
Auchan
Unilever in Uttar Pradesh
Fondo Social del Empresariado Chihuahuense
Phillips Van Heusen

Building partnerships

McDonald's and the Environmental Defense Fund
Marine Stewardship Council (MSC)

Re-measuring wealth: auditing and accountability

Auditing business performance

Environmental auditing

Social and ethical auditing

BT

The ethical audit

The Co-operative Bank
The Body Shop

The social audit

New Economics Foundation
KPMG
Price Waterhouse
The Body Shop

A new global standard for social accountability: SA8000

The CEPAA's guide to SA8000
SGS Yarsley

Developing global standards

Reporting company performance

The Association of Chartered Certified Accountants

Managing the media: how to survive a boycott

Lessons from "McLibel"

Management exercises

Introduction

This chapter covers the management of corporate citizenship from a variety of perspectives. To describe this chapter as a toolkit would aptly describe some of the issues covered, but others require a new approach to business.

The contents of this chapter cover:

- key relationships and stakeholders, including stakeholder mapping and examples of inclusivity in business;
- business and the communities in which they operate;
- partnerships;
- *re*-measuring business performance for financial, social and environmental impact: accountability and auditing;
- a new global social accountability standard SA8000;
- reporting;
- managing the media and avoiding boycotts.

Key relationships and stakeholders

In the world's largest economies there has been a plethora of books, articles and TV programs about stakeholding and "inclusive" versus "exclusive" companies and societies in the last few years. Both the Democratic Party in the USA and the Labour Party in the UK have talked about a stakeholding society. As Britain, Canada and the USA move towards a more inclusive method of management while also expounding the virtues of a flexible labor market, Japan and Germany are adapting their long-running versions of stakeholder economies to make them more flexible.

Neither stakeholding nor inclusivity is particularly new or radical. It is possible to dismiss the debate as just the management fad of the moment, or to take it more seriously and acknowledge that this debate could be about re-evaluating the relationship between individuals, business and society. Some countries have entered a post-industrial era, and the nature of their business organizations has changed, and all countries are engaged in developing strategies for survival in the global economy. When politicians talk about stakeholding they are adopting the language of business, indicating the prominence of business in society and the dominant position of market thinking.

The idea of stakeholding and inclusivity may not be new but its application both to present-day management in the context of globalization has produced some profound developments in the way we view business activity, in the relationship between the individual and the state, and the way in which we approach global problems.

This is a time of economic change, as discussed in Chapter 1. There are new economies waiting to overtake the existing leaders; former colonies are no longer willing to be deferential to old European powers and enlightened customers the world over are asking demanding questions about products. Some have called this "the death of deference,"[1] or the "X-ray environment,"[2] others see it as post-modernism and the fragmentation of ethics and thinking. Perhaps this is one facet of global culture; challenge authority and make institutions, public and private, earn respect. The reality for companies is that relationship capital and brand image are of paramount importance for business success. Stakeholding mapping endeavors to find some ground between different stakeholder perceptions; the problem is, as Hans Kung said in *Global Responsibility*:[3]

> *"If ethics is to function for the wellbeing of all, it must be indivisible. The undivided world increasingly needs an undivided ethic. Postmodern men and women need common values, goals, ideals, visions."*

Engaging stakeholders, through dialogue and consultation is one way of finding a common way forward in a fragmented society.

One of the key advocates of contemporary stakeholding theory is Will Hutton, an economist and Editor of *The Observer*, Britain's oldest Sunday newspaper, who says:

> *"The unifying theory is inclusion; the individual is a member, a citizen and a potential partner. But inclusion is not a one-way street; it places reciprocal obligations on the individual as well as rights – and in every domain and in every social class. These rights can be organized in a voluntary code; or they can be codified into law. The institutions that grow out of these relationships foster relations of trust and commitment; they tend to be high investing, attentive to human capital and highly creative."*[4]

In the context of the company, it means that stakeholders have reciprocal rights and responsibilities.

The seven principles of stakeholding

John Kay and Will Hutton[5] believe the seven essential principles of shareholding to be as follows:

1 *Open economies and democratic societies are the basis for wealth creation.* Economic and political decision making should be decentralized and market organization recognized as the route to innovation and efficiency.

2 *We must all be included in the workings of the economy and society.* To work is to be, because those who are able and want to work have a right to a job and working and earning are central elements in economic and social life.

3 *Ownership confers obligations, including paying taxes.* Ownership confers social obligations, because to own also means to owe.

4 *A good economy is one where you do the right thing without being policed into doing it.* It is better if financial institutions can be responsible for their own activities rather than having to be regulated. As the market does not always bring the greatest benefit to society as a whole there are some areas where there has to be regulation.

5 *Businesses are social institutions, not creatures of the stock market.* As social organizations, companies need to be aware of the obligations of owners to society. Good businesses are bound to make healthy profits but they must share their prosperity. This means that they must share the rewards of success with a range of stakeholders, not just with shareholders.

6 *Good businesses are bound to make healthy profits, but they must share their prosperity.* The sharing of profits must be with a range of claimants, or stakeholders, and not just with shareholders.

7 *Successful market economies rely on a host of intermediate organizations.* There is a third way between the market and the state. Social capital is created by business, the state and a third, growing sector, that has neither the drive for profits of the private sector, nor the agenda of the state but whose existence is based on building civil society.

The idea of stakeholding can be viewed as deriving from the staking of claims for land as Europeans dislodged native Americans and settled across North America. As Paul Hirst, Professor of Social Theory at the University of London says, more modern understanding may come from the development of rules governing modern business, as"applying the principles of democracy to economic life."[6]

Stakeholding acknowledges that capitalism produces winners and losers, and that both need to be guided. Hirst says, "Capitalism is always a mixture of success and failure. Those who suffer from failure have interests and rights too. Wealth creation sounds fine if you have just picked up a big check from your unit trust or life insurance policy. It is less attractive if you are bankrupt or redundant and standing in the middle of a rustbelt."[7] In other words, the best argument for capitalism should be that if it is successful, everyone feels a winner.

The fact is that the unfettered market makes some people very rich, but also produces enormous disparities of wealth, and is not always economic with resources, be they people or the planet. Market efficiency does not necessarily mean environmental efficiency or the observance of human rights. Stakeholding, as a principle, is concerned not to limit the market, or indeed to deny that competitive capitalism can be one of the most efficient drivers of innovation and progress, but to make it work better. This is so that it should reward the many, and not just the few.

There are some who deride the current debate about stakeholding as an attempt by the left to come to terms with the fact that liberal economics has won the battle against socialism. Making companies more accountable to their stakeholders is socialism by the back door. These commentators say that stakeholding theory is "uncontroversial, even banal."[8] This is because good companies have always understood that they operate best when they understand their relationships with employees, contractors, suppliers and customers, so it can be argued that stakeholding is nothing new. These opponents of stakeholding argue that there is a problem with stakeholder corporate governance because it assumes that the interests of stakeholder groups will coincide.[9] This is supported by academics like John Parkinson, Professor of Law at Bristol University, and others who argue that the various stakeholders have different interests: "Lumping all the relevant interests together under the heading 'stakeholder' obscures analysis and hinders the search for appropriate policy responses."[10]

On a more prosaic level Sir Michael Wilson, the chairman of Whitbread (a UK-based brewing, retailing and restaurant group), said: "Just because I go into a newsagent and buy a Mars Bar, it doesn't mean I have a stake in the Mars Corporation."[11] Even writers on the left have doubts about stakeholding theory, including DEMOS, a London-based think-tank, whose members argue that stakeholding has more to do with why the UK and USA have been overtaken and matched by the German and Japanese economies than about how business should operate in the future. Is it a model also of large business, relevant to them, but largely irrelevant to the vast majority of businesses around the world which are small to medium sized and often family run? The DEMOS model for a stakeholding future has four ingredients: a widening share ownership and an increase in shareholder democracy; a focus on employees not companies; the development of a pensions policy so that individuals have ways of paying for life beyond employment; and the development of minimum standards for corporate behavior.[12]

Some critics suggest that stakeholding is incompatible with capitalism because it "would dismantle capitalism by destroying property rights in the capital claims to a firm."[13] These ideas are firmly rooted in the trickle-down theory, that says rewarding shareholders will reward society as a whole. Our inability to tackle environmental problems and close the gap between rich and poor locally and globally seems to show that another more sophisticated, less Darwinian approach is required and desired by enlightened business people.

One of the most vociferous advocates for stakeholder accountability, Anita Roddick, founder and CEO of The Body Shop, is dismissive of criticism of this approach: "What today's corporate reactionaries forget is that long before stakeholding became a political buzzword, it was sound business practice. Victorian philanthropists like Cadbury endowed educational institutions, libraries and hospitals in their local communities, and worked hard to improve the conditions of their employees. They understood that a cohesive society is an essential foundation for business success, and that their companies would thrive with healthier, better-educated and more productive people."[14]

In the debate about stakeholding, corporate governance and profitability, there are some clear points of agreement:

● Business is the engine of society, or at least the dominant force in a market economy.
● Business has responsibilities that go beyond compliance with legislation, economic prudence, ethical behavior and philanthropy.
● Business may not need to recognize claimants as stakeholders, but it would prosper from recognizing that it has to be more accountable to key relationships.
● Different stakeholders often have widely varied claims.
● Business reputation and brand image cannot be taken for granted in a pluralist, information-rich market.

Business prospers if it understands its key relationships: it is in its interests to widen its circle and be more inclusive. Transparency and accountability are business virtues. Corporate citizenship has its greatest momentum in three areas: inclusivity, transparency and accountability.

Defining stakeholders

"A stakeholder society and economy exists where there is a mutuality of rights and obligations constructed round the notion of economic, social and political inclusion. Stakeholder capitalism applies these principles to the operation of free market capitalism and by doing so places its limits on the operation of unfettered markets."

Will Hutton[15]

"A stakeholder is any group or individual who can affect or is affected by an organization's impact or behaviour."

[In the case of The Body Shop this includes] "employees, franchisees, customers, suppliers, shareholders, local communities, and organizations linked through campaigning or charity."

The Body Shop[16]

"In contrast to the stockholder view, a new perspective, referred to as the stakeholder model, suggests that corporations are servants of the larger society. This approach acknowledges that there are expanding demands being placed on business organizations which include a wider variety of groups not traditionally defined as part of the organization's immediate self-interest . . . Businesses are socially responsible when they consider and act on the needs and demands of these different stakeholders."

Buono and Nichols[17]

"An increasingly globalized economy requires a redefinition of the concept of the stakeholder. The community, rather than the corporation, is the starting point in the definition of stakeholder."

ECCR, ICCR, TCCR[18]

"It is a false dichotomy to believe that there is a conflict between shareholders and stakeholders."

Sir Anthony Cleaver[19]

Who are stakeholders?

David Wheeler and Maria Sillanpää work at The Body Shop; they are the architects of the company's social audit process, and responsible for the publication of The Body Shop's *Values Report* 1995 and 1997. In their book *The Stakeholder Corporation: a Blueprint for Maximizing Stakeholder Value*[20] they categorize stakeholders in the following way:

Primary stakeholders

● *Social*
  - shareholders and investors
  - employees and managers
  - customers
  - suppliers and other business partners
  - local communities

● *Non-social*
  - the natural environment
  - future generations
  - non-human species

Secondary stakeholders

● *Social*
  - government and regulators
  - civic institutions
  - social pressure groups
  - the media and academia
  - trade bodies
  - competitors

● *Non-social*
  - environmental pressure groups
  - animal-welfare organizations

Primary social stakeholders can be communicated with directly, and generally, primary non-social stakeholders cannot be. The quality of social stakeholder relationships can be measured in two ways:

● *Quantitatively* – based on benchmarks and performance indicators.
● *Qualitatively* – based on benchmarks and performance indicators, as well as on stakeholders' perceptions.

Five key relationships

These are summed up by Sir Anthony Cleaver:[21]

> *"Almost everything about a company over a period of time can change: the products it makes, the markets it serves, the geography in which it operates, the technology which it employs, the manufacturing processes, the raw materials."*

The one thing that does not change within a company is its five key relationships with:

1 those people who invest in it, the shareholders;
2 those who work for it, the employees;
3 those who buy its goods and services, its customers;
4 the people who supply it with goods and services it does not produce itself, its suppliers;
5 the community at large.

The fate that befell the House of Windsor (see profile below) is not unlike that which has befallen other large institutions in the last few years. Shell was highly surprised by the boycott of its products in Germany and other European countries following the media attention given to the occupation of the Brent Spar oil rig by Greenpeace in 1996. Nike has had to re-write its labor policies following allegations of child labor involved in the manufacture of its shoes in 1995. In contrast Levi Strauss & Co. has worked assiduously to develop overseas sourcing policies that are transparent and honest before press accusations of child labor occurred.

Out of touch with stakeholders?
The House of Windsor and the death of Diana, Princess of Wales

The funeral of Diana, Princess of Wales, on Saturday 6 September 1997 was watched live by 1,000 million people around the world and seen on television at some point by 2,500 million people, 40 per cent of the world's population. Despite the time difference, some 20 million citizens in the USA watched the funeral in the early hours of the morning as well as one-third of all Australians and more than half the British subjects – 31 million people. Diana was possibly the best known person in the world, surpassing religious and political leaders and popular musicians and films stars. The funeral was one of the single largest human-made events ever.

The British Royal Family know themselves as "The Firm" and there is no reason not to apply the lessons of this book to this global organization. "The Firm" is not a profit-making organization, but it has to maintain its income and reputation while managing its public relations. In some respects as the sun finally sinks on the British Empire, with the handback of Hong Kong by the UK to China in 1997 and the growing tide of resentment against the British monarchy as Head of State in Australia, it could be claimed that the House of Windsor still has remarkable popular support around the world. It must also be remembered that membership of the British Commonwealth,[22] separate from the British Royal Family, is rising, as countries see good reason to be part of an English-speaking global club with connections to the key trading countries. The Queen is Head of the Commonwealth.

In the aftermath of Diana's death it quickly became clear that the Queen was out of touch with her key stakeholder group, the British public, and the British government, who every year vote the Royal Family their income in the House of Commons. There was no mention of Diana's death in the church service attended by the Royal Family the next morning; no member of the family said they were upset, sorry or sad in the ensuing few days, and the flag did not initially fly at half mast on Buckingham Palace despite the overwhelming feelings of sorrow expressed around the world. It was reported, although later strenuously denied, that the Queen had decreed that Diana's name must not be mentioned in her presence, forgetting that as Head of the House of Windsor she had more pressing social responsibilities. When the Queen finally made a live statement to the world on the day before the funeral it hardly satisfied the emotional demands of a much-saddened world audience.

On the day of the funeral the Queen and 42 members of her family were forced to join the "People's Princess's" funeral at street level with other members of the public. During the funeral ceremony in Westminster Abbey, Diana's brother, Earl Spencer – a member of the Royal Family's class – put part of the blame for Diana's unhappiness and death on the "The Firm" – and this was in front of half the world's population.

The funeral has been dubbed the "Floral Revolution" as a result of the £50 million worth of flowers that were bought by the British public in Diana's memory (see the Floral Revolution profile in Chapter 1).

There is no hiding place for organizations that are out of touch with their key stakeholders. While acknowledging that the House of Windsor is unique, some of the lessons from this book would prove of value to "The Firm." They do not need a new public relations offensive; it could be argued that they need a new CEO in touch with the world outside the walls of Buckingham Palace and a new flexible approach to managing their key relationships and an understanding of best practice in other democracies which have retained the monarchy – if they are to survive.

In the aftermath of Diana's funeral, royal officials have set up "focus groups," along the lines of advertising agencies and political parties, to find out how they are perceived by their stakeholders. They also established a management group with the title of "The Way Ahead Group" whose aim is to modernize "The Firm."

In touch with stakeholders?
Environmental reporting for IBM (UK)[23]

In an effort to improve communication with stakeholders on environmental reporting, IBM (UK) working with ECOTEC consulted with 75 of IBM's stakeholders, to produce a set of 11 key parameters which were then ranked for IBM's performance.

The stakeholders were chosen from the following range:

- employees
- customers and suppliers
- opinion formers
- neighbors
- legislators and regulators
- the financial and insurance community.

The 11 categories chosen by the stakeholders were:

1 environmental management system
2 IT in pursuit of sustainable development
3 IBM's product stewardship
4 environmental aspects of customer relations
5 IBM and its influence on suppliers' environmental performance
6 energy
7 IBM's global responsibilities
8 transport
9 IBM's commercial activities
10 IBM's manufacturing activities
11 IBM's influence on environmental attitudes in business and society.

Stakeholder mapping

Companies cannot engage with stakeholders unless they have first conducted a mapping exercise. On this map they can plot a range of stakeholders and the relationships of those stakeholders to the company. This requires an open mind; often stakeholders are not recognized as existing by those inside the company. Moreover it is often the case that the company is not able to judge correctly the nature of the relationship with its stakeholders.

Stakeholder mapping can be applied to situations as well as to companies. And, most importantly, though companies tend to want to put themselves at the heart of the web, it may well be illuminating to start with the community and see the company as one contributor to the health and wealth of that community.

Having devised a stakeholder map, it is necessary to decide which stakeholders to consult. How far beyond employees, suppliers, investors, shareholders and customers can the exercise extend? Given our understanding of sustainability how can the natural environment be represented, and how can future generations have a voice in a stakeholder consultation exercise?

Here are three examples of stakeholder mapping, starting with a community exercise, where the development of a sustainable city has been the central concern. This is followed by a very different map of stakeholders from US military healthcare. This is followed by one of the pioneers of social auditing, Traidcraft.

Environmental Risk Assessment for Sustainable Cities: UN Environment Programme (UNEP) International Technology Center[24]

This report uses stakeholder mapping in developing risk assessment. The issues it identifies are directly applicable to corporations.

Stakeholder mapping is described therein as "the identification of the relevant groups and the nature and strength of relationships among them."

The report underlines that:

● effective identification of, and communication with, stakeholder groups is essential;
● stakeholder groups have different interests, expertise, values and agendas. Presented with common information, they may reach different conclusions;
● stakeholder mapping involves understanding social logic as the first step, because different groups have varying levels of social investment, affinity and trust and are governed by different geopolitical, functional and organizational factors;
● risk management requires producing a result favorable to people and the environment based on a risk assessment derived from science-based information.

For the purposes of the sustainable cities programme *stakeholders* are defined as:

● those who are affected by a particular environmental issue or program;
● those who have information, knowledge, resources or positions which are relevant to this issue;
● those who have some control over the outcome of the issue.

Stakeholders are drawn from the business sector, the local community, the region, the public sector, institutions and technical and scientific personnel.

Stakeholder management in military healthcare: the US Department of Defense[25]

"To manage stakeholders, healthcare managers must be involved in a continuous process of internal and external scanning when making strategic decisions . . . Managers must make two critical assessments about stakeholders: their potential to threaten the organization and their potential to cooperate with it."

This case involved the management of a military hospital in the USA. The objective of the task was to protect managers from unpleasant surprises by building a stakeholder map and engaging with stakeholders on an on-going basis as part of strategic management and risk assessment. On this basis they saw that 'power is primarily a function of the dependence of the organization on the stakeholder' whose identity ranges from funding bodies, to physicians, to patients.

The analysis is based on threat versus co-operation, and on the reciprocal rights and responsibilities of stakeholders. A dynamic model was developed using these parameters which identified four types of stakeholder:

- the mixed blessing stakeholder;
- the supportive stakeholder;
- the non-supportive stakeholder;
- the marginal stakeholder.

Using this model successful stakeholder management depended on questions of:

- what the organization does or fails to do;
- what the stakeholder does or fails to do;
- how new information changes the stakeholder groups or the situation in question;
- the issue under discussion.

This model shows that stakeholder management is dynamic, that it requires clear identification of stakeholder groups and their relationships with the organization, and that both management and stakeholders can affect such relationships by their actions and their knowledge base.

The range of stakeholders in this map included physicians, patients, nursing staff, other hospitals, insurance companies, the Department of Defense, Congress and the President of the USA.

Traidcraft plc

Traidcraft is a business which imports crafts, jewelry, paper, clothing, food, teas and coffee from developing countries. It is based in Newcastle, England. Traidcraft only trades on the basis of fair trade (see Chapter 4) and is based on Christian ideas of love and justice in trade. In 1996/97 it sourced $9.075 million worth of goods from developing countries, up 5 per cent on the previous year.

A breakdown of its stakeholders can be seen in Table 5.1.

Table 5.1 Traidcraft's range of stakeholders

Key stakeholders	Other stakeholders	Other interested groups
Customers Fair traders Retailers Mail order customers	Company representatives and retailers' customers European Fair Trade Association (EFTA)	The wider public The development community The business community
Suppliers "Third World" suppliers UK suppliers Other EFTA members Traidcraft Exchange	Producers' communities Producers' environment International Federation for Alternative Trade (IFAT)	International freight agencies
Funders A & B shareholders Personal lenders	Banks European Union	UK government
Staff Traidcraft plc employees	Employees' families Local community	The environment

Shareholders/stockholders

Everyone agrees that shareholders are stakeholders, as they have a property-owning claim over the company. Company law varies from country to country, but in all cases shareholders have significant power, by virtue of their direct ownership of the company, to change the company's operations. When it comes to corporate citizenship it is the shareholders who can often exert the greatest control over both the long-term strategy and the day-to-day management of the company. Owning shares can be one of the most effective ways of overseeing and affecting corporate decision making. It can also be one of the most frustrating for small shareholders as they see large institutional investors failing to take action to correct obviously bad management, poor environmental performance or disregard for human rights in overseas operations. In 1997, shareholders in Shell Transport and Trading in the UK were narrowly defeated on a motion at the Anual General Meeting which would have forced the company to conduct a social audit of its activities.

Under British law, companies are virtually self-regulating and it is shareholders who legitimize corporate action by having control over the appointment of directors and hold them accountable for their actions.

Two UK-based global companies, Virgin and Hanson, have very different perspectives on their stakeholders. Richard Branson, founder and Chief Executive of the Virgin Group, says that he prioritizes his stakeholders as follows:

1 employees, because, if they are treated well they will reward
2 the customers who will remain loyal to the brand and
3 reward the shareholders.

By comparison, Lords Hanson and White of the Hanson Trust (a conglomerate including cement, batteries, tobacco, bricks, electronic equipment, gold and construction) pride themselves on making sure that "management's primary responsibility is to increase shareholder value." Hanson calls this "managerial capitalism"[26] but Hutton describes Hanson as "an operation driven by manipulation,"[27] based on asset stripping and "getting hold of tomorrow's money today." Hanson's adherence to rewarding earnings per share and emphasising that "increasing shareholder value will increase the wealth of society, and thus, of society"[28] means that, in some people's view, such as Hutton's, the company has failed to meet other societal expectations including attempting to provide stable long-term communities for people to work in. But most shareholders have been happy.

The inclusive company

Central to the concept of stakeholding is the idea of inclusivity. An inclusive company is one that consults, and involves, a wide range of stakeholders in its decision making. It makes sure that it understands the effects of its decisions on communities and the environment because it is concerned both for its own long-term profitability and for the long-term health and wealth of society.

The three examples that follow are varied. The first, McKay Nursery, sees its employees, and their welfare, as a source of strength and profitability, and they, in this case, own the company. The second example comes from Europe's largest car manufacturing company, VW, which has combined the idea of a flexible workforce with a long-term benefits package for the employees. The third example is different again and involves the complications and intricacies of industrial change in the heart of the UK's steel industry in the 1980s when workers and managers became owners.

McKay Nursery Co.: responsibility to migrant workers

The majority of socially responsible companies focus their benefits and policies on executives and full-time workers but McKay Nursery is implementing policies for some of the most disadvantaged workers in America: migrant workers. Many migrant workers in the USA are Mexican, who cross the border to work during the harvest season. Growing poverty in Mexico has led to a sharp increase in migrant workers which has depressed wage levels at a time when the cost of living is rising. Newspapers frequently report on patterns of abuse: in May 1997, migrant workers were found enslaved in South Carolina. As borders become more porous, the issue of migrant and guest workers is becoming more critical.

With an annual turnover of $15 million, McKay is an employee-owned business. With 60 full-time employees, the company relies on seasonal labor from Mexico. Employees working more than 1,000 hours receive stock options. According to its President, Griff Mason, these options will compound to $100,000 in 30 years for the lowest paid worker. Each year, employees receive at least $2,000 in stocks or cash.[29] Such benefits build loyalty, with 90 per cent of the workforce returning year after year. One-sixth of the company's full-time workers and managers were once migrant workers.

Wages at the nurseries remain low, albeit in compliance with minimum wage laws. Only 30 hours per week are guaranteed. Despite these factors, McKay is considered to be at the forefront and has won an award from the Business Enterprise Trust, which honors companies that combine a healthy bottom line with social rewards.

VW "workholders"

VW is Europe's largest automobile manufacturer. Under their workholder-value scheme, announced in October 1996, workers receive part of their wages in "time" shares with interest. These can be cashed in to gain early retirement, take an extra holiday or protect themselves against redundancy. In reality, this gives workers a stake in the long-term success and viability of the company, and enhances financial shareholdings. In Germany, shareholdings are often held through local banks which see it as long-term investment that rewards both shareholders and the local community through the payment of workers, who use the banks and the shops and buy houses. The scheme fits in with VW's offer of guaranteed employment in exchange for greater flexibility on working hours on the part of employees.

The difference between Anglo-American shareholder value and VW's new workholding employee scheme is that the former tends to be based on instant liquidity (the ability to buy and sell shares quickly) and the desire for short-term gain, and the latter is based on a long-term relationship. Saying that too much attention had been given to shareholder value in the past, VW's Personnel Director, Peter Hartz, says that the new scheme "combines the notion of workholder value and company value."

VW's major competitor, Mercedes-Benz, Germany's largest industrial group, may be more interested in earnings per share than VW but even it acknowledges the limits of focusing too much on shareholder value. The Chairman of Mercedes-Benz said: "Shareholder value must not be pushed for short-term success at the expense of future viability and future earnings potential." In a reference to all those who had a stake in Mercedes' future he said, "Our future lies not only in chips, machinery, buildings and concepts but also in the heads and hearts of our employees."

Germany has a constitution that demands democratic representation on boards of companies and a long tradition of consensus building in industrial relations, but there is a debate in progress which questions this post-1945 inclusivity. This example of inclusivity at VW may provide a solution for a global economy. If workers are not exploited by the new flexible working arrangements but retain employment and at the same time shareholders are rewarded with profits, this may provide a model for other companies.

The problem that VW has to solve now is the fact that the European car market is almost saturated, and so it must export, but we are probably seeing the beginning of the end for the fossil-fuel-burning internal combustion engine as resources become exhausted and we count the cost of poor air quality and urban congestion. VW will have to be innovative and adaptable if it is to rise to the challenge of mobility in the twenty-first century and fulfil its commitments to shareholders, workholders and the environment. There are other stakeholders to be considered, not least the non-car-owning public.

....

Manganese Steel: closure and close-out are not the only options

The name Manganese Steel has an old and proud lineage. It was the company where Harry Brealey of Sheffield gave stainless steel to the world, but, in 1983, Manganese was an off-the-shelf company name owned by the steelmaking division of the Lonrho Group. The Group closed down one of its companies despite the fact that it had a highly profitable drop-forging operation, many said because it, unlike other Lonrho companies, had supported a trade union call for a national steel strike.

Sheffield City Council, joined local trade unions in a vigorous commitment to the city's economic infrastructure. The decision was taken to make this the steelworks which could successfully re-open, and over £500,000 ($825,000) of public money (a considerable sum at that time) was made available, and a company was formed utilizing the historic name. An agreement was reached with Lonrho for steel billet supply to the new company and a steelworkers' union official, Keith Jones, was appointed as the company director responsible for liaison on workforce matters with the city council. Commercial managers were appointed, including a former trade union convener. Forty-one jobs were created in a slimmed-down forging operation and, significantly, the new workforce voted unanimously to contribute six weeks' work without pay to the new venture.

This was not a workers' co-operative but a commercial venture with a radical difference. The intention was to recreate jobs within the economic process which had been taken away by that process, and all the participants invested what they could in order to derive a benefit. Lonrho provided steel supply at a favorable margin; the workforce committed themselves and their initial wages; the council gave its cash and its imprimatur; others gave their soul to Manganese. Nevertheless, there were critics.

The official Sheffield trade unions pulled away very quickly, condemning the flexible working and unpaid overtime which had to be implemented. Cynical observers in the local business press suggested that the early secretive behavior of the commercial management represented a cabal rather than a shared venture.

But Manganese was a flagship. It was the first, and only, steelworks successfully to re-open and re-employ people. Things did not have to be the way they had been before – dereliction and despair. There was hope.

Manganese lasted eighteen months in all, and a number of factors eventually conspired against it. Sheffield City Council was asked for further funding and, in the atmosphere heightened of attacks on local authorities at that time, this was turned down. Key customers closed down in the prevailing economic climate, for example, a tractor company and a digger manufacturer. Internal disputes broke out with the management, over conditions and pay. Crucially, Lonrho did not renew the terms of the supply agreement but increased them.

Afterwards, the Meadowhall shopping mall was built on the site of the other Lonrho steel plant which also closed. There was talk of Manganese only ever having been a property deal dressed up as something else. In a world where industrial production, particularly in the steel industry, was shifting to other areas of the world and where new business practice and foresight is required, the community of workers, investors, suppliers, government and customers were unable to keep the steel industry alive in Sheffield.

Business and communities

The local community

"Tomorrow's successful company can no longer afford to be a faceless institution that does nothing more than sell the right product at the right price. It will have to present itself more as if it were a person – as an intelligent actor, of upright character, that brings explicit moral judgments to bear on dealings with its own employees and with the wider world."

The Economist[30]

Business has an impact on the local community and vice versa. Social and environmental issues are inherently linked to major strategic considerations.

For example, does the local education system provide an adequate education for future workers? If not, the answer is not only about donating funds, but about getting involved. Encouraging staff to get involved in mentoring, or as governors on local school boards is an important part of staff development as well as a contribution to the local community. In the UK many companies offer secondment to their employees, or working on full pay in a charitable organization or a similar setting, as a way of developing their skills and experience.

Many companies consider corporate social responsibility an exercise in handing out money. While charity is laudable, the key is how a business is run and how the business contributes through its employees, products and promises to the community, not simply through philanthropy.

The global and the local: Marks & Spencer's secondment policy

Marks & Spencer (M & S) is not one of the largest retail outlets in the world, but it is the fourth most profitable. It is also a British institution, and there is a branch in every high street and shopping mall. Prime Ministers Margaret Thatcher and Tony Blair have been happy to tell the world that they buy their clothes there.

M & S is proud of its community involvement. In 1996, M & S supported 1,200 charities, spent $14.0 million on community initiatives, of which $8.1 million were direct donations and they have 35 staff on full-time secondment, and a further 200 staff on part-time secondment (see Appendix 2: Glossary).

The benefits of a secondment are:

- *the company* gains the enhanced capabilities of the returning secondee, and an enhanced image and profile in the community as the secondee becomes an ambassador;
- *the receiving organization* gains professional expertise and skills which it could not otherwise afford. The secondee also brings experience from the commercial sector and a fresh, and perhaps creative, approach to problem solving;
- *the secondee* gains an opportunity to learn about other organizations, normally outside the private sector. He or she is also given the opportunity to succeed outside Marks & Spencer, to develop new skills, to see the business from outside and "improve Company knowledge of, and make a direct contribution to, the local community."[31]

In a global economy, what does "local" mean?

Until fairly recently, most companies based their headquarters in a single city or town. Their activities in the community were primarily geared to that community. In Atlanta, for example, Emory University is known as "Coca-Cola University." With globalization, companies often have multiple bases or headquarters, all of which benefit from the association with the company, but not exclusively. The implications are significant, both for the company and the community.

In order to compete in a global economy, companies are developing multiple headquarters. Even if the company maintains a single HQ, it will increasingly need to address community needs in many locations.

What are the obligations of the company to the local community in which it sources? Even if the company does not wholly own and operate a facility in a poor location, what role should it play in the community?

Engaging the community

Here are some examples of community initiatives from around the world which have benefited both the companies involved and the communities in which they operate. Each community initiative has to be tailored to local circumstances, but there are common themes:

- building partnerships and understanding in the local community;
- earning a licence to operate;
- developing staff skills and opportunities;
- giving back to the community.

These examples come from the USA, the UK, Thailand, France, India, Mexico and Guatemala.

USA

Levi Strauss & Co.'s Community Investment Team

Levi Strauss & Co. has pioneered the idea of the Community Investment Team (CIT) – a group of employees who meet periodically to make decisions about how the company's charitable donations should be allocated. There are over 100 CITs around the world in selected communities where employees of Levi Strauss & Co. live and work.

Steps for engaging the local community

1 Identify local problems such as crime, homelessness, AIDS, poverty, unemployment, inadequate education, racism.

2 How do these problems affect your business? your community? the planet?
   - *Crime* affects employees, customers, shop owners, tourists, and reflects badly on the city.
   - *Homelessness* affects the city or town.
   - *AIDS* affects employees and their families and everyone's health insurance costs.
   - *Poverty and unemployment* affect the customer base.
   - *Environmental problems* affect the health of the workforce and the community; their future costs affect the image of the locality and tourism.
   - *Inadequate educational system* affects quality and caliber of future employees.
   - *Racism* affects employees, customers.
   - *Urban decay* is your company part of the problem?

3 Develop a strategy:
   - work with local groups
   - secondment
   - funding
   - work with other companies
   - playing it safe: investing in the arts.

Building Timberland in the USA

Timberland (see also Chapter 1) manufactures footwear and clothing for markets in 51 countries. The company employs 7,000 people worldwide. The company's mission statement reflects the values of the company: "Each individual can, and must, make a difference in the way we experience life on this planet."[32]

In 1995, Timberland was awarded a Corporate Conscience Award for community involvement. Timberland has created a partnership with City Year, an urban peace corps program of young people working to make a difference in urban areas blighted by poverty. The program includes 600 people between the ages of 17 and 23 who come from diverse backgrounds, from high school drops-outs to those who have attended private schools. The youth corps teaches literacy skills, removes refuse from deserted lots, assists the elderly and, through such activities, learns to work in teams. The corps serves the community and its members are paid a weekly stipend. At the end of the term, they receive a scholarship for college. In 1994, Timberland announced that it would give City Year $5 million over five years.

The partnership is a win–win scenario, benefiting cities and employing the young, many of whom are high-risk. In some instances, Timberland has recruited City Year teenagers when their terms end. Timberland benefits as well. City Year leaders organize workshops for company executives on team building and diversity. The company's executives serve as volunteers in the community, developing a broader range of leadership skills and the ability to interact with a diverse range of people. Each employee is encouraged to volunteer 32 hours per year on company time. In 1996, employees volunteered 10,000 hours. Timberland's goal is to log 40,000 hours of community service per year.[33]

According to Jeffrey Swartz, Chief Operating Officer at Timberland, the partnership with City Year "creates value for us. We don't do any executive training except City Year. We do all our team building with City Year; we consume services from City Year in that regard."[34]

The Timberland–City Year partnership has won the company praise from President Clinton, who often cites the partnership as a model. The company has launched City Year Gear, which is a clothing line that carries inspirational messages. Timberland donates all profits from the sale of this line to City Year. Timberland has a history of using its advertising to promote social causes. When the company found that its boots were becoming *de rigueur* with skin-head groups, some of whom espouse neo-Nazi slogans, the company launched its "Give racism the boot campaign," using the slogan to promote its boot.

Britain

The London Benchmarking Group

The London Benchmarking Group is an informal association between companies taking a leading role in developing corporate community activities. Its members in 1997 were: BP, GrandMetropolitan (now Diageo), IBM UK, Marks & Spencer, NatWest and Whitbread.

The companies came together to try to pool knowledge and experience in good community practice, and to find an effective way of assessing and reporting the value of corporate community involvement, both to internal company audiences, and externally.

The group has declared itself committed to good corporate citizenship, which it defines as:

- running your business lawfully and ethically;
- providing goods and services society wants and needs;
- providing jobs;
- paying taxes which are used to fund social and cultural provision;
- making charitable donations;

,eking mutual benefit, for both the companies and communities, through working
,vith government and the non-profit sector.

The group see the business benefits of good corporate citizenship as:

- building staff skills and motivation;
- building your markets;
- building a license to operate – getting to know complex communities better, and their getting to know you.

The group uses the following categories to describe the range of activities it is involved in:

- *charitable giving*: as a response to appeals from the community such as in donations, social sponsorship, secondments and consultancy, in-kind giving, matched giving, volunteering, collecting for charities from customers;
- *social investment*: meaning sustained involvement in issues important for the community, such as through grants and donations, secondments and consultancy, in-kind contributions, in-house training, supplier development;
- *commercial initiatives*: partnerships to promote and protect commercial interests, such as sponsorship, cause-related marketing, cash/in-kind contributions, and staff development.

Members of the Benchmarking Group feel that the wide scope of these activities is not adequately captured by conventional measures, such as total spending on community activities, or staff hours involved. Effective measures should involve some attempt to assess benefits both to the community and to the business, and should involve benchmarking to help the development of good practice. The group is working to develop benchmarks for its own use, in the belief that these will also be more widely adopted.

The Corporate Community Index

In a separate, but complementary initiative the Corporate Community Index[35] has been developed as a management tool for companies to evaluate and enhance their community involvement programs.

The assessment covers eight areas:

1. purpose and objectives
2. leadership and management
3. programs and activities
4. internal communications
5. external communications
6. measurement and evaluation

7   business benefits

8   community benefits.

All areas are given scores up to 100, based on sampling of projects, interviews with project leaders and company self-assessment.

Thailand

Bata Thailand and the Thai Business Initiative in Rural Development: shoe-in

Three-quarters of the 4 million workers in Bangkok have emigrated from rural provinces. For Bangkok, the consequences are grim: rising rates of unemployment, growth of slum areas, pollution, congestion and increased rates of child labor. The consequences for rural areas are also dramatic: deprived of young adults, rural areas become less able to support their populations, especially the elderly.

Government alone is unable to stem the flow of migration to the cities. But how can the private sector address this complex issue? Enter the Thai Business Initiative in Rural Development (TBIRD), aimed at mobilizing the private sector to provide skills and business expertise to rural communities in need. Through TBIRD, Thai and multinational companies adopt rural villages, providing rural communities with marketing expertise, financial resources, and training to promote job creation. Over 35 companies have adopted rural villages, including the American International Assurance Company, Bangkok Glass, Bata, Bristol Myers-Squibb, Nestlé, and Volvo.

Bata, the world's largest manufacturer and marketer of footwear, with activities in 60 countries, has been in Thailand for over 60 years. Bata has adopted a village in Buri Ram province, and assisted in the establishment of four factories, employing 140 people and manufacturing 8,000 shoe-uppers per day. Three-quarters of the workers are reverse migrants, that is, they were born in the province, migrated to the cities in search of work, and have returned to the province to form part of the co-operative.

The Bata initiative is among the most promising of the TBIRD initiatives, because it is not purely charitable in nature. The result is a win–win proposition, for Bata, the workers, the province and the cities. Bata has increased production by 35,000 shoes per day. Workers now live near their families, keeping their community and way of life intact. By strengthening the capacity of local villages to support families, TBIRD addresses the root causes of migration.[36]

France

Auchan: combating gang warfare

Auchan is France's second-largest hypermarket chain with $24 billion in sales and 120,000 employees. It has over 119 stores throughout France. Since 1981, the company has expanded its international presence, opening stores in Spain, Portugal, Italy, the USA, Poland, Mexico, and Luxembourg. Plans for growth in Hungary, Argentina, Thailand, and China are underway.

Imagine that violent gang warfare has broken out outside your store, leaving customers too frightened to enter. Just when you think it can get no worse, a call comes through from the store manager, informing you that a security guard has been killed in the cross-fire.

Auchan had two choices when faced with this scenario: close the store or take a radical stance. In a spirit of risk, the company decided to seek out the gang leaders and hire them to serve as security guards. The results were excellent and customers began to return to the store. Auchan also provided retail space for several community-owned boutiques. The company was addressing some of the root causes of the problem: poverty, racism and unemployment.

In the Loire valley, Auchan hired ten young people who had not worked for two years. Each youth was mentored by an older employee. Auchan's Director of Human Resources Jean-Marie Deberdt, explains: "When the teenagers first came to us, they did not speak well, could not wake up early, did not bathe. At the end of one year of working and attending training sessions, the results were incredible. Not only did it change the lives of the teenagers, it also changed how managers dealt with people."

Dealing with urban problems is no longer the responsibility of government alone. Business is beginning to take on the challenge of addressing unemployment, crime, poverty and racism that plague the cities and attack profits.

What you see depends upon where you stand.

India

Unilever in Uttar Pradesh

The problem appeared simple enough – Hindustan Lever, a subsidiary of Unilever, had a dairy in a rural part of India which was losing money. This was the kind of clear-cut, routine decision that most managers take when faced with loss: closing the dairy was the only real alternative.

Why was the dairy a failure? The farmers were too poor to adequately feed and care for their cattle. They could hardly afford to purchase the kind of cattle necessary for a productive business. If poverty was the major constraint, what steps could Hindustan Lever take to address this abject poverty?

Hindustan Lever decided to take a radical step: to invest in the development of the rural community, based in the state of Uttar Pradesh. The company provided interest-free loans to the farmers to enable them to feed and care for their cattle, so as to improve the quality and quantity of the milk they produced.

Hindustan Lever assisted in the formation of a five-year plan to improve human and animal health. The company served as a catalyst for attracting government investment for roads, schools and medical clinics.

What made this visionary, long-term approach possible was a deep knowledge of village culture. Each year, Hindustan Lever sends 50 trainees (its annual recruitment of MBAs) to live in the villages of Etah for several weeks. Most of these trainees come from Mumbai and Delhi, so they are experiencing rural life for the first time. Among the best and the brightest, they learn to identify the needs and priorities of the community and then assist in promoting development initiatives. By making use of their government contacts, the trainees have encouraged the government to provide electricity, roads and improved wells. With 50–60 per cent of Hindustan Lever/Lipton's business made in rural communities, future managers gain a valuable perspective on customers. Both company and community benefit.

Within just a few years, the dairy was making considerable profits, which were being reinvested into the community. The development initiative now covers 400 villages in the state of Uttar Pradesh. The company is investing 10 per cent of its pre-tax profits in development initiatives.

With government unable to meet the needs of people, the private sector is able to use leverage to encourage government support and to provide assistance to rural communities for the promotion of the kind of growth which is necessary for business success.[37]

Mexico

Fondo Social del Empresariado Chihuahuense (Chihuahua's Business Social Trust)

Throughout Latin America, the church and the state have been the primary agents addressing social needs. In areas of the world where corruption is a serious problem and where the non-profit sector is weak, forging ties between business, the state, and non-governmental organizations is more difficult.

In the deprived region of Chihuahua, a group of businesses has set up the above Trust to promote social development, together with the state. By adding a 10 per cent surcharge on the business state payroll tax, the Trust will have $2 million to assist nursing homes, drug rehabilitation centers, hospitals, the homeless and indigenous peoples. The Trust seeks to deploy these funds with additional support from both national and international sources of funding.

The Trust is managed by 18 business leaders, two representatives from the state and two local congressmen. "The program is not intended to substitute the state's responsibility, but as a complementary contribution to mitigate pain."[38]

According to Jorge Villalobos Grzybowicz, the Director of the Mexican Center for Philanthropy, corporate philanthropy exists in Mexico, but is not yet a part of the corporate culture, it remains a sporadic and individualized endeavor. The formation of new linkages between business, the State, and non-profit organizations is an important trend. The Chihuahuan model is replicable in other regions of the world.

Guatemala

Phillips Van Heusen

Phillips Van Heusen owns many major clothing lines, including Izod, Van Heusen, and Geoffrey Beene, making a wide range of sportswear and business clothing. The company has 13,000 associates worldwide.

Phillips Van Heusen (PVH) funds an educational program in the highlands of Guatemala to improve the education of indigenous people. With significant sourcing operations in Guatemala, the company seeks to make a difference in a community besieged by poverty. An inadequate educational system fosters poverty. With children receiving only two years of education, the vicious cycle of poverty was being perpetuated. Girls were found to be at a significant disadvantage.

It is a five-year program which targets 34,000 children in seven schools costing $1.5 million. PVH engaged a local consulting firm to conduct a study on child education in the highland region which uncovered several reasons for the failure of the existing educational system: a perception that the school experience is irrelevant, economic pressures which push children into the workforce at an early age, a lack of adequate infrastructure and absenteeism among teachers.

Managed by the American Jewish World Service and funded by PVH, Project New Educational Opportunities (NEO) seeks to improve the opportunities available to children. The project combines five main lines of action: family involvement and community action, pre-school activities, educational methods, improvement of the infrastructure, equipment and materials, and health and nutrition.

Building partnerships
·····························

A number of radical partnerships are mentioned in this book, such as McDonald's work with the Environmental Defense Fund in the USA, the Ethical Trade Initiative in the UK funded by the UK's Department for International Development bringing together multilateral organizations and businesses, and the Council on Economic Priorities' Forum on Global Standards. Faced with social-responsibility issues, many far-sighted businesses are inviting their protagonists into the boardroom in order that dialogue rather than confrontation takes place, and in order that a common solution can be effected.

A partnership for progress: McDonald's and the Environmental Defense Fund

The first McDonald's burger drive-in was opened by Mac and Dick just outside Los Angeles in 1940. By 1995 the chain was able to state in its annual report:

> "McDonald's vision is to dominate the global food service industry. Global performance means setting the performance standard for customer satisfaction while increasing market share and profitability through Convenience, Value and Execution Strategies."

McDonald's products are enjoyed by 33 million people every day around the world, but are regarded by some as cultural imperialists, environmental hooligans and exploiters of child labor. Global corporations often arouse the strongest of passions. But this is the story of the world's first business and environmental group partnership. As Murphy and Bendell[39] have said: "The likelihood of partnership between one of the icons of the throw-away society and a credible environmental group would for most environmentalists seem morally repugnant and quite unthinkable." But corporate citizenship is about a new way of doing business based on partnership, consensus building and the inclusive business. In August 1990, McDonald's signed an agreement with the Environmental Defense Fund to establish a joint task force to address the company's solid waste issues.

In 1995, McDonald's had an annual turnover in excess of $30 billion worldwide. It buys $7 billion worth of food, paper and packaging annually for 21,000 outlets in over 100 countries. In the USA it is the single largest consumer of packaging. As a 1994 leaflet stated: "At McDonald's we believe we have a special responsibility to help protect and preserve our environment for future generations." So, McDonald's understood its responsibilities when it was the object of demonstrations and attacks against the "clamshell" packaging for the burgers. Research showed that the issue was not as straightforward as the protesters or McDonald's might have thought. For instance, if the issue was waste disposal then the fact that in some cases more than 75 per cent of

McDonald's waste is disposed of by customers, away from the restaurant, makes it the responsibility of customers, not the chain to dispose of it responsibly – doesn't it? Or is it the responsibility of McDonald's to produce waste which is easily disposable and non-toxic? If this is the case then is a polystyrene clam shell more environmentally responsible than a paper box? Initial research showed, much to the antagonists' surprise, that the clam shell came out better. So while magazines such as *Rolling Stone* described McDonald's as: "a symbol of ecological evil," McDonald's 1990 annual report said that: "Although some scientific studies indicate that foam packaging is environmentally sound, customers just didn't feel good about it."

In mid-1989 McDonald's Vice-President, Shelby Yastrow appeared opposite Fred Krupp, Executive Director of the New York-based Environmental Defense Fund (EDF), on a cable television program. Krupp and Yastrow decided to work together, to the relief of McDonald's, who had previously found it difficult to find a partner willing to work with them apart from the World Wide Fund for Nature (WWF – USA) with whom they had produced a leaflet on rainforest issues.

The EDF was founded in 1967 on a grant from a Rachel Carson[40] memorial fund. In 1984 it appointed Fred Krupp, a Harvard lawyer, as Executive Director who improved EDF's technical and scientific capabilities, turning it into an expert group, and moved it towards "third-wave environmentalism"[41] where it embraced market-base solutions to business problems. As Krupp said at the time: "We're not ideologues in environmental issues . . . I think environmentalists would become more powerful, more forceful and achieve greater results if we deployed more tools in our tool kit. We should continue to aggressively lobby, aggressively litigate, aggressively criticize corporate malfeasance and promote stricter regulation. We also should be able to problem-solve with corporation."

The guidelines for The Waste Reduction Task Force was that:

- it should evaluate the company's materials use and solid-waste stream and develop a policy;
- no money would change hands;
- either side could terminate the project if it was unhappy;
- both sides would continue their current activities and EDF reserved its right to criticize McDonald's;
- McDonald's requested that EDF's task-force members work in a restaurant for one day each;
- the task force should not look at any other issues, such as global warming, rainforest destruction and food consumption.

The Task Force subsequently arrived at a policy which was endorsed by the company:

- The company should take a "total lifecycle" approach to managing solid waste.
- Reduce waste and volume of packaging.
- Make maximum use of reusable and recyclable materials where possible.

- Conserve and protect natural resources through increased efficiency and conservation.
- Encourage environmental values and practices in local communities by providing educational materials.
- Ensure accountability procedures.
- Maintain productive, on-going dialogue with all stakeholders.

Since the policy agreement, McDonald's has made substantial savings in waste and uses significant amounts of recycled material, all of which are monitored by the EDF. There are those who have criticized the partnership, arguing that it merely provided excellent PR for McDonald's and prostituted the EDF. One thing that is clear, this partnership has set a standard for other agreements around the world and is a model for organizations in all sectors.

As an endnote, it is worth commenting that despite the fact that McDonald's says it dictates environmental policy to its subsidiaries, the plastic clam shell is still used in more than 25 per cent of McDonald's restaurants round the world. The fact is that the clam shell keeps the burgers hotter longer!

....

Shell and road builder Tarmac Construction have employed mediators like the Environment Council to help build links between them and groups opposed to their activities. Sometimes this leads to partnerships, but more often than not it produces positive dialogue where the two sides find common ground, and discover that they share more than they realized. Referring to Shell's decision to dump the Brent Spar oil rig in the North Sea (it is now to become a dock in Norway), its UK Chairman, Chris Fay, acknowledged that his company needed the mediation skills of the Environment Council because previously the company had been "insufficiently sensitive" and that it had learned from that experience, having "tended to communicate at a technical level rather than in ways that people could understand."[42]

Given that it is not uncommon for business people to describe environmentalists and human rights activists as "sandal-wearing, lentil-eating, scruffy luddites," and for the opposing camp to describe the opposition as "suits with the ethics of alley cats," it takes courage and understanding to get opposing groups talking. But it is happening, and showing significant results, many of which are catalogued in David Murphy and Jem Bendell's *In the Company of Partners*.[43] A similar theme is adopted in SustainAbility's study with UNEP *Engaging Stakeholders*,[44] in the work for the Prince of Wales Business Leaders' Forum by Jane Nelson,[45] and in Ashridge's *Partnerships at Work*.[46]

Partnerships at work

Management challenges in partnership have been summarized by Kate Charlton[47] as:

Stage 1:   emergence of the partnership, where partners come together in pursuit of funding, or through recognition of a need.

Stage 2:   establishing a vision for the partnership, in order to produce an agenda for action.

Stage 3:   establishment of a formal structure for the partnership.

Stage 4:   delivery and action plan implemented; policy evolves and remains accountable.

Stage 5:   life after partnership, including continuing the work in hand.

Business as partners in development

"Multi-stakeholder partnerships are not the answer to every problem. Nor are they easy to achieve in practice. If they can be made to work, however, they can offer many benefits both for individual companies and for society at large."[48]

This report highlighted the three partner groups:

- *Government*: national state and local, and multilateral and bilateral governmental organizations;
- *Private sector / business*: corporations and multinationals, business and industry associations, small and micro enterprises;
- *Civil society / Non-Governmental Organizations (NGOs)*: civil society is represented by many different sorts of NGOs with various agendas, local, regional and global, rich and poor. Civil society may also just be individuals, voicing concerns.

A guide to developing partnerships[49]

If planned and implemented appropriately, partnerships can offer both business and different kinds of NGOs useful tools to discuss and promote global sustainability. Although each partnership is different there are some common themes. Accordingly, some common lessons can be learned for the successful management of the partnership process.

Partnerships can be understood as moving through three phases:

1 Initiation: this involves the initial contact between those who will form the core participants. Usually an agreement to co-operate is signed, which outlines the goals of the partnership, along with the respective roles and responsibilities of the partners.

▶

---

2 Implementation: this follows the initiation phase and deals with practical issues, rather than conceptual or process issues. Agreements are implemented, with participants learning from the partnership experience and adjusting goals in light of this experience.

3. Evolution: the end of the partnership often leads to a new form of process, product or project-oriented partnership.

CHECKLIST

Here is a checklist for the successful management of partnerships:

1 Initiation

- Identify partnership purpose: process oriented, project oriented or product oriented.
- Define the problem, the common ground and the opportunity.
- Define clear and defensible objectives and action plans.
- Identify key people to lead the partnership process.
- Engage critical stakeholders in the process and decide on mechanisms for their future input.
- Establish equitable and open decision-making procedures.
- Launch the partnership in an open public forum.
- Establish a basis for continued collaboration.

Suggestions for business

- Inform contacts in trade associations and other professional bodies.
- Consult those involved in similar initiatives to assess the practicality of the proposed goals.
- Find out the levels of expertise held by the proposed NGO partner, assess its campaigns and identify the benefits it can offer.
- Involve departmental managers who will be substantially affected by the partnership.
- Be open with the environmental group partners about problems.
- Recognize the implications for core business practice.
- Do not use the partnership as an endorsement of your company by the NGO partner.

Suggestions for NGOs

- Inform counterparts in environmental groups working on similar issues.
- Identify and target those sectors of the industry with the greatest capacity to act quickly.
- Assess your organizational capacity to perform the required tasks.

►

- Encourage companies to embrace broad principles relating to corporate responsibility for the issue at stake.
- Seek corporate disclosure of information to the environmental group and the public.
- Be open about the potential pitfalls of working with business.

2   Implementation

- Support participant needs and interests with an emphasis on personal contacts.
- Be adaptive and revise goals if necessary.
- Resolve disputes quickly.
- Think creatively about new management systems to facilitate the developing partnership.
- Do not allow partnership managers to act with complete autonomy from senior management.
- Lobby government to support the initiative.

Suggestions for business

- Promote the vision of the partnership to key stakeholders.
- Define responsibility for day-to-day liaison with the NGO.
- Invest in the necessary information technology and training.
- Prepare research reports on the partnership to ensure that lessons are learned.
- See the initiative as a pilot project with potential implications for the future.

Suggestions for NGOs

- Co-ordinate trading, investment, corporate fund raising and campaigning branches of the organization.
- Develop a policy on relations with business if one is not already in place.
- Consult external experts to analyze the implications of the partnership.
- Seek feedback from business partners about your organization's role and contribution to the partnership.
- Do not let financial, resource and skills limitations restrict the growth of the partnership.
- Do not take money for partnerships which involve a public endorsement of participating businesses.

3   Evolution

- Celebrate the success and share the credit.
- Evaluate achievements against initial goals.
- Examine the potential to formalize achievements.
- Publish summaries of successes and failures.

● Support research into the initiative in order to identify lessons learned and new initiatives to be supported.

Suggestions for business

● Communicate successes and limitations to key stakeholders.

● Utilize the skills and knowledge learned.

● Attempt an assessment of costs against benefits.

Suggestions for NGOs

● Attempt an assessment against environmental gains, social development and more abstract goals.

Partnership in progress: Marine Stewardship Council (MSC)

In February 1996 the World Wide Fund for Nature (WWF) formed a conservation partnership with Unilever, the Anglo-Dutch food and detergent conglomerate, to "create market incentives for sustainable fishing"[50] by establishing an independent Marine Stewardship Council (MSC) in February 1997.

The MSC was modelled on the successful Forest Stewardship Council (FSC) formed in 1993 to promote market-led solutions towards sustainable forestry practices around the world. In the case of the MSC two global organizations, WWF and Unilever, with different motivations but the same objective, came together to tackle a shared problem – the decline of global fish stocks.[51]

The issue

● According to the UN's FAO (Food and Agricultural Organization) 70 per cent of the world's commercially important marine fish stocks are fully fished, over-exploited, depleted or slowly recovering.

● This has been caused by overfishing and industrial fishing where the sea floor is vacuumed. This involves sucking up not only fish for consumption but also smaller, undeveloped fish.

● It is estimated that because of this indiscriminate method of fishing one-third of the world's catch is thrown back dead or dying.

● Both WWF and Unilever have an interest in conserving fish stocks, the former because their purpose is to protect bio-diversity and the environment and the latter because fish are their raw material. No fish, no sales.

● Governments have conspicuously failed to halt the decline in fish stocks, the worst culprits being the European Union whose members have continued to argue about country fish quotas while fish stocks have continued to decline.

● According to the MSC governments worldwide pay an estimated US$54 billion each year to subsidize an industry that catches only US$70 billion worth of fish.

The partners

- WWF is one of the world's largest private, non-profit conservation organizations.
- Unilever sells fish to over 150 million people in Europe under labels such as Bird's Eye, Igloo and Gorton's and has some 20 per cent of the European and US frozen fish market with global sales worth $990m. Unilever's turnover was $52 billion in 1996 and its 500 companies operate globally.

The partnership

- The MSC is an independent, non-profit, non-governmental body with the aim of ensuring the long-term viability of global fish populations and the health of the marine eco-systems in which they live.
- Only fisheries meeting strict standards will be eligible for certification by independent accreditation firms.
- Products from accredited fisheries will be able to carry a logo from 1998 stating that the fish is from a sustainable source.
- Sainsbury's, the UK's second largest supermarket chain, has also agreed not to purchase any fish or derivatives, including fish oil, from unsustainable sources.
- Unilever says that by 2005 it will only purchase fish from sustainable sources.

The partnership approach

Unilever's reasons for promoting this partnership are that it wishes to be seen to be contributing to the common effort by working towards a sustainable world and that the MSC approach is based on the precautionary principle. Unilever wants to be seen to be "empowering consumers through a market-led initiative to sustainable fishing."[52] This is good business on Unilever's part and it helps preserve fish stocks and moves the world towards sustainability.

This form of partnership between business and key stakeholders (this is the word both partners have used) could be the future for the solution of many of the world's problems. While there are some who argue that because it is a market-led initiative, and it is the market for fish that has caused the problem, this partnership has succeeded in making progress where governments and the UN have failed in the past. It therefore provides hope and engages the key protagonists in constructive dialogue. If "politics is the art of the possible," then this is highly constructive politics.

This partnership is an example of the network or partnership business outlined earlier where the motive is not purely profit, but the solution to a global problem. In this case it could be argued that the MSC has a corporate identity; it certainly has a mission statement and corporate executives. It is also important in terms of corporate citizenship because it acknowledges the fact that large organizations such as Unilever, through their market position, have a responsibility which is greater than individual consumers.

Some retailers, such as Marks & Spencer in the UK, continue to argue that it is up to consumers to choose what they purchase. Unilever however has accepted that it has a responsibility to use its corporate power to change the situation and to inform customers of the true state of world fish stocks. By refusing to purchase fish from unsustainable stocks from 2005, Unilever, as a market leader, is also taking a stand against unscrupulous suppliers in the market.

It is also worth noting the consensus-building approach by WWF. This partnership has been built on a market-led approach, which may not solve the problem or find approval from some other environmental groups. But this is an issue, along with others, that has been brought to the world's attention by funded research and media activity from other global pressure groups such as Greenpeace, Friends of the Earth, the Sierra Club and the Royal Society for the Protection of Birds.

Re-measuring wealth: auditing and accountability

The International Institute for Management Development annually ranks countries on the basis of 225 competitiveness criteria placing the USA, Singapore, Hong Kong and Japan in the first four places for 1996 and 1997. Britain has slipped to nineteenth place because of, according to the report, "uneven development." It needs to "reassess the viability of its social model and ultimately the role of the state."

A more radical model of economic well-being is the Index of Sustainable Economic Welfare (ISEW). Most economists agree that GDP is not an accurate or sensible measure of a nation's wealth and that other measures are needed. The ISEW was developed in the USA by a group led by Herman Daly, a former World Bank economist, and provides a range of indicators which reflect how people feel about the quality of life. It is intended to highlight the way politicians have mis-sold economic growth to their electorates. The ISEW has been put to the test in many countries around the world, including the USA and the UK where it indicates that the quality of life fell between 1950 and 1996.[53]

Indicators of wealth: GDP versus ISEW

The problems of using the measure of gross domestic product (GDP)

- GDP measures economic change and market activity, not quality of life.
- GDP measures the easily measurable, not what people experience.
- GDP takes no account of what is desirable and what is undesirable.

- GDP is still used to determine national economic policy, and determine the destination of overseas funds.
- According to Herman Daly, GDP "treats the Earth as a business in liquidation,"[54] meaning that we are using up all the Earth's capital assets.
- Examples of GDP's inadequacy:
  - Children watching television enhances GDP, but talking to their parents does not register.
  - A car crash in which the driver is killed and the car demolished causes a rise in GDP.
  - Increased tobacco and arms sales are economic growth, as measured by GDP.

Arguments for the Index of Sustainable Economic Welfare (ISEW)

- ISEW takes into account the increasing proportion of income required to mitigate environmental and social costs.
- ISEW takes into account things which individuals cannot buy, such as poor air quality, loss of wildlife amenities and space and the depletion of natural resources.
- ISEW provides a longer-term perspective than GDP, offsets expenditures caused by a degradation in the environment, reflects disparities in wealth and reflects man-made capital.
- ISEW attempts to indicate aspects of life that affect economic well-being and business success, such as emotional stress, ill-health and the erosion of trust.
- ISEW measures crime rates, youth delinquency and the state of family life.

Using these measures, Daly and colleagues in the USA, and the New Economics Foundation and Friends of the Earth in the UK, say that the growth in GDP from 1950 to 1975 was matched by an increase in the quality of life, as measured by ISEW. Since then, however, ISEW has failed to keep level with GDP, and in the UK's case, ISEW shows a severe decline in the quality of life for the UK's inhabitants.[55]

When Adam Smith, the founder of modern economics, was writing the *Wealth of Nations* in 1776 there appeared to be two certainties. First, natural resources seemed limitless; the rivers were full of fish; the population was small; there was plenty of space and the land offered numerous opportunities for development. Second, business activity was in a position to change the established social structure. Smith also deliberately excluded the service economy from his understanding of the wealth of nations because he said that it did not add value. He maintained that a nation's well-being could not be increased by the accumulation of financial wealth, but by the manufacturing of products, the growing of crops and animal husbandry. However, at the end of the twentieth century, entertainment and service industries have become the real areas of growth for many post-industrial economies, particularly the USA and the UK.

It is now increasingly recognized that there are limits to the growth of human activity on earth and that development has to be measured for standard of living *and* quality of life. For instance, companies interested in investing or building facilities in overseas markets require more information than figures for average personal income or the country's gross domestic product (GDP). According to various guides to business, companies seeking to relocate are interested in a range of issues including ease of access to clients and customers, transport infrastructure, quality of telecommunications, the training and skills of local staff, freedom from pollution and the quality of life for employees.[56] As business people move from one city to another they are likely to compare the metro system in Paris to that in New York and Tokyo, the air quality in Beijing, Kuala Lumpur and London, and the risk of being mugged in Sydney, to Los Angeles and Reykjavik.

Some people in the world are starting to think about adopting strategies for sustainable development, so we must develop indicators that allow continuous monitoring and reporting of the state of the environment. We also need to be able to make international comparisons. In some areas, such as air quality, this is relatively straightforward because the measurements, being scientifically and quantitatively based, have some agreed parameters. Other indicators, such as transport use, are less easy to compile because they depend on local conditions and social use (see Table 5.2).

We are making a link between indicators of the quality of life in communities and business performance. Increasingly, companies are required to provide information which goes beyond an historical financial account: "The market will expect more depth and complexity of information covering a broader front and all against a backcloth of more competition, often coming from areas not previously anticipated."[57]

Much of this information is based on environmental sustainability and indicators of social impact which have been developed at a local community level and by global institutions such as the United Nations, and nongovernmental organizations, such as Amnesty International and the International Chamber of Commerce.

Table 5.2 The UK's indicators for sustainable development[58]

These include economic measurements and the quality of life:

● the economy	● acid deposition
● transport use	● air quality
● leisure and tourism	● freshwater quality
● overseas trade	● marine quality
● energy	● wildlife and habitat
● land use	● landscape
● water resources	● soil
● forestry	● minerals extraction
● fish resources	● waste
● climate change	● radioactivity
● ozone layer depletion	

The trend towards new ways of measuring the standard of living *and* the quality of life across society as a whole is reflected in new attempts to re-measure business activity using criteria that are not based simply on financial profit and loss. Just as GDP is slowly being discredited as an accurate portrayal of the state of a country, so there are moves to supplement financial accounts with other information about a company's performance. There is a need to improve the depth and breadth of financial accounts so that they are more comprehensive, and this is a corporate citizenship issue, but we want to look at three areas of innovation in corporate reporting on the environment, ethics and social impact. Just as societies need more information than cash flows in order to make sensible strategic decisions, so too do companies and their shareholders and other stakeholders. Managers who are genuinely intent on proceeding down the responsible corporate-citizenship route need tools for change. These include new auditing, reporting and verification systems, as well as aptitudes for partnership building and envisioning a different future.

The economics of breastfeeding: why we need alternative indicators of economic well-being

It is possible to have economic growth and for some businesses to be profitable while the long-term health of society declines. Here is an example.

Marilyn Waring, in *If Women Counted*,[59] has highlighted the example of breastfeeding versus infant-milk formula as a way of explaining the deficiencies in measuring wealth using the current GDP formula. Infant-milk formula has provided business opportunities over the last 50 years for companies like Nestlé, Meiji and SMA. These companies have marketed their products aggressively in

▶

the past, particularly in poor countries with low levels of literacy, and recently to busy employed mothers in other countries.

Obviously, some mothers need to use infant-milk formula, but, in general, all the evidence shows that "breast is best." As Waring says: "Studies of infant feeding patterns around the world indicate that breastfeeding generally is the most satisfactory food supply for infants, at least for the first four to six months of life."

Breastfeeding babies is better than infant-milk formula, when possible, for these reasons:

● It is more nutritional than other milk, including infant-milk formula.

● It is well-packaged.

● It is cheaper, having little, or no, market value.

● It does not require the purchase of bottles, teats or sterilizing equipment.

● Breast milk passes on the mother's immunities to the child.

● Breast-fed babies not only have a greater chance of surviving the first few years of life, but are also likely to be healthier in later life, so breast-fed babies are less of a drain on a country's health services.

● Breast-fed babies have better developed brains, and learn faster.

Breast milk has not been thought of as a food by economists and so has never been measured as part of GDP, until of course, it is replaced by infant milk formula. At this point, short-term economic growth is heralded by the government and the World Bank forgetting that in the longer term this move will put an increased strain on the services, such as healthcare and education.

For women, there are other issues associated with breastfeeding, including the fact that women are less likely to get pregnant while lactating and can, therefore, choose to have a break from what is often a life-threatening series of pregnancies. Obviously, the responsibility lies with men in this case, but breastfeeding sometimes gives women a short rest. This is a particular issue in countries with strong male cultures, oppression of women and low levels of literacy. When it comes to companies selling infant-milk formula, it is these same women that have often been convinced, for various reasons, of the efficacy of bottle milk, but have either been unable to read the instructions properly or have not had access to clean water to mix the formula with.

However breastfeeding versus infant-milk formula is not just an issue for women in developing countries; it is also an issue for all women working away from home. Most employers will not allow breastfeeding at work, and in many countries, it is often considered unacceptable to breastfeed in public places, such as restaurants and shopping malls.

None of these would be an issue if we were able to value mothers and future generations using non-financial criteria, within the criteria for ISEW. Supporting breastfeeding is one of the most significant long-term investments any society can make for the future. Companies that irresponsibly promote infant-milk formula, at the expense of breastfeeding, need to examine their shareholders' short-term profits against the long-term benefits to society as a whole.

Auditing business performance

Corporate citizenship requires openness and accountability in order to build long-lasting, trusting relationships with stakeholders.[60] We now live in the information age and it can be argued that we are awash with information, but we are also less sure about the future. Both governments and companies have to manage the flood of information and the increasing complexity of the global economy.

Just as society is interested in information which goes beyond financial data and looks at issues like resource use, environmental protection and social issues, so too business is more frequently being asked to provide more information about its performance, operations and impact.

Business performance can be audited against a variety of criteria and with a range of methodologies. In an audit, any organization, including a company, can be measured against:

● company policies
● regulations
● external benchmarks
● professional standards
● programs and targets, internally or externally devised
● stakeholder expectations.

An audit is simply an examination of the accounts, financial or otherwise, of an organization. It usually denotes third-party verification, as in financial accounts, although it may not with some types of audit. Financial auditing is relatively straightforward as it involves measurements of money within agreed parameters, laid down by regulations and professional standards. *Interpreting* financial accounts can be a different matter, depending on the expectations of a wide range of stakeholders, or key relationships.[61]

All organizations, apart from those that are informal or privately funded, have to conduct financial audits, and if they are public or private companies, they have to publish a set of accounts in all countries. These accounts should have been audited by a registered auditor, under a system sanctioned by the government of that country.

While this book is primarily concerned with global business organizations, the principles of corporate citizenship are also being applied to public and non-profit organizations. The auditing procedures and systems described here are suitable for any organization, of any size, operating in any area. It is for this reason that the European Eco-Management and Audit Scheme

(EMAS) (described on page 236) has been adapted for local authorities in the UK. Social auditing has also been pioneered by companies in different sectors and with a range of constitutions. Social and ethical auditing has also been used in public services such as healthcare trusts in the UK.

In the 1970s in California a few companies began conducting environmental audits and publishing them alongside their financial audits. The main impetus for this innovation were liability laws in the USA, and California in particular. Some companies, like Shell, began auditing and reporting on their environmental performance beyond compliance with regulations in the early 1980s.[62]

Environmental auditing has now been accelerated by the introduction of local, regional and global standards on environmental performance and a significant number of larger companies, although not all, now publish an environmental report as part of their annual accounts, or as a separate document. These reports have not, except in a few cases, had the status of audited reports, as they have not been verified independently. There is no legal requirement, in any country, to publish an environmental audit, but it is becoming part of a company's strategy to demonstrate best practice, benchmarking and the earning of approval from society, namely a "licence to operate."[63]

More recently, a few companies on both sides of the Atlantic have conducted ethical and social audits and published the results. These companies include Traidcraft,[64] The Body Shop, Ben & Jerry's and Shared Earth. Simon Zadek, research director at the New Economics Foundation (NEF),[65] estimated in 1997 that between 7 and 15 per cent of FTSE[66] companies are examining or experimenting with the idea of social audits. If this figure is correct, we can expect an explosion of published social audits in the next few years. Professor Kirk Hanson of Stanford University, who externally verified NEF's social audit of The Body Shop in 1996 said: "Social performance today has profound importance for commercial performance . . . the social audit will eventually be done much as the financial audit is now done."[67]

Social and ethical monitoring of companies has been taking place for some years and there have been many published comparisons of companies including the Council on Economic Priorities (CEP) *Shopping For A Better World*,[68] which sold nearly 1 million copies in the USA, *The Green Consumer Guide* by Elkington and Hailes,[69] which was a bestseller in the UK, *Changing Corporate Values* by Adams *et al.* in the UK,[70] which was based on CEP's US work, and *The Ethical Consumer Guide to Everyday Shopping* by the Ethical Consumer Research Association.[71]

Some large companies now publish reports on their community or citizenship work, a few of which are audited, and most of which are published with public relations in mind.

Before discussing environmental, ethical and social audits it is worth pointing out that these discrete areas overlap significantly and sometimes it is difficult to separate them out. For instance, an environmental audit will very likely refer to the company's acknowledgment of the principle of sustainability. As was discussed in Chapter 2, sustainability is concerned with issues of social justice, equity as much as with resource use and environmental degradation. As environmental, ethical and social auditing all require consultations with stakeholders this makes these audits significantly different from financial accounting. In this sense all three types of audit, that is excluding financial audits, can be categorized as forms of social audit because their compilation requires dialogue with stakeholders and developing an understanding of their perceptions and values. Environmental audits also involve monitoring against regulations, standards and objective targets.

Environmental auditing

The commonly accepted definition of an environmental audit comes from the International Chamber of Commerce (ICC) in 1989:

> *"A management tool comprising a systematic, documented, periodic and objective evaluation of how well environmental organization, management and equipment are performing with the aim of helping to safeguard the environment by: (I) facilitating management and control of environmental practices; and (II) assessing compliance with company policies, which includes meeting regulatory requirements."*[72]

The International Chamber of Commerce (ICC) made clear that in adopting the systems approach to environmental auditing it was crucial that "management at the highest levels overtly supports" the program. The key words in the definition, which apply to all audits, environmental or otherwise, are *systematic*, *documented*, *periodic* and *objective*, although objectivity may have to be determined in consultation with stakeholders.

The introduction of environmental auditing has seen a revolution in organizational accountability because it requires an examination of so many areas of activity. Environmental management also overlaps with health and safety, where there is considerable regulation and inspection in many countries, but not all.

The most important objectives of an environmental audit are:

- to measure a company's activities against regulations;
- to measure a company's activities against the company's policies;
- to monitor the effectiveness of a company's environmental management system;
- to lessen a company's environmental impact through continuous improvement.

However, the most important aspect of an environmental audit, and of all auditing, is to find areas for improvement. Auditing is only worthwhile as a systems-based activity if it is built on an appreciation of continuous improvement. There are few organizations that cannot improve on their environmental performance in some way.

The advantages of carrying out an environmental audit and producing an independently verified statement are:

- gaining management commitment;
- increasing employee confidence and raising morale;
- verified reports are likely to be believed; public relations reports less so;
- companies believe their own public relations and, most important, directors, managers and employees can talk the same language.

There are also significant financial advantages resulting from an audit:

- It lessens the likelihood of prosecution, which can be expensive in terms of public relations and court costs.
- Auditing often makes organizations aware of best practice and industry benchmarks and therefore increases competitiveness.
- It provides reassurance for customers, who are increasingly making choices based on brand image.
- Mergers and acquisitions are often only possible after the reassurance that an audit can bring.
- Insurance and investments costs are lower as environmental auditing reduces risk.

Environmental management standards

The first national environmental management system was devised in the UK under the title of BS 7750 (British Standard 7750) and was based on the quality management standard of BS 5570. This was adopted in the UK and in some other European countries. This has been superseded in the UK and Europe by the Eco-Management and Audit Scheme (EMAS) and the ISO 14000 series (International Standards Organization). The two new systems, EMAS and ISO 14000, are both systems-based and designed to build in continuous improvement (see Table 5.3). However, neither system is mandatory, despite the fact that EMAS was originally conceived as a standard which would be compulsory for certain industrial sectors, such as chemicals and aggregates.

Business lobbied hard against the introduction of mandatory environmental auditing and reporting and argued that self-regulation and benchmarking enforced by the market would bring about the necessary improvements in environmental performance. The business case dictated the outcome of the negotiations for ISO 14000 to an even greater extent, in order to provide a standard that was acceptable to industry in the USA where the threat of litigation based on environmental reporting was strongest.

Table 5.3 A comparison of ISO 14000, the global environmental standard and EMAS, the European scheme[73]

ISO 14000 series	EMAS
A recognized global standard	The European Union Regulation requires all member states to set up the necessary assessment procedures. The scheme is voluntary
Applies to organizations and sites	EMAS applies to sites only
Open to all organizations	Open to certain industrial sectors (and local government authorities in the UK)
No initial review is necessary	Initial review is mandatory
No register of environmental effects or legislation	Requires register of environmental effects and legislation
Only the environmental policy must be publicly available	Policy, program and EMAS must be publicly available
Requires an audit	Requires an audit more frequently than ISO 14000 and the methodology is more tightly defined
Only requires communication with contractors and suppliers	Requires certain levels of control over contractors and suppliers
Does not require an independently validated environmental statement	Requires an independently validated environmental statement

Social and ethical auditing
●●●●●●●●●●●●●●●●●●●●●●●●●●●●●●●●●●●●

When, in 1996, BT announced that it was to undertake a social audit its Chairman, Sir Ian Vallance said: "I believe that in today's society, companies not only need to operate in an ethical manner, but also need to demonstrate this publicly." BT's concern was a reflection of the bad publicity that companies like Nike, Shell and BP have attracted over their perceived insensitivity to social issues like exploitative child labor, poverty, other human-rights abuses and their lack of communication with key stakeholders.

Social and ethical auditing looks beyond the financial accounts at how companies affect their stakeholders as a reflection of society as a whole. The fact that systems of social auditing are being developed by the largest accountancy and consultancy firms means that this form of accountability is coming of age. As Keith Rosmarin of KPMG's Global Edge in South Africa, says: "A paradigm shift needs to take place whereby measurement and assessment methods which are standard practice in accounting and strategic development are also applied to social involvement." For KPMG in South Africa the advantages of social auditing mean: "Undertaking this work by necessity gives companies a greater openness to skills development. They begin to see factors like racial diversity in the workforce as an asset."[74]

Social auditing in its broadest sense covers social *and* ethical aspects of an organization, auditing procedures and management systems, accounting and reporting. For all these areas standards and methodologies are being developed in individual companies, in the public sector, by private consultancy firms, in multilateral organizations and in a number of countries. It is reasonable to say that no clear standard or methodology has emerged, although some patterns are emerging, which are being hotly debated. There are significant differences emerging in the current debate.

> *"The environmental report is merely one element of what really should be provided: a social audit, a way of expressing the impact a company has on society in every facet of it operations. The pressure to provide such a report in inexorable."*
>
> Sir Anthony Cleaver[75]

BT's social audit: working within a "robust ethical framework"

In December 1996 BT, the telecommunications giant, announced that it was going to conduct a social audit (see also profile in Chapter 2).

BT's chairman said that he believed that "commitment to ethical behavior has to become nothing more nor less than 'business as usual'. . . .Those who manage companies have a responsibility to underline the importance of ethics to our enterprises. There can be no question of simply paying lip service to the idea. We must, in our actions as well as our words, show our employees, our customers, and indeed, all our stakeholders what our company stands for what are our values. It is BT's view that everyone associated with the company has – and lives by – a robust ethical framework."

BT is a founder member of the Institute for Social and Ethical AccountAbility, established in 1969 by the New Economics Foundation (NEF) (see profile later in this chapter).[76] BT's interest in social accounting and social responsibility will be put the test when it publishes its first independently verified set of social accounts. At the launch of the social audit the people at BT were anxious to make sure that no one thought they had lost sight of their primary objective – "to provide good and competitively priced services. Beyond this, social responsibility is a factor that we think is growing to grow."

Of BT's annual advertising budget of between $248 million and $330 million, only $3.3 million is being spent on the social-responsibility campaign. Some indication was given at the launch by BT's director of corporate relations that social responsibility was seen as a public-relations campaign. Having advertised itself very heavily in the UK under the theme "it's good to talk," BT discovered that some people had had enough of BT's ads – enough to make it start a campaign to "stem the upward (negative) trend early on."[77]

According to an opinion poll carried out for BT in 1996, 80 per cent of people asked thought it was important to know about a company's attitude on issues of social responsibility, a figure which apparently has remained the same since 1989.[78] BT thinks that its campaign on social responsibility could become an issue in its own right, and if customers are concerned about the relationship between business, society and society's problems BT wants to be seen to care about them, and to have a better understanding of their social impact. This is the reason for its social audit.

The difference between social and ethical auditing

All audits, apart from financial audits, are in some way social and have ethical components, because they deal with stakeholders' values. But a distinction can be made between ethical and social audits. Ethical audits are essentially internal management tools, and a way of listening to the views of stakeholders, particularly those who work in the company, while social audits are primarily designed to make the organization account for its social impact. How it does this depends on what it is accountable for – regulations, policies, standards, benchmarks or stakeholders' expectations. In both cases dialogue takes place with stakeholders, in the case of the ethical audit internally, and in the case of the social audit, internally and externally.

While the term social audit has been in use since the 1960s, and there are references to it from the 1930s,[79] ethical auditing is a more recent phenomenon. Ethical audit tests the consistency of values throughout the organization.

The ethical audit

The specific questions that need to be addressed in an ethical audit are:

● what are the values of the organization?
● how were they derived?
● are they consistent with the way the organization works and what it does?
● do they conform with the values of the people working in the organization?

Sheena Carmichael, a consultant in ethics, with significant experience of carrying out ethical audits, says:

> *"The purpose of ethical audit is to inform senior management about ethical vulnerabilities. It will uncover ways in which organizational structure and processes prevent staff from doing the right thing. It can also be used to report on the ethical performance of the organization: in this case, the social effect, the effect on external stakeholders, will be measured."*[80]

The Co-operative Bank's ethical audit of customers and non-customers

When the Co-operative Bank (the Co-op) in the UK was 120 years old in 1992, it launched an ethical policy. The launch of the new policy was aimed at securing its long-standing customers and gaining new business. In the years since it has been spectacularly successful seeing an increase in customers through an advertising campaign which has branded its image on British banking. In 1997 it won a prestigious Corporate Conscience Award from the Council on Economic Priorities in the USA.

With its roots in the co-operative movement, the Co-op was based on the values of collectivism, tolerance and civil rights; of providing a service to customers in public service, trade unions and like-minded individuals. Through its innovations like being the first telephone banking service in the UK and distributing the first fee-free Gold Visa card for life, it has also gained the respect of the larger banks.

During 1990 and 1991 the bank carried out five market research surveys, three qualitative and two quantitative. These involved in-depth discussions with key stakeholders, both customers and non-customers, to find out what perceptions people had about banking in general, and about the Co-operative Bank in particular.

The findings have a bearing on the relationship between citizenship and corporate citizenship:

● Customers have little idea where banks invest their money.
● For many current customers there are specific issues that concern them:
  – 90 per cent were concerned about human rights;
  – 87 per cent were concerned about arms exports to oppressive regimes;
  – 80 per cent were concerned about animal exploitation.
● For non-customers 10–15 per cent said that an ethical policy would be a strong "pulling point," 75 per cent said that the issues of human rights, arms sales and animal exploitation were not important to them, and 10 per cent said that focusing on these issues would put them off opening an account at the bank.[81]

Since 1992 the Co-op has realized that it also has to concentrate on issues such as customer service and quality in order to be perceived as a responsible company (see also profile in Chapter 4).

The Co-op's survey of ethics in business

In 1992 the Co-operative Bank commissioned from the University of Westminster a survey of attitudes to ethics among Britain's managers in private business, 85 per cent of whom in the survey were male, aged between 35 and 54.

The results of the ethical survey were:

● 90 per cent said that business should pay for causing environmental damage, but only 7 per cent were willing to cycle to work;
● 39 per cent said that helping the poor was not the role of their company;
● 86 per cent said that positive discrimination should not be give to disabled people;
● 7 per cent said that it was OK to sell arms to repressive regimes and export pesticides banned in the UK overseas;
● 60 per cent said that they did not agree with boycotts against countries with poor records in human rights;
● 93 per cent said that tax evasion was unnecessary or illegitimate;
● 20 per cent said that they would rather cheat on their domestic partner than the Inland Revenue (the tax man);
● 23 per cent said that deviousness was necessary to be promoted;
● Among company directors, 72 per cent saw no reason not to drive large cars, and 68 per cent did not advocate banning products that consumed the world scarcest resources.

As the bank's managing director (now retired), Terry Thomas, said: "The business maxim 'win at all costs' is down but not yet out, and it is clear that more British businesses need to clarify their ethical stance."[82]

These two surveys show how a company can conduct partial ethical surveys, using external agencies, in this case to find out how the values of the company accord with their customers and society in general.

The Body Shop: social-responsibility criteria

The Body Shop is audited against the following criteria of social responsibility:

- Compliance with regulatory and international standards.
- Active disclosure to allow all stakeholders to make informed judgements.
- Active engagement in the community.

The social audit

A social audit measures the following aspects of an organization's activities:

- how employees and other stakeholders perceive the organization;
- how the organization is fulfilling its aims;
- how the organization is working within its own values statements.

> "Social auditing assesses the social impact and ethical behavior of an organization in relation to its aims, and those of its stakeholders."[83]

A company that proceeds down the social auditing road, completes the full cycle and publishes the results is a company that is not frightened to face the world, understands that it will find strength through consulting stakeholders and that the process itself will help determine the relationship between the company and society. In the same way that individuals really know themselves through their reflection in other people's eyes, so corporations can know themselves by listening to those closest to them. In this sense the social audit is very much a listening exercise, after which the company retires to process the information and re-examine its policies and activities to see how it can improve its performance.

The origins of social auditing lie in attempts to balance the costs associated with the company's social activities. The problems of this approach are that some social costs cannot be accounted for financially, but this method does have merit in encouraging companies to re-analyze their financial accounts with a view to looking beyond the financial performance.

The principles of social auditing have to be founded on disclosure, or openness, as the dialogue with stakeholders has to be reciprocal, continuous and honest. The audit outcome and the process has to be conducted by an independent agent, and verified by a third party. It is so important that all the stakeholders have confidence in the audit.

At the heart of social auditing is the contract between business and society. In an age where business has to earn its reputation, where maintaining brand image is vital to commercial success and where some prominent companies have lost market share due to failures in areas of public perception on social and environmental issues, the social audit is one way of building confidence among stakeholders.

The benefits of social auditing can be summarized as:

- an input of systematic information on what is happening outside the company;
- recognizing and working with stakeholders;
- feedback to stakeholders on the company's achievements;
- strengthening loyalty and commitment among stakeholders;
- continuous risk assessment;
- improving management performance through informed decision making;
- allying increased profitability with social concern;
- gaining legitimacy in the eyes of society;
- cyclical audits should enable continuous improvement to take place, if cognizance is taken of the results of the audit.

These benefits are illustrated by the audit cycle in Figure 5.1.

The social statement

The social statement which results from the social audit should contain:

- the company's values and missions;
- definitions of the stakeholders to be consulted;
- the scope of the audit;
- an overview of the audit results;
- stakeholders' perspectives or indicators;
- management's comments on the report and management's commitments for the future;
- a report from an independent auditor.

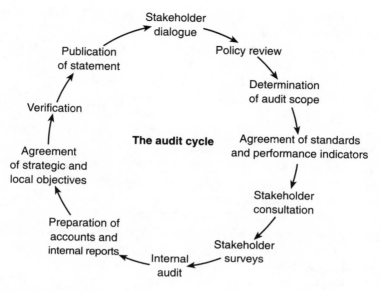

Fig 5.1 The audit cycle[84]

The practice of social auditing

New organizations are springing up, more in Europe than in the USA, to provide research and consultancy services to companies interested in social auditing. Foremost among these is the New Economics Foundation, which along with BT and The Body Shop, have established the Institute of Social and Ethical Accountability. Ready to take advantage of a growing business trend and to sell their services, the world's larger consultancy companies are hurriedly setting up social auditing facilities. Here we profile KPMG's work in this area. NEF and KPMG are followed by a look at The Body Shop's social-auditing process.

New Economics Foundation

The New Economics Foundation (NEF), based in the UK, is an independent non-profit organization which is dedicated to establishing methods and practices of economics based on key principles of social justice and environmental sustainability. NEF aims to identify what is wrong with current approaches to economics, and establish what the practical alternatives are, by carrying out research, publishing reports, running conferences and training events, providing consultancy, and acting as a major resource and information centre on the ideas and initiatives of new economics.

NEF was established following The Other Economic Summit (TOES) in 1984, an annual event which now runs parallel to the G7 summit meetings, and which is convened by grassroots organizations as an expression of discontent with the limitations of economic policy advanced by the mainstream meeting. TOES in June 1997 in Colorado, for instance, took as its theme "Working alternatives: a world that works," and offered public-education workshops and cultural events, using a dynamic and participatory approach to express the community's desire to advance positive alternatives to what was seen as the "big business as usual" approach of the G7. In 1998 TOES will be in the UK, on the topic "Sustainable Consumption."

NEF's research and development work is divided into programs, each of which involves working with community groups and other organizations, and produces reports and packages of written materials designed to help people put the ideas into practice. Two main – closely related – programs are on indicators and social auditing.

The indicators program involves identifying signs and measures which better account for and communicate human welfare and progress, and which give people clearer signals as to how they should be acting to bring about greater ecological sustainability and social justice. For instance, at the local level and supported by the Environmental Action Fund, the Worldwide Fund for Nature and the Local Government Management Board, NEF developed and tested a community indicators resources pack. At the national and international policy level, it has championed the use of the Index of Sustainable Welfare (ISEW) as an alternative to conventional indicators such as GDP.

NEF has taken an active role in the development of social auditing in the UK, devising a methodology which assesses the social impact of an organization – for-profit or non-profit – relative to its own aims and those of its stakeholders. NEF has served as the external verifier of The Body Shop's social audit in 1995 and 1997, and was auditor of Ben & Jerry's social accounts in 1996. It was also a catalyst for the creation of the Institute for Social and Ethical Accountability, founded in 1996, whose mission is to "strengthen the social responsibility and ethical behavior among organizations" by devising guidelines and standards for social and ethical accounting, auditing and assessment. The Body Shop and British Telecom are among the Institute's founding members.

NEF operates a mail-order book service, covering books and reports on sustainability, community action, globalization and social auditing, and produces a quarterly magazine for subscribers to the NEF.

Accounting for a change: KPMG

In The Netherlands, KPMG, the international accountancy and consultancy firm, offers *integrity consulting* to both the private sector and government agencies. A major focus of the consulting work is to prevent ethical problems by assessing the corporate culture and state of affairs. KPMG provides the following services:[85]

- *Integrity thermometer* which describes the moral context of the organization. There are currently 25 Dutch companies using the thermometer.
- *Measures scan* which describes the company's formal procedures and examines if there is a danger of unethical behavior.
- *Stakeholder reflector* assesses the company's reputation with key groups by consulting stakeholders.

  Among criteria for the stakeholder reflector are:
  - unity: is conduct consistent across the company?
  - openness: does the organization provide relevant data to the stakeholders, and is it open to criticism?
  - honesty: does the company literature provide a true picture of the organization?
  - liberty: are stakeholders under pressure by the company to make decisions?
  - subsidiarity: is the company adequately decentralized?
  - equality: does the company treat major stakeholder groups equally?
  - reciprocity: does the organization employ the same standards internally as it does to its stakeholders?
  - adequacy: does the company respond in an appropriate manner and in a timely fashion to the needs of stakeholders?
  - solidarity: does the company address the social needs of the community in which it operates?
  - faithfulness: does the company meet the expectations of its stakeholders?
  - sustainability: does the company compensate the stakeholders it harms?
  - readiness to learn: does the company repeat mistakes or does it learn from them?

The CARE framework: Price Waterhouse

Price Waterhouse (UK), international accountancy and management consultancy, has developed a methodology for putting corporate citizenship at the heart of strategy. The principle behind this methodology is: "translating total reputation management into increased stakeholder value."

Pressure groups, media, and governments are demanding that firms re-evaluate their decision making to ensure that a profitable bottom line is not realized at the expense of other stakeholder demands. The framework:

- integrates corporate initiatives;
- is based on the company's stakeholders including shareholders, customers, employees, society and partners;
- is based on the quality management process;
- links "the effectiveness of a firm's corporate responsibility programs to direct business results."

The Body Shop's social audit

In 1995 The Body Shop International carried out its first full social audit, and published the results as a *Social Statement*, alongside its *Environmental Statement* and *Statement on Animal Protection*. Together these three documents constituted what the company termed its *Values Report*. In publishing its Social Statement, the company became the first publicly listed company in Britain to do so.

The Body Shop's purpose in undertaking the social audit was: "to systematically audit, verify and disclose the company's performance on social matters . . . we have taken as our philosophical starting point the belief that all stakeholders should have an effective voice in commenting upon and shaping a company's behaviour." To this end "we have provided a platform for all views, including critical and minority views."

Performance was judged against the company's mission statement and trading charter, as well as more specific policies on health and safety at work, human resources, and community trade. The audit process involved consultation with the following ten stakeholders: customers, staff, franchisees, sub-franchisees, shareholders, suppliers, community trade partners, local community, UK non-governmental organizations, and charities which had been supported by The Body Shop Foundation.

The method involved holding focus groups to identify issues salient for each stakeholder group, then administering questionnaires designed to capture perceptions of the company's performance against both these specific stakeholder issues and core values articulated by the company.[86] In addition, documentary information relating to agreed quantitative and qualitative standards was taken from company departments. The process was independently verified.

The main lessons The Body Shop took from the exercise were that they needed to pay more attention to their relationships with their franchisees, and that although most of their employees strongly supported the company's ethical stance, many were not happy with the level of staff development they were receiving. Both of these became central to the action plans developed by the company as a result of the audit.

The reaction of the business press was generally positive, applauding the company's openness in publishing its "warts-and-all" report. One newspaper described it as "nothing less than a road test for stake-holding," while another commented that "influential voices within industry are already saying that where The Body Shop has ventured, others will soon follow."[87]

A second full audit was conducted in 1997; the results were published in 1998.

A new global standard for social accountability: SA8000

Launched by the Council on Economic Priorities Accreditation Agency in October 1997, SA8000 is a collective initiative, aimed at bringing together increasingly fragmented codes of conduct, and at providing clear definitions of terms in the area of workers' rights including child labor, forced labor, and health and safety.[88] The need for external monitoring and, therefore, transparency of results allows standardization across companies, and creates a universal benchmark upon which to marshal support for social accountability. Several major companies have adopted SA8000, including Avon, Toys 'Я' Us and Otto Versand. The CEPAA Accreditation Agency Board consists of representatives from business, NGOs and academics, including Reebok, Amnesty International, Toys 'Я' Us, Sainsbury's, Avon, KPMG and SGS.

SA8000 evolved through the development of criteria for measuring company performance around the world, by non-governmental organizations such as the Council on Economic Priorities, and a number of global businesses and unions which had been developing their own criteria for sourcing. Bringing together these sets of organizations was a natural next step in agreeing common standards across geographical, industry-sector and company-size boundaries. However the development of the standard has not been easy. Agreeing on definitions and standards across geographical and industrial boundaries is complex.

SA8000 is a third-party social accountability code which can be applied internationally across all commercial sectors to evaluate whether companies and other organizations are complying with basic standards of labor and human-rights practices and, eventually, with a wider range of issues. As an initial auditing position, SA8000 concerns itself only with the core issues of human rights and associated health and safety and equal opportunities issues.

The business case for SA8000

SA8000 allows business to do what it does best: increase the health and wealth of society and assure continued profitability. Business works best when there is a level playing field, and SA8000 does just that by providing a global standard.

Businesses that adopt SA8000 recognize that it will protect brand image and company reputation. Among the business benefits are:

● an improved relationship with contractors and suppliers;
● increased information, and thus confidence, for customers;
● better supply-chain management;
● assurance for the company and its investors.

By protecting workers' rights, companies are working towards more stable global business conditions.

Compliance with the requirements of the standard will produce certification and public accreditation of meeting social accountability requirements, in the same way that the quality and environmental management systems are accredited already. Auditing bodies accredited by the Council on Economic Priorities Accreditation Agency (CEPAA) to audit organizations to SA8000 will issue the SA8000 certificate in such circumstances. The CEPAA is the accrediting agency, and the organization which has ownership of the new social accountability standard. The CEPAA will accredit certification bodies which will confirm an organization's certification, following the appropriate audit and reporting process.

The basis for SA8000

The normative elements established by SA8000 which will form the basis against which organizations are audited are taken from established ILO conventions on forced labor, freedom of association, and other relevant criteria, as well as from the UN's Universal Declaration of Human Rights and The United Nations Convention on the Rights of the Child.

The standard sets out working definitions and core elements against which companies and organizations will be independently audited and identifies those criteria which will be the bases of the auditing judgement, leading ultimately to the award of the SA8000 certificate. Therefore, a core element is child labor, the criteria for which include the following:

- The company shall not engage in or support the use of child labor.[89]
- The company shall establish, document, maintain, and effectively communicate policies and procedures, where appropriate, for promotion of education for children who are either subject to the local compulsory education laws or are leaving school, including means to ensure:
  - that their combined hours of daily work time, school time and transportation time to and from either activity does not exceed ten hours a day;
  - that, in relevant work activities, no work shall be permitted that is unhealthy, unsafe, or hazardous to children, inclusive of transportation.

The CEPAA's guide to SA8000[90]

In 1998 SA8000, and the accompanying guidance document, were subjected to a two-year consultation period during which CEPAA welcomes suggestions from any individual organization. For a full version of the standard please contact CEPAA (see address details in Appendix 3).

SGS Yarsley and the development of SA8000

SGS Yarsley ICS is the UK arm of SGS, (Société Général de Surveillance) the world's largest certification and inspection body and a global third-party auditing organization, with a major UK base in the Yarsley operation, together with a reputation for innovation and development in the sphere of management systems.

Recognizing the significant development that social accountability auditing represented, SGS made a commitment to initiate the development of an independently monitored code or standard against which commercial companies' performances could be measured and assessed. To oversee the initial development, meetings of interested commercial organizations were convened in June 1996. Substantial early support was given to the project by Jeff Horner, Corporate Director of SGS ICS, to which SGS Yarsley belonged, this support proving invaluable in the later worldwide development of the new standard.

The Council on Economic Priorities (CEP) was also active in these early meetings and quickly became established as the organization best suited to own and maintain the proposed new standard. CEP's importance was underlined by its profile as an NGO which bridged the world of NGOs, which were responsible for the most significant developments in social auditing that had taken place, with commercial enterprises. Its organizational presence in the UK, Europe and the USA was also significant.

Accordingly, a Standards and Accreditation Advisory Board was set up by the CEP to monitor and oversee the development of the new standard, known as the CEPAA (see profile above). A significant majority of American companies expressed an initial interest in the application of the new standard, so this body met first of all in the USA.

The outcome of this activity was the standard and a program of pilot audits at "beta" sites, from which valuable hands-on auditing experience would be gained and integrated into the new code.

Developing global standards

SA8000 has been developed with reference to quality management standard ISO 9000,[91] and the environmental management standard ISO 140001[92] series. While SA8000 was not an ISO standard when launched it had been developed in full consultation with business, international standards organizations and non-governmental organizations. It is another example of a global agreement being developed with the support of some governments, but without their direct involvement. In the USA some members of the SA8000 team had served on the White House's Apparel Industry Task Force, establishing criteria for global sourcing for clothes and shoes, and in the UK some participants in the SA8000 process were involved in the UK government's Ethical Trading Initiative.[93] In both cases there was communication between the different groups.

The increasing convergence between company law and financial accounting practice regionally and globally, coupled with global standards on quality and the environment is increasingly being complemented by standards addressing social issues. All these procedures require third-party verification.

There is a significant qualitative difference between the European Eco-Management and Audit System (EMAS) and ISO 140001 series in that the former requires a pre-audit and a final public statement[94] while the latter is very much more a lowest common denominator standard (see Table 5.3 on page 236 for a comparison). It can be argued that the development of global standards of social accountability will inevitably try to please too many different interest groups at the same time without solving any of the problems that they are designed to tackle, such as exploitative child labor or the right to collective bargaining. Within months of the SA8000 being launched, a significant number of companies had requested applications to be accredited to perform audits, including many of the world's largest consulting firms.

While the SA8000's launch was welcomed by most of the NGOs working in areas of human rights, fair trade and ethical trade there was some recognition this was only the start of a global initiative to change the terms on which world trade is conducted. The limitations of SA8000 were acknowledged by the CEP's Director, Alice Tepper Marlin, when she said that "setting the standard is only five per cent of the process. Auditing for compliance is the next step."[95]

The development of social-accountability standards and social auditing has become a global affair and addresses what was referred to earlier as "the triple bottom line" of financial, environmental and social accountability.[96]

This is an issue that some successful responsible companies are willing to seriously address. Tom DeLuca, Vice President of Toys 'Я' Us, said that his company was asking its 5,000 suppliers to be certified to SA8000. Avon has made similar demands on its suppliers and will audit all of its own factories.

The Dutch-owned C&A group said it had inspected 1,900 factories up to the end of 1997, and that if made aware of a problem it could get an auditor to any factory within 24 hours.[97]

Two major US companies, Toys 'Я' Us and Otto Versand, the world's largest mail order company, have argued that adopting SA8000 now was cheaper than compliance problems in the long run. As Fitzroy Hillaire from Avon said: "Cheap labor becomes more expensive in the long run."[98]

What a difference an audit makes!

An audit of social accountability can confer advantages and benefits:

● In the market: it increases competitive advantage, increases access to global markets, meets buyers' requirements, creates product and process differentiation, improves consumer satisfaction, anticipates customers' interest, and enhances public image.

● Legal benefits: it improves understanding of legal requirements and regulatory compliance, reduces pressure from enforcement agencies, enhances risk management, and lowers liabilities.

● Financial benefits: it increases shareholders' confidence, lowers insurance costs and facilitates access to finance.

● Strategic benefits: a company gains worldwide recognition; an audit enhances both short- and long-term management and facilitates future change.

● Ethical benefits: an audit addresses stakeholders' concerns and increases honest, informed communications.

Reporting company performance

"Firms must have the highest international standards of disclosure and governance. In so doing, they will reduce risk from the investors' perspective, reduce their cost of capital and enhance their valuation."

Paul Myners[99]

A company has consulted its stakeholders, has understood the need for an audit of its activities in all areas and is now about to report the state of its affairs to the wider public in an open, honest document.

As a recent worldwide analysis of corporate reports said:

"To engage stakeholders effectively and demonstrate performance and leadership, reporting must address stakeholder groups in the languages and

*areas of relevance specific to each target audience and use benchmarks or
indicators that are credible."*

SustainAbility, UNEP and the New Economics Foundation[100]

In future, reporting on a company's financial, environmental and social
affairs will be done more frequently and eventually all the time. In this section there are some guidelines for reporting. Reporting honestly and openly,
with the same message to all stakeholders is not a choice, but a necessity for
companies that want to remain in touch with their key stakeholders and provide information easily for other stakeholders.

There are four main criteria for reporting:

- Be honest: the world is transparent; admit areas in which you need to
  make progress or changes.
- Be clear: your report will be read by possible investors and school children.
- Give the same message to *all* stakeholders.
- Make sure the report is certified by a third party, otherwise it will be seen
  as company public relations and not an honest account of the company's
  activities.

Engaging stakeholders through reporting

*"As we look forward into the next five years of company environmental
reporting, there is every indication that we are moving squarely into an age
of accountability in which the full spectrum of a company's activities and
relationships is likely to be increasingly monitored and questioned by
stakeholders."*

SustainAbility, UNEP and the New Economics Foundation[101]

TEN RECOMMENDATIONS TO REPORT MAKERS

1 Be open and honest: "Avoid collective self-delusion."

2 Include a very stringent review of legal compliance and problem areas.

3 Show performance against targets.

4 Focus on significant issues for your sector and company, contextualize information and flag up gaps.

5 Adopt standardized reporting formats, ensuring information is comparable
from year to year.

6 Distinguish between local and global impacts.

▶

> 7 Normalize information (for example, against unit of product) and use common ratios and sector benchmarks.
>
> 8 Go for independent, third-party verification.
>
> 9 Tailor reports to different stakeholders, with clear and user-friendly signposting, and remember that paper can be a very poor medium for communication.
>
> 10 Discuss stakeholder relationships and start informed dialogue on sustainability.

Table 5.4 gives an example of how to represent different stakeholder interests in a single report. Different stakeholders have different concerns, for instance, regulators will be interested in the qualitative measurement of emissions and effluents; shareholders will be particularly interested in the management of environmental risk.

Corporate environmental disclosure: The Association of Chartered Certified Accountants[102]

Winners 1996

Main award: British Airways plc

Runner up: London Electricity plc

First time reporter: J. Sainsbury's plc

Commendations: Inveresk plc and Shared Earth plc

Short-listed: Anglian Water, The Body Shop, Borealis, BT, Nesté Oy., Novo Nordisk, Rank Xerox, SAS, Thorn EMI, Traidcraft Exchange, Yorkshire Electricity.

Criteria used in the selection of award winners by the panel of judges:

1 Environmental policies and references to other standards such as ICC, Responsible Care etc.
2 Management commitment and systems and reference to audits, reviews and EMAS, ISO 14001.
3 Narrative, or the impact of the core business and the value of understandability.
4 Factual data, both good and bad news.
5 Historical trends at global and site level.
6 Targets, capable of verification.
7 Performance against targets.
8 Explanation of variances.
9 Financial linkages between environmental and financial data.
10 Liabilities and provisions.
11 Environmental expenditure.

Table 5.4 Environmental reporting matrix WICE – The World Industry Council for the Environment[103]

Key audiences/	Customers/ consumers	Employees	NGOs	Financial institutions/ Shareholders	Local communities	Press/ media	Regulators	Scientists	Suppliers JV partners dealers	Trade associations
Contents										
Qualitative										
Foreword										
Profile of enterprise										
Environmental policy										
Environmental targets and objectives										
Views on:										
– environmental issues										
– community relations										
Management										
Environmental management systems										
Management of environmental risks										
Office and site practices										
Quantitative										
Environmental indicators and targets:										
– emissions, effluents, energy consumption,										
– transportation and waste minimization										
Use of energy and natural resources										
Compliance with regulations and permits										
Financial indicators										
Products										
Products, processes and services										
Giving more information										

254

12 External verification.

13 Sustainability.

14 Lifecycle / mass balance / eco balance sheet showing the organization's environmental impact and commitments.

15 Extras, including information via reports, Internet and newsletters.

Managing the media: how to survive a boycott

Boycotts are common in many countries around the world, but are most effective in North America and parts of Europe where it is possible to mobilize public opinion effectively against a product or a company. They are often ineffective in the UK, where consumers are hard to mobilize on moral issues. Craig N. Smith catalogued the history of boycotts globally since the 1960s in *Morality And The Market*[104] and US magazine *Boycott Quarterly*[105] provides a regular update on boycotts in North America.

A sample of successful boycotts around the world includes:

- *Japan, 1970s*: Shufuren (Japanese consumers' association – mostly women) organized a boycott against a whole range of products for excessive prices through to poor product labelling. Shufuren had some 6 million members and the campaign was largely successful.

- *Britain, 1970s*: Friends of the Earth organized a boycott of soft-drinks company Schweppes (now Cadbury-Schweppes) over the introduction of non-returnable bottles (previously all bottles were returnable and reusable). The world is full of non-returnable bottles.

- *USA, 1983*: the United Farm Workers organized a boycott of Lucky Super-markets because of its support for the Bruce lettuce-growing company, which did not support unions.

- *USA, 1960s*: a consumer boycott of Dow occured over its manufacture of napalm for use by the US government in the Vietnam War. The Vietnam War ended with the withdrawal of US forces. Awareness of the horrors of the war was heightened by nightly TV coverage.

- *Switzerland, 1977*: the Swiss Federation organized a boycott of food products that failed to show a full list of ingredients. This resulted in the rapid introduction of tighter legislation.

- *South Africa, 1982*: Rowntree-Mackintosh was boycotted by black trade unions over the refusal of the company's subsidiary, Wilson-Rowntree, to recognize trade unions. Pressure on international companies slowly helped to bring about the end of apartheid and liberate the country's black majority.

▶

- *International, 1983–4*: an international boycott of Canadian fish products was organized in protest of seal hunting by Canadian fishermen. In the UK, Tesco and Findus stopped using Canadian cod; Sainsbury's said it was for consumers to choose.
- *Europe and North America, 1990s*: a boycott of Shell gasoline stations was instigated over Shell's disposal of the Brent Spar oil rig in the North Sea and its support for the Nigerian military regime which was suppressing and murdering the Ogoni people. At the height of the boycott, Shell gasoline sales were reported to be $50 million a day down, particularly in Germany and The Netherlands, where support for the boycott was highest. Shell decided not to dispose of the oil rig at sea, and now incorporates a statement on human rights in its operating policy.
- *USA, 1990s*: a boycott of PepsiCo took place in protest of its business in Myanmar (Burma); and a boycott of associated company Starbucks Coffee was organized as a result of its business with PepsiCo.
- *USA, 1990s*: a boycott of Disney by groups such as the American Family Association and the Southern Baptist Conference was organized because the company gave healthcare benefits to partners of gay employees; sold cruises where alcohol was drunk; and as a result of suggestions that the film *The Lion King* implied a homosexual relationship between the cartoon characters.

THE *Corporate Citizenship* GUIDE TO AVOIDING THE THREAT OF A BOYCOTT

Corporate Citizenship suggests a strategy, which avoids the threat of boycotts, and which is founded on the belief that business is part of, not apart from, society and has to earn its licence to operate:

1 Understand and review the company's key relationships, or stakeholders, on a regular basis, aware that the longest-running, most profitable companies are those that are flexible and adapt to changing values and markets.

2 Tell the truth. Just as campaigning organizations have a responsibility to tell the truth about business activity, so business has a responsibility to tell the truth. In the long run, in a world with fewer hiding places, companies are exposed if they tell lies.

3 Develop partnerships with organizations, perhaps pressure groups or multi-lateral organizations, where you and they can gain by sharing experience.

4 Publish externally audited and publicly accessible reports on finance, environment and social impact regularly.

5 Don't be defensive of the profit motive; just make sure the profits were made responsibly.

Lessons from "McLibel"

Are you an industry leader?

Campaigners tend to target not the worst companies, but those that are most well-known, and those companies that have made some previous commitment to social or environmental causes. There are undoubtedly fast food chains with a worse record of social responsibility than McDonald's. Although it had already responded to public pressure by working with the Environmental Defense Fund, McDonald's being among the most well-known fast food chains, is always vulnerable. Targeting an industry leader puts the whole industry on warning. Companies like McDonald's make good pressure points because they are industry leaders, because they have solid brands with a global identification and because people expect more from them.

Media action or the courts?

Once a company is attacked in the press, or by a campaign group, the usual recourse of taking legal action can backfire. Legal action keeps the story in the public domain, feeding the perception of truth.

For example, in 1996, a television program ran a story alleging that the retailer Marks & Spencer used child labor in Morocco. The company sued for libel, thereby keeping the story in the public domain. Pentland, which owns Mitre soccer balls, was charged with using child labor in Pakistan. Rather than suing, the Chairman of Pentland, Stephen Rubin, thanked the newspaper for bringing the issue to his attention, highlighting the company's commitment to combating child labor. "We will investigate this immediately," he told the press. Within a matter of hours, he and several other Pentland executives boarded a jet to track the story. They found that the photo of children working in their factories had been staged. The moral of the story? Actions speak louder than court cases.

● MANAGEMENT EXERCISES ●

1 Identifying your stakeholders

To think about how a stakeholder approach applies to your business, it helps to get very concrete.

Using Wheeler and Sillanpää's list of "primary social stakeholders" on pages 198–99 in this chapter, see if you can answer the following questions:

a   In addition to your employees and managers, who are your five most significant:

►

    – investors?

    – customers?

    – suppliers and business partners?

    – members of the local community?

b Can you rank them in order of importance to the successful functioning of your company?

c What do you think the main expectations of your company are on the part of:
  – employees and managers?
  – investors?
  – customers?
  – suppliers and business partners?
  – members of the local community?
  (Do you know?)

d What would you need to change, in order to meet the expectations more fully of:
  – employees and managers?
  – investors?
  – customers?
  – suppliers and business partners?
  – members of the local community?

e How do these expectations fit with your company mission? Do they contain any obvious conflicts of interest? If so, how do you intend to resolve them?

2 Do you know what your stakeholders think of you?

Knowing what your key stakeholders think of you is not only the basis for building an inclusive way of operating, but it is also a means of gaining important commercial information. Many companies now have a strong customer focus, but fewer extend this intelligence gathering to other important relationships. There are also many smaller scale ways in which you might discover what your stakeholders have to say about you. How many do you currently use?

Employees and managers:

● open-door management, management-by-walk-about;

● formal and regular appraisal processes;

● suggestions schemes;

● exit interviews;

● 360-degree feedback systems;

● confidential telephone hotlines;

● access to board members.

▶

Investors:

- attendance at and participation in annual general meetings;
- record of proposals submitted for voting at annual meeting, and questions raised;
- questionnaires to solicit feedback.

Customers:

- market research, panels, focus groups;
- suggestions schemes;
- evaluations by independent consumer organizations.

Suppliers and business partners:

- questionnaires to solicit feedback;
- joint activities and discussions;
- specific people to act as liaison.

Members of the local community:

- company tours, open days for community groups, schools etc.;
- internship program for students;
- talks to schools, community groups;
- volunteer program for employees;
- employees encouraged to sit on school and community group boards.

3 Auditing dilemmas

Here are three dilemmas based on real incidents in social auditing. What is the best resolution to the situations?

a Ventilating an accountability issue in China

The facility being audited was a manufacturer in central southern China, part of the inland region that has been the showpiece recipient of so much development on the part of the Chinese government. The audit team was small, consisting only of the lead auditor and an interpreter/ auditor from China.

The journey to the factory was made using local taxis, notable for their cheapness and for the fact that the drivers locked themselves into a steel-mesh cage for protection. The journey was over several hundred miles and, for their return, the team was obliged by the factory owner to use coach transport, as he pointed out that in the remote regions through which they travelled, there was a strong possibility of robbery and murder.

The factory itself was a modern highly developed facility with on-site dormitory accommodation for the employees and over 3,000 staff on site. The area surrounding it was still rapidly being developed with roads mostly unnamed and tower blocks

▶

of flats thrown up all around. Postal addresses were invariably only box numbers. The address of the facility when translated turned out to be "next to the petrol station"!

The factory's owners were based in Hong Kong, and senior executives arrived to meet the social-accountability auditors by hydrofoil. This turned out to be significant, first, because it shortened the time available for the audit, and later, for a more profound reason. The company was a principal supplier to the client, manufacturing 70 per cent of the inflatable products stamped with the client's cartoon characters, bathing rings, water wings, balls, etc.

Most of the workforce were women, who undertook hand-pressing and cutting in teams of eight or more with little automation. Final trim and fit was by hand, using scissors. All the manufacturing materials were PVC based, with special PVC bonding adhesive in widespread use. The result was a suffocating atmosphere heavy with plastic and bonding fluid fumes.

The company management agreed that the fumes were oppressive and undoubtedly a hazard. They pointed out that face masks could be made available for the women but, when these had been tried, the workforce had refused to use them because of their make-up and hairdos. The auditors had noticed that discipline was strict in the factory and that, at lunchtime, the staff immediately formed into columns of two at a time and marched briskly to the canteen. It seemed implausible that, with such discipline, a refusal to wear safety equipment would be tolerated.

There was a heated debate between the management and the auditors on the subject of the fumes, during which the main factor seemed to be the management's desire to make the last hydrofoil back to Hong Kong. The auditors indicated that their report would very likely include a requirement to install adequate ventilation equipment which, given that the factory was on three storeys in a large building, would represent a substantial cost.

This was what the audit report finally stated. In discussion with the client, the lead auditor emphasized that the installation of ventilation was vital to provide even a minimum level of fume disposal in the company. The improvement could be staged over a period of time, perhaps 12 to 18 months, but there had to be an agreement that it would take place. The client noted the competitive price offered by the supplier.

Follow-up audits confirmed that, despite a written assurance from the supplier, the only ventilation in the factory was still through open windows, and no protective masks or other breathing equipment were in use.

b Keeping it in the family, Chinese style

The factory being audited produced over 90 per cent of the plastic inserts in breakfast-cereal packets, and depicted the cartoon animals and characters that were the client's trade mark. They did this in conditions of great hygiene and efficiency in a

▶

modern, airy facility which, while it was not automated, in keeping with other comparable facilities in China, was at least a pleasant place to work.

The company turned over more than $2 million per month in orders from the client and was a key supplier. Hours of work, associated health and safety systems and wages all seemed satisfactory, as did most aspects of the facility's operations. Interviews with the employees revealed a workforce that, on the face of it, was happy, healthy and, by the standards of the region, indeed the country as a whole, was well-paid, because the production bonuses associated with the high level of orders were good. Company records were meticulous and included copies of birth certificates as well as health registration and identity cards.

Nonetheless, the lead auditor was unhappy because his team had told him that more than one employee had given a birth date on request as something like 1978, 1977 or 1980. When checked against their company records their ages appeared as 24 or 26 years, but the photograph on the ID card seemed the same, and all other details matched.

When faced with this dilemma the management of the facility confessed that, yes, there was indeed an issue. The law in China, as everyone knew, permitted only one child per family. The director pointed out that this remained true provided that the child born was a boy. If a girl was born, Chinese families had the habit of continuing to procreate with the result that there might be one, or two girls of similar age and appearance, cared for in extended families who officially did not exist, born in vain hope of a male offspring .

What then happened, the director pointed out, the "official" girl would take a job and register, and when her time came to have her baby, she went home to her village and her place would be taken by the "unofficial" sister who did not officially exist. He explained ruefully that, while the company had an idea that this was happening, they could do little about it, and if they tried, they could not eliminate the practice. In any case, the company still got its production out!

c House and home in Manila

The social-accountability audit team had the address of a supplier which proved to be a suburb of Makita, the industrial city in the Philippines adjacent to Manila, the capital city. The facility was responsible for the production of labels for clothing and other uses that bore the distinctive logo of the client's characters. The factory was the principal supplier in a niche area and was noted as a key supplier.

On arrival in the suburb, the team had some difficulty in locating the address in a leafy, tree-lined avenue of domestic, albeit expensive and up-market, residences. There was no sign of a commercial factory, not even a small one, but the street name was the same and a check with the local police and a road map confirmed that no other route had the same name. The social-accountability team had four members in all, with two lead auditors in attendance and two national auditors from the certification body's Makita office. Undaunted, the team approached the address in question and found that this was, in fact, the correct label manufacturer.

The company was responsible for $250,000 of sales turnover per month in a key range of products. It employed 12 people in all, but only three of these were in manufacturing. Its processes included the use of specialist inks for clothing and cloth articles, decorated with the client's logos. The company's operations were fairly sophisticated, mainly printing processes, but involving various temperatures and a requirement for laboratory testing. All of this took place in a relatively small detached property, what one of the lead auditor's described in his hand-written notes as "essentially a domestic house!."

The company's management was enthusiastic about the audit and keen to receive any recommendations for improvement. Approval would have to come from the company's chief executive who lived in New York, where the corporate offices were located.

A key aspect of the process involved 24 operations and, on questioning the manager, the lead auditor was unable to assess how this was achieved as the process was not fully automatic and needed constant supervision. He was told that the supervisor slept on the premises. This interview was conducted in the living room of the house, with paint and solvent stores in the adjacent yard and the family's bedrooms upstairs. Pressing to find out where the supervisor's dormitory accommodation might be for the all-night shifts, the team leader was told: "You're sitting on it!."

The audit team noted that the dormitory accommodation in question was the fold-down sofa which appeared quite acceptable!

Notes to Chapter 5

1 "The death of deference" is the phrase used in the *Tomorrow's Company Report* (1996) Royal Society of Arts, London: RSA, and refers to the fact that governments and companies can no longer take for granted the support of their populations or customers.

2 Elkington, John (1998) *Cannibals with Forks.* London: SustainAbility.

3 Kung, Hans (1991) *Global Responsibility: In Search of a New World Ethic.* London: SCM Press.

4 Hutton, Will (1996) "Raising the stakes," *Guardian*, 17 January.

5 Kay J. and Hutton W. (1997) "The seven deadly principles of stakeholding," *The Observer*, John Kay is the author of (1993) *Foundations of Corporate Success: How Business Strategies Add Value* and with A. Silberston (1995) "Corporate governance," *National Institute Economic Review*, August.

6 Hirst, Paul (1997) "From the economic to the political," in Kelly, Gavin *et al.* (1997) *Stakeholder Capitalism*. London: Macmillan.

7 Ibid.

8 Willets, David (1997) "The poverty of stakeholding," in Kelly, *Stakeholder Capitalism*. London: Macmillan.

9 Ibid.

10 Parkinson, John (1996) "The stakeholder business," Employment Pol

11 Sir Michael Wilson quoted in the *Journal of the Centre for Tomorrow's Company*, May 1997.

12 Leadbetter, Charles and Mulgan, Geoff (1996) *Whatever Happened to Labour's Big Idea?* October. London: DEMOS.

13 Jensen, Michael C. and Fagan, Perry L. "Whose world is it anyway?" *The World in 1997*. London: The Economist.

14 Roddick, Anita (1966) "Openness, the true meaning of business stakeholding," *The Times*, 28 September.

15 Hutton, Will (1997) "An overview of stakeholding," in Kelly, Gavin *et al.* (1997) *Stakeholder Capitalism*. London: Macmillan.

16 The Body Shop (1995) *Values Report*. Littlehampton, UK The Body Shop.

17 Buono, Anthony F. and Nichols, Lawrence T. (1985) "Stockholder and stakeholder interpretations of business's social role," in Hoffman, W. Michael and Mills Moore, Jennifer (eds) (1990) *Business Ethics*. Maidenhead: McGraw-Hill.

18 Ecumenical Committee for Corporate Responsibility (ECCR), with the Interface Centre on Corporate Responsibility (ICCR) and the Task Force on the Churches and Corporate Responsibility (TCCR): Fareham, UK (1995).

19 Cleaver, Sir Anthony, Chairman of IBM UK and Chairman of the RSA's *Tomorrow's Company Inquiry* (1996).

20 Wheeler, David and Sillanpää, Maria (1997) *The Stakeholder Corporation: Blueprint for Maximizing Stakeholder Value*. London: Pitman Publishing. See also New Economics Foundation (1995) *Social Auditing for Small Organizations*. London: NEF.

21 Cleaver, Sir Anthony, Chairman AEA Technology and Chairman of the RSA's *Tomorrow's Company Inquiry* (1996).

22 The British Commonwealth was born of the British Empire and now represents 25 per cent of the world's population. Its meetings are attended by heads of state and is presided over by the Queen.

23 ten Brink, Patrick *et al.* (1996) "Consulting the stakeholder: a new approach to environmental reporting for IBM (UK) Ltd," in *Greener Management International*, Sheffield: Greenleaf Publishing.

24 UNEP International Environmental Technology Centre (1996) *Environmental Risk Assessment for Sustainable Cities*. IETC Technical Publication Series, 3. Osaka/ Shiga: UNEP.

25 Blair, John D., Stanley, Jay and Whitehead, Carlton J. (1992) "A stakeholder management perspective on military health care," *Armed Forces and Society*, 18, No.4.

26 *Harvard Business Review* (1991) November–December, p. 142.

27 Hutton, Will (1996) *The State We're In*. London: Vintage.

28 *Harvard Business Review* – see note 26.

Feder, Barnaby J. "Putting stock in migrant workers," *International Herald Tribune*, 27 June.

30 *The Economist* (1995) 18 June 1995.

31 Marks & Spencer (1993) *Secondment Policy and Code of Practice*. London: Marks & Spencer.

32 Will, Rosalyn (1995) *Stellar Companies: The 1995 America's Corporate Conscience Awards*. Research Report. May. New York: Council on Economic Priorities.

33 Ministry of Social Affairs, Denmark (1997) *Partnership for Social Cohesion: Business Initiatives in the USA, Europe and Japan*. International Conference on Social Commitment of Enterprises. Copenhagen, 16–18 October.

34 Makower, Joel and Business for Social Responsibility (1994) *Beyond the Bottom Line: Putting Social Responsibility to Work for your Business and the World*. New York: Simon & Schuster.

35 Bruce Naughton Wade (1997) *The CCI Index*. London, September.

36 Leipziger, Deborah (1996) *Canadian Companies on the Cutting Edge: Bata Promotes Development*. Research Report. July/August. New York: Council on Economic Priorities.

37 Wells, Phil (1995) "Integrated Rural Development Programme in India, the transnational corporation in a host country: policy and practice in developing countries," *New Consumer*, August.

38 Fondo Social del Empresariado Chihuahuense, *Una missione solidaria*. Mexico: Fondo Social del Empresariado Chihuahuense.

39 Murphy, David and Bendell, Jem (1997) *In the Company of Partners*. Bristol: Policy Press.

40 On Rachel Carson, see the section on "Environment" in Chapter 4 on page 97.

41 For a full discussion of third-wave environmentalism, see Murphy and Bendell (note 39).

42 Slavin, Terry (1997) "Business comes to terms with green activists," *The Observer*, 1 June. Slavin (1997); see also the Environment Council's courses and pamphlets on consensus building and mediation.

43 Murphy and Bendell – see note 39.

44 UNEP – see note 24.

45 Prince of Wales Business Leaders' Forum, The World Bank and the United Nations Development Programme (1997) *Creating Wealth for Countries, Companies and Communities*. See also the work at the Ashridge Management Centre on developing partnerships.

46 Charlton, Kate (1997) *Partnerships at Work*, London: Ashridge Management College.

47 Ibid.

48 See note 45.

49 This guide draws heavily on the work of Murphy and Bendell (see note 39).

50 Statement of Intent on MSC signed by WWF International and Unilever plc, February 1997.

51 For a comprehensive discussion of both the FSC and the MSC, see Murphy and Bendell (note 39).

52 Presentation to an ICC/UNED conference in London, October 1996.

53 New Economics Foundation (1998) *Sustainable Economic Welfare in the UK*. London: NEC.

54 Cobb, Clifford W., Halstead, Ted and Rowe, Jonathan (1990) "If the GDP is up, why is America down?," *Resurgence*, No. 175. See also Daly, Herman E. and Cobb, John B., Jr. (1990) *For the Common Good*. London: Green Print.

55 Ibid.; New Economics Foundation and Stockholm Environmental Institute (1991) *Growing Pains? An Index of ISEW for the UK, 1950–1990*. London: NEF; Jackson, Tim and Marks, Nic (1997) *Measuring Sustainable Economic Welfare – A Pilot Index*. London: NEF.

56 For instance, see *The Economist* guides and the Healey & Baker annual *European Real Estate Monitor: Europe's Top Cities*.

57 Cleaver, Sir Anthony (1998) "Challenges for the board in the new millennium," in *Performance Measurement in the Digital Age*. London: Institute of Chartered Accountants.

58 This is the HMSO (1996) list of Indicators for Sustainable Development for the United Kingdom. © Crown copyright.

59 Waring, Marilyn (1989) *If Women Counted: A New Feminist Economics*. London: Macmillan, pp. 207–10, reissued as (1988, 1990, 1993) *Counting for Nothing (What Men Value and what Women Are Worth)* New Zealand: Bridget Williams Books, p. 168.

60 See this chapter, page 193, for a discussion of stakeholders, which are also described as key relationships and claimants.

61 See this chapter, page 193, for a discussion of stakeholders. In corporate citizenship, it includes key relationships, relationships with people or organizations which may have an impact on a company, or vice versa (a company could have an impact on them).

62 Welford, Richard and Gouldson, Andrew (1993) *Environmental Management and Business Strategy*. London: Pitman Publishing, p.99.

63 The idea that companies should be required to have a "licence to operate" was one of the conclusions of the *Tomorrow's Company Inquiry* (see note 19).

64 See profile of Traidcraft in this chapter on page 204.

65 See profile of the New Economics Foundation on page 243, this chapter.

66 FTSE: Financial Times Share Index.

67 Hanson, Kirk (1996) *The Times*, 19 September.

68 Council on Economic Priorities (1994) *Shopping for a Better World*. New York: Sierra Club Books.

69 Elkington, John and Hailes, Julia (1989) *The Green Consumer Guide*. London: Gollanz.

70 Adams, Richard, Carruthers, Jane and Hamil, Sean (1991) *Changing Corporate Values*. London: Kogan Page.

71 Ethical Consumer Research Association (1993) *The Ethical Consumer Guide to Everyday Shopping*. Manchester: ECRA.

72 International Chamber of Commerce (1989) *Environmental Auditing*. Geneva: International Chamber of Commerce.

73 Welford and Gouldson (see note 62); Institute of Environmental Management (1995) "Eco-management and audit scene: enhancing the impact of environmental management?," 3, No.3; Wheeler and Sillanpää (see note 20).

74 Prince of Wales Business Leaders' Forum (1997) *Reporting Good Practice: KPMG Social Auditing at the Cutting Edge*. London: PWBLF, Spring.

75 Cleaver – see note 21.

76 See profile of the New Economics Foundation on page 243, this chapter.

77 Smith, Alison (1997) "BT seeks to reassure 'caring' consumers," *Financial Times*, 13 January.

78 Ibid.

79 Carmichael, Sheena (1997) "Ethical auditing: uncovering the shadow side of the organisation," *RSA Journal*, July.

80 Ibid. Carmichael is the director of ETHOS, a London-based consultancy in business ethics.

81 Information from the Co-operative Bank.

82 Hotten, Russell (1993) "Firms reveal they put profits before ethics," *Independent on Sunday*, 3 January.

83 New Economics Foundation and the New Academy of Business (1996) *The Audit Cycle*. London: NEF and NAB.

84 Ibid.

85 Interview with Kaptein Muel of KPMG, Amsterdam, 17 September 1997; Muel, Kaptein (1997) *Ethics Management: Auditing and Developing the Ethical Content of Organizations*. Ph.D. dissertation, Erasmus University, Rotterdam, p.136.

86 See The Body Shop (1995) *Values Report*, for full details of method.

87 *The Observer* (1996) February; *Independent on Sunday* (1996) February.

88 The social accountability requirements cover:

a) child labor; b) forced labor; c) health and safety; d) freedom of association and the right to collective bargaining; e) discrimination; f) disciplinary practices; g) working hours; h) compensation; i) management systems covering policy, management review, company representatives, palling and implementation, control of suppliers, addressing concerns and taking corrective action, outside communication, access for verification and record keeping.

89 Define "child" as any person less than 15 years of age, unless the minimum age law stipulates a higher age for work or mandatory schooling, in which case the higher age would apply.

90 *SA8000*, CEPAA (Council on Economic Priorities Accreditation Agency), October 1997. A full copy can be obtained for $20.00 from CEPAA (see Appendix 2: Glossary for full address).

91 See Appendix 2: Glossary and Index.

92 See Appendix 2: Glossary and Index.

93 See Appendix 2: Glossary and Index.

94 For an analysis of the differences between EMAS and ISO 14001, see Chapter 4.

95 Crowe, Roger (1997) "New moves to protect labour in Third World," *Guardian*, 16 October.

96 For a brief exposition, see Appendix 2: Glossary; for a full discussion, see Elkington (note 2).

97 *Guardian* (1997) "Slow move to ethical trade," 7 November.

98 Matthews, Virginia (1997) "Framework for ethical sourcing," *Financial Times*, 12 December.

99 Myners, Paul (1998) "Improving performance reporting to the market," in *Performance Measurement in the Digital Age*. London: Institute of Chartered Accountants. Myners is Chairman of Gartmore Investment Management plc.

100 SustainAbility, UNEP and The New Economics Foundation (1996) *Engaging Stakeholders*. London: SustainAbility.

101 Ibid.

102 Owen, David, Gray, Rob and Adams, Roger (1997) *Corporate Environmental disclosure: Encouraging Trends*. London: Association of Certified Accountants.

103 WICE (1994) *Environmental Reporting: A Manager's Guide*. Geneva: International Chamber of Commerce.

104 Smith, Craig N. (1990) *Morality and the Market*. London: Routledge.

105 *Boycott Quarterly,* published by the Centre for Economic Democracy, PO Box, 30727 Seattle, WA, USA.

6

BUSINESS AS IF THERE'S A FUTURE

It is possible to envision different futures

Managing change and complexity

Five principles for corporate citizenship

Five management imperatives for corporate citizenship

"In the twilight of the twentieth century, making globalization work humanely is quickly becoming the dominant issue of our time."

Jeffrey E. Garten[1]

"What is a world order without a binding and obligatory ethic for the whole of humankind – without a world ethic? What is the use of prohibitions with an ethical foundation in one country if they can be got round by going to other countries?"

Hans Kung[2]

It is possible to envision different futures

Here are four hypothetical possibilities.

Hedonism and happiness: we're all on holiday!

In the first vision of the future everyone drinks Coke, flies British Airways and eats Big Macs while watching CNN's choice of news items. In this vision, everyone listens to the latest global pop idols, chews Wrigley's, works using Microsoft and drives a Toyota. In this vision, the world has been homogenized around particular consumer items; there is mass mobility as everyone goes on holiday, and world poverty has been solved as big business, in partnership with governments, builds water wells and supports a benign world government based on the Universal Declaration of Human Rights.

Working hard: I'm all right!

The second vision of the future is apocalyptic. In this vision, the disparity between rich and poor grows, both between countries *and* within countries. The world population divides even further into three groups of the super-affluent, the affluent and the poor. The first two groups have a high life expectancy, live under the rule of law and have mass mobility. The third group represents perhaps one-quarter of the world's population and often do not have access to clean water, medical services or education. Many of them do not live under the rule of law and are not citizens, but are subjects both of their governments and the global economy. The combination of a lack of basic human rights and absolute poverty consigns this group to total misery.

To each his or her own: that's the way it should be!

The third vision is also apocalyptic and sees increased power and control of world affairs devolved to largely uncontrolled financial markets and big business. In this vision, large corporations rule the world, often managed by well-meaning executives who are neither in control of their own professional destinies nor the destinies of their companies. There are significant regional conflicts, as the poor try to migrate to the rich countries that they have supported over years by paying the interest on debts. This leads to greater barriers around the three trading blocs of Europe, North America and Japan, and increased military intervention by the USA in small-scale conflicts.

These are easily recognizable visions, partly because some aspects of them are already here. There is, however, *another way*.

Another way: business as if there's a future

This other way is based on three simple principles:

1 a new partnership between business, government and civil society;
2 an acceptance by business that it has both political and financial power;
3 agreement that at present globalization has its winners and its losers.

Managing change and complexity

How can business combine its responsibility to be profitable with "thinking interdependence," protecting human rights and supporting the rule of law?

Remember that a senior Shell executive said after their débâcle over the Brent Spar oil rig in the North Sea and, in a separate incident, after the Nigerian government's murder of Ogoni activists: "It's a CNN world. It's not a trust-me world. It's a show-me world." It is also a world of uncertainty as the CEO of Siemens Nixdorf, Gerhard Schulmeyer, has said: "We are moving from managing what is known, to the management of uncertainty."

The nature of globalization is such that we can expect greater homogenization *and* a greater emphasis on difference and diversity as international capital spreads its tentacles and has to adapt to local conditions. This paradox means that globalization has been matched by *glocalization* as global corporations allow subsidiaries to manage themselves in ways appropriate to local conditions.

The thought that "we are all global citizens" has different starting points in history. For some it is 1945 and the dropping of thermo-nuclear bombs on

Hiroshima and Nagasaki; for others it is 1492 and the European discovery of America; and for yet others, it is the laying of the first transatlantic telegram cable in 1895. International trade has taken place for thousands of years, and business people have visited markets for just as long, but the process has reached such a level of activity that, for almost everything we do, there is a global implication. As Professor Stuart Hall, British academic and social commentator, has said:

> *"I think that at the heart of it is the fact that none of the processes we are interested in – economic, political, cultural – are containable or frameable within the confines of the nation-state. The terrain on which all the fundamental processes now operate is global, not local, not national, not confined by the nation-state."*[3]

The idea of global citizenship resonates differently around the world. For the British and Japanese, many of whom feel a certain geographic homogeneity, the idea of globalization is one of going from home territory into a wider world. For Afro-Caribbeans in Britain and Koreans in Japan, there have always been other places as referents in their sense of identity. For North Americans, recent history means that the vast majority have some sense of ethnic identity beyond their immediate shores.

Identity is important and, in a global economy, business knows only too well how good it feels for people to identify with a particular lifestyle. This is why brand names such as Coca-Cola, McDonald's and Mercedes-Benz have become so important. Every individual now has both a global and a local identity, the global identity often being based on a particular lifestyle and the consumption of global brands. The local identity is based on community, ethnicity and local climatic and geographic conditions. We are perhaps as much constituted by our global identification, if we can personally recognize it, as by our local affiliations.

If we accept that we are all local and global citizens, so too are companies, hence the title of many company reports and this book, *Corporate Citizenship*. All companies have ethnic origins and all brands have images based on marketing, but no two businesses are the same, and on the global stage there is enormous variety. Global brands are dominated by mass-consumer items like soft drinks, fast food and entertainment (Coca-Cola, McDonald's and Disney), but the world's largest companies, in terms of turnover, are in energy and manufacturing (Shell, General Motors, General Electric and Ford).

There is a difference between national, international, transnational, multinational and global companies according to where they are based, whether they are horizontal or vertically managed and the products they sell.[4] For instance Boeing, one of only two major aircraft manufacturers, is firmly based in the USA, but it sources globally. No one would disagree that Boeing is a global brand, that it is American and that it has helped achieve extraordinary safety levels in its product area. Nestlé, by contrast, has a Swiss identity but nearly 87 per cent of its assets are foreign based and 97 per cent of its workforce operate outside Switzerland. Both Boeing and Nestlé are major players in the global economy, but the notion that all the world's largest companies are able to move rapidly to new markets, employ new labor and are resistant to local differences is untrue.

Just as globalization means something different to each individual, it represents different things to different companies. One thing that distinguishes American and Japanese global companies from many other companies is that in most cases their domestic markets represent more than 50 per cent of their turnover. For European companies the global economy, outside their domestic territory, is much more important. This is one reason why, in general, Europeans are more internationalist than people from the USA; why there are more international product lines in European supermarket shelves; and why corporate citizenship is a hotter topic in Europe than in most other parts of the world.

The other reason that re-thinking the role of business in society has become so important in Europe is because the nature of the contract between business and the community is based both on entrepreneurial freedom *and* on community benefits. As Robert Reich, former secretary in the Clinton administration, says, the USA has swung too far in promoting the values of the individual, rather than the community, such that "economic apartheid is becoming the rule" in the USA.[5] If this is true then according to the UN's 1997 *Human Development Report*, economic apartheid is being practiced globally.

Rioting in Indonesia following the collapse of the Indonesian rupee, and the chaos caused by the collapse of other Asian currencies in 1997 and the devaluation of European currencies in the late 1980s, highlighted how many people's lives are dependent on a stable global financial system. A Japanese finance minister described the situation as "a global crisis of capitalism."[6] Perhaps that crisis can only be solved through a coalition of governments and business, working to protect communities from the vicissitudes of global capitalism?

So what are the solutions? Anyone who has worked for, or with, the world's largest companies knows how strong their sense of corporate identity and community is. Corporate man and woman might be a little on the wane, but companies like Shell and Mitsubishi prosper because they combine economies of scale, with strong brand identity and the commitment of their employees. In other words, many corporations are good model communities, often operating across nation-state boundaries. So the first solution could be for them to promote themselves, and their systems of corporate governance, based on management review and accountability, as good examples to some of the governments they have to deal with, where human rights are violated or there is environmental indifference.

However, enlightened business leaders know that global capitalism is facing a crisis on two fronts. First, it is reliant on increased production to meet consumer demands, which in many cases the companies have created, and this is incompatible with sustainability and ecological realities. Second, competitive capitalism, without social controls, creates social disharmony, and global business activity may destroy local communities. It is very much in businesses's interests to ensure that the market is controlled by a balance of government and civil society.

The second solution is for business to be more inclusive, by seeking to involve itself in communities and by looking for solutions to its problems from a wide range of stakeholders. This means that responsible corporations would show recognition of the principles on which civil society operates and that those principles of mediation, negotiation, accountability and justice should be supported and not undermined by business. As Hutton has argued: It "could be possible to develop a new capitalist model in which market flexibilities are integrated with webs of trust and commitment, and where society acknowledged the imperative of sharing risk and income as fairly as possible."[7] This may be easier for countries in the affluent North (see "North–South dialogue" in Appendix 2: Glossary), represented by North America, Europe, Japan and much of South East Asia and Australia, to develop, as their production has shifted from manufacturing to services in the second half of the twentieth century. For instance, in the UK more people work in creative industries such as film, design and rock music than in the automobile industry. Design alone earns nearly $20 billion a year for the UK and employs some 300,000 people, and rock music is bigger than steel. These industries are inherently based on fashion, change and innovation, and are used to adaptation. Subsistence farmers in the poorer South involved in growing bananas, rice or coffee need stability in global markets to maintain and raise their standards of living.

These ideas coalesce: (1) business works best when there is a level playing field, when the rules are known and agreed; (2) business needs a strong civil society to supply educated employees and consumers, as well as healthcare and the administration of the rule of law; (3) in the information age most organizations rely on the ability of their employees to think, learn, innovate and implement to give them competitive edge; (4) if we put the global and local communities at the centre of attention, rather than the company, we can begin to tackle the growing wealth disparity that exists at present.[8]

The companies and other bodies profiled in this book support just these principles. A global economy needs global non-business organizations to monitor business and, among others, this book has profiled Amnesty International, Greenpeace, the World Wide Fund for Nature (WWF), the Council on Economic Priorities and some of the work of the United Nations. How can we marry these thoughts to those of the Chairman of BT, Sir Ian Vallance, when he says: "I believe that a commitment to ethical behavior has to become nothing more nor less than 'business as usual'. . . . We must, in our actions as well as our words, show our employees, our customers, and indeed, all out stakeholders what our company stands for and what our values are."

There are many examples of businesses that have found ways of working which acknowledge their role and power. For this reason we have included a profile of McDonald's work with the EDF in the USA in Chapter 5 (but questioned the "McLibel" prosecution in Chapter 5), detailed Shell's problems in the North Sea and Nigeria (but pointed out the inclusion of human rights and sustainability in their business principles since then), catalogued The Body Shop's initiatives on social auditing (but made it clear that other businesses such as Marks & Spencer, BT, GrandMetropolitan [now Diageo], The Co-operative Bank and VanCity are also showing imagination in this area), and provided examples of community initiatives from around the world of business working to solve social problems – Auchan in France, Hindustan Lever in India, Levi Strauss & Co. in Colombia and Bata in Thailand.

There may be some surprise at the inclusion in this book of profiles on the US Department of Defense, the UK's Ministry of Defence, London's Metropolitan Police, the community organization of Abrinq in Brazil and Medecins sans Frontières. However, these are organizations facing the same issues as business: how to build local and global societies based on social justice and fair play and deal with internal problems of equal opportunities, racism and environmental protection. They too are accountable to their stakeholders. Each sector has something to learn from the others, and each sector has to learn to talk to the others.

Five principles for corporate citizenship

Despite the diversity of emergent managerial and organizational forms, the profiles in this book indicate that there are some concepts that underpin, and give credibility to, the idea that there is a new model of corporate citizenship, beyond philanthropy and voluntarism. As the CEO of BP says: "[Our] efforts [in developing a more coherent and transparent relationship between business and communities] have nothing to do with charity, and everything to do with our long-term self-interest."[9]

We think that the profiles in this book, taken together, support the following propositions:

1 Business is a major player in world affairs, and there is a new balance of power between business, government and civil society

The changing relationship between business, government and civil society reflects a new balance of power and influence. We know that the role and scope of business in world affairs is greater now than it has ever been, and that in some major trading countries government is finding a now role, if it is not in retreat. These facts, coupled with increased stakeholder empowerment, mean that business is having to redefine its role in world affairs.[10]

2 Businesses and individuals are thinking globally

The globality of thinking, by which we mean the ability to use the globe as a theoretical reference point, has developed rapidly. For instance, we have been implored to "think globally and act locally," if we can.[11] This can also be referred to as connectivity or the ability to conceptualize the world as one interconnected system, linking balanced ecological systems with balanced social systems.

3 Business thrives where society thrives

The most successful societies – and businesses – are ones with high levels of trust and mutuality, education and training, and which are supported by good infrastructure and the rule of law.[12] Business needs a strong civil society.

ᴊmental imperative requires the saving of the natural environ- order to support human life. Human life is dependent on a healthy environment, and vice versa, but while the world can (and may) coɴ. ᴊue without humans, the reverse is not true.

5 Businesses are communities of people

Large business organizations are communities of people who share the desire not to be dysfunctional, unhappy or inefficient with other communities, including residential communities, non-profit organizations and single-issue non-governmental organizations, so that they can maximize their profits.

The title of "responsible corporate citizenship" applies to those companies, and other organizations, that recognize and act on the five points outlined above. Other companies, operating outside this framework, may claim corporate citizenship, and many companies do, but they are undermining the system that supports them. In this respect, they are not responsible. As an individual citizen in the community, I may claim citizenship, but by driving too fast through a residential area, cheating on my tax, failing to feed my children properly or not recycling my domestic waste, I am not being a *responsible* citizen. The same applies to companies.

The five themes outlined here are the basis both for profitable business *and* healthy communities.

Five management imperatives for corporate citizenship

Drawing on these five themes we can identify the following management principles:

1 Be accountable

All companies, and other organizations (including government), must incorporate transparent accountability into their operating principles. Ownership varies from organization to organization, but they are all accountable to everyone, even though different groups may be interested in specific areas. They must allow for comparability with other organizations and ensure honest and accurate reporting. Continuous improvement, through monitoring, reporting and third-party verification requires new management systems. New forms of measurement are required based on financial, environmental and social accountability – for business, government and community.[14]

2 Think interdependence

Companies do not operate alone, or in a vacuum. Think systems. Think interdependence. Think ecology. Out of sight should not be out of mind – when you have sold your product, you are still responsible for its disposal.

3 Have clear principles

Operate on clear principles, but acknowledge the rich diversity that provides balanced systems. Without some global values-based framework, we will descend into chaos, but there also must be tolerance for difference. Finding a balance is the task for the next century.

4 Embrace change and complexity

Managers need to be able, more than ever, to handle change and complexity and develop new skills accordingly. This includes hearing voices that have been ignored or marginalized previously. The manager must try to envisage other social realities, far distant from the boardroom.

5 Be educated and knowledgeable

Education, training and the distillation of knowledge must be at the heart of any organization's operations. There is much to consider within business practice for the future.

There is no clear view of the future, but there are signposts. The issues which have been identified in this book are at the heart of the debate about the future of business, the future of government *and* the future of civil society. Business, however, because of its pre-eminent role in the development of local communities and global society, has the greatest leap of faith to make. Corporate citizenship will determine how the next century evolves.

Notes to Chapter 6

1 Garten, Jeffrey E. (1998) "Globalism doesn't have to be cruel," *Business Week*, 9 February. Garten is Dean of Yale School of Management. He also served as a Deputy Secretary of Commerce during the first Clinton administration.

2 Kung, Hans (1991) *Global Responsibility: In Search of a New World Ethic*. London and Munich: SCM Press.

3 Hall, Stuart (1997) In conversation with Martin Jacques, "Les enfants de Marx et de Coca-Cola," *New Statesman*, 28 November.

4 See definition in Chapter 1 on page 26.

5 Reich, Robert (1997) Interviewed in *New Statesman*, 14 November.

6 Elliot, Larry (1998) "No asylum from world's sickness," *Guardian*, 31 January.

7 Hutton, Will (1997) *The State to Come*. London: Vintage.

8 See Chapter 1 for figures on the growing wealth disparity which is occurring as the global economy develops.

9 Garten – see note 1.

10 See Chapter 1. Consider, for instance, the situation of 100 companies having turnovers which are greater than the smallest 50 countries.

11 "Think globally, act locally" is a rallying call from the environmental movement, aware that environmental problems can only be solved on an international basis, but believing that we must set an example by starting somewhere – locally.

12 See Chapter 1. See also Fukuyama, Francis (1995) *Trust*. Harmondsworth, UK: Penguin, and Hampden-Turner, Charles and Trompenaar, Fons (1993) *The Seven Cultures of Capitalism*. New York: Piatkus, as well as the indicators for the 29 member countries, which show that, in some countries, more than 80 per cent of 25 to 64-year-olds have completed at least an upper-secondary education, whereas in some less well performing countries, such as Greece and Turkey, fewer than 50 per cent have done so (*Financial Times* (1997), 11 December).

13 The natural environment means the physical world, specifically all that which is non-human. Although, of course, humans are natural!

14 See "The Index of Sustainable Economic Welfare," on page 227 in Chapter 5.

APPENDIX 1
Recommended reading

Capra, Fritjof (1982) *The Turning Point: Science, Society and the Rising Culture*. London: Flamingo.

Castells, Manuel (1996) *The Rise of the Network Society*. London: Blackwell.

Centre for Social Management and New Consumer (1995) *Good Business? Case Studies in Corporate Social Responsibility*. Bristol: Policy Press.

Council On Economic Priorities (1994) *Shopping for a Better World*. San Francisco: Sierra Club Books.

Elkington, John (1998) *Cannibals with Forks*. London: SustainAbility.

Gray, John (1998) *False Dawn: the Delusions of Global Capitalism*. London: Granta.

Hawken, Paul (1994) *The Ecology of Commerce*. London: Phoenix.

Henderson, Hazel (1996) *Building a Win-Win World: Life Beyond Economics*. San Francisco: Warfare Berrett-Koehler.

Kelly, Gavin, Kelly, Dominic, and Gamble, Andrew (eds) (1997) *Stakeholder Capitalism*. London: Macmillan.

Korten, David (1995) *When Corporations Rule the World*. London: Earthscan.

Murphy, David F. and Bendell, Jem (1997) *In the Company of Partners*. Bristol: Policy Press.

Prince of Wales Business Leaders' Forum (PWBLF) (1996) *Business as Partners in Creating Wealth for Countries, Companies, and Communities*. London: PWBLF with the World Bank and UNDP.

Schumacher, E.F. (1962) *Small is Beautiful*. London: Blond and Briggs.

Stead, W. Edward and Garner Stead, Jean (1992) *Management for a Small Planet: Strategic Decision-Making and the Environment*. London: Sage.

Wheeler, David and Sillanpää, Maria (1997) *The Stakeholder Corporation*. London: Pitman Publishing.

Zadek, Simon, Pruzan, Peter and Richard Evans (1997) *Building Corporate Accountability*. London: Earthscan.

APPENDIX 2
Glossary

Alternative trade organization (ATO)

An ATO is an organization that trades on the basis of fair trade, developing a trading relationship with producers that give them more control, security and income. Examples of ATOs are Oxfam, Traidcraft, Equal Exchange and Twin Trading in the UK.

CERES

CERES stands for the Coalition for Environmentally Responsible Economies. The CERES Principles were born in the wake of the Exxon Valdez accident in Prince William Sound, Alaska in 1989. They can be seen as important trendsetters and a precursor to the International Chamber of Commerce's Business Charter for Sustainable Development.

The CERES Principles cover:

1 protection of the biosphere
2 sustainable use of natural resources
3 reduction and disposal of waste
4 wise use of energy
5 risk reduction
6 marketing of safe production and services
7 damage compensation
8 disclosure
9 the appointment of environmental directors and managers
10 assessment and audit.

Child labor

The International Labour Organisation (older than the UN, as it was founded in 1919) estimates that there are 100 to 200 million children under the age of 15 working around the world, about 95 per cent of them in developing countries. Child labor is also becoming a significant problem affecting immigrant communities in many industrialized countries.

Definitions are important in assessing the problem: standards for minimum employable age established by the International Labour Organisation have been ratified and incorporated into national legislation by many countries. Briefly, the age standards for developed countries are:

13 years old   for light work
15 years old   for regular work
18 years old   for hazardous work.

For countries where social and educational services are not well developed, the age standards are:

12 years old   for light work
14 years old   for regular work
18 years old   for hazardous work.

Increasingly, the standard for industrialized countries, 15 years of age, is being applied without qualification to developing country producers.

Closed loop technology

An industrial complex operating under the principles of closed loop technology recycles all its waste materials and emits, discharges or disposes none to the air, water or land.

Complexity

A situation where there is a large number of continually varying circumstances that may not all be easily understood.

Co-operative

A co-operative is a business owned and run by its employees.

Corporate citizenship

The new corporate citizenship is not about philanthropy, it is not about attaching a glossy community affairs report to the annual financial report as an after-thought managed by public relations. The new corporate citizenship is about citizenship at the heart of strategic planning. The new model may well represent a paradigm shift, although we are talking about radical evolution, rather than revolution. The word "new" implies modern, progressive and development, but one of the qualities of the current corporate citizenship situation is its post-modernity - that there is no clear view of the future and that rationality in management decision-making must be tempered with caution, emotion and unreason.

Corporate governance

Corporate governance is concerned with the relationship between business and society. Central to this concern is: who owns the company? Who benefits from its activities? To whom is the company accountable? How are directors appointed?

Corporate social responsibility (CSR)

The social responsibilities of companies range from compliance with health and safety regulations for employees, to environmental protection to corporate governance. All companies have economic, social, ethical and environmental responsibilities, some of which require compliance with the law, others requiring discretionary action to ensure that the company does not knowingly operate to the detriment of society. At the heart of the CSR movement are the issues of transparency and accountability so that all stakeholders, and the company itself, audits and reports on its ethics and financial, social and environmental affairs.

Corporation

A corporation is a group of individuals acting as one entity. In the context of corporate citizenship, corporate refers to any organization whether in the business, public or voluntary, the for-profit, the not-just-for-profit and the not-for-profit sectors. All organizations are accountable to society for their operations, whether they be a global company, a government department or a local pressure group. Their ownership and key relationships may determine their reporting priorities.

Disability

A disabled person is "someone who experiences significant disadvantages in employment as a result of medical or physical impairment." (Employers' Forum on Disability)

EMAS (European Union's Eco-Management and Audit System)

The European Union's EMAS regulations are voluntary and apply to all companies, but have been adapted for local government in the UK and Germany. They require organizations to be audited for their environmental effects and to report publicly. At present this must happen every three years, but this may change to annual reports in the future. In the first year there were nearly 1,000 EMAS registrations of German companies, followed by 50 in the UK.

Environmental audit

The commonly accepted definition of an environmental audit comes from the International Chamber of Commerce (ICC) as quoted in 1989: "A management tool comprising a systematic, documented, periodic and objective evaluation of how well environmental organization, management and equipment are performing with the aim of helping to safeguard the environment by:

● facilitating management and control of environmental practices; and
● assessing compliance with company policies, which includes meeting regulatory requirements."

Ethical audit

Ethical audits are essentially internal management tools, and a way of listening to the views of stakeholders, particularly those who work in the company, while social audits are primarily designed to make the organization account for its social impact. Ethical audit tests the consistency of values throughout the organization.

Ethical investment

Although ethical investment only represents some 10 per cent of total investment in the world today, it is a useful indicator of future thinking. While traditional ethical investment criteria range from issues such as not investing in armaments, tobacco, oppressive regimes and environmental policy, increasingly outside the ethical investment field, investment is being channelled to companies that have reported on their social and environmental impacts. This accounts for some 8 per cent of companies trading on the London Stock Exchange.

Ethical Trade Initiative (ETI)

The Ethical Trading Initiative is a forum composed of several development and campaigning organizations in the UK with the aim of improving working conditions in developing countries by developing a forum for discussion, analysis, and training. The ETI is a process rather than a product, providing a common framework for addressing codes of conduct and monitoring. The Initiative hopes to provide a road map for companies seeking to develop best practice in the area. The UK Ministry for International Development has endorsed the Ethical Trading Initiative and provided significant financial support.

Externalities

Economists term externalities as effects that are outside, or external to, decision-makers. Externalities can be both positive and negative, but have come into focus through decision-making that does not take into account the full social and environmental costs of resource use and the creation of pollution. No longer can the environment be regarded as a large sink for the disposal of emissions and effluents. For responsible companies, the task is to think both upstream and downstream and "internalize externalities" by taking responsibility for all social and environmental costs. There is, therefore, a link to be made between corporate social responsibility, life cycle care and supply chain management.

Fair trade

Fair trade is based on the principle of rewarding producers for their efforts. Fundamental to the fair trade movement is the fact that supermarket shoppers have a choice; they can choose to buy fair traded products for reasons of ethics, quality, price or life style. By rewarding producers at source and strengthening their position through direct trade, fair prices and by providing credit, fair trade is seen as the best way of promoting development.

Gay

Person involved in a relationship with, or merely having a sexual preference for, people of the same sex.

Global company

Some companies may be described as global, rather than international. Global companies may also be transnationals or supranationals, manufacturing different components in different countries to make a final product which is sold globally. It is difficult in these cases to say "this product is 100 per cent American or Spanish." Most large automobile manufacturers and electronics companies are now global.

Globalization

Globalization is the process of increasingly large organizations dominating trade and social relations, most of them businesses, and the development of electronic webs that provide the basis for a 24 hour economy and instantaneous cross-border communications.

Global Action Plan (GAP)

GAP is a program established by the United Nations Environment Programme to encourage individuals and households to measure and improve their environmental impact on the basis of "think global, act local."

Glocalization

Glocalization is the process where a company with a global perspective and operating policies develops policies and actions sensitive to local conditions.

International Labour Organisation (ILO)

The ILO predates the United Nations having being formed in 1919. Through international conventions it has established criteria for global governance on issues such as exploitative child labor, working conditions, collective bargaining and health and safety.

ISO 14001 series

The ISO 140001 series succeeds ISO 9000, the quality management system, by providing a globally recognized environmental management system. The series is based on the principles of a register of environmental effects, including inputs, processes and outputs, and measurable continuous improvement based around an audit, monitoring and management system. Unlike the European Union's Eco-Management and Audit Scheme (EMAS) it does not require a third party verified public statement. In the UK, ISO 14001 and EMAS superseded BS 7750.

ISO 9000

The ISO 9000 series provides a globally recognized quality management system based on the principles of continuous improvement, auditing, monitoring and a management system.

Lesbian

Person (female) involved in a relationship with, or merely having a sexual preference for, people of the same sex.

Life cycle analysis (LCA)

LCA is a management tool for understanding the total environmental impact of a product or service from inception to disposal. This means accounting for the use of energy, biosphere reserves, transport and disposal costs. It is a necessary factor in awarding eco-labels in order to establish which product has the least environmental impact. It can also be a useful management tool in supply chain management and understanding social and environmental responsibilities.

Montreal Protocol

The Montreal Protocol, signed in 1987, set standards for protecting the ozone layer.

Multinational corporation

A multinational corporation (MNC) is a company that may be based in one country but has bases in other countries, for management, manufacturing or distribution.

Natural Step

The principles of the Natural Step have been adopted by companies like IKEA, Scandic Hotels, Electrolux and Swedish McDonald's. The organization was founded by Dr Karl-Henrik Robert who developed a set of non-negotiable principles, or systems conditions, for environmental sustainability. The starting points were that there were certain impediments to change, around the world: a general lack of knowledge regarding the fundamental conditions of life; an absence of a comprehensive overview of environmental science which leads away from integration to arguments over detail, rather than agreement on principles; negative expectations and resignation; the individual's sense of disempowerment.

Non-government organization (NGO)

An NGO is an organization which is neither a business nor represents a government. Often NGOs are single issue pressure groups working for issues such as human rights, the environment or fair trade, but an NGO can also represent mainstream activities such as business. In this way both the International Chamber of Commerce and Greenpeace are NGOs.

North-South dialogue

The affluent North is normally defined as North America, Europe, Australia, New Zealand and Japan while the South is those countries which have not benefited from post-1945 "development." The UN Development Reports show that the wealth disparity between the affluent North and the poorer South continues to increase. Advocates of a North-South dialogue argue that there is a moral imperative to redistribute wealth to the South and this is an issue of power, as much as access to global markets. As the UN Development Reports show, there have been winners and losers in the development of the global economy. The winners have been multinational corporations and people living in the North.

Philanthropy

Philanthropic business activity is the distribution of excess profits after other claimants, such as shareholders, have been paid. It is a voluntary activity on the part of business and is not normally part of its everyday business functioning.

Polluter pays principle

The polluter pays principles states that the creator of polluter should pay for any clean up or disposal that is necessary. On this principle all industrial or consumer waste should be the responsibility of the producer.

Precautionary principle
Established in 1974 by the Organization for Economic Co-operation and Development (OECD) the precautionary principle basically says "if in doubt about the environmental effects of an activity, don't do it."

Secondment
A term used in the UK for employees fully paid by their company to work on community projects.

Social auditing
A social audit measures the following aspects of an organization's activities: how employees and other stakeholders perceive the organization; how the organization is fulfilling its aims; how the organization is working within its own values statements.

Social auditing assesses the social impact and ethical behavior of an organization in relation to its aims, and those of its stakeholders.

Stakeholder
Stakeholders are described as people or organizations that have an impact on, or are impacted on, by the company. There is also a debate as to the true meaning of stakeholding: does it mean that any company has a wide range of key relationships or that these key relationships have a stake in the company? They certainly have a stake in its financial, social and environmental performance; whether they have an ownership stake is a matter of great debate.

Stakeholder corporation
A stakeholder corporation is a company which engages its stakeholders in consultation and provides information geared to satisfying stakeholder interests. By remaining in touch with stakeholders, the company hopes to improve its management systems and decision-making procedures, and ensure that it is more in tune with society's demands.

Stakeholder map
A stakeholder map allows an organization to understand its stakeholders and their relative and reciprocal positions vis-à-vis the organization. Much of the process of devising stakeholder maps is based on understanding resource and wealth distribution and the use of power.

Sullivan Principles
The Sullivan Principles were launched in 1997 by the Reverend Leon H. Sullivan and supported by 12 major US corporations. They provided principles for conducting business in South Africa.

Supranational corporation
Supranationals appear to recognize no home base and operate in many countries. See also *multinationals* and *global companies*.

Transgenerational

Transgenerational equity means providing for future generations, and ensuring that we leave the world in a better state than we found it. This is one of the fundamental principles of sustainable development.

Transnational corporation (TNC)

A transnational corporation (TNC) is a company that has its headquarters in one country but operates most of the time outside that home country in a number of other countries (Nestlé for instance only has two per cent of its operations in Switzerland, its home base).

Voluntarism

Voluntarism is based on philanthropy and involves business donating money and resources after other claimants have been satisfied. While business donations for social causes and the arts are obviously welcomed by voluntary organizations working in those areas, at the heart of the new corporate citizenship is the fundamental idea of the company as being responsible and responsive to society's needs through its whole aims, ideals and operating methods.

APPENDIX 3
Contact addresses

AIESEC International
40 Rue Washington, B-1050 Brussels, Belgium
Tel: +32 2 646 2420 Fax: +32 2 646 3764
Email: aiesec@ai.aiesec.org
Website: http://www.aiesec.org

AIESEC is the world's largest student organization. It strives to build youth leadership and develop values such as social responsibility, cultural understanding, entrepreneurship and active and life-long learning. This primarily happens through AIESE's international traineeship exchange program.

Amnesty International (International Secretariat)
1 Eastern Street, London WC1X 8DJ, UK
Tel: +44 (0)171 413 5500 Fax: +44 (0)171 956 1157
Email: amnestyis@amnesty.org
Website: http://www.oneworld.org/amnesty/

Amnesty International is a worldwide movement of people who campaign for human rights. Its appeals on behalf of victims of human-rights violations are based on accurate research and on international law.

Asahi Shimbun Foundation
Tokyo Kenikyo-in, Medical and Public Health Centre, 4-8-32 Kudan-Minami, Chiyoda-Ku, Tokyo 102, Japan
Tel: +81 (3)5210-6670 Fax: +81 (3) 5210-6679

The Asahi Shimbun Foundation has been awarding Japanese companies for their attention to social responsibility issues since 1991.

Ashoka (UK) Trust
7th Floor Windsor House, 83 Kingsway, London WC2B 6SD, UK
Tel: +44 (0)171 405 3477 Fax: +44 (0)171 242 0503
Email: info@ashoka.org
Website: http://www.ashoka.org

Ashoka finds and supports outstanding individuals with ideas for far-reaching social change by electing them to a fellowship of public entrepreneurs.

Ashoka: Innovators for the Public

1700 North Moore Street, Suite 1920, Arlington, VA 22209, USA
 Tel: +1 703 527 8300 Fax: +1 703 527 8383
 Email: info@ashoka.org
 Website: http://www.ashoka.org

Ashoka finds and supports outstanding individuals with ideas for far-reaching social change by electing them to a fellowship of public entrepreneurs.

Ashridge Centre for Business and Society

Ashridge Management College, Berkhamstead, Herts HP4 1NS
 Tel: +44 (0)1442 843491 Fax: +44 (0)1442 841209
 Website: www.ashridge.org.uk

Situated within Ashridge Management College, the Centre conducts research into the link between corporate competitiveness and accountability to stakeholders, and the role of business as a stakeholder in society. Director: Andrew Wilson.

BP Centre for Corporate Citizenship

Warwick University Business School, Centre for Corporate Citizenship, Warwick Business School, University of Warwick, Coventry CV4 7AL
 Tel: +44 (0)1203 524158 Fax: +44 (0)1203 524393
 Website: www.warwick.ac.uk

Established in 1996, the mission of the unit is to promote good corporate citizenship through active involvement with companies, research and teaching. Corporate citizenship is defined as understanding and managing as positively as possible a company's external influences for the benefit of both itself and society as a whole on society. The Director of the Unit, Chris Marsden, runs discussion group on email entitled "Teaching Corporate Citizenship."

The Business Enterprise Trust

706 Cowper Street, Palo Alto CA 94301, USA
 Tel: +1 650 321 5100 Fax: +1 650 321 5774
 Website: www.betrust.org

A non-profit organization created to highlight and promote the study of good business practices. The trust makes an annual award to outstanding companies and individuals, and produces video documentaries, business-school cases and educational materials to illustrate how sound management and social vision can result in business success.

Business for Social Responsibility

609 Mission Street, 2nd Floor, San Francisco, CA 94105, USA
 Tel: +1 415 537 0888 Fax: +1 415 537 0889
 Email: dhudson@bsr.org
 Website: http://www.bsr.org

Business for Social Responsibility is a membership organization for companies of all sizes and sectors. BSR's mission is to help its member companies achieve long-term commercial success by implementing policies and practices that honour high ethical standards and meet their responsibilities to all who are impacted by their decision.

Business in the Community
44 Baker Street, London W1M 1DH, UK
  Tel: +44 (0)171 224 1600 Fax: +44 (0)171 486 1700
  Email: information@bitc.org.uk
  Website: http://www.bitc.org.uk

Business in the Community is a registered charity whose purpose is to support the economic and social regeneration of communities by raising the quality and extent of business involvement and making that involvement a natural part of successful business practice.

Catholic Institute for International Relations
Unit 3, Canonbury Yard, 190a New North Road, London N1 7BJ, UK
  Tel: +44 (0)171 354 0883 Fax: +44 (0)171 359 0017
  Email: ciirlon@gn.apc.org

An independent charity which works to overcome human-rights violations, armed conflict, poverty and injustice in the South (see "North–South dialogue" in Appendix 2: Glossary.

Center for Corporate Community Relations at Boston College
36 College Road, Chestnut Hill, MA 02167, USA
  Tel: +1 617 552 4545 Fax: +1 617 552 8499
  Website: www.bc.edu/ccr

A non-profit membership association serving corporations committed to community involvement and corporate social responsibility. Services include professional development, custom research and information services, and an annual international Leaders' Conference.

Centre for Social and Environmental Accounting Research
University of Dundee, Dundee, Scotland DD1 4HN, UK
  Tel: +44 (0)1382 344789 Fax: +44(0)1382 224419
  Email: CSEAR@acc.dundee.ac.uk
  Website: http://www.dundee.ac.uk/Accountancy/csear.htm

A networking institution which gathers and disseminates information about the practices and theory of social and environmental accounting, and provides a mechanism for academics and practitioners to make contact and support each other.

Centre for Tomorrow's Company (CTC)

19 Buckingham Street, London WC2N 6EF, UK
   Tel:+44 (0)171 930 5150 Fax: +44 (0)171 930 5155
   Email: ctomco@ctomco.demon.co.uk
   Website: http://www.tomorrowscompany.com

CTC came out of the RSA Tomorrow's Company Inquiry, a three-year business-led project exploring the roots of sustainable business success.

Coalition for Environmentally Responsible Economies (CERES)

711 Atlantic Avenue, Boston, MA 02111, USA
   Tel:+1 617 451 0927 Fax: +1 617 482 2028
   Email: ceres@igc.apc.org
   Website: http://www.ceres.org

A non-profit membership organization comprising leading social investors, environmental groups, religious organizations, public pension trustees and public interest groups. It focuses on ways investors could help implement environmentally and financially sound investment policies, and promotes responsible corporate activity for a safe and sustainable future for our planet.

Consumers International

24 Highbury Crescent, London N5 1RX, UK
   Tel: +44 (0)171 226 6663 Fax: +44 (0)171 354 0607
   Email: consint@consint.org.uk
   Website: http://www.consumersinternational.org

Consumers International is an independent, non-profit organization which exists to support and strengthen member organizations and the consumer movement, and to fight for policies at the international level that respect consumer concerns.

Council on Economic Priorities (CEP)

30 Irving Place, New York, NY 10003, USA
   Tel: +1 212 420 1133 Fax: +1 212 420 0988
   Email: cep@echonyc.com or cep95@aol.com

CEP is a non-profit research organization which rates the corporate social responsibility and environmental performance of companies, providing data to investors, companies and consumers.

Council on Economic Priorities Accreditiation Agency (CEPAA)

30 Irving Place, New York, NY 10003, USA
   Tel:+1 212 420 1133 Fax: +1 212 420 0988
   Email: info@cepaa.org or sa8000@aol.com

The accrediting agency which has ownership of the new social accountability standard, SA8000, and which accredits auditing bodies to audit organizations and issue SA8000 certificates accordingly. The Board consists of representatives from business,

NGOs and academics including Reebok, Amnesty International, Toys 'Я' Us, Sainsbury's, KPMG and SGS.

Ecumenical Council for Corporate Responsibility

11 Burnham Wood, Fareham, Hants PO16 7UD, UK
  Tel: +44 (0)1329 239390 Fax: +44 (0)1329 238711
  Email: ECCR@geo2.poptel.org.uk

ECCR was formed to create a British focus for the study of corporate responsibility in both the churches and transnational corporations. It produces educational material on the issues raised by TNCs and aids appropriate representations and campaigning by churches in the British Isles, especially where these churches are shareholders in British-based TNCs.

EIRIS Services Ltd

504 Bondway Business Centre, 71 Bondway, London SW8 1SQ, UK
  Tel: +44 (0)171 735 1351 Fax: +44 (0)171 735 5323
  Email: ethics@eiris.win-uk.net

EIRIS is a research organization dedicated to helping people invest according to their ethical principles.

Equality Foundation

PO Box 164, St Lawrence House, 29-31 Broad Street, Bristol BS99 7HR, UK
  Tel: +44 (0)117 929 7780 Fax: +44 (0)117 922 6664
  Email: enquiries@ef.westec.co.uk

Using systems of diversity and inclusion to drive quality improvement and pursuit of excellence.

Ethibel

Vooruitgangstraat 333, Bus 7, B-1030 Brussels, Belgium
  Tel: +32 2 201 04 44 Fax: +32 2 201 04 00
  Email: ethibel@bitserv.com

Independent ethical research association carrying out company profile studies using social, ecological and ethical criteria. Also holds a quality label for ethical or green investment funds.

Ethics Resource Center

1747 Pennsylvania Ave, NW, Suite 400, Washington DC 20006, USA
  Tel: +1 202 737 2258 Fax: +1 202 737 2227
  Website: http://www.ethics.org

The ERC is a non-profit, non-partisan educational organization whose vision is an ethical world. Its mission is to serve as a catalyst to improve the ethical practices of individuals and organizations from the classroom to the boardroom. The organization fulfils its mission through three distinct areas of expertise: as a leader in the fields of organizational/business ethics consulting; as a provider and facilitator of character education programs; and as an ethics information clearing-house.

EthicScan Canada Ltd
PO Box 54034, Toronto, Ontario M6A 3B7, Canada
  Tel: +1 416 783 6776 Fax: +1 416 783 7386
  Email: ethic@concentric.net
  Website: http://www.ethicscan.on.ca

EthciScan Canada Ltd is a business ethics, research and consulting clearing-house that monitors social and environmental performance of 1,500 companies in Canada.

European Institute for Business Ethics
Nijenrode University, Straatweg 25, 3621 BG Breukelen, The Netherlands
  Tel: +31 3462 91290 Fax: +31 3462 265453
  Email: eibe@nijenrode.nl
  Website: www.nijenrode.nl

This organization exists to support business in behaving with integrity and how to listen to stakeholders. It gives advice on how to integrate business ethics as competitive advantage, and it provides research, consulting and training.

FairTrade
7th Floor Regent House, 89 Kingsway, London WC2B 6RH, UK
  Tel: +44 (0)171 405 5942 Fax: +44 (0)171 405 5943
  Email: fairtrade@gn.apc.org
  Website: http://www.gn.apc.org/fairtrade/

The aim of FairTrade is to alleviate poverty in the Third World by encouraging industry and consumers to support fair trade.

Forum for the Future
Thornbury House, 18 High Street, Cheltenham GL50 1DZ, UK
  Tel:+44 (0)1242 262729 Fax: +44 (0)1242 262757
  Email: annemariedabrowska@forumche.demon.co.uk

Forum for the Future is a UK charity founded by Jonathon Porritt, Sara Parkin and Paul Ekins. Its mission is to accelerate the building of a sustainable way of life by taking a positive solutions-oriented approach to today's environmental challenges.

Human Rights Research and Education Center
University of Ottawa, 57 Louis Pasteur, PO Box 450, Station A, Ottawa, Ontario K1N 6N5, Canada
  Tel: +1 613 562-5772 Fax: +1 613 562-5125
  Email: hrrec@human-rights.cdp.uottawa.ca
  Website: http://www.uottawa.ca/~hrrec

Headed by Professor Errol Mendes, the Center operates a range of programs, corporate round tables, research and publications, in the belief that university-based centres can act to bridge the mechanism between the corporate community and the public sector/civil society. It offers a program on business ethics and stakeholder relations.

Human Rights Watch

485 Fifth Avenue, New York, NY 10017, USA
   Tel: +1 212 972 8400 Fax: +1 212 972 0905
   Email: HRWNYC@hrw.org HYPERLINK mailto:HRWNY@hrw.org
   Website: http://www.hrw.org

Human Rights Watch, the largest US-based international human-rights monitoring and advocacy organization, is dedicated to promoting respect for international human rights and humanitarian law worldwide. Five divisions cover Africa, the Americas, Asia, Central Asia, Europe and the Middle East.

IMUG

Escherstr. 23, 30159 Hannover, Germany
   Tel: +49 511 911 15 0 Fax: +49 511 911 15 95
   Email: imug.hannover@t-online.de
   Website: http://www.home.t-online.de\home\imug.hannover

The Institute researches responsible consumer behavior and corporate social responsibility. It develops a scientific basis for a comparative company test, researches on social and ecological behavior of companies offering goods on the German market and publishes data for consumer information.

The Institute for Global Ethics

PO Box 563, Camden, Maine 04843, USA
   Tel: +1 207 236 6658 Fax: +1 207 236 4014
   Email: wethics@globalethics.org
   Website: http://www.globalethics.org

An independent, non-sectarian, and non-political organization that is dedicated to elevating public awareness and promoting the discussion of ethics in a global context.

Institute for Policy Studies

733 15th Street, NW, Suite 1020, Washington DC 20005, USA
   Tel: +1 202 234 9382 Fax: +1 202 357 7915
   Email: http://www.igc.org/ifps

IPS is dedicated to ushering in a new progressive era by strengthening the country's most important social movements, providing them with strong intellectual ammunition.

Institute for Social and Ethical AccountAbility

1st Floor Vine Court, 112-116 Whitechapel Road, London E1 1JE, UK
  Tel: +44 (0)171 377 5866 Fax: +44 (0)171 377 5720
  Email: Secretariat@AccountAbility.org.uk
  Website: http://www.AccountAbility.org.uk

An international professional body committed to strengthening social responsibility and ethical behavior of the business community and non-profit organizations. It does this by promoting best practice, social and ethical accounting and auditing, and the development of standards and accreditation procedures for professionals in the field.

Interfaith Center on Corporate Responsibility

475 Riverside Drive Room 566, New York, NY 10015-0050, USA
  Tel: +1 212 870 2293 Fax: +1 212 870 2023
  Email: info@icca.org

ICCR co-ordinates the work of religious and socially responsible investors assisting them to be shareholder advocates on issues like the environment and diversity.

International Institute for Environment and Development

3 Endsleigh Street, London WC1H 0DD, UK
  Tel: 44 (0)171 388 2117 Fax: 44 (0)171 388 2826
  Email: mailbox@iied.org
  Website: http://www.oneworld.org/iied

IIED is an independent, non-profit organization which seeks to promote sustainable patterns of development through research, policy studies, consensus building and public information.

International Institute for Environment and Development America Latina

Piso 6, Cuerpo A, Corrientes 2835, 1193 Buenos Aires, Argentina
  Tel: +54 1 961 3050 Fax: +54 1 961 3050
  Email: mailbox@iied.org
  Website: http://www.oneworld.org/iied

IIED is an independent, non-profit organization which seeks to promote sustainable patterns of development through research, policy studies, consensus building and public information.

International Labour Office

4 route des Morillons, CH-1211, Geneva, Switzerland
  Tel: +41 22 799 6111 Fax: +41 22 798 8685
  Email: http://www.ilo.org

ILO was founded to work for social justice as a basis for lasting peace. It carries out this mandate by promoting decent living standards, satisfactory conditions of work and pay and adequate employment opportunities. Methods of action include the creation of international labor standards; the provision of technical co-operation services; and research and publications on social and labor matters. In 1946 ILO became a specialized agency associated with the UM. It was awarded the Nobel Peace Prize in 1969.

Investor Responsibility Research Center
Suite 700, 1350 Connecticut Avenue, NW, Washington DC 20036–1701, USA
Tel: +1 202 833 0700 Fax: +1 202 833 3555
Email: mkt@irrc.org
Website: http://www.IRRC.org

IRRC is the leading source of impartial, independent research on corporate governance, proxy voting and corporate social responsibility issues.

Keidanren Kaikan
1-9-4 Ote-machi, Chiyoda-ku, Tokyo 100, Japan
Tel: +81 3245 0144 Fax: +81 3279 3611
Website: http://www.eco-web.com/register/01729.html

Kinder, Lydenberg, Domini & Co.Inc.
129 Mt Auburn Street, Cambridge, MA 02138-5766, USA
Tel: +1 617 547 7479 Fax: +1 617 354 5353
Email: sri@kld.com

A provider of social research for institutional investors which meets the needs of social investors, KLD provides performance benchmarks, corporate accountability research, and consulting services analogous to those provided by financial research service firms.

Lawyers Committee for Human Rights
333 7th Avenue, 13th Floor, New York, NY 10001-1050, USA
Tel: +1 212 845 5200 Fax: +1 212 845 5299
Email: nyc@lchr.org
Website: http://www.lchr.org

Carries out work to protect and promote fundamental human rights. It focuses on building the legal institutions and structures that will guarantee human rights in the long term.

Minnesota Center for Corporate Responsibility
1000 LaSalle Avenue, Minneapolis, MN 55403-2005, USA
Tel: +1 612 962 4121 Fax: +1 612 962 4125

New Academy of Business
3-4 Albion Place, Galena Road, London W6 0LT, UK
Tel: +44 (0)181 563 8780 Fax: +44 (0)181 563 8618
Email: New-academy@compuserve.com
Website: http://www.new_academy.ac.uk

The New Academy of Business offers management education and development to individuals and organizations which want to combine high-quality business performance with a commitment to human values.

New Economics Foundation
Vine Court, 112-116 Whitechapel Road, London E1 1JE, UK
   Tel: +44 (0)171 377 5696 Fax: +44 (0)171 377 5720
   Email: neweconomics@gn.apc.org

The New Economics Foundation is an independent research institute for developing and promoting innovative work and practical approaches to economics which are responsive to social, ethical and environmental issues.

NPI Global Care
PO Box no. 227, 48 Gracechurch Street, London EC3P 3HH
   Tel: +44 (0)171 665 3235 Fax: +44 (0)171 665 3301
   Email: tony_belsom@npi.co.uk
   Website: http://www.npi.co.uk/globalcare/

NPI, founded in 1835, is a mutual company, owned by its 500,000 policy holders, offering investments in companies that do not adversely affect people, animals or the environment. Its unit trusts are researched by NPI in co-operation with EIRIS, the ethical investment research service. It consistently outperforms "conventional" funds, although past performance is not necessarily a guide to the future.

Office for Public Management
252b Gray's Inn Road, London, WC1X 8JT, UK
   Tel:+ 44 (0)171 837 9600 Fax: +44 (0)171 837 6581
   Email: office@opm.co.uk
   Website: http://www.opm.co.uk

An independent centre providing organizational development, management education and research. The Office works to improve management practice and thinking in public, private and charitable organizations committed to the achievement of explicit social goals.

Panos Institute
1025 Thomas Jefferson St NW, Suite 105, Washington DC 20007, USA
   Tel: +1 202 965 5177 Fax: +1 202 965 5198
   Email: panos@cais.com

The Panos Institute specializes in information for development, and stimulates public debate by providing accessible information on environmental and social development issues. Also has offices in London, Paris, Washington, Africa, South Asia and Latin America.

Prince of Wales Business Leaders' Forum
15-16 Cornwall Terrace, Regent's Park, London NW1 4QP, UK
  Tel: +44 (0)171 467 3656 Fax: +44 (0)171 467 3610
  Email: info@pwblf.org.uk
  Website: http://www.oneworld.org/pwblf/

The mission of PWBLF is to promote continuous improvement in the practice of good corporate citizenship and sustainable development internationally, as a natural part of successful business operations.

Rights and Resources
2253 North Upton Street, Arlington, VA 22207, USA
  Tel: +1 703 524 0092 Fax: +1 703 524 0092

Social Investment Forum
1612 K Street NW, Suite 600, Washington DC 20006, USA
  Tel: +1 202 872 5319 Fax: +1 202 331 8166
  Email: info@socialinvest.org
  Website: http://www.socialinvest.org

A national non-profit membership association which is dedicated to promoting the concept, practice and growth of socially responsible investing. Administered by Co-op America, SIF comprises investment practitioners and institutions from across all fields who seek to use their investment dollars to encourage positive social and environmental change in society.

Social Venture Network Europe
4 Great James Street, London WC1N 3DA, UK
  Tel: +44 (0)171 242 4990 Fax: +44 (0)171 242 5010
  Email: svneurope@freedom2surf.co.uk

An international network of socially and environmentally engaged entrepreneurs and business leaders dedicated to changing the way they and the world do business. They integrate the values of a socially and environmentally sustainable society into day-to-day business practices.

Social Venture Network
PO Box 29221, San Francisco, CA 94129-0221, USA
  Tel: +1 415 561 6501 Fax: +1 415 561 6435
  Email: svn@well.com
  Website: www.svn.org

An international network of socially and environmentally engaged entrepreneurs and business leaders dedicated to changing the way they and the world do business to create a just, humane and sustainable society. SVN integrates the values of a socially and environmentally sustainable society into day-to-day business practices.

Students for Responsible Business
Tel: +1 415 778 8366 Fax: +1 415 778 8367
Email: webmaster@srbnest.org
Website: http://www.srb.org

SRB was created as a community of graduate and undergraduate business school students and alumni who believe that a new model is emerging in business today, and that they can and should be at the forefront of changing the role of business in society.

SustainAbility
49–53 Kensington High Street, London, W8 5ED, UK
Tel: +44 (0)171 937 9996 Fax: +44 (0)171 937 7447
Email: info@SustainAbility.co.uk
Website: http://www.sustainability.co.uk

Much of SustainAbility's work focuses on environmental strategy and management. As the area evolves, it is helping to define the sustainable development agenda around the "Triple Bottom Line" (business solutions which are socially responsible, environmentally sound and economically viable).

Swiss Info Center
Rue de Romont 2, CH-1700 Fribourg, Switzerland
Tel: +41 26 322 06 14 Fax: +41 26 322 39 62
Email: centreinfo@bluewin.ch

Investor and corporate responsibility research and information.

UK Social Investment Forum
1st Floor, Vine Court, 112-116 Whitechapel Road, London E1 1JE, UK
Tel: +44 171 377 5907 Fax: +44 171 377 5720
Email: uksif@gn.apc.org
Website: http://www.arq.co.uk/ethicalbusiness/uksif/

Primary purpose is to promote and encourage the development and positive impact of socially responsible investment throughout the UK.

United Nations Development Programme
One United Nations Plaza, New York, NY 10017, USA
Tel: +1 212 906 5064 Fax: +1 212 906 5657
Website: http://www.undp.org.unso_www.html

World Business Academy
PO Box 19210, San Francisco, CA 94119-1210, USA
Tel: +1 415 227 0106 Fax: +1 415 227 0561
Website: http://www.worldbusiness.org

A research and educational institution that engages the business community in a better understanding and practice of the new role of business as an agent for social transformation. The WBA delivers self-learning educational resources, and conducts research projects, forums and seminars in the areas of corporate social responsibility, leadership, and the development of human potential at work.

World Development Movement
25 Beehive Place, London SW9 7BR, UK
   Tel: +44 (0)171 737 6215 Fax: +44 (0)171 274 8232
   Website: http://www.oneworld.org/wdm/

The World Development Movement achieves justice for the world's poorest people through campaigns that tackle the fundamental causes of poverty.

World Resources Institute
1709 New York Avenue, NW, Washington DC 20006, USA
   Tel: +1 202 638 6300 Fax: +1 202 638 0036
   Email: philip@wri.org
   Website: http://www.wri.org

An independent centre for policy research and technical assistance on global environmental and development issues, WRI is dedicated to helping governments and private organizations of all types cope with environmental, resource, and development challenges of global significance.

INDEX

Aberdeen Ordinance Center 145
Abrinq Foundation 132–4, 276
accessibility 141–2
accountability 278–9
  and stakeholders 61
acid rain 96–7
Action Aid, and ETI 154
Advertising Standards Authority (ASA)
    162
Africa, child labor 129
ageism 142
Agenda for Action 47
AIDS and HIV in the workplace 18,
    147–50
  disease management 147–50
  National AIDS Trust Employment
      Initiative 148–9
AIP *see* Apparel Industry Partnership
Al Yamamah arms deal 169–70
alcohol 162
Alliant Techsystems, and landmines 169
alternative trade organization (ATO),
    definition 283
American Express, brand image and
    reputation 63
Amnesty International
  arms trade 168, 171
  brand image and reputation 63
  human rights and the workplace
      113–17
  profile 119–20
amoral business 50–1
animal welfare and protection 23, 173–7
  ethical investment 163
  farm animals 174–5
  Hormel 175
  Land O'Lakes 175
  RSPB 176–7
  testing 175–7

Tom's of Maine 175–6
Apparel Industry Partnership (AIP) 132,
    250
Arbor International, sourcing 11
arms trade 23, 83, 162, 167–71
  control 171
  and Indonesia 170–1
  landmines 169
  sales 169–71
  and Saudi Arabia 169–70
  solutions 171
  UK policy 168–70
  UN 168
ASA *see* Advertising Standards Authority
Asahi Foundation 46–7
asbestos 97
Ashridge Centre for Business and Society
    180
Asia, child labor 129
Asia Monitor Resource Centre 129
Association of Chartered Certified
    Accountants, company performance
    253–5
Auchan 216, 276
auditing and accountability 227–31
  benefits 251
  indicators of wealth 227–31
auditing business performance 232–4
Australia
  ecotourism 105
  greenhouse gases 97–8
Avon
  accountability 3, 250–1
  profile 37
AVX, and landmines 169
azo dyes 107

B&Q, ageism 142
BA *see* British Airways

Banana Republic, Tagua Initiative 112
Bangladesh
    annual revenue 15
    malnutrition 16
    poverty 153–4
banking with a conscience 164–7
    Co-operative Bank 164–6
    VanCity 166–7
banks, and laundering 14
Barclays Bank
    brand disasters 67
    and disability 139
Barings Bank, collapse 88, 93
Bata and Thailand 215, 276
Bath Environment Centre 108–9
Bath University 108
BCCI, collapse 88, 93
Beijing Conference 145
Ben & Jerry's
    accountability 3
    auditing business performance 233
    and BSR 44
    disabled employees 141
    mission statement 36–7
    and sexual orientation 144
Benenson, Peter 119
Bhopal and Union Carbide 69–70
Bible 20
Big Issue, The 51–2
Bismarck, Otto 21
Blair, Tony 210
BMW 9, 65
    sustainable business 103
boards
    accountability 86
    complacency 88–9
    power 86–7
Body Shop, The
    accountability xix, 3, 276
    and AIDS 149
    animal welfare 175–6
    auditing business performance 233
    brand image and reputation 62
    ethical audit 241
    and fair trade 156

mission statement 36
    social audit 156, 246
    stakeholders 197
Boeing 274
Bolivia, corruption 95
bovine spongiform encephalopathy
    (BSE) 174
boycott 255–7
    guide to avoidance 256
    lessons from McLibel 257
    media action or courts? 257
BP
    accountability xix, 3, 39, 43
    and Colombia 120–2
    London Benchmarking Group 213–15
    new corporate citizenship 35
BP Centre for Corporate Citizenship,
    Warwick University 180
Braille 139
    Barclays Bank 67
    British Airways 66
    Dow Corning 67
    Ford Pinto 65
    Heineken 66
    Mercedes-Benz 65
    Prudential Assurance 66–7
brand image and reputation 61–5
    American Express 63
    Amnesty International 63
    Burger King 64
    Coca-Cola 63
    Greenpeace 63
    Heinz 67
    Hungry Jack's 64
    Kellogg's 67
    Levi Strauss & Co. 63
    Marks & Spencer 63
    Nike 62–3
    Pizza Hut 64
    Premier Beverages 63
    Virgin 63
    Volvo 63, 65
Branson, Richard
    and Amnesty International 119
    Virgin image 66–7

Brazil
and Abrinq Foundation 132–4
ecotourism 105
breastfeeding 230–1
Brent Spar oil rig 36, 68, 221, 272, 276
bribery 87
British Aerospace 169–70
British Airways (BA)
brand image 67
protecting reputations 66
software sourcing 12
British Army, racism and sexual
harassment 146–7
British Gas, and disability 140
British Union for Abolition of Vivisection
(BUAV) 175
British-American Tobacco (BAT) 172
Browne, John 122
Brundtland, Gro Harlem 97
Brundtland Report 100
BS 7750 235–6
BSE see bovine spongiform
encephalopathy
BSR see Business for Social Responsibility
BT
accountability 3, 17, 42–3, 276
social audit 237–8
BUAV see British Union for Abolition of
Vivisection
building partnerships 219–21
business as partners in development
222–7
guide to developing partnerships
222–7
Marine Stewardship Council 225–7
partnerships at work 222
Burger King, brand image and reputation
64
business
changes xxii–xxiii
four models 5–05
global 18–19
virtues 19
Business Charter for Sustainable
Development 104

business and communities 209–18
Auchan 216
Bata Thailand 215
Chihuahua's Business Social Trust
217–18
Corporate Community Index 214–15
engaging the community 211–18
Hindustan Lever 216–17
Levi Strauss & Co. 211–13
local community 209–11
London Benchmarking Group 213–15
Marks & Spencer 210
Phillips Van Heusen 218
Timberland 212–13
Business in the Community 136
Business Enterprise Trust 178
business future see future
Business for Social Responsibility 43
and AIP 132
profile 44

C&A
human rights and the workplace 113
social accountability 251
Cadbury 197
Cadbury Committee, and corporate
governance 91–2
Cadbury Report on Corporate
Governance 89
Cadbury, Sir Adrian 89
Café direct
coffee 151
Oxfam 151
Traidcraft 151
CAFOD, and FairTrade 155
CALPERS, and corporate governance
90–1
campaign groups xxiii
Campbell, Mark 146
Campbell's Soup, and corporate
governance 90
Canada, education 178–9
capital, movement 19
carbon dioxide 97–8
CARE framework 245

Carlyle, Thomas 20
Carson, Rachel, memorial fund 220
Casanare 2000 120–2
Catholic Institute for International
    Relations 154
Center for Corporate Community
    Relations at Boston College 178
Centre for Tomorrow's Company 43,
    47–8
Century Textiles, environmental
    management 07, 105, 107
CERES see Coalition for Environmentally
    Responsible Economies
CFCs 10, 97
Chandler, Geoffrey 114–15, 119
change 19, 281
    business xxii–xxiii
    global connectivity 19
    world xxii–xxiii
change management 274–9
Charter for Good Corporate Behavior
    45–6
Chernobyl 18, 69
Chihuahua's Business Trust 217–18
child labor 68, 95, 126–9, 257–8
    Africa 129
    alternatives 128–9
    ascertain whether a problem 127–8
    Asia 129
    definition 283–4
    Latin America 129
    provide protection 128
    SA8000 248
    workplace action 128
China
    and English language 12
    and foreign investment 26
    grain imports 20
    gunpowder and printing 20
    human rights 115
Christian Aid 154
    and fair trade 154–5
    and FairTrade 155
Churchill & Friend, and disability 140
CI see Conservation International

CIDESA see Foundation for Socio-
    Environmental Training, Research
    and Development
Clark, Alan 115
Cleaver, Sir Anthony 47
Clinton, Bill 115
closed loop technology, definition 284
co-operative, definition 284
Co-operative Bank
    banking with a conscience 164–6,
        276
    Corporate Conscience Award 239–41
    ethical audit 239–41
Co-operative Wholesale Society
    and ETI 154
    and FairTrade 155
Coalition for Environmentally
    Responsible Economies (CERES)
        103–4
    definition 283
    VanCity 167
Coca-Cola 24, 173, 273
    brand image and reputation 63
    global company 24
Coca-Cola University 211
coffee 151–4
    Cafédirect 151
Colombia
    BP 39
    and BP 120–2
    corruption 95
    floriculture 10, 12–13
Colombian Human Rights Committee
    121
community 209–11
    engaging the community 211
    Marks & Spencer 210
    what does local mean? 211
    see also business and communities
community business 52
Community Investment Team 211
community involvement, ethical
    investment 160
Community Trade Programme 15
Companies act! 148–9

company
  global 23–6
  inclusive 48
  successful 75–4
company boards, diversity 137–8
company performance 251–5
  Association of Chartered Certified
    Accountants 253–5
  engaging stakeholders 252–5
  ten recommendations to report makers
    252–3
competences 86
competition, change xxiii
complexity, definition 284
Confucianism 20
connectivity, global 18–20
Connolly, Edward v. Rossing Uranium
  (RTZ) 24
Conservation International (CI) 112
consumerism xxiii
Consumers International 154
Cook, Robin 168, 171
Corby, Sir Brian 124
corporate citizenship xxii, 33–58
  categories 84–5
  definition xxi–xxii, 284
  five management imperatives 278–9
  five principles 277–8
  introduction xix–xxv
  models of social responsibility 50–5
  and organizations 40
  responsibilities 40–3
  social responsibility 43–9
  tomorrow's organization 43
  who said this? 38–40
Corporate Community Index 214–15
Corporate Conscience Award 111
  Co-operative Bank 239–41
  Timberland 212–13
corporate environmental disclosure,
    Association of Chartered Certified
    Accountants 253–5
corporate governance 23–4, 83, 85–95
  Cadbury Committee 91–2
  CALPERS 90–1

Campbell's Soup 90
  corruption 93–5
  definition 284
  ethical investment 160
  Hampel Committee 92–3
corporate social responsibility (CSR),
    definition 284–5
corporation, definition 285
corruption 93–5
  corporate governance 93–5
cost control 62
Costa Rica, Cafédirect 151
Council on Economic Priorities (CEP) 43,
    219
  animal welfare 174
  Corporate Conscience Award 111, 149,
    239
  and ETI 154
  SA8000 73
  SGS Yarsley 249
critical issues xxiv, 91–190
  animal welfare 173–7
  arms trade 167–71
  corporate governance 85–95
  education 177–80
  the environment 95–6
  environment and last 30 years 96–113
  fair trade and ethical investment
    150–67
  human rights and workplace 113–50
  tobacco 172–3
CSR see corporate social responsibility
currency, speculation 23
customer service 62

Daewoo, global business 15
Daly, Herman 100, 227–8
Davis, Peter 66–7
DDT 97
deafness 139
DeLuca, Tom 250
DEMOS 196
Department for International
    Development (DfID) 171
desertification 96

developing world 14–18
  global business 15–16
development *see* sustainable
  development
DfID *see* Department for International
  Development
Diageo
  accountability xix, 3
  see also GrandMetropolitan
Diana, Princess of Wales
  floral tributes 10, 12–13
  House of Windsor 200–1
  landmines 64, 167
dinkies 144
disability 138–40
  definition 285
disabled employees 140–2
discrimination 136
disease, global 18
Disney 273
  boycott 256
  and sexual orientation 143–4
diversity
  company boards 137–8
  what companies can do 137
DKNY, Tagua Initiative 112
Dominican Republic, Cafédirect 151
Domino's Pizza, and CERES 103
Dow, boycott 255
Dow Corning, protecting reputations 67
drugs, illegal 13–14, 23
Dyno Nobel, and landmines 169

Earth Summit, Rio de Janeiro 96–8
East Timor 170
Eco-Tex certification 107
Ecoflor 12–13
ecology, global 18
ecology of commerce 102–3
economic responsibility 40–1
Ecopetrol 120
ECOTEC 203
ecotourism 105
  Natural Step 105
  Scandic Hotels 105

Ecotourism Society 105
education 177–80, 279
  Canada 178–9
  ethical investment 160
  Netherlands 180
  UK 179–80
  USA 178
efficiency 62
Electrolux 98
ELN 120
EMAS *see* European Eco-Management
  and Audit Scheme
Emory University 211
employee relations, ethical investment
  160
English, global language 20–1
environment 95–6
  and ethical investment 161–2
  and McDonald's 39
  standards 83
Environment Council, and Shell 221
environment and last 30 years 96–113
  business and environmental
    management 105
  Century Textiles 107
  Coalition for Environmentally
    Responsible Economies (CERES)
    103–4
  ecology of commerce 102–3
  ecotourism 105
  Gaia 99–100
  International Chamber of Commerce
    104
  Merck 106
  Natural Step 98–9
  NatWest, Marks & Spencer, Bath
    Environment Centre 108–9
  Nortel 110
  Novo Nordisk 111
  Scandic Hotels 105–6
  SmithKline Beecham 112
  steps towards sustainable business
    102
  sustainable business 101
  sustainable development 100

Tagua Initiative 112–13
three sustainability shifts 101
environmental audit 234–6
  BT 42–3
  definition 285
  environmental management standards
    235–6
  see also auditing business performance
environmental damage xxii, 68
Environmental Defense Fund, and
    McDonald's 3, 54
environmental management standards
    235–7
equal employment opportunities 134
  women and minorities 135–6
Equal Exchange, Cafédirect 151
ERC *see* Ethics Resource Center
Esso, and National Trust 71
ethical audit 237–41
  Co-operative Bank 239–41
  definition 285
  The Body Shop 241
ethical investment 150–67
  animals 163
  definition 285–6
  environment 163
  negative criteria 162
Ethical Trade Initiative (ETI) 153–4, 219
  definition 286
Ethics Resource Center (ERC) 178
ETI *see* Ethical Trading Initiative
European Eco-Management and Audit
    Scheme (EMAS) 101, 232–3, 236
  definition 285
European Institute for Business Ethics
    180
exchange rates 19
externalities, definition 286
Exxon Valdez 68–72, 103–4, 121

fair trade 150
  definition 286
  Nestlé 150
  Philip Morris 150
  Unilever 150

fair trade and ethical investment 95,
    150–67
  banking with a conscience 164–7
  Cafédirect 151
  Christian Aid 154–5
  Co-operative Bank 164–6
  coffee 151–2
  ethical investment 157
  Ethical Trading Initiative 154
  fair trade 150
  FairTrade 155
  four investment funds 160–4
  Max Havelaar 153
  negative criteria 157–60
  positive criteria 157–60
  The Body Shop 156
  VanCity 166–7
FairTrade 73–4, 154
  profile 155
FARC 120
Fay, Chris 221
Findus, boycott 256
fish stocks 54, 225–7
floriculture
  Colombia 10
  Netherlands 13
food miles 9
food poisoning 72
Ford 273
Ford Pinto 65, 69
  brand image and reputation 62
Forest Stewardship Council (FSC) 225
Foster's, and Nomura 8
Foundation for Socio-Environmental
    Training, Research and
    Development (CIDESA) 112
France
  Auchan 216, 276
  pollution 9
fraud 88
Freeport-McMoRan, and Rio Tinto 8
Friedman, Milton xi
Friends of the Earth
  and MSC 227–8
  Schweppes 255

FSC *see* Forest Stewardship Council
future xxv, 269–80
    different futures 271–2
    five management imperatives for
        corporate citizenship 278–9
    five principles for corporate citizenship
        277–8
    managing change and complexity 27–9

Gaia theory 99–100
gambling 162
GAP *see* global action plan
Gap, Tagua Initiative 112
Gates, Bill 21
gay, definition 286
gay and lesbian issues 143–4
Gay Pride 143
General Electric 273
    and landmines 169
General Motors 273
    brand image and reputation 62
    and CERES 103–4
    global business 15
    global company 24
generally recognized as safe (GRAS) 176
geophysiology 100
George, Eddie 14
Germany
    and bribes 87
    greenhouse gases 97–8
    shareholders 87
    takeovers 87
Giddens, Anthony 23
Gilford, Yvonne 169
Glaxo 87
global action plan (GAP) 108
    definition 287
global communication 20–1
global company 23–7
    definition 286
global connectivity 18–20
    change 19
    movement and mobility 19
    wealth disparity 19–20
global and corporate governance 23–4

global economy
    change xxii
    and changing perspectives 7–9
    changing perspectives 7–9
global economy and social responsibility
    1–58
Global Environmental Charter: Japan 45
global organizations 4–6
    Greenpeace 4–5
    Levi Strauss & Co. 4
    Marks & Spencer 5
    NEC 5
    Nesté 4
    UK Ministry of Defence 5
global sourcing 9–14
    Arbor International 11
    Ecoflor 12–13
    four examples 10–14
    illegal drugs 13–14
    IT from India 11–12
global standards 251–3
    audit of social accountability 251
global warming xxii, 97
globalization, definition 287
glocalization, definition 287
Gola, human rights and the workplace
    113
Golding, William 100
Goodworks International 130
governance, global and corporate 23–4
grain imports, China 20
Grajew, Oded 134
Gramstrup, Marianne 111
GrandMetropolitan
    accountability xix, 3, 16–17, 276
    brand image and reputation 64
    London Benchmarking Group 215–17
    and Nomura 8
Greenbury Code 92
greenhouse gases 97–8
Greenpeace
    accountability xix
    brand image and reputation 63
    equal opportunities 40
    global organization 4–5

and MSC 227
new corporate citizenship 35
growth, global 22
Guatemala, Phillips Van Heusen 218
Guinness, fraud 93
Gulf War 41
gunpowder 20

Hall, Richard 42
Hampel Committee on Corporate
  Governance 92–3
Hampel, Sir Ronald 92
Handy, Charles 15
Hanson Trust, shareholders/stockholders
  205–6
Hart, Peter 207
Harvey-Jones, Sir John, and Amnesty
  International 119
health and safety, ethical investment 160
healthcare, ethical investment 160
Heineken, protecting reputations 66
Heinz, brand image and reputation 67
Hilbre Farms 11
Hillaire, Fitzroy 37, 73, 251
Hindustan Lever 216–7, 276
HIV and AIDS in the workplace 147–50
Hoffman, Lord 24
Honda 47
Hong Kong Christian Industrial
  Committee 129
honne 45
Hormel, animal welfare 175
Horner, Jeff 249
House of Windsor 200–1
Howard Kennedy Enterprise 37
Hughes Aircraft, and landmines 169
Human Rights Research and Education
  Center 178–9
Human Rights Watch 113–17
  arms trade 168
  and landmines 169
human rights and the workplace 68,
  113–50
  Abrinq Foundation 132–4
  additional human rights 117

ageism 142
AIDS and HIV 147
Amnesty International 119–20
Apparel Industry Partnership 132
BP in Colombia 120–2
British Army 146–7
business action on human rights 124–5
business case 120, 135
business and overseas workplace 129
child labor 126–9
Churchill & Friend 140
disability 138–40
disabled employees 140–2
disease management 147–50
diversity on boards 137–8
equal opportunities 134
Levi Strauss & Co. 131–2
National AIDS Trust Employment
  Initiative 148–9
Nike 129–31
Opportunity 2000, 136–7
sexual harassment 144–7
sexual orientation 143–4
Shell in Nigeria 122–4
UN Universal Declaration of Human
  Rights 117–19
US Army 145–6
women and minorities 135–6
Hungry Jack's, brand image and
  reputation 64

IBM 47
  and board 88
  brand image and reputation 62
  environmental reporting 201–2
  London Benchmarking Group 213–15
  and sexual orientation 143
ICC *see* International Chamber of
  Commerce
IKEA 98
images, global 18
IMF *see* International Monetary Fund
INBio *see* National Biodiversity Institute
inclusive company 48, 206–9
  McKay Nursery 207

inclusive company – *contd*
  Manganese Steel 208–9
  Volkswagen 207–8
Index of Sustainable Economic Welfare
    (ISEW) 227, 228–31
India
  corruption 95
  Hindustan Lever 216–17, 276
  information technology (IT) 11–12
Indian National Association of Software
    and Service Companies 11
indicators of wealth 227–31
Indonesia
  and arms trade 170–1
  corruption 95
  smog 9
Industry Cooperative for Ozone Layer
    Protection (ICOLP) 110
INFACT 172
information sources
  change xxii
  and English language 20–1
information technology (IT), India 11
Institute of Petroleum 14
Institute for Social and Ethical
    AccountAbility 238
integrity consulting, KPMG 244
integrity thermometer, KPMG 245
interdependence 279
Interface, sustainable business 102
Interfaith Center on Corporate
    Responsibility, and AIP 132
international business, change xxii
International Chamber of Commerce
    (ICC) 120
  Business Charter for Sustainable
    Development 104
  environmental auditing 234–6
  and global rules 22
international company 26–7
International Convention on the Rights of
    the Child 134
International Cooperative for
    Environmental Leadership 110
International Institute for Management

Development 227
International Labour Organisation (ILO)
    126
  definition 287
International Monetary Fund (IMF)
  and Malaysia 5
  and Mexico 8
  SAPs 22
  and Thailand 8
International Network of Street Papers 52
Internet, standards 117
ISEW *see* Index of Sustainable Economic
    Welfare
ISO 9000 xii, 249
  definition 287
ISO 9002 107
ISO 14000 xii, 101, 249–50
  definition 287
issues *see* critical issues
Ito Yokado 47

Jackson, Michael 64
Japan
  greenhouse gases 97–8
  Keidanren's Code of Corporate
    Behavior 45–6, 88
  shareholders 87
  takeovers 87
  women and minorities 135–6
Japan Airlines 47
Jasco 47
Jennings, John 124
John Paul Mitchell Systems, animal
    welfare 175–6
Jones, Keith 208
Jones of New York, Tagua Initiative 112
Jospin, Lionel 171

Keidanren's Code of Corporate Behavior
    45–6, 88
Kellogg's, brand image and reputation 67
Kennedy, John F. 116
Kentucky and Metropolitan Sewer
    District, and CERES 103–4
Kernet, and landmines 169

Kerr, Margaret 110
key relationships and stakeholders 48,
    193–98
  defining stakeholders 198
  seven principles of stakeholding 195
King, Lord 66
King, Rodney 114
Kiss My Face, animal welfare 175–6
Korea, global business 15
KPMG
  Global Edge 237
  profile 244–5
  seven deadly sins 94
Krupp, Fred 220

labour costs, sourcing 9–14
Land O'Lakes, animal welfare 175
landmines, and social responsibility 41,
    64, 83
language, global 20–1
Latin America, child labor 129
laundering, drugs money 14
LCA see lifecycle analysis
learning organization 74–5
Leeson, Nick 93–4
legal responsibility 41
lesbian, definition 287
lesbian and gay issues 143–4
Levi Strauss & Co.
  accountability xix, 3, 276
  brand image and reputation 63
  code of conduct xii
  Community Investment Team 211
  country selection 131
  global organization 4
Levi's, brand image and reputation 64
life cycle analysis (LCA) 112
  definition 287–8
Ligget Group 172
liquidity 88
Liz Claiborne
  and AIP 132
  code of conduct xii
  and Myanmar 125
LL Bean, and AIP 132

Lockheed Martin, and landmines 169
London, financial center 26, 88
London Benchmarking Group 213–15
Lonrho Group 208–9
Lotus Development, and sexual
    orientation 144
Louisville and Jefferson County, and
    CERES 103–4
Love Canal 69
Lovelock, James 100

McDonald's 273
  accountability xix, 3, 17, 39
  and animal welfare 174
  brand image and reputation 62, 64, 67
  Environmental Defense Fund 3, 54,
    219–21, 257, 276
  global company 24
  McLibel 257, 276
McDonalds Sweden 98
McKay Nursery 206–7
Magna Carta 115
Mahathir Mohammed, Prime Minister of
    Malaysia 8
Malaysia
  and International Monetary Fund (IMF)
    5
  smog 9
manager, corporate citizen 39–40
managing change and complexity 272–7
managing corporate citizenship xxv,
    191–267
  auditing and accountability 227–31
  auditing business performance 232–4
  building partnerships 219–27
  business and communities 209–18
  developing global standards 249–51
  environmental auditing 234–6
  the ethical audit 239–41
  the inclusive company 206–9
  key relations and stakeholders 193–98
  managing the media: boycott 255–7
  reporting company performance
    249–51
  SA8000 246–8

managing corporate citizenship – *contd*
the social audit 241–6
social and ethical auditing 237–9
who are stakeholders? 198–200
Mandela, Nelson 120
Manganese Steel 208–9
Marine Stewardship Council (MSC) 225–7
marketing 162
Marks & Spencer
accountability xix, 276
Bath Environment Centre 108–9
brand image and reputation 63
environmental management 105
global organization 5
human rights and the workplace 113
London Benchmarking Group 213–15
media or courts? 257
and MSC 226
sourcing 11
Marlboro 173
Marlin, Alice Tepper 250
Matsushita 47
Maucher, Helmut O. 17, 120
Max Havelaar, fair trade 153
Maxwell, Robert 88, 93
measures scan, KPMG 245
Medecins sans Frontières (MSF) 53–4, 276
media management 255–8
Mehta, Dewang 11
Meiji, and breastfeeding 230–1
Mendex, Errol 178
Mercedes-Benz 207, 273
brand image and reputation 62
protecting reputations 65
Merck
environmental management 105
rainforest 106
Metropolitan Police, Statement of Values 37–8
Metropolitan Sewer Corporation, and CERES 103
Mexico
Cafédirect 151
Chihuahua's Business Social Trust 217–18

corruption 95
and International Monetary Fund (IMF) 8
and McKay Nursery 207
Max Havelaar 153
Microsemi, and landmines 169
Microsoft, and English 12, 21
Ministry of Defence (MOD) *see* UK Ministry of Defence
minorities, and Avon 37
mission statements 36–8
Mitsubishi 275
MNC *see* multinational company
MOD *see* UK Ministry of Defence
models of social responsibility 50–5
amoral or responsive business 50–1
Big Issue, The 51–2
business as community 52
business as moral activity 51
Medecins sans Frontières (MSF) 53–4
network or partnership business 53
money movement 19
monitoring, global 18
Monitoring and Verification Working Group 154
Monks, Bob 85
Montreal Protocol 97, 110
definition 288
moral business 51
Motorola, and landmines 169
movement and mobility 19
MSC *see* Marine Stewardship Council
multilateral organizations 19
multinational company (MNC) 26–7
definition 288
Mumby, Phil 74
Myanmar (Burma)
boycott 256
human rights 115, 125

National AIDS Trust Employment Initiative 148–9
National Anti-Vivisection Society 176
National Biodiversity Institute (INBio) 106

National Growers Association, Colombia 12
National Health Service (NHS), equal opportunities 40
NATO, and landmines 41
Natura 133
Natural Step 96, 98–9
    definition 288
    ecotourism 105
    environmental management 105
    and Gaia 99–100
NatWest
    Bath Environment Centre 108–9
    and disability 139
    environmental management 105
    London Benchmarking Group 213–15
NatWest, accountability 36
NEC, global organization 5
Nesté, global organization 4
Nestlé 274
    accountability 17, 120
    and breastfeeding 230–1
    fair trade 150
    transnational 26, 87
Netherlands
    education 180
    floriculture 13
network business 53
New Academy of Business 43, 179
New Consumer, and FairTrade 155
new corporate citizenship see corporate citizenship
New Economics Foundation (NEF) 154, 228, 238
    auditing 233
    social audit 243–4
New England Corporate Consortium for AIDS Education 150
NGO see non-governmental organization
Nicaragua, Cafédirect 151
Nicole Miller, and AIP 132
Nigeria
    corruption 95
    Ogoni activists 122–5
    poverty 15

and Shell 36, 68, 122–4, 276
Nike
    and AIP 132
    brand image and reputation 62–3
    human rights and the workplace 113
    subcontracting 129–31, 237
Nike Corporation, financial performance xi
Nomura, UK pubs 8
non-governmental organizations (NGOs) 7
    definition 288
    development 19
    Keidanren 45–6
Nortel 110
North Sea, and Shell 36
North-South dialogue, definition 288
Novo Nordisk, environmental management 105, 111
NTT 47

Occidental Petroleum 121
OECD see Organization for Economic Co-operation and Development
Olin Ordnance, and landmines 169
Oliveira Roxo 133
Opportunity 2000 136–7
oppressive regimes 162
Organization for Economic Co-operation and Development (OECD) 87
organizations, and corporate citizenship 40, 42
Otto Versand 107
    social accountability 251
outsourcing 19
Oxfam 154
    Cafédirect 151
    and FairTrade 155
ozone layer 97

Paine, Thomas 116
Pakistan, corruption 95
paradigm shift xxii, 36
Parchment, Mark 146
Parker, Gary 112

partnerships 53
see also building partnerships
PCP 107
Pentland, media or courts? 257
Pepsi-Cola 18
PepsiCo, boycott 256
performance *see* company performance
personnel training 62
Peru 151
philanthropy, definition 288
Philip Morris, fair trade 150
Phillips Van Heusen, Guatemala 218
pirating 23
PIRC (Pensions and Investments
    Research Consultants) 124
Pizano, Marta 13
Pizza Hut
  brand image and reputation 64
  disabled employees 141
Polaroid
  and AIDS 149–50
  and CERES 103
policy, ethical investment 160
polluter pays principle 288–9
pollution xxii, 101
  France 9
  Royal Dutch/Shell 9
population 96
pornography 162
post-modernism xxii, 36, 196
poverty 96
Power Company of Sao Paulo 133
precautionary principle, definition 289
Premier Beverages
  brand image and reputation 63
  and FairTrade 155
  quality 73–4
Price Waterhouse, social audit 245
Prince of Wales 146
Prince of Wales Business Leaders' Forum
    43, 48–9
Prince William Sound and Exxon, risk
    management 71–2, 103–4
principles 277–9
printing, invention 20

productivity 72–4
protecting reputations 65–8
Protestant work ethic 20
Prudential Assurance
  and disability 139
  and Shell 124
  protecting reputations 66–7

QAP *see* quality assurance project
quality 72–4
  Premier Beverages 73–4
quality assurance project (QAP) 73–4

racism and sexual harassment, British
    Army 146–7
Raytheon, and landmines 169
Reagan, Ronald 168
Red Crescent, and landmines 41, 64, 167,
    169
Red Cross, and landmines 41, 64, 167,
    169
Red Lobster, disabled employees 141
Reebok
  and AIP 132
  and BSR 44
  code of conduct xii
  human rights and the workplace 113
  software sourcing 12
  subcontracting 130
Reich, Robert 274
relationship management 49
Renlon, profile 42
reporting 252–5
reputation 61–5, 65–8
  management 48
resource efficiency and enhancement 49
responsibilities
  economic, legal, social, environmental
    40–3
Renlon 42
responsiveness 49
Rice, David 121
Rio Conference 96
Rio Tinto, and Freeport-McMoRan 8
risk management 68–72

Bhopal and Union Carbide 69–70
Prince William Sound and Exxon 71–2
Union Carbide and Exxon 68–72
Robert, Karl-Henrik 98
Roddick, Anita
and Amnesty International 119
New Academy of Business 179
stakeholder accountability 197
Rosmarin, Keith 237
Rowntree-Mackintosh, boycott 255
Royal Dutch/Shell
accountability 3, 40
and environment 71
pollution 9
Royal Society of Arts, Manufactures and
Commerce (RSA) 47
Royal Society for the Protection of Birds
(RSPB)
and MSC 227
profile 176–7
RTZ see Rio Tinto
Rubin, Robert 8
Rubin, Stephen 258
Russia, corruption 95
Ryding, Frank 169

SA8000 see Social Accountability
Sainsbury's
animal welfare 175–6
and disability 140
and ETI 154
and FairTrade 155
and MSC 226
Sakamaki, Hideo 8
SAPS see structural adjustment
programmes
Saro-Wiwa, Ken 122–5, 272
Saudi Arabia
and arms 169–70
human rights 115
Save the Children, and ETI 154
Scandic Hotels 98, 105–6
ecotourism 105
environmental management 105
School of Oriental and African Studies

(SOAS) 21
schools traffic accident reduction (STAR)
program 108
Schulmeyer, Gerhard 272
secondment, definition 289
seven deadly sins 94
seven principles of stakeholding 195
Seveso chemical plant 69
sexual harassment 144–7
British Army 146–7
US Army 145–6
sexual orientation 143–4
and Ben & Jerry's 144
and Disney 143–4
and Lotus Development 144
and United Airlines 143–4
sexual preference policy 143
Shared Earth, auditing business
performance 233
shareholders/stockholders 205–6
Sharma, Mahesh 107
Sharp 47
Shell 273, 275
accountability 3, 36, 40, 87
boycott 256
Brent Spar 36, 68, 221, 272
environmental audit 233
global company 24
Nigeria 36, 68, 122–4, 276
shareholders/stockholders 205
and Tarmac Construction 221
Shiseido 47
Short, Clare 153–4
Shufuren, boycott 255
Sierra Club, and MSC 229
Simpson, Ann 124
Singapore, smog 9
SMA, and breastfeeding 230–1
Smith, Adam 228–9
Smith and Hawken, and CERES 103
SmithKline Beecham, environmental
management 105, 112
Social Accountability 8000 (SA8000)
xii–xiii, 117, 246–9, 251
basis 248–9

Social Accountability – *contd*
business case 247–8
CEPAA 249
SGS Yarsley 249
Toys 'Я' Us 73
social audit 237–9, 241–6
benefits 242
definition 289
New Economics Foundation (NEF)
243–4
practice 243–6
Price Waterhouse 245
social statement 242–3
The Body Shop 156, 246
social and environmental responsibility
41
social and ethical auditing 237–9
BT 238
social responsibility 72–4
interest in 43–9
Asahi Foundation 46–7
Business for Social Responsibility
(BSR) 44
Centre for Tomorrow's Company 47–8
Charter for Good Corporate Behavior
45–6
Prince of Wales Business Leaders'
Forum 48–9
UN Development Programme 48–9
World Bank 48–9
World Business Council for Sustainable
Development 49
social responsibility in global economy
xxii, 1–58
changing perspectives 7–9
definition of company types 26–7
developing world 14–18
everyday examples 6–7
global company 23–6
global connectivity 18–20
global and corporate governance 23–4
global growth 22
global language 20–1
global organizations 4–6
global sourcing 9–14

what has become globalized 18–20
social responsibility, interest in 43–9
Business for Social Responsibility 44
social statement, social audit 242–3
Société Général de Surveillance (SGS)
249
sokaiya 8
Sony 47
and English 21
Soros, George 23
sourcing
ethical 74
see also global sourcing
South Africa, Sullivan Principles 103
stakeholder corporation, definition 289
stakeholder mapping 202–5
definition 289
Traidcraft 204–5
UNEP 203
US Department of Defense 203–4
stakeholder reflector, KPMG 245
stakeholders 48, 198–206
and accountability 61
definition 198, 289
five key relationships 199–202
IBM 201–2
and key relationships 193–98
primary 199
secondary 199
shareholders/stockholders 205–6
stakeholder mapping 202–5
The House of Windsor 200–1
Traidcraft 204–5
UNEP International Technology Center
203
US Department of Defense 203–4
standards 61
see also global standards
STAR *see* schools traffic accident
reduction
Starbucks Coffee, boycott 256
Stokes, Richard 146
strategy xxii, 61–80
brand disasters 65–8
brand image and reputation 61–5

ethical investment 160
learning organization 74–5
managing risk 68–72
quality, productivity, social
responsibility 72–4
successful companies 75–6
Stride Rite, and BSR 44
structural adjustment programs (SAPs) 22
successful companies 75–6
keys to success 62
Sullivan Principles 103
definition 289
Sumitomo copper trading 93
Sun Company, and CERES 103
supply chain 61
supranational company 26–7, 87
definition 290
sustainability shifts 101
sustainable business 101–2
sustainable development 100, 227–8
Sutherland, Peter D. 35
Swartz, Jeffrey 213
Swedish Match 173
Swiss Federation, boycott 255

Tagua Initiative 112–13
environmental management 105
Tanzania, Cafédirect 151
Tarmac Construction, and Shell 221
tatamae 45
technological revolution, change xxii–iii
telecommunications, global 18
Tesco
animal welfare 175–6
boycott 256
and disability 140
Thailand
Bata 215
International Monetary Fund (IMF) 8
Thatcher, Margaret 169, 173, 210
The Body Shop *see* Body Shop
The Other Economic Summit (TOES) 244
Thiokol, and landmines 169
TIAA-CREF 90
Tiananmen Square 18, 114

Tikki Café 155
Timberland 212–13
accountability 3
mission statement 37
TNC *see* transnational company
tobacco 70, 83, 162, 172–3
TOES *see* The Other Economic Summit
Tokyo Marine and Fire 47
Tomorrow's Company 1996 Inquiry 89
Tom's of Maine
accountability xix
animal welfare 175–6
Total 120
toxics 73
Toyota 87
Toys 'Я' Us
code of conduct xii
social accountability 73, 250–1
trading conditions, change xxiii
Traidcraft
auditing business performance 233
Cafédirect 151
and Fair Trade 155
transgenerational, definition 290
transnational company (TNC) 23–7
definition 290
transparency 61, 86
Transparency International 94–5
Triton 120
Trudeau, Garry 130
Truman, Harry 116
Twin Trading, Cafédirect 151
Typhoo/Cadbury group 73

Uganda, Cafédirect 151
UK
ecotourism 105
education 179–80
and foreign investment 26
greenhouse gases 97–8
shareholders 87
takeovers 87
UK Ministry of Defence (MOD)
accountability xix, 276
global organization 5

UN, arms trade 168
UN Conference on Human Environment,
    Stockholm 96
UN Conference on Trade and
    Development (UNCTAD), index on
    transnationality 23–6
UN Development Programme 48–9
UN Drug Control Programme 13–14
UN Environment Programme 108
UNCTAD, see UN Conference on Trade
    and Development
unequal opportunities 136
Unilever 87
    accountability 3
    fair trade 150
    software sourcing 12
    World Wide Fund for Nature (WWF)
        54
Union Carbide and Bhopal 69–72
United Airlines, and sexual orientation
    143–4
United Farm Workers, boycott 255
Universal Declaration of Human Rights
    83, 115, 117–19
US Army, sexual harassment 145–6
US Department of Defense
    accountability xix, 276
    equal opportunities 40
USA
    arms trade 168
    Bill of Rights 116
    ecotourism 105
    education 178
    and foreign investment 26
    greenhouse gases 97–8
    shareholders 87

Vacca, Asdrubal Jimenez 121
Valdez principles 103–4
Vallance, Sir Ian 237, 276
VanCity
    banking with a conscience 166–7,
        276
    and CERES 103–4
Venezuela, corruption 95

Vickers Defence Systems 169
Vietnam, corruption 95
Vietnam War 41
Virgin
    brand image and reputation 63
    shareholders/stockholders 205–6
Volkswagen 65, 87, 206–8
voluntarism, definition 290
Volvo, brand image and reputation 63,
    65
Vosper Thorneycroft 169

Ward, Barbara 100
water 96
WBA see World Business Academy
wealth disparity 19–20
Wheeler, Sir Roger 146
Whitbread 196
    London Benchmarking Group
        213–15
Wilson, Sir Michael 196
Wilson, Woodrow 116
women, and work 19
workholders, and VW 207–8
working methods xxiii
World Bank 48–9
    and SAPs 22
World Business Academy (WBA) 178
World Business Council for Sustainable
    Development (WBCSD) 49
World Development Movement 154
    and FairTrade 155
World Health Organization (WHO)
    and Colombia 13
    and disease 18
    smog 9
World Network Services, Mumbai 12
World Tourism Organization 105
world trade 26
World Trade Organisation (WTO), and
    global business 22
World Wide Fund for Nature (WWF)
    220
    and Nigeria 123
    Unilever 54, 225–7

yakuza 8
Yastrow, Shelby 220
Young, Andrew 130
yuppies 144

Zadek, Simon 233
Zimbabwe, maize 11
Zolty, Barbara 173